F. B. Sanborn

THE

RESULTS OF SLAVERY.

BY

AUGUSTIN COCHIN,

EX-MAIRE AND MUNICIPAL COUNCILLOR OF PARIS.

WORK CROWNED BY THE INSTITUTE OF FRANCE
(ACADÉMIE FRANÇAISE).

TRANSLATED BY

MARY L. BOOTH,

TRANSLATOR OF COUNT DE GASPARIN'S WORKS ON AMERICA, ETC.

BOSTON:
WALKER, WISE, AND COMPANY,
245 WASHINGTON STREET.
1863.

UNIVERSITY PRESS:
WELCH, BIGELOW, AND COMPANY,
CAMBRIDGE.

TRANSLATOR'S PREFACE.

The warm welcome accorded by so many of our most patriotic statesmen, as well as the general public, at this crisis, to "The Results of Emancipation," together with the reiterated demand for its complement, justify me in offering to American readers the translation of the second part of M. Cochin's useful book, "The Results of Slavery."

As both volumes were published together in the original form, under the collective title, *L'Abolition de l'Esclavage*, it may be proper to state that the publication of the translation of the first volume separately, under its individual title, was done with the approbation of the author, who at the same time expressed the hope that it might "soon be possible also to publish the translation of the second volume, since the proof seems more striking when the results of emancipation are placed in the presence of the results of slavery, — the good face to face with the evil." This hope I am glad to realize by presenting to the American public a book which cannot fail to interest it, devoted as it is, in great part, to the able discussion of our affairs at a time when the wise suggestions and earnest sympathy of European friends are of incalculable value to us.

The chapter on the United States was completed during the summer of 1861. The addition in the translation of a vigorous article, written by M. Cochin in August, 1862, during the dark days that followed the reverses near Richmond, continues the work wellnigh to the present time, and brings us strong and cheering counsel from amid the then prevailing discouragement. As more "last words" of the author, concerning the existing position of affairs, I may be permitted to quote from a private letter dated February 7, 1863: —

"We are occupied with your affairs as if they were our own; and, indeed, they are really the affairs of the whole human race. Unhappily, we know little of general events, except through the English journals, and of particular facts, except through correspondence from French sheets established in Louisiana, or letters from merchants occupied solely with their cotton affairs. Several of our Departments are suffering greatly. If the manufacturers were assembled, and the question were put to them, 'Do you wish that slavery should be perpetuated and you should have cotton?' the greater part, I fear, would answer, 'Give us cotton!' On the contrary, if the operatives were assembled and asked, 'Do you wish that slavery should endure and you should have bread?' I believe that all would answer, 'Free the slaves!' It is the same in England, where, notwithstanding, thanks to the freedom of assemblage, a happy agitation is recommencing by meetings and addresses in favor of the abolition of slavery. Here, the cause will be pleaded before the *Corps Legislatif*, petitions to the Senate are being prepared, several bishops intend speaking; in a word, public opinion is not dead, but it is not free, and policy, at the instigation of England, despite her apparent refusals, has entered upon a path of mediation which can end only to the profit of the South. A decisive victory, should you obtain it, by the grace of God, will incline minds towards you; but this is long in coming. What we should do, it seems to me, we convinced advocates of human freedom, is to defend its cause, and to strive to make it come out victorious, whatever may be the issue of the war. Now we can hope that neither peace nor separation nor mediation can be wrought without slavery having received a death-blow. Let us not cease to direct our efforts in this direction, in order that liberty may progress *at all events*."

The chapters devoted to the slaveholding countries other than the United States, the slave-trade, the immigration of free negroes, and the colonization of Africa, afford much useful and interesting information touching the beginning, growth, and effects of slavery, while the portion of the work entitled "Christianity and Slavery" is an able exposition of slavery in the evangelical point of view, which, designed for a Catholic, is equally useful in a Protestant community. M. Cochin, who is as sincere a Catholic as M. de Gasparin is a sincere Protestant, is a broad and liberal-minded man, ready to recognize good wherever found; and, while especially striving to clear his Church of the stigma of complicity with slavery, the arguments which he deduces to prove the antagonism of this institution and Christianity are alike interesting and applicable to believers of all creeds. It is a hopeful sign when churches and institutions are seen, not only to cease to tolerate, but also to disavow all former sanction of, an existing abuse.

With the firm conviction that this volume will be of use to my countrymen in the solution of the great problem which is now before us, and will aid them, by its lucid details and kindly tone, more clearly to discern the happy practical results which must ultimately proceed from the great principles of truth and justice which they are so nobly struggling to maintain through the horrors of a civil war, and the loss of so much that is dear to them in the present, I submit the work to their perusal and approval.

MARY L. BOOTH.

NEW YORK, March 15, 1863.

CONTENTS.

BOOK FIRST.

THE UNITED STATES OF AMERICA.

CHAPTER IV.

CHAPTER V.

BOOK SECOND.

BOOK THIRD.

BOOK FOURTH.

BOOK FIFTH.

BOOK SIXTH.

THE SLAVE-TRADE.—IMMIGRATION.—AFRICA.

BOOK SEVENTH.

CHRISTIANITY AND SLAVERY.

CHAPTER I.

CHAPTER II.

CHAPTER III.

CHAPTER IV.

APPENDIX.

RESULTS OF SLAVERY.

BOOK FIRST.

THE UNITED STATES OF AMERICA.

INTRODUCTION.

THE United States are rarely judged with impartiality in Europe. As this great nation is the only powerful republic founded in modern times, monarchists will not speak well of it, republicans dare not speak ill of it. The first carefully note, and loudly express, every defect and scandal; and present them as continual and logical. In their eyes, the country of Washington is a tumultuous and execrable community, open to slavery, polygamy, and atheism, the tranquil abode or hospitable refuge of bankrupts and robbers; a community founded by a handful of fanatics to end in a horde of filibusters. The second, no less ultra, extol the marvellous growth of this nation without neighbors and without bounds, enriched by the increase of a population fleeing to its shores from the too narrow limits of Europe; — a nation which more than pays its expenses;* triples

* The receipts into the Treasury, from all sources, during the fiscal year ending June 30, 1859, including the loan authorized by the act of June 14, 1858, and

in twenty years the number of its inhabitants and cities; knows no social distinctions, and little of the hierarchy of powers; surpasses in half a century nations numbering fourteen hundred years; and, arrived at a like grandeur, with greater future, may be regarded as the queen of coming times, and the land of Canaan for the liberty of the world.

The United States have taken upon themselves to disconcert by turns their detractors and their courtiers. To calumny they reply by gigantic progress, and by the rapid accomplishment of prodigious destinies.

But how far they also deceive the best hopes of their friends!

For my part, I hold to preserving the sympathy which led France to take part in the American Revolution. I continue to represent America to myself under the noble traits which M. de Tocqueville has drawn in one of the greatest books of the age. It must be admitted, however, that sad events have occurred to overshadow this radiant image. Evidently, for a quarter of a century, the esteem which Europe bore America has been daily decreasing.

Since this epoch, even before the late events which have brought about the separation of the Northern and Southern States, every steamer has brought us echoes of coarse affrays and shameful scenes, — the torture of a missionary, the caning of a Senator, the deifying of a *danseuse;* under

the emissions of Treasury-notes authorized by the existing laws, have been about $ 81,692,400; this sum, with the balance of $ 6,398,366 remaining in the Treasury at the commencement of the fiscal year, makes the total service of the year $ 88,090,787.

During the fiscal year ending June 30, 1859, the public expenses have therefore amounted to $ 83,751,511.57. Of this sum, $ 17,405,285 have been applied to the payment of the interest on the public debt, and to the redemption of the notes issued by the Treasury. For all other branches of the public service during this fiscal year the expenses have been $ 66,346,226.13. The balance remaining in the Treasury, July 1, 1859, the commencement of the present fiscal year, was $ 4,339,275.54. — *President's Message*, Dec. 19, 1859.

senseless names, disorderly factions oppressing the freedom of suffrage; lawyers shamefully protecting thieves; mobs burning hospitals; commerce multiplying its frauds, its bankruptcies, and its dupes; every species of jugglery in honor; every species of crime increasing, — the country of Franklin seems transformed into the stage of Barnum.

It cannot be doubted that American society contains within itself permanent elements of moral perturbation; it is a prey to one of those diseases of which it may die, or, much worse, like many other nations, may fall, without dying, into incurable dissolution.

One of the causes of this dangerous state is assuredly the natural effervescence of a nation still so young. Subjected to a crisis unique in history, it unites under the same name, but under independent and diverse constitutions, every extreme, from the millionnaire of New York to the gold-digger of California; from the statesman of Washington to the adventurer of Salt Lake, — the freest citizens and the most miserable slaves on earth. On a territory which daily shifts its frontiers, five or six races mingle pell-mell; the last tribes of Indians recede before the full tide of Germans and Irish that roll upon the shores, and the maintenance of order in this chaos is confided to the most liberal laws, placed in the keeping of a private citizen in a frock-coat, without civil list or army.

But these agitations also prove vigor of constitution; they certainly attest a powerful civic and Christian spirit in the people that resist them.* The disease is not here; this is not the fever of death, but the fever of youth.

We might, with distinguished publicists, point out the destruction of the ancient laws, and above all of the ancient customs which presided at the foundation of this new community. We might also allege the state of faith in a moment

* As was so strongly and eloquently demonstrated by the illustrious Père Lacordaire, in his opening oration before the French Academy, January 24, 1860.

of painful transition, when minds are gradually becoming detached from dissenting Christianity, without yet proceeding with resolute tread to the complete Christianity of the Roman Church.* With Channing,† with Senior,‡ we might signal the rage for speculation and aggrandizement, the disappearance of great statesmen.

But all of these existing circumstances are consequences, not causes.

The principal cause of these evils, and of so many others, the secret poison which is gnawing the very vitals of this community, and threatening it with shame, decay, and dissolution, I affirm is *Slavery*.

Everywhere else in the whole Christian world, slavery is disappearing or diminishing; in the United States, it endures, it is increasing, and, by the terrible ascendency of its individual effects, is ruling over and menacing the very existence of the nation.

Men have sought to deny it; they can no longer doubt it to-day. The work of Washington is endangered, the Union is rent asunder, the Constitution is violated, the national suffrage is contemned, civil war is at hand. What, I ask, is the origin of such calamities? What is the cause of this most miserable decay in the bosom of this most magnificent development?

It is *Slavery*.

I shall endeavor rapidly to sketch the picture of the progress and ravages of this scourge.

In tracing this picture, I can choose between two different methods: —

Either to analyze the laws, describe the manners, and calculate the forces of each of the Southern Slave States; to study the evils of slavery in the family; to show that laws

* Brownson's Quarterly Review, Mission of America, 1857.

† Slavery, translated by M. Edouard Laboulaye.

‡ American Slavery, Edinburgh Review, 1856.

become less human, creeds less solid, morals more corrupt, the material condition more critical, under its influence, and thus to render it manifest, that the same evil shakes at once in these States laws, creeds, morals, and wealth, — that is, all that sustains and all that composes a regular community.

Or else to show how the question of slavery, passing beyond the boundaries of the Slave States, rules over and endangers the entire confederation ; how it has come to affect its whole policy, the greatness of its character in the world, the concord and peace of the States which it comprises, and the growth of its magnificent destinies.

The second method is newer ; it gives less room for emotion, but leads more directly to a practical conclusion.

To seek to prove to men that they are injuring themselves, is in general to lose one's trouble, for they believe themselves good judges of their own interests, and if they are mistaken, if they do themselves harm, this harm, by punishing them, is its own sufficient warning. The Slave States appear indifferent to the counsels which are lavished upon them, and reply, "It is our own business!"

On the contrary, it is just to accuse those openly who do wrong to others. If the slaveholder injures, not only himself, not only the unfortunate race which he retains captive, but the whole confederation ; if he debases, by his obstinacy, one of the first civilizations in the world ; if he urges on to civil war a community the growth of which has been incomparable ; if he violates Christianity ; if he outrages nature ; if he is an obstacle to the progress of the human race, —his monstrous crime creates against him who commits it a legitimate right, and this right belongs to every American, to every Christian, to every man. There is not a conscience which should not league itself with the justice of God, to denounce and combat his crime.

The influence of slavery on the politics and social condition of the American Union;

The reasons alleged for maintaining it;

The means proposed to abolish it;

The final crisis of the separation of the States on account of slavery; —

Such is the scope of the following work.

CHAPTER I.

INFLUENCE OF SLAVERY ON THE WHOLE POLICY AND LEGISLATION OF THE UNITED STATES.

§ 1. From the Adoption of the Constitution to the Missouri Compromise.

1787 - 1820.

By a striking coincidence, slavery and liberty, good and evil, were born in the same year in the United States. In the winter of 1620, the bark *Mayflower* landed on Plymouth Rock a handful of pious, honest, intelligent men, lovers of justice and equality, — these were the founders of the illustrious nation which takes the name of the United States of America. The same year, another ship, supposed to be Dutch, touched at Jamestown in Virginia, and landed nineteen negro slaves, the first that ever set foot on and polluted the soil of North America. These two powerful influences still endure, and unceasingly divide the country. From the decks of the *Mayflower* has issued one of the freest and most flourishing nations that the world has ever seen, composed at present of nearly thirty million men. The sad passengers of the negro vessel have had four million successors. Virginia, which was destined to become the cradle of independence, was also that of slavery.*

The example was rapidly imitated, and the custom of employing slaves was propagated from the South to the

* Beverley, History of Virginia. P. Van Biervliet, *Etudes sur l'esclavage aux États Unis*, (Louvain, 1859,) p. 31. Charles Sumner's Speech, September 19, 1860 (Boston).

North. In 1639, political rights were already refused to slaves in Maryland. The two Carolinas became the principal market of the slave-trade. From the middle of the seventeenth century, slavery existed in all of the Southern States. It was propagated more slowly in the Northern States, where the number of slaves never reached that of freemen, while it greatly exceeded it in the South. It cannot be doubted that the English government warmly encouraged the importation of negroes. Virginia several times remonstrated against this, and in 1776,* among the grievances enunciated against George III., the Williamsburg Convention reproached him with the inhuman use of the royal prerogative which had prevented Virginia from prohibiting by law the introduction of negroes. The same opposition is found in a declaration of Congress, dated October 8, 1774.†

In Georgia, a law interdicted the importation of negroes and that of spirituous liquors ; it became necessary to abrogate this in 1749.

Massachusetts, Connecticut, Rhode Island, Delaware, and Pennsylvania succeeded by degrees in freeing themselves from the contagion. Sustained by more lively religious principles, having a less imperative need of laborers accustomed to the climate, these States triumphed over the invasion, example, and pressure of the mother country.

After the Declaration of Independence, when the immortal founders of the American Republic were framing the Constitution of September 17, 1787, — a law which still rules and secures to the most modern people of earth the honor of possessing one of the most ancient constitutions, — Jefferson, having proclaimed in solemn terms that "all

* Channing, Introduction of Slavery, Laboulaye's translation.

† *Bibliothèque de l'Arsenal*, Documents collected by Gregory, ex-Bishop of Blois, Tom. VIII. of the French documents. I owe access to this curious collection of documents of the eighteenth century to the courtesy of M. P. Lacroix, librarian of the Bibliothèque de l'Arsenal.

men are created equal, and endowed by their Creator with inherent and inalienable rights, among which are liberty," etc., wished to add an article condemning slavery.

A majority of a single vote rejected this resolution. Interest prevailed then, as since, over the convictions of the most illustrious fathers of American liberty. Washington emancipated his slaves by testament, Franklin wrote against slavery, the celebrated judge, John Jay, and many other great men, shared the same feeling. But, in the fear of weakening or breaking the bond of federation, already so fragile, they did not insist on it, and the monstrous nuptials of liberty and servitude were hallowed.

This arrangement was disguised like a shameful deed under the evasive silence of an equivocation. No article of the Constitution is polluted by the word *slavery*. The abolition of the slave-trade, in the year 1808, is shadowed forth in these words of Article I. Section IX. § 1: "The migration or importation of such persons as any of the existing States shall think proper to admit, shall not be prohibited by Congress prior to the year 1808." Furthermore, in Article I. Section II. § 3, by which the representatives are distributed in proportion to the amount of population, we read that "to the whole number of free persons shall be added *three fifths of all other persons*." This is all! "A stranger might read the Constitution," says Channing,* "without suspecting that slavery exists among us."

Thus the Constitution, like the Gospel, is silent upon slavery; but the Gospel does not speak of it because, in its sight, all men are equal; the Constitution is silent because, in its sight, slaves are not men!

Happily, the blast of liberty that swept over Europe made itself felt in America. The American Congress of 1794 prohibited the slave-trade; the same principle entered into the treaties contracted in 1814 and 1842 between Eng-

* Note to a letter to Mr. Clay, p. 349, Laboulaye's edition.

land and the United States, but without the latter having ever consented to submit to the right of search, at length abandoned in the sequel of the diplomatic disputes and negotiations of 1858.

At the same time, the Northern States set a memorable example. In 1780, before the end of the Revolutionary war, Pennsylvania and Massachusetts voted the gradual extinction of slavery. All the States situated north of the Delaware followed this example in succession ; at the census of 1820 slavery had virtually become extinct in seven of the thirteen States which originally composed the confederation; viz. Pennsylvania, Massachusetts, Connecticut, Rhode Island, New Jersey, New Hampshire, and New York.

Slavery remained confined within the six other States: Delaware, Maryland, Virginia, North and South Carolina, and Georgia.

But at this epoch the federation already numbered in these States alone 1,620,340 slaves ; * while in 1790 it did not include, in both North and South, more than 670,633 in all.†

Divisions and annexations have increased the number of the States of the Union to thirty-four, ‡ nineteen free States,

*	
Delaware	2,290
Maryland	90,368
Virginia	472,528
North Carolina	288,548
South Carolina	384,984
Georgia	381,622

(Helper, Compendium, Table 12.)

† Oration delivered at New Haven, in 1790, by Rev. James Dana. *Bibliothèque de l'Arsenal*, Gregorian Collection, English documents, Tom. III.

‡ Without counting several Territories. The following are the dates of birth of the several States, with their extraction: —

1564. A colony of French Protestants, under Ribault, settled in Florida.
1565. St. Augustine founded by Pedro Melendez.
1584. Sir Walter Raleigh obtains a patent, and despatched two ships to the coast which received the name of Virginia.
1607. First establishment of the London Company at Jamestown, Virginia.
1614. A fort founded by the Dutch on the site of New York.
1615. Fort Orange built near the site of Albany, New York.

and fifteen slave States; viz. *Free States,* California, Connecticut, Illinois, Indiana, Iowa, Kansas, Maine, Massachusetts, Michigan, Minnesota, New Hampshire, New Jersey, New York, Ohio, Oregon, Pennsylvania, Rhode Island, Vermont, Wisconsin; *Slave States,* Alabama, Arkansas, Delaware, Florida, Georgia, Kentucky, Louisiana, Maryland, Mississippi, Missouri, North Carolina, South Carolina, Tennessee, Texas, Virginia.

It was hoped that, if the example of the Northern States did not suffice, the abolition of the slave-trade would check the increase of slaves at the South, and bring about the gradual disappearance of the negro race; inasmuch as rice

1619. First General Assembly convened in Virginia.
1620. Arrival of the Puritan Pilgrims at Plymouth Rock.

FREE STATES.

1614. New York settled by the Dutch.
1620. Massachusetts settled by the Puritans.
1623. New Hampshire settled by the Puritans.
1624. New Jersey settled by the Dutch.
1636. Rhode Island settled by Roger Williams.
1636. Connecticut settled by the Puritans.
1682. Pennsylvania settled by Wm. Penn.
1791. Vermont admitted into the Union (from New York).
1803. Ohio admitted into the Union.
1816. Indiana do. do.
1818. Illinois do. do.
1820. Maine admitted into the Union (from Massachusetts).
1837. Michigan admitted into the Union.
1845. Iowa do. do.
1847. Wisconsin do. do.
1848. California do. do.
1858. Minnesota do. do.
1859. Oregon do. do.
1861. Kansas do. do.

SLAVE STATES.

1607. Virginia settled by the English.
1627. Delaware by the Swedes.
1634. Maryland by the English Catholics.
1650. North Carolina by the English.
1670. South Carolina by the Huguenots.
1733. Georgia by Gen. Oglethorpe.
1792. Kentucky admitted into the Union.
1796. Tennessee admitted into the Union.
1812. Louisiana admitted into the Union.
1817. Mississippi admitted into the Union.
1819. Alabama admitted into the Union.
1821. Missouri do. do.
1836. Arkansas do. do.
1845. Florida do. do.
1845. Texas.

and indigo, the principal productions of the South at this epoch, were beginning to be furnished as cheaply from the East Indies.*

An obscure mechanic of Massachusetts, Whitney, intervened to foil this expectation, by inventing, in 1793, the *saw gin*, or machine for picking cotton.†

Until this time, the United States had exported scarcely 200,000 pounds of cotton; to-day, they export more than 1,400,000,000 pounds. Without speaking of rice, tobacco, and, above all, sugar, see what is produced by the labor of the unhappy slaves! But see, too, what produces, encourages, and decuples slavery! It pleases God that we should recognize human solidarity in even the smallest details, and we shudder to think of the suffering that a piece of cotton cloth has caused to human beings on the other side of the globe, without speaking of the so-called freemen whom the manufacturers of Manchester employ to weave what slave hands have gathered.

The growth insured by such a commerce to the Southern

* Agriculture proper, the cultivation of grain and the vine, has been in no place and no time suited to slavery. The Romans, although their landed property was extensive, were ruined, despite the number of their slaves, for lack of being able to employ enough free laborers in the culture of their fields, or rather despite this very number, for it was necessary to maintain during the entire year hands that were only useful during a part of the year. Thus, sugar, cotton, and coffee, things with which man can at need dispense, are the products of slave labor; bread and wine, the necessary aliments, are, by the grace of God, the gifts of free labor.

† The *long-staple* cotton is cultivated with difficulty; and yields scarcely one tenth as much as the *short-staple*. But in the latter, the cotton adheres so strongly to the seed that a man cannot pick more than a pound a day with the hand. Even with the rollers and wheels employed by the Indians, the expense is still excessive; so that, until the invention of Whitney, America exported but little of this kind of cotton. In 1794, the exportation increased from 187,000 to 1,601,760 bales. In 1800, it reached 17,000,000 bales; in 1810, 93,000,000 bales; and at present it exceeds 1,400,000,000 pounds.

The *saw gin* is now perfected; as it has the disadvantage of cutting the long staple, Macarthy's *roller gin* is used in preference to this. (American Slavery, by Senior, p. 11 (1856). *La Question du coton en Angleterre*, by John Ninet, *Revue des Deux Mondes*, March 1, 1861.)

States may be imagined; the cession of Louisiana by France, and of Florida by Spain, added to this prosperity.

But how furnish to the demand the labor that it necessitated? and how obtain slaves enough without the slave-trade? *

This was done, first, through a clandestine trade; secondly, by another abominable means, *the raising of negroes.* Negroes were raised like horses elsewhere, one male to ten females, reproduction was stimulated by every means, products were multiplied, then sold. Like our counties devoted to the raising of cattle, a number of States received the name of *slave-raising States.*† An infamous practice, unknown to the ancients, and a hundred times worse than the slave-trade, since it leads men to sell the children whom they have seen born, and have caused to be baptized, — necessitates the separation of families, and transforms society into a productive stud!

By these two means, despite the mortality which in all countries diminishes the slave races more rapidly than the free, the demand for this animated merchandise was provided for successfully; as we have already said, there were less than 700,000 slaves in the United States in 1790; in

* The Rev. J. Dana, in the oration of 1790, before cited, estimates that, to keep up the supply of slaves in the United States and the West Indies, which numbered together at that time 1,601,302, a yearly importation of from 70,000 to 80,000 from Africa was needed. He thence concludes, that from the beginning of the slave-trade, in 1620, to 1790, Africa had furnished some 20,000,000 slaves, which, at £30 per head, would amount to a value of £600,000,000.

† The number of negroes raised and imported from one State into another by means of this infamous trade is estimated at 120,000 annually. Virginia alone sells from 40,000 to 50,000 per year; North Carolina, Maryland, and Kentucky furnish the greater part of the remainder; these are purchased by Louisiana, Arkansas, Alabama, Mississippi, and the other Southern Slave States. A few of the slave-breeding States see their black population rapidly diminishing by reason of this sale and of white immigration. In 1850, Delaware had but 2,290; Missouri 87,422 slaves to 592,000 freemen. A diminution has taken place in North Carolina, Maryland, Kentucky (which has but 210,981 slaves to 761,403 whites), and Virginia (which has 472,528 slaves to 894,800 whites).

1850, the South alone possessed 3,200,364. The whole number of *persons of color* at that time was 3,591,000 ; it had risen, in 1860, to 4,490,000.

Doubtless the North continued its opposition. In 1787 Jefferson caused a law to be passed organizing the territory northwest of the Ohio, and declaring that slavery should never be introduced into this section of country. Six great States, peopled by a few thousand savages in 1790, and inhabited by five million freemen in 1850, now divide this territory.

But by degrees the influence of the Southern States gained on legislation, and its steps may be counted by the number of laws and measures which succeeded each other.

§ 2. From the Missouri Compromise to the Election of President Buchanan.

1820 - 1857.

From 1818 to 1820, a great controversy arose on the question of the admission of the State of Missouri. We know that, on attaining a population of 40,000 inhabitants, a Territory can demand to be admitted as a State. Missouri, in its constitution, had permitted slavery. Twice the House of Representatives refused it admission ; twice the bill was passed by the Senate. At length it was admitted on the proposition of Mr. Clay, but with the agreement, known as the *Missouri Compromise,* that henceforth slavery should not be established north of the parallel of 36° 30′ north latitude, to the east and west of Missouri. "Fine justice !" said Pascal, formerly, "which is bounded by a mountain or a river ; truth on this side the Pyrenees, error on that !"

The South accepted this compromise, which secured to it two more votes in the Senate. The North voted for it through weakness, hoping that the vast territories of the

West would insure the preponderance to liberty in the future. But it is the fatality of this sad history, that every act of weakness results in irremediable crime. Servitude and liberty thus having each its domain, the question was, which should more speedily form new States to gain new votes in Congress and win the majority.

We know that there are two Senators for each State, whatever may be the population, and only one Representative to a number of inhabitants which cannot be less than 30,000, and which the law, which determines it every ten years (see the Constitution, Art. I. Sect. II. § 3), has raised by degrees to about 90,000.

The result is, that a new State, but just admitted, and having less than 100,000 inhabitants, may have as much weight in Congress as the oldest and most populous State, and that the minority of the nation may thus rule over the majority, and paralyze the whole. On the other hand, when the candidate for the Presidency does not obtain a majority of votes, the House of Representatives elects, voting again by States (Constitution, Art. II. Sect. I. § 3), — a new opportunity for the minority of the population to insure the triumph of its wishes. From this, we comprehend the extreme interest attached to the annexation of new States to the South, as additional weight in its side of the balance. The instrument of this policy of annexation was violence; Mississippi, Alabama, and Arkansas were wrested from the Indians, and a servitude unknown to savages was established there by civilized men. Texas was *stolen* from Mexico.

Stolen! The word is Channing's. Read this great citizen's admirable letter to Mr. Clay on this crime.* Texas

* "The annexation of Texas will extend and perpetuate slavery; it is for this that it is desired. On this point there can be no doubt. Since 1829 the annexation of Texas has been talked of in the Southern States and in the West. They have declared that nine Slave States, as large as Kentucky, could be formed from it. . . . . . They have calculated the rise that this would cause in the price of slaves," etc.

belonged to Mexico. Now Mexico, giving a lesson in liberty to the American republic, on shaking off the yoke of Spain, had nobly decreed that *henceforth no person should be born a slave, or introduced as such, in the Mexican States.*

To open a new territory to slavery,* to furnish prey to speculators, the United States went to the aid of what was grandiloquently called the independence of Texas, that is, the revolt of a feeble minority of the inhabitants, urged on by American colonists. And to whom was the conquest given? To these valorous citizens, as the price of their guilty rebellion? Not at all. The generous United States took possession of the territory, under the pretext of protecting it.

"In the army of eight hundred men who won the victory which scattered the Mexican force, and made its chief a prisoner, not more than fifty were citizens of Texas, having grievances of their own to seek relief for, on that field. The Texans in this warfare are little more than a name, a cover, under which selfish adventurers from another country have prosecuted their work of plunder.

"Some crimes, by their magnitude, have a touch of the sublime, and to this dignity the seizure of Texas by our fellow-citizens is entitled. Modern times furnish no example of individual rapine on so grand a scale. It is nothing less than the robbery of a realm. The pirate seizes a ship. The colonists and their coadjutors can satisfy themselves with nothing short of an empire."†

Listen again to these prophetic words: —

"By this act, our country will enter on a career of encroachment, war, and crime. . . . . We boast of our rapid growth. Our people throw themselves beyond the bounds of civilization, and expose themselves to relapses into a

* Revolutionary gatherings of Texans granted four hundred square leagues of the public lands to speculators for $ 20,000.

† Channing's Works, Vol. II. p. 202.

semi-barbarous state, under the impulse of wild imagination, and for the name of great possessions. . . . . . It is full time that we should lay on ourselves serious, resolute restraint. . . . . . The annexation of Texas will be the beginning of conquests which, unless arrested and beaten back by a kind Providence, will stop only at the Isthmus of Darien. . . . . . Henceforth we must cease to cry, Peace, peace. Our Eagle will whet, not gorge, its appetite on its first victim; and will snuff a more tempting quarry, more alluring blood, in every region which opens southward. To annex Texas is the first step towards Mexico. . . . . . Is she prepared to be a passive victim? . . . . . Do we expect England to remain a spectator of a measure which will resuscitate the slave-trade, and render void her struggles for long years in the cause of humanity? . . . . .

"But in adding Texas to Florida, we shall encircle the Gulf of Mexico. . . . . . The West Indian archipelago will necessarily enter into these daily increasing schemes for empire. . . . . . Will England and the other nations of Europe witness our encroachments without alarm? . . . . . It is said that nations have their destinies; that the stationary Turk must sink under the progressive civilization of Russia. . . . . . That the Indians have melted before the white man, and the mixed, degraded race of Mexico must melt before the Anglo-Saxon. Away with this vile sophistry! There is no necessity for crime."

Channing penned these eloquent pages in 1837, a year after the insurrection of the Texans, supported by an army sent, in full peace with Mexico, by the United States. In 1843, the annexation of Texas was refused after lively agitation and stormy debates. It was admitted as a Slave State, December 29, 1845. Almost immediately the prophecies of Channing were accomplished: Texas claimed of Mexico the territory of New Mexico, and war was declared by Mr. Polk, then President.

When peace was concluded, the abandonment of California and New Mexico to the United States was conceded. An angry discussion having arisen between the North and South with respect to the proposition of Mr. David Wilmot, by which Congress declared that the subsidies necessary to the war should only be accorded on condition of the prohibition of slavery in all territories which might be conquered, the House of Representatives repeatedly passed this formula, known by the name of the *Wilmot Proviso;* this was rejected by the Senate, but was taken up again by the House on the occasion of the treaty with Mexico, and the new Territories remained provisionally without organization. The agitation and struggles increased until, in 1850, California demanded admission as a State, *without slaves;* a clause which had been unanimously adopted. A manifesto of unheard-of violence, drawn up by Mr. Calhoun, was addressed to the Southern States by a convention of delegates and senators from these States, threatening the rupture of the federal bond. They did not fear to discuss the bases of a new organization, in case of separation. The North replied by indignation meetings. In Congress, the Southern delegates proposed a resolution tending to declare that the adoption of the measures projected by the Northern States would be considered as rightfully effecting a separation. After long resistance, the compromise proposed by Mr. Clay was adopted, by the terms of which California was admitted with its constitution, New Mexico was detached from Texas, which received an indemnity of $ 10,000,000, the *proviso* was set aside, the organization of new Territories was recognized as a right of the inhabitants, and the constitution, after being accepted by them, was to be submitted to Congress. Slavery was maintained in the Federal District ; that is, in the city of Washington and the separate District of Columbia. A stringent law against fugitive slaves was promised to the Southern States.

Mr. Clay was proclaimed the saviour of the public peace; he had saved it for the present moment by rendering war inevitable at a not very distant future. The nation had trafficked in sacred rights as it would in vulgar interests; it had paved the way for a new debate to every new demand for annexation, — debates in the territory before the constitution, debates in Congress on the examination of this constitution. Slavery was aggravated by a law against fugitive slaves. All of these evils must unavoidably break forth after a momentary pacification; when fresh fuel is thrown upon the fire, it is stifled for a moment, then blazes anew, and burns more fiercely.

The *Fugitive Slave Law* was passed in 1850; it authorized the master to pursue and seize upon fugitive slaves in the Free States, placed the federal officers at his service, and delivered up the fugitive to him without defence, without judgment, and without appeal. This detestable enactment violated the right of asylum, forcibly rendered the Free States accomplices of the Slave States, transformed judges into judicial bloodhounds, and placed the liberty of every man at the mercy of the calumnious denunciation of the first knave that might come. As Theodore Parker says,* in delivering up his Master for thirty pieces of silver, Judas Iscariot only fulfilled constitutional obligations; he was not a traitor, but a patriot!

The South went further. On constituting the Territories of Kansas and Nebraska in 1854, the Missouri Compromise was abolished; that blissful line, at the north of which all were free, was effaced; the inhabitants of a Territory were declared perfectly free to organize for themselves their *peculiar institutions*,† while respecting the Constitution of the United States.

* Cited by M. Laboulaye, Introduction, p. 51.

† The words *peculiar institution* have come, by a hypocritical euphemism,

The consequences of this act were not long in appearing. The Territory of Kansas was organized, May 30, 1854. On the 29th of the following November it had to elect a delegate to demand its incorporation as a State.* About a thousand armed men made a descent from a neighboring State, hustled out votes and voters, and elected Mr. Whitfield, a partisan of slavery. On the 30th of March, 1855, the inhabitants were to elect their Territorial legislature. More than four thousand men from the same State invaded the ballot-box in arms, and of 5,500 votes collected, less than 1,000 belonged to Kansas. What did the legislature, thus installed, decide? It declared that no one could be sworn without affirming that slavery was a right; that to maintain the contrary involved the penalty of two years of hard labor; four years for printing or circulating any writing against slavery; four years for giving shelter to a fugitive slave; *death* for aiding in his flight and concealment; *death* for stirring up slaves to insurrection; disfranchisement for refusing to swear to support the Fugitive Slave Law.

To commit such crimes is odious, but to commit them with impunity is monstrous. The central authority interfered little; it despatched an order to Governor Walker to send a few troops to protect the ballot-box, violated a third time at the end of November, 1855, on the election of a new delegate to Congress. This called forth the eloquent speech of Senator Charles Sumner, who, in protesting eloquently against this crime, exclaimed: "In truth, we are all in-

to be the pseudonyme of slavery. Men dare not say, "I am the champion of slavery!" but exclaim, "You attack our peculiar institutions!"

In one of Dickens's novels, Martin Chuzzlewit, a Southern delegate, the Hon. Elijah Pogram, when accused of always having dirty hands, replied, "What an antipathy you have to our peculiar institutions!"

* There are two degrees of political initiation for countries annexed to the Union. The one consists in the establishment of a provisional system, called *Territorial* government, the other in the establishment of the definitive system, called *State* government. (M. Mignet, notice on Edward Livingston, read June 30, 1838, before the Academy of Moral Sciences. *Mémoires*, Tom. III. p. 16.)

cluded in the common title of men, as spaniels, lapdogs, mastiffs, and bloodhounds are included in the common name of dogs." He did not know how soon he was to learn it by experience, for, two days after delivering this speech, he was assailed in his place in the Senate-chamber, close by the seats where Washington and Jefferson had sat, by Mr. Brooks, a member of Congress from South Carolina, who beat him over the head with a cane, and stretched him senseless.

"We approve of Mr. Brooks's conduct," said the *Richmond Inquirer*, of June 12th, — "we approve it without reserve. The act was good in conception, better in execution, perfect in results. *It was a proper act, done at the proper time, and in the proper place.*"

Meetings of approval were held in the South. A cane of honor was presented to Congressman Brooks. He was not expelled from Congress, but was acquitted with a fine of three hundred dollars; — that was buying celebrity at a cheap rate.

Debates of this kind did not greatly advance matters in Kansas. Murders and acts of violence remained for the most part unpunished.

The President's Message of 1858 recounts in diffuse language the continuation of this turbulent and bloody story. The Constitution of Topeka was succeeded by the Lecompton Constitution; election followed election, sometimes for, sometimes against slavery; the latter annulled on account of the withdrawal of the inspectors of the elections, the former opposed by tumultuous protests. The question, carried to Congress, where it occupied nearly two entire sessions, did not receive there a clearer solution. The President contradicted in his official capacity the course of conduct which he had counselled as a private individual. Should the Territory be admitted as a State, with its patched-up constitution, leaving it to the people to amend it afterwards in a new convention, or should all amendments be required to be made before admission? The President advocated the first course, Congress had voted for the second; and on the 4th of May, 1858, by means of an act called the *English Compromise,* an expedient was found. Resting on the fact that the people of Kansas had demanded for the support of the common schools twice the quantity of "public lands ever before accorded to any State upon entering the Union," Congress decreed that Kansas should not be admitted until after a new election, by which its inhabitants should accept lesser grants, equivalent to those made to Minnesota. Congress reserved to itself the right of approving this constitution, without interfering with the question of slavery, in conformity with the principle of non-intervention, known as the Nebraska Bill.

The election took place August 2d, 1859, and the people rejected the proposition of Congress. It was necessary, therefore, to make a third constitution.

But a new difficulty was raised by the Presidential message.

Did the Territory contain the number of inhabitants required to elect a member of the House of Representatives, namely, 93,420? To be certain of this, a preliminary census was necessary; but it was quite probable that, during this succession of elections, riots, and constitutions made, broken, remade, and to be remade, since 1854, a large number of the inhabitants had quitted so disturbed a country, and that the census would result in a new postponement. The President proposed to Congress to extend the census to all the new Territories; he was shocked at the idea that hordes spread over a country scarcely cleared should have the same privilege of sending members to the Senate as the ancient State of Virginia; he added, that, the Senate having in certain cases to elect a Vice-President of the United States from among its number, who might become President in case of the death of the President during his term of office, the proud confederacy was thus exposed to the danger of having for its head a citizen chosen by the ignoble ballot of Kansas or Utah.

But would Congress adopt this resolution? Would Kansas accept this new delay? Would the census be taken peaceably? Behold the extremity to which a people come thither to labor and to live, a fertile and extensive territory, the neighboring States, in short, the whole confederation, was reduced; — and why? Because Congress had abandoned, for the discussion of vulgar interests, the question whether men endowed with souls could be slaves!

§ 3. From the Election of President Buchanan to the Insurrection at Harper's Ferry.

1856-1860.

Since the Kansas question was raised, the Presidency, in 1857, had changed hands. The election which gave the majority to Mr. Buchanan was another most significant incident of this lamentable drama, which strongly resembled the prelude to civil war. M. de Tocqueville says truly: "The choice of the President matters little to each citizen. . . . . . But parties make use of the name of the Presidential candidate as a symbol. They personify their theories in him." *

The whole struggle, like that of the preceding elections, hinged upon the question of slavery. All the old party denominations were effaced before those of the Free-Soilers,† and the partisans of what was called, by a contemptible subterfuge, the *peculiar institutions* of the South. Party

* Tom. I. p. 218.

† The Free-Soilers are the Republican, their adversaries the Democratic party. The Northern States are designated as the *Labor States*; the Southern as the *Capital States*.

spirit, on the rostrum and in the press, rose to a pitch of violence exceeding all imagination; while the Abolitionists were not a whit behind their adversaries, thus endangering in the highest degree the cause of emancipation.

It is well known that the victory remained with the partisans of slavery. On the 4th of March, 1857, they elected President Buchanan. Sixty-six years of age, Secretary of State of President Polk at the time of the annexation of Texas, and afterwards Minister to England, this old diplomatist had, besides his eminent talents, three claims to their favor. He was openly known to be in favor of the annexation of Cuba; he had been one of the *Ostend Conference*, which encouraged the adventurer Lopez, to whom Mr. Marcy, then Secretary of State, dared write, November 13, 1854, "to oppose the abolition of slavery in Cuba, before any one should take a fancy that such a measure would not be prejudicial to the interests (say, rather, *covetousness*) of the United States"; and he had for his political motto the *Monroe Doctrine*,* which may be summed up in the maxims, *The Americanization of America; America for Americans;* that is, the appropriation of the whole continent, and the expulsion of foreigners. Lastly, he was of a genuinely diplomatic character, and, always irresolute,† he vibrated between the two parties, saying to the Slave States, "Keep your slaves, the Constitution permits it"; to the Free States, "Do not meddle with the slaves, the Constitution forbids it"; to the new States, "Vote as you please, I confide in the ballot-box, the American remedy, always sure to redress all wrongs."

Elected on account of these qualities, and in these circumstances, President Buchanan saw the four years of his administration glide by, neither satisfying nor dissatisfying

* The first and most exact formula of this doctrine is found in the message of President Monroe, 1823.

† See his letter, *Journal des Débats*, Aug. 15, 1857.

any one, provoking Spain by degrees, and endeavoring to hold equally balanced the scales that leaned more and more to the side of slavery.

However, the time came to create for himself a new claim, either to a new election,* or to a grateful remembrance if he were not re-elected, — his last messages lay down more boldly the policy to which he was ambitious to set the seal and bequeath his name.

The Kansas election appears to us as an exact picture of political customs within. The messages of President Buchanan in 1858, 1859, and 1860 are the characteristic exposition of American politics abroad.

We know what clearness and brevity distinguish the official communications of the European governments ; the art of saying everything in a few words, or sometimes of saying nothing in grandiloquent language, has been carried to a great length in England and France. The diplomatic portfolios, closed unfortunately even after events have taken their place in history, contain treasures and finished models, too little known, of perfect literature. Very different from these documents, the messages to the United States are interminable, monotonous, and confused papers. To penetrate, wade through, and understand them needs the patience and resolution of an explorer of the virgin forests, advancing step by step, and making his way axe in hand. This courage does not always meet its reward. The messages of 1858, 1859, and 1860 deserve the trouble of

* "It is impossible to regard the ordinary course of events in the United States without perceiving that the wish to be re-elected rules the thoughts of the President; that all the policy of his administration tends to this point, that his slightest movements are subordinated to this object; that especially, as the critical moment approaches, private interest takes the place of public interest in his mind. Being re-eligible, he is nothing more than a docile instrument in the hands of the majority; he loves what it loves, hates what it hates, forestalls its pleasures, anticipates its complaints, yields to its slightest wishes; intended by the lawgivers to guide, he follows it." (De Tocqueville, I. p. 223.)

analyzation ; beneath the enormous mass of subjects, facts, figures, and words are discovered declarations of vast importance to the repose of Europe and the world, as in the army of Macbeth, ambushed behind the tangled wood, swords and lances are found. It may not be uninteresting to extract and sum up, to render them more conspicuous, the articles of the programme of Mr. Buchanan's foreign policy.

In China and Japan, the plenipotentiary, with incomparable shrewdness and address,* has profited by the demonstrations of two great nations to obtain the same advantages for his own without striking a blow. America has played the part of Austria in the Eastern war, —that of winning without hazarding a stake. Concluded at Tientsin on the 18th of June, 1858, and ratified by the President by advice of the Senate on the 21st of the following December, the treaty has been returned to Pekin by Mr. John Ward, and the ratifications exchanged at Peit-sang on the 16th of August, 1859.†

The President has achieved a notable diplomatic success in 1858 in negotiating the abandonment of the right of search by England ; on which he congratulates himself by saying, very justly : "No two nations have ever existed on the face of the earth which could do each other so much good or so much harm." He adds, that "the repeated acts of British cruisers in boarding and searching our merchant-vessels in the Gulf of Mexico and the adjacent seas are so much the more injurious and annoying, as these waters are traversed by a large portion of the commerce and navigation of the United States, and their free and unrestricted use is essential to the security of the *coastwise trade* between the different States of the Union." This coastwise trade might remind us somewhat of that on the Coast of Africa.

* Message of 1858.

† Message of 1859.

In 1859, a new difficulty has arisen with respect to the possession of the island San Juan, but these are in process of arrangement.

The relations between England and France continue friendly. This is not the case, either in 1858 or 1859, with Spain. An amicable arrangement is resolved on, *if possible;* hitherto it has been found impossible to realize it. To a distinguished citizen of Kentucky has been confided the task of essaying for *the last time* to obtain justice from the Spanish government. What, then, are the grievances of the affair of the *Black Warrior*, declared by the President to be of a nature, if reparation be not made, to justify an *immediate appeal to war?* The reclamation of custom-house duties, illegally collected. Then Spanish functionaries, *placed under the control of the Captain-General of Cuba,* have insulted the national flag.

Behold Cuba arraigned for trial!

Listen to the sequel. It is very disagreeable to have to make reclamations at Madrid, so far distant and before a cabinet that changes so often, for, in short, "Cuba is almost within sight of our shores; our commerce with it is far greater than that of any other nation, including Spain itself, and our citizens are in habits of daily and extended personal intercourse with every part of the island."

A grasping farmer does not plan more adroitly how to efface the boundary-lines of the field of his neighbor, upon the latter's refusal to sell him this field so near his own, so necessary to his convenience, so much frequented by his children; — he too alleges the interests of agriculture: the field will be better cultivated in his hands, he will not suffer it, like its present possessor, to be run down by weeds or by obsolete methods of farming.

Mr. Buchanan takes higher ground: he invokes morality and philanthropy, he points out the error of Europe. She fancies that the United States covet Cuba in order that there may be one more Slave State in the Union. She recalls the letter to Mr. Soulé that we have cited. No, no, it is through abhorrence of the slave-trade that the United States wish to acquire Cuba.

"It is the only spot in the civilized world where the African slave-trade is tolerated, and we are bound by treaty with Great Britain to maintain a naval force on the coast of Africa, at much expense both of life and treasure, solely for the purpose of arresting slavers bound to that isle. . . . .

"As long as this market shall remain open, there can be no hope for the civilization of benighted Africa. Whilst the demand for slaves continues in Cuba, wars will be waged among the petty and barbarous chiefs in Africa, for the purpose of seizing subjects to supply this trade. In such a condition of affairs, it is impossible that the light of civilization and religion ever penetrate these dark abodes."

The message of 1859 repeats these considerations, so philanthropic and pious: —

"But we are obliged, as a Christian and moral nation, to consider what would be the effect upon unhappy Africa itself, if we should reopen the slave-trade. This would give the trade an impulse and extension which it never had even in its palmiest days. The numerous victims required to supply it would convert the whole slave-coast into a perfect pandemonium, for which this country would be held responsible in the eyes both of God and man. Its petty tribes would then be constantly engaged in predatory wars against each other, for the purpose of seizing slaves to supply the American market. All hope of African civilization would thus be ended.

"On the other hand, when a market for African slaves shall be no longer furnished in Cuba, and thus all the world be closed against this trade, we may then indulge a reasonable hope for the gradual improvement of Africa. The chief motive of war among the tribes will cease whenever there is no longer any demand for slaves. The resources of that fertile, but miserable country, might then be developed by the hand of industry, and afford subjects for legitimate foreign and domestic commerce. In this manner, Christianity and civilization may gradually penetrate the existing gloom."

Our suspicions are put to rest; it is through interest for Africa that America wishes to despoil Spain; it is through aversion to the slave-trade that the South burns to annex one Slave State more!

With these pious views is mingled, however, a less exalted sentiment; already expressed, it appears again a second, then a third time. Mr. Buchanan speaks of the principles of America, before speaking of its appetites, as one says grace before meat; but hunger cries more loudly, and stifles the moralizing.

"The island of Cuba, from its geographical position, commands the mouth of the Mississippi, and the immense and annually increasing trade, foreign and coastwise, from the valley of that noble river, now embracing half the sovereign States of the Union. With that island under the dominion of a distant foreign power, this trade, of vital importance to these States, is exposed to the danger of being destroyed in time of war, and it has hitherto been subjected to perpetual injury and annoyance in time of peace. Our relations with Spain, which ought to be of the most friendly character, *must always be placed in jeopardy, while the existing colonial government over the island shall remain in its present position.*

"Whilst the possession of the island would be of vast importance to the United States, its value to Spain is, comparatively, unimportant. Such was the relative situation of the parties when the great Napoleon transferred Louisiana to the United States. Jealous, as he ever was, of the national honor and interests of France, *no person throughout the world* has imputed blame to him for accepting a pecuniary equivalent for this cession."

It is easy to divine the rest. The United States are to haggle for Cuba, like a merchant for a bale of cotton ; or to abduct it as a lover carries off a beauty.

"It has been made known to the world, by my predecessors, that the United States have, on several occasions, endeavored to *acquire Cuba from Spain* by honorable *negotiation.* We would not, if we could, acquire Cuba in any other manner. This is due to our national character. All the territory which we have acquired since the origin of the government has been by fair purchase from France, Spain, and Mexico ; or by the free and voluntary act of the independent state of Texas,* in blending her destinies with our own. This course we shall ever pursue, UNLESS *circumstances should occur, which we do not now anticipate, rendering a departure from it clearly justifiable, under the imperative and ruling law of self-preservation.*" †

Astuteness and covetousness could invent no more adroit and audacious language than this. In truth, one asks himself whether he is reading a genuine historical document or a scene in a farce.

* Mr. Buchanan puts his own interpretation on the history of the capture of Texas and the sale of Louisiana. We have seen how *free and spontaneous* was the annexation of Texas. As to Louisiana, it is well known that Napoleon I., at the time of the rupture of the Peace of Amiens (March, 1803), embarrassed how to defend Louisiana against the probable aggressions of the English, and unwilling to ask credit for the resources of war, determined, despite the warm opposition of M. Decrès, his Minister of the Marine, to sell this beautiful territory for eighty million francs. Mr. Monroe, who had visited France to regulate the question of transit on the Mississippi, was greatly surprised by this unexpected proposition, which he had the shrewdness to accept on the spot. The necessities of war and financial distress were the causes, therefore, of this lamentable cession, which rendered the United States masters of the mouths of the Mississippi and the Gulf of Mexico, and left them with no other neighbor than Spain. (Thiers, *Histoire du Consulat et de l'Empire*, Tom. IV. Liv. XVI. p. 320.)

† In 1859 this policy is confirmed. "I need not repeat the arguments which I urged in my last annual message in favor of the acquisition of Cuba by fair purchase. My opinions on that measure remain unchanged. I therefore again invite the serious attention of Congress to this important subject. Without a recognition of this policy on their part, it will be almost impossible to institute negotiations with any reasonable prospect of success."

These petty grievances summed up, amplified, and transformed into a *casus belli;* this adroit persistence in setting forth the seductious of the coveted object; morality invoked at the moment when it is least expected; then these prosaic offers of sounding silver; the unfortunate reminiscence of the *free and spontaneous* action of Texas; these protestations of fidelity to the national reputation, — all compose a perfect drama, concluding with this ineffable stroke.

"This course we shall ever pursue, UNLESS *circumstances should occur which should authorize us to depart from it*"!

This is the explanation given the world. Had the adventurer Lopez been President, would he have used other words? It is probable that, in the confidence of his political councils, the President held a still clearer, more explicit, and more practical language.

We involuntarily recall the last scene of the second act of Casimir Delavigne's "Louis XI.," where the king, who has just made a treaty with the Duke of Burgundy through the mediation of the Count de Nemours, schemes with his compeer Tristan to regain the treaty and rid himself of the Count.

"Both are at your mercy."

"Respect the right of nations! No, no, not here." He interrupts himself to offer a prayer, then continues: "But who knows? on the road." — "He is proud —" "Arrogant —" "He may insult you in a lonely wood, — himself or friends." — "*He will.*" — "Defend yourself." — "Count on me." — "I do."

Thus Spain, forced to be a vender despite herself, might see her property, should she resist, slip through her fingers with its price. For the message does not even foresee the possibility of hesitation. The President submits the question to Congress, because, says he, "it may become indispensable that I should find myself clothed with the faculty of making advances to the Spanish government, directly after the signature of the treaty, without waiting till it be ratified by the Senate."

Nevertheless, what does Spain reply? On the 31st of December, 1858, on being interrogated by the House of Representatives, the Minister of Foreign Affairs declares that "the government is disposed to demand the satisfaction due such an insult, ... that it decidedly rejects propositions so dishonorable, and that, if need be, it will oppose, *even by force,* the dismemberment of the smallest portion of the Spanish territory."

M. Olozaga proposes to Congress to assent to these words, and the proposition is *unanimously* adopted.

On the 4th of January, 1859, the Minister repeats his declarations to the Senate, and affirms that no misunderstanding exists between the United States and Spain. He adds, that no offer has been made for the sale of Cuba, and exclaims, in conclusion: —

"If any representative of a foreign power had attempted to make me an offer for the alienation of Cuba, I should have interrupted him at the first word, to tell him the effect that such insinuations would produce on the mind of Spaniards. The preservation of the island of Cuba is not to us a question of interest or convenience, but of dignity and honor; all the interest that might result from it, all the gold that might be heaped up from it, would not suffice to persuade Spain to make the sacrifice of this glorious relic of the precious discoveries and surprising and magnificent conquests of our sires. The alienation of Cuba! Such an insane thought could only enter the minds of those who know nothing of Spain, and have never penetrated her inmost thoughts." *

* In Cuba, the authorities instigated protests. In an address to the Queen, the corporation of Havana remonstrated indignantly against the project of selling freemen like a *vile herd of slaves.* Was this the comparison to be chosen by men who did not blush to buy and sell other men, and to whom reverts the shame of having given meaning and application in human speech to the phrase, "vile herd of slaves"?

Thus all that Mr. Buchanan affirms, Marshal O'Donnell denies; all that the United States ask, Spain refuses. Who is mistaken here? how avoid a collision? Alas! I greatly fear that this is one more proof that the reason of the strongest is always the best.

Let us hope for better things, however; let us believe that right will be the stronger, and that the nations *neighbors* to Cuba by their colonies and to Spain by their territory will not suffer this noble nation to be despoiled. Whatever may be the future, we will not digress from our subject, but draw from these events the lessons which they contain.

Had Spain followed the example of Christian nations, had she emancipated her slaves, it is probable that, after the sacrifices of a few transitional years, the prosperity of this magnificent colony, like that of Jamaica, Bourbon, and Mauritius, would have resumed its course. It is also probable that the negroes, in general better treated in the Spanish colonies than elsewhere, would have readily gathered about their ancient masters. Instead of this, the Spaniards have persisted in lulling themselves to sleep with their proverb, *Que los esclaves se acaben cuando el tiempo los acabe,* — "Slavery will be destroyed when the time comes."

They have found pleasure in wringing the greatest possible profit from this glorious relic of their ancestors' discoveries, as they would squeeze an orange; and but few voices were raised in Spain in favor of emancipation, when England and France were resounding with triumphant huzzas.

At this time Spain could not free her slaves; emancipation would have been the signal of insurrection or betrayal; either the slaves would have made Cuba a second San Domingo, or the Cuban slaveholders, desirous at the same time of keeping their slaves and of ridding themselves of functionaries and imposts, would have stretched their hands to the United States. Now the latter did not wish Spain to emancipate her negroes, for fear that the example would be contagious in the Southern States; it proposed to buy them; it reserved to itself the right to take them. Spain was as it were hedged in one crime by another.

As for the United States, they were also impelled fatally to one crime by another. At any price, it was necessary to aggrandize themselves, as we have already said; for every increase of territory augmented the influence in Congress, in the Senate, in the Presidential vote, in the public functions. The North and South vied with each other in hastening to organize new States; the question was, which should be the first to attain them: it was a veritable territorial race.

Cuba, therefore, was not alone menaced. Mexico was weak and agitated; it was the moment to turn her weakness to account, and to profit by her disturbances. Listen again to the insinuations of President Buchanan.

"Our position in relation to the independent states south of us on this continent, and especially those within the limits of North America, is of a peculiar character. The northern boundary of Mexico is coincident with our own southern boundary from ocean to ocean, and *we must necessarily feel a deep interest* in all that concerns the well-being and fate of so near a neighbor. *We have always cherished the kindest wishes for the success of that republic,* and have indulged the hope that it might at last, after all its trials, enjoy peace and prosperity under a free and stable government. We have never hitherto interfered, directly or indirectly, with its internal affairs, and it is a duty which we *owe to ourselves* to protect the integrity of its territory against the interference *of any other power.* Our geographical position, our direct interest in all that concerns Mexico, and *our well-settled policy in regard to the North American continent,* render this an indispensable duty. . . . . . The truth is, that this fine country, blessed with productive soil and a benign climate, has been reduced by civil dissension to a condition of almost hopeless anarchy and imbecility."

Pecuniary reclamations are not satisfied. American citizens have been the victims of murder, imprisonment, and pillage. Provoking contributions have been exacted. The American Minister, Mr. Forsyth, advises his countrymen not to pay them; he protests against the banishment and seizure of the goods of an American citizen; he quits Mexico.

The President awaits the end of the struggle, and hopes for justice, if the Constitutional party be victorious.

"But for this expectation, I should at once have recommended to Congress to grant the necessary power to the President to take possession of a sufficient part of the remote and unsettled territory of Mexico, to *hold in pledge*, until our injuries shall be redressed and our just demands satisfied."

The moderation of such counsels seems praiseworthy.

The Constitutional party have a gloomy prospect for the morrow of their triumph, in having to answer to reclamations, in respect to which it is declared that "*all gentle means are henceforth exhausted.*"

We do not clearly comprehend by what right President Buchanan reserves the power of refusing to recognize the government or Absolute party as legitimate, if it triumphs. Nevertheless, we willingly compliment him on awaiting the end of the struggle. But is this all?

"There is another point," says the message, "which calls for immediate action."

On the southwestern frontier, in the Mexican states of Chihuahua and Sonora, are a few whites and bands of natives who take advantage of the state of anarchy to commit depredations. This lack of security hampers the colonization of Arizona, and may be an obstacle to the transit of the mail recently established between the Atlantic and Pacific.

"I can imagine," writes Mr. Buchanan, "no possible remedy for these evils . . . . . but for the government of the United States to assume a temporary protectorate over the northern portions of Chihuahua and Sonora, and to establish military posts within the same. This protection might be withdrawn as soon as local governments shall be established in these Mexican states, capable of performing their duties *towards the United States.*"

Protect! The Czar, too, wished to be the protector of Turkey, Turkey protects the Principalities, and England exercises a protectorate over the Ionian Isles. Before long this word *protect* will pass from the language of honest men, to remain the exclusive property of diplomatists.

The message of 1859 repeats, defines, and renders the insinuations more and more transparent.

"Mexico ought to be a rich and prosperous and powerful republic. She possesses an extensive territory, a fertile soil, and an incalculable store of mineral wealth. She occupies an important position between the Gulf and ocean for transit routes and commerce. Is it possible that such a country as this can be given up to anarchy and ruin, without an effort from any quarter for its *rescue* and *safety?* Will the commercial nations of the world, which have so many interests connected with it, remain wholly indifferent to such a result? Can the United States especially, which ought to share most largely in its commercial intercourse, allow its immediate neighbor thus to destroy itself and injure them? Yet, *without support* from some quarter, it is impossible to perceive how Mexico can resume her position among nations, and enter upon a career which promises any good results. The aid which she requires, and which the interests of all commercial countries require that she should have, it belongs to this government to render, not only by virtue of our neighborhood to Mexico, along whose territory we have a continuous frontier of nearly a thousand miles, *but by virtue, also, of our established policy, which is inconsistent with the intervention of any European power in the domestic concerns of the republic.*

"The wrongs which we have suffered from Mexico are before the world, and must deeply impress every American citizen. A government which is either unable or unwilling to redress such wrongs is derelict to its highest duties. The difficulty consists in selecting and enforcing the remedy. We may in vain apply to the constitutional government at Vera Cruz, although it is well disposed to do us justice, for adequate redress. Whilst its authority is recognized in all the important ports and throughout the sea-coasts of the republic, its power does not extend to the city of Mexico and the States in the vicinity, where nearly all the recent outrages have been committed on American citizens. *We must penetrate into the interior* before we can reach the offenders, and this can only be done by passing through the territory in the occupation of the constitutional government. The most acceptable and least difficult mode of accomplishing the object will be to act in concert with that government. Their consent and their aid might, I believe, be obtained; but if not, our obligation to protect our own citizens in their just rights, secured by treaty, would not be the less imperative. For these reasons, I recommend to Congress to pass a law authorizing the President, under such conditions as they may deem expedient, *to employ a sufficient military force to enter Mexico* for the purpose of obtaining indemnity for the past and security for the future.

"Mexico is now a wreck upon the ocean, drifting about as she is impelled by different factions. As *a good neighbor*, shall we not extend to her a helping hand *to save* her? If we do not, it would not be surprising should some other nation undertake the task, and thus force us to interfere at last, under circumstances of increased difficulty."

What are we to say of this kind neighbor, who, with the intent of *piloting, aiding, saving, delivering,* a state without support, demands to introduce into its territory military forces which the *protected* do not ask? — to succor it? No, no, to *obtain indemnities and guaranties!*

Upon another point, again, President Buchanan advises protective measures.

Europe knows little of the five republics of Central America, — Nicaragua, Costa Rica, New Granada, San Salvador, and Honduras, — which occupy, under the brightest skies of earth, a space as broad as France, and hold between the two parts of America the key of two seas and two continents, — that curious bridge called the Isthmus of Panama. This bridge, so convenient for the neighboring states which it connects, is an obstacle, on the contrary, to the intercourse of nations in general; it is time that Cape Horn, like the Cape of Good Hope, should be avoided, and that a canal should intersect Panama like Suez.

This would shorten the distance from New York to San Francisco * 3,600 leagues; from New York to Jeddo, 3,400 leagues; from New York to Canton, 3,200 leagues; from Bordeaux to San Francisco, 3,400 leagues; from Havre to San Francisco 3,500 leagues; from Cadiz to Manilla, 2,000 leagues; from London to San Francisco, 3,500 leagues; from London to Jeddo, 3,000 leagues; from London to Canton, 2,800 leagues; from London to Sydney, 2,200 leagues; from Amsterdam to Jeddo, 2,400 leagues. We can comprehend the importance that all nations must attach to preserving the neutrality of these countries, that no petty interest, no local disorder, may occur to put a

* See the very interesting memoir of our countryman, M. Belly, (Paris, 1858,) who has obtained from the governments of Nicaragua and Costa Rica a treaty, signed May 1, 1858, for the grant of a maritime canal by the river San Juan and Lake Nicaragua, — a treaty which I hope that France will not suffer to become a dead letter. See also the learned paper published in England (1846) by Prince Louis Napoleon Bonaparte, now Emperor of France.

barrier in the way of the commerce of the world; yet without wounding the sovereign rights and lawful remuneration of the States of Central America. To this end, on the 19th of April, 1850, Mr. Clayton of the United States and Mr. Bulwer of England signed the treaty known by their names. But since this time, how many different interpretations have been given to this treaty! Mr. Buchanan began by disputing with England its ancient protectorate over the Mosquitos. For an insignificant claim, Greytown was bombarded. The adventurer Walker was not disavowed, and the patriotism of the citizens of Nicaragua and Costa Rica, commanded by President Mora, alone served to oppose him and drive him to Santa Rosa and Rivas (1855). Walker wrote after his defeat, "I may not live long enough to see the end of the war, but I feel that my comrades will not leave the result uncertain." The President of the United States seems ready to receive this legacy; he establishes clearly, in his message of 1858, the advantages of the neutrality of the Isthmus; but we feel that every attempt of any other nation, every treaty, every movement on the part of the sovereign states, will be considered as an infringement on neutrality, for which the Union will take it upon itself to demand reparation. She says to the ancient republics of Guatemala, as children do to each other in play, *The first that stirs shall pay a forfeit.*

The President asks Congress to authorize him to employ the land and naval forces of the United States to prevent transit from being obstructed or closed by illegal violence, and to protect the life and property of American citizens travelling this route. He goes still further. He pretends that the Americans have already suffered serious losses; they are entitled to indemnity, in something the same manner as the man who demanded indemnity for having torn his coat in knocking down his neighbor. The American Minister has demanded reparation, and the President does not hesitate to declare: —

"Unless this demand shall be complied with at an early day, it will only remain for this government then to adopt such other measures as may be necessary, in order to *obtain for itself* the justice which it has in vain attempted to secure through peaceful means."

We will go no further. This somewhat lengthy analysis of these messages indicates precisely how low the policy of the United States, interpreted by a President who represented at once the ancient and modern American spirit, but who, above all, personified the views and passions of the Southern States, had fallen.

To buy or seize upon Cuba, to settle Mexico, to intimidate, then occupy, Central America, — such was the scheme. What the end thereof? On the one hand, immeasurably to aggrandize the American Union, to lay hands on an immense portion of the terrestrial globe before having the power to people or defend it, to realize at any cost that unbridled ambition which impels the Saxon race to be everywhere the first occupants; and, above all, to aggrandize the South, to create for the South new Slave States, to bring a reinforcement in Congress to the power of the South; thus, in brief, to extend at once the country and servitude.

An audacious policy, imprudent and unjust, which, availing itself of every means, estranges and repels great citizens, inspires and gives birth to adventurers, transforms into piracy the part of a noble nation, and lessens its glory more rapidly than it extends its surface!

See, therefore, what slavery had made the policy of the United States on the eve of the great crisis which signalized the year 1860.

But before recounting this decisive event, let us inquire what influence slavery has had on the material and moral prosperity of the Union.

CHAPTER II.

THE NORTH AND SOUTH.

Slavery exists only in the Southern States of the confederation. How is it, then, that, ruled by this culpable interest, these States in their turn rule the whole confederation? Whence comes the preponderance manifested in the Federal legislation and policy? Is it that the South is richer, more populous, more intelligent than the North? Strange position! Socially, the North is progressing, the South declining. Politically, the North is conquered, the South victorious.

Proofs of this strange contrast abound.

The Slave States have a superficies of 851,448 square miles, or 544,926,720 acres; the Free States, 612,597 square miles, or 392,092,080 acres. Consequently, the first have 238,851 square miles, or 152,834,640 acres more than the second. Notwithstanding, the white population of the second amounts to 18,669,061, while that of the first is but 8,038,996, that is, 10,630,065 less inhabitants; and if the colored population, slave and free, be added, the North has in all 18,893,856 inhabitants, or 30.84 per square mile; the South, 12,240,294, or 14.34 per square mile; that is, 6,653,562 less inhabitants.

SUPERFICIES AND POPULATION OF THE STATES IN 1860.

I. Free States.

	Square Miles.	Inhabitants per Square Mile.	Whites.	Free Colored.	Total.	Ratio of Increase from 1850 - 1860.		
						White.	Free Colored.	Total.
California	188,982	2.01	361,353	4,086	305,439	294.34	324.74	310.37
Connecticut	4,674	98.45	451,420	8,627	460,147	24.35	12.14	42.10
Illinois	55,405	30.90	1,704,323	7,628	1,711,951	101.45	40.32	101.06
Indiana	33,809	39.93	1,339,000	11,428	1,350,428	37.03	1.47	36.63
Iowa	55,045	12.26	673,844	1,104	674,948	251.18	231.53	251.14
Kansas *			106,579	625	107,206			
Maine	30,000	20.94	626,952	1,327	628,279	7.76	*l*.2.14	7.74
Massachusetts	7,800	157.83	1,221,464	9,602	1,231,066	23.95	5.93	23.79
Michigan	56,243	13.32	742,314	6,799	749,113	87.89	163.22	88.38
Minnesota	83,531	2.08	173,596	259	173,855	2,775.06	709.38	2,760.87
N. Hampshire	9,280	35.14	325,579	494	326,073	2.56	*l*.5.00	2.55
New Jersey *	8,320	80.77	646,699	25,318	672,035	38.92	6.33	37.27
New York	46,000	84.36	3,831,730	49,005	3,880,735	25.70	*l*.0.18	25.29
Ohio	39,964	58.54	2,302,838	36,664	2,339,502	17.79	41.12	18.14
Oregon	95,274	0.55	52,337	128	52,465	299.92	*l*.38.16	294.65
Pennsylvania	46,000	63.18	2,849,266	56,849	2,906,115	26.18	6.01	25.71
Rhode Island	1,306	133.71	170,668	3,952	174,620	18.62	7.68	18.35
Vermont	9,056	34.79	314,389	709	315,098	0.31	*l*.1.25	0.31
Wisconsin	53,924	14.39	774,710	1,171	775,881	154.20	8.44	154.06

II. Slave States.

	Square Miles.	Population per Sq. Mile	Whites.	Free Colored.	Slave.	Total.	Ratio of Increase 1850 - 1860.			
							White.	Free Colored.	Slave.	Total.
Ala.	50,722	19.01	526,431	2,690	435,080	964,201	23.43	18.76	27.18	24.96
Ark.	52,198	8.34	324,191	144	111,115	435,450 † 14,555	99.88	81.25*l*.	135.91	107.46
Del.	2,120	52.93	90,589	19,829	1,798	112,216	27.28	9.72	*l*.21.48	22.60
Fla.	59,268	2.37	77,748	932	61,745	140,425	64.70		57.07	60.59
Ga.	58,000	18.23	591,588	3,500	462,198	1,057,286	13.42	19.41	21.10	16.67
Ky.	37,680	30.67	919,517	10,684	225,483	1,155,684	20.76	6.72	6.87	17.64
La.	46,431	15.25	357,629	18,647	331,726	708,002	39.98	6.78	35.50	36.74
Md.	9,356	73.43	515,918	83,942	87,189	687,049	23 14	12.35	*l*.3.52	17.84
Miss.	47,156	16.78	353,901	773	436,631	791,305	19.68	16 88*l*.	40.90	30.47
Mo.	67,380	17.54	1,063,509	3,572	114,931	1,182,012	79.64	36.44	31.47	73.30
N. C.	45,000	22.06	631,100	30,463	331,059	992,622	14.12	10.92	14.73	14.20
S. C.	24,500	28.72	291,388	9,914	402,406	703,708	6.13	10.65	4.53	5.27
Ten.	45,600	24.34	826,782	7,300	275,719	1,109,801	9.24	13.67	15.14	10.68
Tex.	237,321	2.55	421,294	355	182,566	604,215	173.51	10.58*l*.	213.89	184.22
Va.	61,352	26.02	1,047,411	58,042	490,865	1,596,318	17.06	6.83	3.88	12.29

* The census for 1860 enumerates two slaves in Kansas and eighteen in New Jersey.

† Indians.

Territories.

	White.	Free Colored.	Slave.	Total.	Ratio of Increase 1850 - 1860.			
					White.	Free Colored.	Slave.	Total.
Colorado	34,231	46		34,277				
				a.2,261				
Dakota	2,576			2,576				
Nebraska	28,759	67	15	28,841				
Nevada	6,812	45		6,857				
				a.10,507				
New Mexico	82,924	85		83,009	34.73			51.94
Utah	40,214	30	29	40,273	254.18		11.53	253.89
				a.426				
Washington	11,138	30		11,168				
Dist. of Col.*	60,764	11,131	*3,185	75,080	60.15	10.66	*l*.13.62	45.26
Total	26,975,575	487,996	3,953,760	31,445,080	37.97	12.33	23.39	35.59

Let us compare the moral and intellectual condition of the North and the South.

In 1850, the sixteen Free States had 62,433 public schools, 72,621 teachers, and 2,769,901 pupils.

At the same time, the fifteen Slave States numbered only 18,507 schools, 19,307 teachers, and 581,861 pupils.†

In the first, 422,515 *white* adults could not read or write ; in the second, 512,882.

* Now freed by Act of Congress.

† These figures, with nearly all in this chapter, are taken from a work of infinite value for the ample official information which its author has ably collected, *A Compendium of the Impending Crisis of the South*, by Hinton Rowan Helper of North Carolina, published in New York in 1860, of which 100,000 copies were sold by subscription in the North, while it was strictly interdicted in the South. Although Mr. Helper was a native of a Southern State, and partly wrote his work in Baltimore, he was restricted from publishing it in this city by the following provision in the laws of Maryland, enacted in 1831, only thirty years ago: "It is enacted by the General Assembly of Maryland, that, after the promulgation of this act, no citizen of this State shall print or engrave, or cause to be printed or engraven, any picture, nor write or print, or cause to be written or printed, any pamphlet, journal, tract, or writing whatsoever of an inflammatory character tending to excite discontent or rebellion among the colored population of this State, or of any other State or Territory, nor carry or send, or cause to be carried or sent, such pictures or writings, under penalty of being declared guilty of felony, and condemned to imprisonment for a period of not less than ten or exceeding twenty years." (December, 1831.)

The whites, therefore, suffer from slavery as well as the blacks. How many whites under twenty in each State can neither read nor write?

In Connecticut,	1 in 568	In Louisiana,	1 in 38½
Vermont,	" 473	Maryland,	" 27
New Hampshire,	" 310	Mississippi,	" 20
Massachusetts,	" 166	Delaware,	" 18
Maine,	" 108	South Carolina,	" 17
Michigan,	" 97	Missouri,	" 16
Rhode Island,	" 67	Alabama,	" 15
New Jersey,	" 58	Kentucky,	" 13½
New York,	" 56	Georgia,	" 13
Pennsylvania,	" 50	Virginia,	" 12½
Ohio,	" 43	Arkansas,	" 11½
Indiana,	" 18	Tennessee	" 11
Illinois,	" 17	North Carolina,	" 7

The cost of churches in the Free States in 1850 is estimated at $67,773,477; in the Slave States, at only $21,674,581.

The subscriptions for Bibles and religious tracts, the support of missionaries, and the return of free negroes to Africa, amounted, in 1855, to $1,005,743 in the Free States; while in the Slave States they did not exceed $222,402.

In the first, the number of journals in 1860 amounted to 2,888, issuing 735,520,708 copies annually; in the second, to 1193, issuing 192,430,840 copies per year.

At the North, there were, in 1850, 14,911 public libraries, containing 3,888,234 volumes. In the South, 695 public libraries, containing 649,577 volumes.

In 1855, $4,670,725 were collected for mail service in the North. In the same year, $1,553,198 were collected for mail service in the South.

The number of patents issued for new inventions in 1856 amounted in the North to 1,929; in the South, to 268.

To these figures let us add proofs of the industrial, agricultural, financial, and economical inferiority of the South.

"Compare," says Theodore Parker,* forcibly, "these two systems of machinery; the North has reduced iron and fire to slavery; the South has transformed men into machines; compare the machinery of the nineteenth century *after* Jesus Christ, with the machinery of the nineteenth century *before* Jesus Christ; calculate how far the productive power of the North prevails over the productive power of the South."

To begin by an almost incredible disproportion, mark the profits yielded to the customs by the commerce of the different States: —

Custom-house receipts for 1854: —

Free States	$ 60,010,489
Slave States	5,136,939
Difference . . .	$ 54,873,550

In 1855, the banking capital of the Free States amounted to $ 230,100,340; of the Slave States, $ 107,078,940.

At the same date, the North had excavated 3,682 miles of canals; and had expended $ 538,313,647 in the construction of 17,855 miles of railroads. The South had only 1,116 miles of canals, and 6,859 miles of railroads, at a cost of $ 95,252,581.

In the manufactures of the North (1850), with 780,576 workmen, and a capital of $ 430,240,051, the value of the products amounted to $ 842,586,058; while in the Southern States, with a capital of $ 95,029,879, and a corps of 161,733 workmen, they did not exceed $ 165,413,027.

The North in 1855 exported $ 167,520,693, and imported $ 236,847,810; represented by a tonnage of 4,252,615 tons. The exportations of the South amounted to $ 107,480,688 only, its importations to $ 24,586,528, and its tonnage to 855,517 tons.

It is true that the South is chiefly agricultural, and that its products pass in a great part through the North. Thus

* Letter to the American People, III. 42.

New York, which is the London of the United States, represents in itself alone the amount of

Imports	$ 164,776,511
Exports	113,731,238
Tonnage	1,404,221
Manufactured products	237,597,249
Expense of railroads	111,882,503
Banking capital	38,773,288

This alone is a proof that the South has suffered all commercial and maritime activity to drift to the North, although it possesses excellent seaports and important cities.

Thus, let us compare the oldest and most flourishing of the Slave States, Virginia, so favored by its great seaports, its position between the North and South, the West and the Atlantic, the richness of its soil and its mines, and the mildness of its climate, — let us compare Virginia with the most prosperous of the Free States, New York : —

New York had, in 1790, 340,120 inhabitants; in 1860, 3,880,735 inhabitants.

Virginia had, in 1790, 748,308 inhabitants; in 1860, 1,596,318 inhabitants.

New York exported, in 1791, $ 2,505,465; in 1852, $ 87,484,456.

Virginia exported, in 1791, $ 3,130,865; in 1852, $ 2,724,657.

In 1791, the imports of New York and Virginia were equal.

In 1853, the imports of the first amounted to $ 178,270,999; of the second, to $ 399,004.

Shall we compare two less important States, — Massachusetts and North Carolina?

The first has a superficies of but 7,800 square miles; the second, of 50,704 square miles.

Nevertheless, the first has seen its population increase from 378,717 souls in 1790, to 1,231,066 in 1860; in the second it was 393,751 in 1790, while it was but 992,622, of which 331,059 were slaves, in 1860.

Both States possess excellent harbors. Boston has become the second commercial city of the United States; Beaufort is scarcely known by name.

The imports of the first State amounted in 1855 to $ 45,113,774, its exports to $ 28,190,925, representing a tonnage of 970,727 tons. The imports of North Carolina did not exceed $ 243,088, its exports, $ 433,818, and its tonnage, 60,077 tons.

In 1850, the products of the arts, manufactures, and mines of Massachusetts amounted to $ 151,137,145; the same products in North Carolina amounted to $ 9,111,245. Six years later, in 1856, the amount had increased in the first State to $ 288,000,000, that is, more than twice the value of the whole cotton crop of the Southern States. The value of property in the first State amounted to $ 573,342,286; in the second, it did not exceed $ 226,800,472, including negroes; and as the property in the city of Boston alone may be estimated at $ 250,000,000, we see that this city alone might buy up the whole State of North Carolina.

The first State, in 1850, numbered but 1,861 illiterate inhabitants under the age of twenty; there were 80,063 in North Carolina, without counting its 288,548 negroes, kept *legally* in perfect ignorance.

The results are analogous, if we compare Pennsylvania and South Carolina, Philadelphia and Charleston, — the latter a declining city, the imports of which, amounting to $ 2,662,000 in 1760, decreased to $ 1,750,000 in 1855.

But it is constantly affirmed that the North is a manufacturing region, unfitted for cultivation, and depending entirely on the South for subsistence.

This is the answer: —

AGRICULTURAL PRODUCTION OF THE UNITED STATES IN 1850.

General Products.

	Free States.	Slave States.	Value.
	Bushels.	Bushels.	$
Wheat	75,157,486	27,904,476	1.50
Oats	96,905,371	49,882,799	0.40
Indian Corn	242,618,650	348,992,282	0.60
Potatoes	59,033,170	44,847,420	0.38
Rye	12,574,623	1,608,240	1.00
Barley	5,002,013	161,907	0.90
Buckwheat	8,550,245	405,357	0.50
Beans and Peas	1,542,295	7,637,227	0.75
Grass-seed	762,265	123,517	3.00
Linseed	358,923	203,484	1.25
Garden Stuff	3,714,605	1,377,260	
Pot Herbs and Fruits	6,332,914	1,355,827	

Total Difference of Quantity and Value.

Free States,	499,190,041 bushels,	valued at	$ 351,709,703
Slave States,	481,766,889 "	"	306,927,067
	17,423,152		$ 44,782,636

Special Products.

	Free States.	Slave States.
	Pounds.	Pounds.
Hay	28,427,799,680	2,548,636,160
Hemp	433,520	77,677,520
Hops	3,463,176	33,780
Flax	3,048,278	4,766,198
Maple-Sugar	32,161,799	2,088,687
Tobacco	14,752,087	185,023,906
Wool	39,647,211	12,797,329
Butter and Cheese	349,860,783	68,634,224
Wax and Honey	6,888,368	7,964,760
Cotton *		978,311,600
Cane-Sugar		237,133,000
Rice		215,313,497

* Alabama	564,429 bales.
Georgia	499,391 "
Mississippi	484,292 "
South Carolina	300,901 "
Tennessee	194,232 "
Louisiana	178,737 "
Other States	223,797 "
Total,	2,445,779 bales, weighing each 400 lbs.

Total Difference of Weight and Value.

Free States,	28,878,064,902 lbs.,	valued at	$ 214,422,523
Slave States,	4,338,370,661 "	"	155,233,415
	24,539,694,241 lbs.		$ 59,189,108

Total Balance of the Value of General and Special Products.

Free States	$ 566,132,226
Slave States	462,150,482
Difference in favor of the Free States .	$ 103,981,744

Thus, in short, far from the South having furnished more agricultural products than the North, the total value of Northern products exceeds by more than $ 100,000,000 the total value of the products of the South.

Except in *cotton,* its principal wealth, *cane-sugar,* and *rice,* which the South alone produces, and *Indian corn, beans and peas, hemp, flax, tobacco,* and *wax,* which the South produces in greater quantity, — except in these products, the North has the advantage. The South has cotton, which is the bread of machinery; the North has wheat, which is the bread of man.

It may be even remarked, that the quantity of hay produced by the Free States is in itself alone superior to the *total* quantity of the *special* products of the Slave States.

Product of hay in the Free States . . .	12,690,982 tons.
Which, at $ 11.20, is worth . . .	$ 142,138,998
Special products of the South* . .	$ 138,605,723
Difference . . .	$ 3,533,275

* Cotton, ...	2,445,779 bales at $ 32.00	$ 78,264,928
Tobacco, ...	185,023,906 lbs. at 10 cts. per lb.	18,502,390
Rice, ...	215,313,497 " 4 " "	8,612,539
Hay, ...	1,137,784 tons at $11.20 per ton	12,743,180
Hemp, ...	34,673 " 112.00 "	3,883,376
Cane-sugar, ...	227,133,000 lbs. at 7 cents per lb.	16,599,310
Total, ...		$ 138,605,[illegible]

3 D

The result is again in favor of the North, if we compare the agricultural products per acre.

	Free States.	Slave States.
Wheat	12 bushels per acre.	9
Oats	27 " "	17
Rice	18 " "	11
Maize	31 " "	20
Potatoes	125 " "	113

To this difference of products naturally corresponds an enormous difference in the revenues and capital value of lands.

	Real and Personal Property.	Revenue.
Free States . . .	$ 4,102,172,108	$ 18,725,211
Slave States . .	2,936,090,737 *	8,343,715
Difference . .	$ 1,166,081,371	$ 10,381,496

In 1850, the average value of land per acre was, —

In the Northern States	$ 28.07
" Northwestern States	11.39
" Southern States	5.34
" Southwestern States	6.26

We might also compare the number and value of animals, the value of farming materials, etc.

It is enough to have demonstrated by manifold proofs : —

1st. That even the agricultural strength of the North is superior to the agricultural strength of the South ;

2d. That if the South has specific products, cotton most of all, these products are far from possessing the importance assigned them ;

3d. That progress is manifesting itself more and more in the North ; that the disproportion is increasing from day to day in the South.

4th. That the inferiority of the South injures the whole confederation, the prosperity of which would be doubled if

* If the value of slaves, estimated at $ 1,600,000,000 be deducted, a difference remains of $ 2,766,081,871.

the same progress was manifested in the South as in the North ;

5th. That this inferiority is especially injurious to those of the inhabitants and landholders of the South who have no slaves, and whose property is depreciated by reason of this scourge. Now landholders of this sort are numerous, for it is estimated that, of 544,926,720 acres which compose the superficies of the Slave States,

173,024,000	acres are	held by	slaveholders,
40,000,000	"	"	Government,
331,902,720	"	"	non-slaveholders.

It remains to be proved that this increasing inferiority is due to slavery.

Now this is not doubtful ; it is incontestable. We comprehend without proof that forced and hopeless labor produces less than labor guided by will, spurred on by gain, served by intellect. On listening to testimony, it is impossible to doubt that masters and slaves vie with each other in indolence, that the spirit of enterprise is extinguished in the South, that neither capital nor immigration flows thither.

Lastly, judging by facts, we become sure that slavery destroys prosperity, whether we compare a State with itself at different epochs,* or draw a parallel between two neighboring States, placed in like conditions of fertility, climate,

* KENTUCKY.

	Wheat.	Rice.
Crop of 1840 . .	4,803,152 bushels.	1,321,373 bushels.
" 1850 . . .	2,142,822 "	415,073 "
Diminution . .	2,660,330	906,300

TENNESSEE.

	Wheat.	Tobacco.
Crop of 1840 . .	4,569,692 bushels.	29,550,432 lbs.
" 1850 . .	1,619,386 "	20,148,932 "
Diminution . .	2,950,306	9,401,500

and population. Figures have spoken, let us listen to witnesses; they have had under their eyes spectacles still more striking than figures.

"Compare," said Gouverneur Morris, in 1797, to the National Convention, — "compare the free regions of the Middle States, where rich and opulent culture denotes the prosperity and happiness of the people, with the destitution and sterility which the vast territories of Virginia, Maryland, and the other Slave States present to the gaze. Travel over the whole American continent, and you will see the aspect change continually, according as slavery appears or disappears. From the moment that you quit the Eastern States, and enter New York, the effect is striking. Cross New Jersey, and enter Pennsylvania; you will find new progress, new proofs of a different system. Go down to the South, at every step, in these vast slave countries, you will discover a desert more and more desolate in comparison to the increased proportion of these unhappy creatures."

Sixty years later the contrast is more striking. Mark this beautiful passage from M. de Tocqueville, whom one is never weary of citing: * —

VIRGINIA.

	Rice.	Tobacco.
Crop of 1840 . .	1,482,799 bushels.	75,347,106 lbs.
" 1850 . . .	458,930 "	56,803,227 "
Diminution . .	1,023,869	18,543,879

ALABAMA.

	Wheat.	Rice.
Crop of 1840 . .	838,052 bushels.	51,000 lbs.
" 1850 . . .	294,044 "	17,261 "
Diminution . .	544,008	33,739

* Tom. II. p. 298. On both banks, the air is alike healthy, the climate temperate, the soil inexhaustible; each of them forms the extreme boundary of a vast State; on the left, Kentucky, in which slaves are admitted; on the right, Ohio, which has rejected them from her midst. Kentucky was founded in 1775, Ohio not till 1787; the latter has already 250,000 inhabitants more than the former.

"The traveller who, embarked on the Ohio, suffers himself to be floated down the river by the current to its confluence with the Mississippi, steers, we may say, between liberty and slavery, and he has only to cast his eyes about him to judge in an instant which is more favorable to the human race.

"On the left bank of the river the population is thinly scattered; from time to time, a group of slaves are seen wandering with a careless air over the half-barren fields; the primitive forest constantly reappears; one would say that the community was asleep; man seems inactive, and Nature alone offers the image of activity and life.

"On the right bank of the river, on the contrary, arises a confused hum proclaiming from afar the presence of manufactures; rich harvests cover the ground, elegant residences announce the taste and care of the workman; on every side, competence reveals itself, man appears wealthy and contented; — he labors."

Leaving property, agriculture, manufactures, and commerce, if we ask Southern men what share the North bears in the most trifling habits of their life, they reply: —

"It is a well-known fact," writes a Southerner,* "that we are compelled to go to the North for almost every article of utility and adornment, from matches, shoe-pegs, and paintings, up to cotton-mills, steamships, and statuary, that we have no foreign trade, no princely merchants, nor respectable artists. The North is the Mecca of our merchants, and to it they must and do make two pilgrimages per annum, — one in the spring and one in the fall. We want Bibles, brooms, buckets, and books, and we go to the North; we want pens, ink, paper, wafers, and envelopes, and we go to the North; we want shoes, hats, handkerchiefs, umbrellas, and pocket-knives, and we go to the North; we want furniture, crockery, glass-ware, and pianos, and we go to the

* Helper, p. 21.

North; we want toys, primers, school-books, fashionable apparel, machinery, medicines, tombstones, and a thousand other things, and we go to the North for them all. . . . . .

"In infancy we are swaddled in Northern muslin; in childhood we are humored with Northern gewgaws; in youth we are instructed out of Northern books; at the age of maturity we sow our 'wild oats' on Northern soil; in the decline of life we remedy our eyesight with Northern spectacles; in old age we are drugged with Northern physic; and finally, when we die, our inanimate bodies, shrouded with Northern cambric, are stretched upon the bier, borne to the grave in a Northern carriage, entombed with a Northern spade, and memorized with a Northern slab!"

Thus in every manner, in an economical point of view, the North is the stronger, the South the weaker.

But if we look at political influence, by an incredible contrast, the South rules, the North is worsted.

In seventy-two years (1789–1861) of eighteen elections or re-elections, twelve have given the Presidency of the United States to Southern slaveholders, six to Northern men.*

In the election of 1856, of 4,049,204 votes cast, the North counted 2,958,958, the South only 1,090,246. The North gave the majority to the Republican candidate, Fremont, by 1,340,618 votes against 1,224,750 given to the Demo-

* 1789. Washington (Virginia), re-elected.
1797. John Adams (Massachusetts).
1801. Thomas Jefferson (Virginia), re-elected.
1809. James Madison " "
1817. James Monroe " "
1825. J. Q. Adams (Massachusetts).
1829. Andrew Jackson (Tennessee), re-elected.
1837. Martin Van Buren (New York).
1841. Wm. H. Harrison (Ohio).
1845. James K. Polk (Tennessee).
1849. Zachary Taylor (Louisiana).
1857. James Buchanan (Pennsylvania).
1861. Abraham Lincoln (Illinois).

cratic candidate Buchanan; but the South cast but 1,194 votes in all for Mr. Fremont, because he was opposed to slavery, giving Mr. Buchanan a balance of 609,587 votes, which determined his success. The American candidate, Mr. Fillmore, had, besides, 873,055 votes, 393,590 of which were cast in the North and 479,465 in the South.

We know that the Supreme Court is composed of district judges, assembled once a year in solemn session, and that being empowered to judge of law and fact without appeal, between States and individuals, as regards the constitutional point of view, this court has a political importance of the first order, of which the *rôle* of no sovereign tribunal in Europe gives any idea. We know also that these judges, whose function and action are alike immutable, are appointed by the President of the United States.

Now the boundaries of these districts are drawn in such a manner that five judges belong to the Slave States, and but four to the Free States, despite their superiority of every kind.

The post of Secretary of State, the highest in the Cabinet, charged with external relations, since 1789 has been filled twenty-three times during forty years by slaveholders; and nine times only during twenty-nine years by men from the Free States.

Since 1809, the Presidency of the Senate has been continually filled by Southern men, with the exception of three or four sessions.

Mark the proportion of the other principal functions: Speakers of the House, 21 in 23, 44 years against 24; Attorney-Generals, 14 in 19, 42 years against 27; Ministers to foreign countries, 80 in 134.

Seventeen Free States, with a population of 13,288,670 white inhabitants, have 34 Senators, or 1 in 413,708.

* Federal Constitution, Art. II. Sec. II. 2; Art. III. Sec. I. 11. De Tocqueville, Tom. II. Chaps. VI., VIII. pp. 157, 188, 241.

Fifteen Slave States, with a population of 6,186,477 inhabitants, have 30 Senators, or 1 in 206,215.

In the House of Representatives, the Free States have 146 members, or 1 in 91,935 inhabitants ; the Slave States have 90 members, or 1 in 68,725 white inhabitants, the slaves representing the rest, and thus aiding to send to Congress the representatives who vote against them.

We see by these last figures that the cause of emancipation might have gained a majority both in the Senate and in the House of Representatives. But this has not been, for two reasons.

The first is, that a large number of the inhabitants of the North have had interests in the South. The South numbers 205,924 inhabitants originally from the North, while in the North there are 609,223 inhabitants originally from the South ; these last have doubtless quitted the South on account of slavery, but a large number of them are still in its interests, and consequently all the representatives of the Free States are not disinterested in the question.

In the second place, there is a powerful reason, established unanimously by writers, and which alone explains why the South, despite so striking a social inferiority, preserves its political superiority. This is that the North has manifold interests, is obedient to influences which conflict among themselves, is divided into parties which do not attach the same importance to the same questions ; while to the South, the maintenance of slavery is a point which rules over all others and silences all secondary divisions : the men of the North vote in different ways ; the men of the South vote as one man.

It should be added, that the Abolition party, apart from respectable exceptions, has been in the wrong in confounding itself too frequently with the party of abuse, agitation, and disorder, and thus, under the pretext of abolishing servitude, threatening honest men with another kind of intolerable servitude, — anarchy.

It results at once, from this preponderance of the South and brutality of parties, that men of intellect and heart, of noble character and refined talent, inspired with a disgust of public life, have abandoned it, and live in retreat, devoting themselves to isolated labors. A handful of merchants produced Washington and his illustrious contemporaries. A rich and powerful nation has not a single statesman!

CHAPTER III.

REASONS FOR MAINTAINING SLAVERY. — OBJECTIONS AND REPLIES.

One hesitates to believe in such a subversion of justice, religion, and honor. He asks himself whether there is not some powerful reason, some sacred interest, involved in the support of slavery ; he gladly hears it said, that all stories are exaggerated, and that, if the name of slavery exists, the thing is metamorphosed ; he seeks, too, for some tokens of a peaceful solution.

I experience these doubts and wishes.

Ah ! it is by no means to accuse America, it is by no means for the base pleasure of calumniating a great nation, that I probe its wounds : it is with the eager desire to see this young and powerful community cured of the malady which is consuming it. Let us enter, then, upon this new examination : after the history of slavery, let us draw its portrait ; let us listen to its defence, and pass judgment on its cause.

Slavery is usually defended by a few general arguments, by a few special reasons, and by a few practical difficulties.

§ 1. The Origin History, and Theory of Slavery.

I.

Open history, it is said, — slavery has existed everywhere ; it is the infancy of races, — must we complain because all men are not born twenty years old ? Slavery is a natural and universal fact ; it is the education of barbarism by civilization ; it is the novitiate of Liberty.

In fact, slavery appears in history in the position of universal fact, — like idolatry, like polygamy, — in a word, like evil! But history acquaints us, that slaves in ancient times were from conquered races, subjugated by arms; American slaves are from races purchased or bred by their masters: the ancient slaves came from war; the modern slaves come from the counter or the stud.

History teaches, again, that it has not been the barbarian races that have been enslaved by civilized nations, but, on the contrary, the most polished people that have been invaded and reduced to slavery by barbarians.* The Assyrians fell under the yoke of the Medes; the Medes, the Bactrians, the Lydians, the whole of Asia Minor and Egypt, under the yoke of the Persians; the Arabs rule where Alexander reigned; the Turkish hordes progress in nothing but slavery; the Moguls carry death and servitude from the Mediterranean to the farthest bounds of India. In Europe, the Pelasgians were driven out by the Hellenes; the Achaians became slaves. Barbarian Rome enslaved Etruria, Sicily, Carthage, then Greece. Almost everywhere, the subjugated race has been the most advanced, and has civilized the conquering race; when the barbarian has been vanquished, he has corrupted the victor. Such is the lesson of history, which never presents servitude to us as the first step towards civilization, but only as the victory of force.

The lesson, again, which arises from modern history is still more striking; it presents to us all the great nations of modern Europe practising slavery at once during three centuries, without the education of the subjugated race having been elevated a single degree, advanced a single step, by servitude; while wherever it has been established, especially in the United States, this servitude has corrupted and

* *Histoire de l'esclavage dans l'antiquité*, by M. Wallon, Introduction, p. xix.

debased the ruling race, and brought it back towards barbarism.

We cannot insist too strongly on this striking lesson. It was hoped that the black race would people America, and that the white race would civilize the black: let us open our eyes and look at the facts.

Four centuries have not yet passed since America was revealed to the world. All the races, all the tongues, all the creeds of Europe, then already arrived at a high degree of civilization, have shared in this admirable gift of the Creator. When we read the extensive statistics collected by Humboldt; when we follow, grouped in unequal numbers, the whites, the blacks, the Indians, the mixed breeds, the Catholics, the Protestants, the idolaters, into the vast and magnificent regions of the three Americas, — Northern, Southern, and Insular, — where are spoken the English, Spanish, French, Portuguese, Dutch, Danish, and Swedish tongues, all the languages of Latin origin, and all those of Germanic stock, without counting the Indian dialects, — we exclaim, with the illustrious author of these researches: "There is something solemn and prophetic in these inventories of the human race; the whole future of the New World seems written in them." * Yes, the whole future; but the past also. For, at the date that Humboldt wrote, the white race was to the black in Continental and Insular America as 38 to 19. What, then, had become of the black race? for it was this, — it was the African race that had really colonized America. For three centuries, America had received ten Africans to one European. At the time of its discovery, Europe had not a population numerous enough to spare; the people were neither accustomed to long voyages, nor had they the means for them; missionaries, public functionaries, merchants, and criminals were for a long time the sole travellers. In Africa had been found a numerous, wretched,

* *Voyages de Humboldt*, Tom. III. pp. 339, 340, 344.

and docile race, ready or easily constrained to change countries and masters; men persuaded themselves that to subject this race to Christians was to subject it to Christianity. The most reliable authors agree in estimating at about 40,000,000 the number of Africans transported to America during three centuries, and the number of deaths during the passage at more than 20 per cent. Since then several millions more have been carried thither by the slave-trade, according to official documents.* In the hands of the whites, those two unfortunate races, the Indians and the Africans, have been, the one driven back, the other enslaved: both are on the road to decrease and extinction. There are not to-day 10,000,000 of blacks in all America. In the United States there are only 4,000,000 in 20,000,000 inhabitants. Since the suppression of the slave-trade, as yet very incomplete, this population, no longer receiving any increase except from births, has been decreasing, as the births have been everywhere exceeded by the deaths.† In the United States alone there has been, and still is, an increase, because entire States make a trade of *raising* and selling negroes, — the domestic thus taking the place of the foreign slave-trade. Yet, notwithstanding, in this, as in all countries which receive slaves by thousands, laborers are lacking, and the States are driven to extremities. In Europe, labor is also scarce; yet we do not think of mingling Chinese or Indians among our honest peasantry. In the Southern States, as in Cuba and Brazil, the reopening of the slave-trade is demanded, immigrants are called for, conquests are projected.

It is a law of nature, that the human species (and some species of the animal kingdom share in this title of nobility)

* In the documents on Slavery, collected by Gregory, ex-Bishop of Blois, is found a curious speech, delivered at Philadelphia in 1790, by the Rev. Dr. Dana, estimating the slaves imported into America at more than 80,000 per year. (*Bibliothèque de l'Arsenal, fonds Grégoire.*)

† In Brazil and Cuba, this amounts to more than 5 per cent. (Don José Saco.)

does not increase in servitude. It is a second law of nature, that, where the servile labor of the blacks prevails and flourishes, the whites disappear, for the reason that the rich have no need of the poor; thus South Carolina, now so audacious, which had, in 1790, 107,094 slaves, and 140,178 whites, has now more than 400,000 slaves to 300,000 whites. It is a third law of nature, that the free race, when not suffered by God to become entirely corrupted and the victim of its own misdeeds, finally gains the ascendency over the black race in numbers as in activity, and forces it to fall back and lose ground. Renewed in vigor during the last half-century by generous struggles, and by larger loans from the blood and ideas of Europe, North America has received, since 1819 alone, nearly 4,000,000 of Europeans, — a number equal to that of its slaves. Compare the figures of the census of 1850 with that of 1860: —

	1850.	1860.
Free population . . .	19,987,563	27,463,571
Slave population . .	3,204,313	3,953,760
	23,191,876	31,417,331

The whole population had increased, therefore, in the ratio of 36 per cent. in ten years; but while that of the *Free* States had increased in the ratio of 41 per cent., in the *Slave* States the *free* population had only increased in the ratio of 32 per cent., and the progress of the slave population had not exceeded 22 per cent.

If the Southern States should become masters of Mexico, of Cuba, of all the lands they covet, they would lack negroes to occupy them. The number of slaves introduced with great effort into Texas, since its annexation in 1847, is estimated at less than 50,000, while it might have received in the same time more whites who would have cost nothing. There are now some Slave States which have scarcely any slaves, — as Delaware, Maryland, Missouri, and some parts of Kentucky, Virginia, and Tennessee; in the Border States, liberty almost everywhere passes beyond the frontier, and servitude recedes. The black population, therefore, is no longer kept up by the slave-trade; the surface which it occupies is diminishing; its increase is becoming more and more inferior to that of the white population.

It may, therefore, be affirmed, that the black race, in the sad conditions in which it has been condemned to live, has finished its mission. It has not even served to people America, and, decimated, brutalized, repressed, it has not itself been civilized by the white race.

The argument which the defenders of slavery in the United States seek from history, history condemns and contradicts on the very soil where it is invoked.

II.

After history, religion is appealed to, and we hear repeated to satiety: "God condemned man to labor; Noah cursed Ham; the Jewish nation permitted slavery."

This grave point will be the subject of a special study.* We confine ourselves here to a few words.

Yes, God has condemned man to labor, but not to serve. Now it is precisely to exempt himself from labor that man reduces his fellow to servitude. Noah cursed Ham; but where is the parish register that establishes Ham's lineage? "More than one pretended historian," says Voltaire somewhere, "does not hesitate to say *we, our ancestors, our sires,* in speaking of the Franks who overrun and took possession of Gaul. The Abbé Vely says *we.* Ah, my friend, is it quite certain that you are descended from a Frank? Why may you not be of a poor Gallic family?" Where, then, is the American family that may not have a little of the blood of Ham in its veins? If Ham was accursed, what malediction was powerful enough to outlive the pardon of Jesus

* Part II. Christianity and Slavery.

Christ? The Jewish people had slaves; so be it: do you claim to be also of the Jews?

Men dare seek in the New Testament the defence of slavery.

The New Testament recommends patience, and not servitude. The duty of enduring does not infer the right of oppressing. Because a prisoner is enjoined not to burn his prison, is his captivity declared just? The Apostles say to slaves, "Be patient!" Did they say to masters, "Buy, sell, whip, separate?" They recommend obedience to princes; yet the prince of that time was Nero: does this mean that they justify Nero?

It is persistently repeated, "Can you deny that, without slavery, the negroes would have remained heathens? They owe to servitude baptism and Christianity."

This is a mistake; slaves owe to servitude an abhorrence of Christianity. Transport missionaries to Africa, go instruct the negroes at Zanguebar or Gaboon, imitate the children of Claver and Libermann; this is the true way to carry them the Gospel. But to ravish from them all the gifts of God, country, family, and liberty, and say to them, whip in hand, "Work!" then, with the same exhortation, "Pray!" — do we call this horrible constraint conversion?

Testimony abounds to prove that religion thus preached is sterile and despised.*

God desires free souls, and souls desire a father in God; the slave, if he utters the name of God, either accuses him in a whisper of injustice, or senselessly adores him as an

* In some curious Memoirs, recently published, Count de Vaublanc remarks the difficulty experienced by the negroes of St. Domingo in learning religion, and adds naively: "There would certainly be some danger in persisting to persuade them of that which it is impossible that they can comprehend. Their teachers take good care not to do so. In general, all the Gospel preached to the negroes is a commentary on the texts upon patience: I do not imagine that much use is made in their presence of the texts relating to equality." (Part I., *La religion aux Colonies avant et après l'abolition de l'esclavage*, p. 285.)

invisible slave-driver, — a religion of hypocrisy, of superstition, of servility, never of love! Some poor negroes are pious; converted in spite of servitude, and not by it, —having no difficulty in imagining a better life for themselves than the present, they look forward to heaven, they bless death; the words of the sacred writings seem to them a mysterious chant, the echo from a distant country, which lulls them with dreams of future liberty. Then they become pious; but St. Paul was obliged to recommend to the best of them *not to despise their masters;* they love their condition as the martyr loves his chains. Ah! let us not speak of religion; if we do evil, let us not mingle in it the sacred name of God; above all, let ministers of whatever faith be silent; their nauseous dissertations prove but one thing, — that, instead of converting the blacks, slavery has corrupted the priesthood.

III.

The advocates of slavery gladly fall back on more vague and convenient argument.

The race of blacks is inferior, — slavery is neither a question of history nor religion, it is a question of *race.*

It is very fashionable at the present time to talk of races. I strongly commend this tendency, not only because we owe to it admirable researches and valuable discoveries, but, besides, it appears to me an involuntary return to Christian ideas concerning the unity of the human race. The time is not far distant when philosophy and history will join hands to reduce man to his simple self; a book which has made some noise in Germany bears the perspicuous title, "The Individual and his Individuality." To believe that several million men are of the same race, is to be on the road to the opinion that all men are of the same family; it is to admit that those that have gone before us have influenced us, as we shall act upon those that follow us; it is closely to approach the doctrine which affirms the unity and solidarity of the human race.

But what moral inferences may not be drawn from the theory of races? An Englishman is insolent, — how can he help it? he belongs to the Saxon race. A Frenchman is blustering, — how can he help it? he is of the Gallic race. An Italian is indolent, — he springs from the Latin race. Fatalism thus re-enters conscience and history in the grossest and most convenient manner. The seven capital sins become a question of race. Poor negro, thou art a slave! how can it be helped? Thou art of the negro race; thou canst not deny it.

Nevertheless, it is persistently repeated: "Look at the face of the negro; admit that he is black, repulsive, that you would not take a negress for a wife; the instinctive repugnance is as strong at the North as at the South. The color of the skin, the shape of the skull, the nature of the hair, denote in the negro a race different from our own, and science confirms the evidence."

Linnæus, Buffon, Cuvier, Lamark, the two Geoffroy Saint-Hilaires, Müller, Humboldt, and Flourens, four thousand years after Moses, reply with a common voice, that men are of the same species, that this species was born of a single couple, and that this single couple was created in a single place. A *polygenistic* school also exists; it flourishes in the United States; it supports the practice of servitude by scientific arguments. All crimes have their theory; there is a philosophy, there is also a physiology of slavery. But the most recent and most profound works proclaim* and

* See the lessons given in 1856 by M. Isidor Geoffroy Saint-Hilaire, and the fine, perspicuous, and earnest studies of M. de Quatrefages, especially his arguments against the theory of the illustrious Swiss savant, M. Agassiz, now professor in the United States, which maintains that all men form part of one species, but are the issue of several couples, and were created by *nations*, in eight zoölogical centres. (*Revue des Deux-Mondes*, December 15, 1860; January 15, February 15, March 15, 1861.)

place beyond all dispute the noble doctrine, I will even say the sacred dogma, of the unity of the human species.

Science has demonstrated, that between the most perfect of animals and the most imperfect of men there is an infinite difference, that the animal races offer greater variations between different individuals of the same family than the most remotely allied human peoples. In the black and the white the faculties are similar, the language is the same; the skull differs little, the limbs, the proportions, the stature, are the same; marriage is fruitful, and the organ which seems the most distinct, the skin, is composed of the same particles, the same integuments, arranged in the same order, formed of the same elements, grouped in the same manner, and presenting only a different coloring, the tint of which varies greatly, is seen on certain parts of the epidermis of the white, and appears, disappears, or at least is modified under the influence of the surroundings, age, or growth.

And even though the black were not of your race, by what argument would you conclude from this difference that he ought to be your slave?

No physical proof can demonstrate that the color of a man is a badge of servitude; man does not bear his titles of nobility on the parchment of his skin. Has he a soul? Herein is the whole question. A man cannot be a slave because he is a man; does he who fails to comprehend this deserve himself the name of man?

"Is it not certain that through his faults still more than through his figure the negro is an inferior being? He is indolent, inactive, drunken, cruel, incapable of labor or virtue without compulsion. He is truly formed for his inferior condition; the little education of which he is susceptible he owes to servitude."

I know this argument; and I read in the before-cited message of Governor Adams, dated Columbia, November 24,

1856, these incredible words: "Until Providence decides otherwise, the African must continue to be a hewer of wood and a drawer of water. . . . . . There was a time when a canting philosophy almost inclined our minds to believe that slavery was unjust. Investigations have wholly changed the common opinion on this point. The South now believes that a mysterious Providence has mingled the two races together on this continent with some wise view, and that their mutual relations have been profitable to both. Slavery has elevated the African to a degree of civilization which the black race has never attained in any age or in any country."

Touching profession of faith, and well worthy a namesake of that illustrious Adams who, in 1835, delivered a memorable discourse against slavery! At least you should agree upon the bases of this virtuous theory. If you have educated the slaves, how is it that they are still so indolent and thievish? If slavery has no other end than education, be consistent, and affranchise all those who become instructed and intelligent, those who carry on your households and save your fortune; keep none but the vicious, the ignorant, and the imbecile. But how long have our faults been a reason for servitude? At this rate, how many whites deserve chains and the whip! How many entire nations need to be sent to this beneficent school! The Southern States, as I know, and as Mexico and Cuba know still better, are willing to devote themselves to become the preceptors, in this manner, of the human family. What will they teach them? The answer is simple: they will teach them to be slaves, or to be *hewers of wood and drawers of water;* this will assuredly elevate them to a degree of civilization which they must despair of attaining in any other time or country.

No, slavery does not correct the vices of the African race; it increases them: degradation is not the cause of servitude, but its result.

I am aware of the deficiencies of this unfortunate branch of the human family, and do not expect very soon to hail an African Bossuet, Raphael, or Newton. But we are beginning to become better acquainted with the blacks, not only through the admissions of those who employ them, but by the recitals of those who visit them at home.

It is not in vain that Mungo Park and Caillé have roamed over Soudan, through Kacundy and Timbuctoo; that Denham and Clapperton have penetrated to Lake Tsad; that the brothers D'Abbadie have explored Abyssinia; that Barth, Overweg, and Vogel have followed the fantastic course of the Niger; that Livingstone has traversed South Africa from Loando to Quillimane; that Raffenel, Loarer, Hecquard, Admiral Bouet, and Captain Guillain have visited the coasts of Senegal, Guinea, and Dahomey; that Mgr. Massaïa is evangelizing the Gallas, and Mgr. Kobès the two Guineas. We are no longer reduced to the recitals of Herodotus concerning the voyage to the country of the Nasamons, nor even to the interesting, but incomplete, observations of Père Labat, Barbot, Tillotson, and other travellers of the sixteenth and seventeenth centuries.*

We know now, that, divided into numerous tribes, some a prey to abominable tyrants, and to the horrors of a fetichism in which the serpent recalls the ancient symbol of the demon, and in which human sacrifices are a figure of the instinctive confidence of humanity in an atoning blood, others subjected to the yoke by the invasion of Mussulman hordes, all the black nations resemble each other in great kindness and gentleness, remarkable bodily vigor, a sobriety equal to that of the Indian, and enough love of labor and commercial intelligence to have cultivated vast regions, and founded towns of twenty or thirty thousand souls. We know, too, that the sale of slaves to Europeans is the chief origin and example of the pillages and atrocities which weigh down the blacks

* See *L'Histoire des Voyages*, in 50 vols. Didot, 1751.

of Africa. We know lastly, that, despite the debasement of long centuries of darkness, blood, superstition, and oppression, several tribes are handsome, intelligent, and worthy of the most elevated types of the human family.

IV.

Habitually, after speaking of race, the defenders of slavery speak of the *climate*. "White men cannot endure the burning heats of the sun; the climate necessitates the employment of blacks."

Let us examine facts.

Cotton suffers from cold, but no temperature is too high for its vegetation; it succeeds especially in alluvial lands in the neighborhood of the sea; beyond the parallels of 35° on the eastern coast, and 39° on the western coast of America, it cannot be cultivated; while under the excessive heats of the southwest of Texas it grows marvellously. But are these heats wholly insupportable to white men? We may be permitted to doubt it,* for, before the introduction of negroes, whites were employed for ten years in Cuba, and for eighteen years in St. Domingo; in the French colonies, and even in Guiana, white apprentices were used in the beginning; the same was true in Brazil, and also in Cuba, where there are as many whites as blacks. Certain documents prove that black labor was introduced, not on account of the mortality of the whites, but of their indolence.

Lastly, there is no doubt that, wherever labor is hard for the whites, it is also very hard for the blacks; it is for this reason that they are compelled to it by force.

Let us admit, moreover, since it is true, that there are some localities where the blacks alone can support the heat. Thence result three conclusions: —

* See particularly the work of M. de Nouvion on Guiana, and the *Traité de Géographie et de Statistique médicales,* by Dr. Boudin.

1. Wherever the sun has not the same intensity, the argument ceasing to be applicable, the slavery of the blacks should disappear. Now in Virginia, Kentucky, Maryland, North Carolina, Delaware, and Florida the temperature is perfectly adapted to white labor, as every one can convince himself by looking at the map. If blacks are employed, it is not because the sun scorches the whites, but because indolence freezes them!

2. The rays of the sun divide labor, the earth, and its products among men, but they do not draw a compulsory line between liberty and servitude. This is to calumniate the sun. Wherever it exacts black hands, it also permits white hands.

3. If there be a climate which the Creator has rendered habitable to the blacks alone, let it be left to the blacks alone, let them dwell in it as masters, and let the whites abandon it. Do we found colonies on the shores of Lake Tsad? Do we buy houses in Kano or Timbuctoo? Let us not mingle the black and the white worlds together, nor demand arguments from the sun to subjugate the one to the other, but bounds to live in peace, wherever God has fixed us.

Away, then, with all arguments of education, race, and climate, which are fit to lead man to subdue horses, to tame apes, and to acclimate swans and lamas, but not to authorize him to lay sacrilegious hands on his brother-man!

In his *Voyage aux Antilles*, M. Granier de Cassagnac has elaborated an argument, more honorable to the blacks, which is now widely diffused over the United States. Slavery had been deduced from inequality. He deduces it from equality. It is a treaty, a mutual contract, between a vender and a purchaser, one of the modes of organization of labor, advantageous to both parties.

"The slaves sold by the African kings are their superfluous slaves, who have labored for them and been born among them; there are here and there a few prisoners of war, but these are rare exceptions. . . . . .

"The slave-trade, that pretended commerce in human flesh, becomes reduced, in the eyes of men of good sense, to *a simple translocation of workmen, of incontestable advantage to the latter*.* Servitude does not constitute a condition of violence to those subjected to it; it is a method of organization of labor which guarantees the maintenance of the laborer during his natural life, in consideration of the sum of efforts of which he is capable. . . . . . The establishment of liberty in Europe has destroyed the ancient economical organization which resolved the problem of the material assistance of men by obligatory labor, but has not yet found a new and equivalent solution; for at the present time the free laborers consume more than they produce, which is proved by the fact that they receive from society in addition alms, vagrant institutions, foundling asylums, and hospitals. . . . . .

"Nothing less than the impenetrable crust of absurdity which envelops the brain of European philanthropists could prevent them from discerning these truths."

After history and religion, the question of color and of races, behold us then in the presence of a new science, — *political economy!* This provides us fresh enlightenment.

Full as they are of ingenuous cynicism, the preceding assertions would excite the laughter, if laughter on such a subject were possible, of three classes of readers, — travellers, jurisconsults, and economists.

We will not exculpate the philanthropists, but will leave their brains enveloped in the *impenetrable crust,* and only congratulate them that they do not wear it upon their hearts.

I. What do travellers reply to this cool imposture concerning prisoners of war and slave-hunts?

Denham, Oudney, and Clapperton witnessed one of these

* *Voyage aux Antilles*, 1842, pp. 137 – 139.

ghrazia,* they heard the most intelligent of the chiefs, El Kanemi, the regenerator of Bornou, chant his triumph, exclaiming :—

"The blood of my enemies has fed my chiefs and quenched their thirst ; their flocks, their houses, their wives, are our booty. . . . . . I have destroyed five kingdoms. . . . . . I return after humbling my enemies and reducing them to slavery. The enemies of my people stood in its presence like sheep without a shepherd before the hyena ; they were devoured."

They found on the road to Fezzan and Bornou, especially near wells, sinister landmarks, — hundreds of skeletons of slaves who had died on the way of fatigue and thirst.

"These unfortunates," said Oudney, "are dragged through the deserts with less care and attention than we give to the droves that are led to the shambles. . . . . . I have counted by one well nearly a hundred skeletons, the skin still clinging to the bones, yet no one ever thought of throwing a little sand over the sad remains. The horror that I manifested excited the laughter of the Arabs. 'Bah!' they exclaimed, 'they were nothing but negroes! curses on their fathers!' Then, with the utmost indifference, they set about stirring the bones with the but-end of their muskets, exclaiming, 'This was a woman, this was a young man.'

"The greater part of these unfortunates had formed the booty of the Sultan of Fezzan, returning from a *ghrazia* in Ouadey ; on setting out, a quarter of a ration only had been provided for each individual, and they had died rather from hunger than fatigue. They marched, chained together by the neck and legs ; the most robust alone reached Fezzan in a state of complete emaciation and weakness ; these were fattened for the Tripoli slave-market."

* *Le Niger*, by M. Tugnot de Lanoye.

All these horrors, however, were subsequent to the abolition of the slave-trade!

II. What do jurisconsults reply to this new theory concerning contracts?

That a contract is null when it does not involve the equal liberty of the contractants; that a contract is personal, and does not bind the wife, the children, nor the descendants; lastly, that nothing can be sold except that which is salable. "The title of the acquirer," says M. de Broglie,* wisely, "can be no better than the title of the seller; and if the title of the seller be founded on violence or fraud, if the object sold be not venal in its nature, if it be not lawfully an article of commerce, the party interested always has a right to make reclamation."

III. What, in fine, do masters of political economy reply to this pretended theory of the organization of labor?

History and science agree on two capital facts, the demonstration of which is perhaps the greatest service rendered by political economy: —

The first is, that of property has its origin in the nature of man and labor. Man possesses the fruit of his faculties, only because he possesses these faculties themselves; whence it follows, that he can neither sell himself without ceasing to be a man, nor buy another man without destroying the basis itself of all right of property.†

Says a judge, "I ask any one to show me a bill of sale, signed by the hand of the Creator."

The second is, that all the marvels of modern civilization, all its superiority, are due to *freedom of labor*. What makes the irremediable inferiority of slave labor to free labor is, that of the two motive powers which nature has set in play to impel us to action, fear and hope, slavery employs but one, namely, fear.‡

* Rapport, p. 4. Raynouard, *Du Droit Industriel.*

† *Justice et Charité*, by M. Cousin. *La Proprieté*, by M. Thiers.

‡ Baudrillart, *Manuel de économie politique*, p. 75.

Slavery is rather a question of *wages*. The calculation is simple: the negro costs little to raise, little to acquire, and little to transport; he is docile, or if he be not, he becomes so through the lash; the expense of his food and lodging is the least to which it is possible to reduce a human being. It seems as though labor could never contend with a lower price than this. Notwithstanding, the speculation has failed. The labor which costs least produces least; political economy has established these admirable laws, — the earth is of value chiefly through man; man is of value chiefly through the soul; task-labor is that of the free and moral man, and is the best; day-labor is that of the inferior workman, and is less profitable both to the hireling and the master; servile labor is the lowest of all, with no energy, no interest, no stimulus but fear. If the expenses of purchase and education, the interest of the capital employed, and the cost of maintaining the slave, be divided by the whole number of days that he has been useful, it will be seen that gratuitous labor is very dear. There can be no comparison, to use the before-cited saying of Theodore Parker, between the labor forced by free men from iron and fire, those machines of the nineteenth century *after* Jesus Christ, and that yielded by slaves, those machines of the nineteenth century *before* Jesus Christ.

At the same time, while the scarcity of food has augmented its value, the increase of the free population has diminished the wages of the latter, and the influence of these two causes united is such that, in several States, servile labor is beginning to be no longer remunerative. An American author has calculated the date when free labor will be cheaper than servile, which he declares will be in 1923.* This is purely hypothetical. Wages do not decrease with the increase of population, when the demand for labor increases still more, and we could never become

* Cited by Weston, *Progress of Slavery*.

resigned to see the wages of white men reduced to the means of subsistence of negroes. Compulsory labor, without *wages*, is monstrous injustice; it must be prohibited; this is the true question. But this bad deed becomes also a bad speculation.

America offers a striking proof of the truth of these doctrines: they are of consequence enough to claim an entire chapter, which we have devoted to them in the preceding pages.

Thus the pretended theory that slavery is founded on history, right, and political economy, is refuted by travellers, jurisconsults, and economists.

Without doubt, free communities are acquainted with wretchedness: charity entered into the world together with liberty; and charity does not suffice for all. But I wish to know whether sick slaves are everywhere treated better than our poor, in Christian hospitals? Is the artisan alone exposed to beggary? may it not also become the lot of the millionnaire? Why does not the author of the argument become himself a slave, through prudence, in order to avoid the risk of dying in a hospital?

VI.

It is of America herself that we shall ask in fine the answer to the strange political theory which dates back to Aristotle: It is right that part of mankind should be slaves in order that the rest may devote themselves, without care for material life, to the arts, and especially to the exercise of political rights. This strange compensation reminds one of Hogarth's caricature of fat men and lean men. It is necessary to the equilibrium of the world that every fat man should have a lean man to counterbalance his weight.

We shall not invoke the examples of Asia and Africa,

formerly slave countries, nor those of Sparta and Athens,* we shall not refer to the picture of the democracies which slavery threatens with exhaustion and disorder, nor of the aristocracies which it kills by corruption and insurrection. What we have already written concerning the state of America will suffice. What strokes might we add to this lamentable picture!

The frequency of crime, the decay of justice, the state of the clergy, and the corruption of the family in the Southern States are written in authentic and ineffaceable words in every document.

It is especially admitted, as we have already said, that to slavery may be attributed the decline of public spirit, the violence of parties, the disgust of enlightened men for a system of politics in which brutality has more share than intellect.

Here the system of compensation would find again a more exact application; it is not true that domestic servitude is the support of public liberty, but it is true that civilization recedes before barbarism, that angels flee before demons, that virtue disappears before vice, talent before grossness, that the party which aims to keep the blacks has prevailed over the party which wished to lead the whites to progress, that Washington and Franklin have given place to Walker and Lopez.

We have given too much space, perhaps, to this discussion of the *general and theoretical arguments* which the partisans of slavery have put in circulation. One experiences real pain in honorably discussing things which his conscience declares to be dishonorable. But he is well recompensed if he succeed in expelling from the pure region of the soul, of thought, and of science, a theory which had crept in through specious arguments. Disavowed by the

* Wallon, XXVI.

history, by the philosophy, by the political economy which it in turn invoked, despoiled of its borrowed garb like a thief of the garments of an honest man, this theory is reduced to a pure and simple fact, — a fact gross, formidable, difficult to overcome, but at least deprived of the aid of the two strongest weapons on earth, — conscience and reason.

Let us come to the point, and, after *general and theoretical arguments*, examine *special and practical arguments*.

These are reduced to two, most especially in use, the one by the ladies, the other by the citizens of the United States.

The most feeling among the ladies of Havana and New Orleans comfort their hearts by saying, "*The slaves are not unhappy.*"

The most philanthropic among the American divines exclaim, "Slavery is an evil, but *emancipation is impossible. There is no legal remedy.*"

We will give these two objections the reply which they merit.

§ 2. The Happiness of the Slaves.

Nothing is more common in American books than the following sentence : —

"The slave is not unhappy ; he would have been much more wretched in Africa, France, or England : is the free laborer less to be pitied ?"

I.

It will be supposed that I am about to borrow facts in reply from the celebrated novels of Mrs. Stowe, and reasons from Channing's work on slavery.

The work of Channing is in my eyes one of the most admirable ever inspired by religion and patriotism, and the novels of Mrs. Stowe are among the most eloquent appeals that ever proceeded from woman's pen; nevertheless, I am resolved not to make the slightest use of them.*

I am ready for every admission, every temperament, every concession that may be wished; let us keep to the truth, — the truth, alas! is lamentable enough.

I am willing, therefore, to believe that the negro was more unhappy in Africa; but the question is, not to know how he was treated in the land of Mahomet, but how he should be treated in the land of Jesus Christ.

If our cities contain wretches more to be pitied than some negroes, it is a reason for ameliorating the condition of the whites, by no means for maintaining the condition of the blacks.

I consent not to speak of laws. Open the collection of these odious laws! We read there with horror enactments unknown to heathen legislators; we see the slave deprived of rights like a chattel, yet weighed down with more duties than a man; in Louisiana, in South Carolina, in Florida, almost everywhere, affranchisement fettered, marriage impossible, instruction interdicted; in Maryland, the author or the propagator of a writing in favor of liberty punished by an imprisonment for twenty years; free blacks banished from Arkansas, Missouri, and many other States.†

If there are laws which protect the rights of masters, there are some without doubt which hinder the abuse of their power. But, as Bentham has justly said: "Under the rule of the most excellent laws, the most crying infrac-

* I do not wish to place the Americans alone on defence; I recognize their arguments for and against slavery in contests which the same debates excited formerly in Europe; perhaps slavery has never been justified with more spirit and obstinacy than in France; also, in order to avoid translations, to spare the Americans, and to inflict on the French authors who maintained this cause, now so dishonorable, the shame of a reperusal after the lapse of long years, a large number of my quotations are borrowed from them.

† Stroud, Laws of Slavery. See in Appendix an extract from the Code of Louisiana.

tions alone will ever be punished, while the ordinary course of domestic oppressions will brave all the courts of justice." Is it enacted, moreover, that the judges shall not themselves have slaves?

I consent not to cite the statistics which prove the extreme mortality among the negroes, the excess of deaths over births, which has occurred, moreover, wherever there have been slaves, even in the colonies where they have been best treated. It would be answered, that statistics prove nothing, and contradict each other; it might be answered, besides, that the birth or death of a negro is not considered a fact of sufficient importance for particular note; this I believe true, particularly of the deaths.

I consent, in fine, not to speak of the cruelties of masters or their agents. "Do not believe a word of Mrs. Stowe's tales," it is said; "to judge America from her stories is like judging France from the Police Gazette, or a catalogue of criminal cases. To listen to her, every master is a demon, and every slave an angel, as on the stage every rich citizen is a villain, and every poor man a saint. Can you not see that, feeling aside, interest alone would lead the master to take good care of his slave?"

I accept all this; let us not judge slavery by its *abuses*, but exclusively by its *results*.

"Without doubt," exclaims M. de Vaublanc, in his *Mémoires*, "there are unfortunates among the negroes; but how many such do you not see in France? . . . . . The men who skim the caldrons where sugar is made respire a balsamic odor as healthy as agreeable. I have seen a physician order Bordeaux wine for a negro. Doubtless some Frenchmen have abused their authority, and ordered cruel chastisements; this was criminal, but how rare!

"The house, the windows, every place is open. If the negroes were maltreated, they would shed the blood of their abhorred masters; but these masters sleep tranquilly. . . . .

Tell us, then, enlightened philosophers, what is the result of a comparison between this extreme confidence and your doors, your locks, your bolts, your walls mounted with glass, your watch-dogs?" &c.

Then he exclaims anew, "Exceptions may have been noticed, but how rarely!"

The author of the *Voyage aux Antilles* has consecrated his pencil to the same melting scene of the Creoles sleeping tranquilly in the midst of the negroes, then warms in the same manner with the subject: "Behold the creatures whom European philanthropists represent as loaded with chains, lacerated by the whip, with hearts full of vengeance and hatred against their masters! We would like to know what men in Europe would dare let armed servants sleep in their chamber by the side of themselves and their money?" *

He says elsewhere: —

"Those who have seen European and tropical agriculture, and compared the toil of the laborer who harvests corn and wine with that of him who gathers sugar, coffee, and spices, are forced to acknowledge that God has done almost everything for the latter, and almost everything against the former, taking pity perchance on the insufficiency of the black race, which amasses immense riches with little effort." †

These arguments appear and reappear in all American books. Without contesting them, how can we make them agree. To prove that the blacks are needed, it is affirmed that the whites would succumb to tropical agriculture; to prove that the negroes are happy, it is declared that this labor is much less fatiguing than that of the whites; when it is sought to demonstrate the inferiority of the negro, he is charged with vices; to prove that he is contented, his good character is extolled, &c., &c.

Why should we be moved by the scene of these peace-

* *Voyage aux Antilles*, pp. 93, 95. † Ibid., p. 119.

able nights of the New World? how can the negro help sleeping soundly? He is wearied, and is not sleep his time of happiness? Sir Walter Scott says: "Do not awaken the sleeping slave; he dreams, perhaps, that he is free!" If the slave lets his master sleep tranquilly, it is not to the credit of the master, but of the slave.

But we will not dispute; we will draw the same picture of the slave that he willingly draws to himself of the rich man,—the negro is happy; he eats well, he sleeps well; during his whole life, he has no care for the future, no suffering to endure; he is almost constantly singing, drinking, and dancing light-heartedly while his master lives in peace.

This happiness is the most revolting thing of all!

I complain of both for sleeping so tranquilly and living so happily. Yes, what makes me most indignant is, not the cruel master, unjustly chastising the innocent slave,—it is the master without remorse, and the slave without care; it is the young beauty selling a negro to obtain a bracelet, innocently criminal and ingenuously atrocious; it is the rude negro, intoxicating himself, singing, dancing, ready to truckle all other liberties for the single liberty of vice; it is the virtuous father of a family, who fancies himself also a father to his blacks, ready to exclaim naively, with M. de Vaublanc: "If these negroes had been unhappy, I should have been very wicked, for I myself was happy. I should have enjoyed this happiness in the midst of two hundred wretched men." *

Yes, this it is which renders me indignant, because this mutual blindness is the lowest degree to which the wretch and the culprit can descend through the fatal habit of the wrong which the one endures and the other inflicts.

What sentiment of liberty ought I to expect of the citizen habituated to this position of absolute despot? What respect for the law can I find in the judge who violates

* *Voyage aux Antilles*, p. 95.

without scruple the right of the man? What army can be formed in the heart of such a population? What energy, what activity, can animate the heart of a man indulged in all its caprices? What sensibility remains in the heart of the woman tender towards herself to excess, whose rosy lips order the whipping of a slave, or babble about the price and inconveniences of this kind of domestic animal, as it is the fashion in France to talk of one's sheep and chickens?

Beautiful Creole ladies nonchalantly murmur the hackneyed phrase, "A negro is not a man." Yes, in passing a brutalized slave, one finds himself repeating, "This man is no longer a man!" But in the presence of the indifferent master, I say alike, "This man is no longer a man!" Slavery produces happiness only by annihilating the sentiment of human dignity in both master and slave.

The degradation of him who serves and of him who is served in the very midst of the most common, most supportable, most vaunted condition, — such is not an abuse of slavery, but its first result.

II.

The second and gravest is this: —

Servitude radically destroys the family, and this in two ways, — by immorality and by separation; both inevitable.

In slave countries, immorality corrupts both the family of the white man and that of the negro.

How can it be denied? The proofs are living. The blacks and the whites abhor intermarriage. But whence come the mulattoes? We are apparently forced to answer, From licentiousness.

How avoid it? In this respect, the man who can do as he will, is strongly tempted to do all he can. If he has children, he increases his riches. If he abuses his power, who restrains him? who punishes him?

Then the masters are such fascinating fellows! as the author of the *Voyage aux Antilles* formerly assured us.

"The whites," writes he, "have failed in their duties of morality and continency as Christians, I admit; but it is unjust to make their fault greater than it is; and if God pardons them, the negresses will not be the ones to hold malice against them. . . . . . They consider themselves *very naturally* as the wives of those who feed and lodge them; and when we see the kind of spouses to which they are accustomed in their own country disembark from the slave-ships, we need not carry fatuity very far to believe that the latter can be replaced with them without striking disadvantage. This is, besides, their most sincere and scarcely disguised opinion, and if philanthropists believe them very unhappy in finding themselves exposed to the ardor of their new masters, a short voyage to the Antilles will radically convince them to the contrary."*

I pause at this convenient morality. I might add repulsive details, and cite fathers facilitating the first lapses of their sons, rich men mingling vice with the pleasures of a sumptuous entertainment, plantations where the children know very well that the slaves about them are their brothers and sisters, whole cities where an entirely exemplary household is quoted as an exception. But I have not the art to speak decorously of things that are indecorous, still less the inclination to laugh at them.

What shall we say of the family of the black, when he has one? What shall we say of the injuries beyond reparation to which he is exposed, of the dissimulated griefs which he stifles, of the concentrated rage with which his soul is overburdened, when he has not the baseness to accept or complaisantly aid in these outrages? What shall we say of that abominable fact, — *negro raising?* It is well known that, among horses and cows, a fine stallion suf-

* Pp. 237, 240.

fices for a drove. Some slave-holders have in the same manner one sire to several mothers; and the methods for raising the bovine and equine races are now brought into use for the human race, on the soil of liberty.

The family of the unhappy slave is also destroyed by *separation.* I will believe that this was rare in the Antilles; I know that it was not permitted to separate an infant from its mother, before a certain age. I know also that in America the colonists endeavor to keep and not to separate the negroes; I pass over in silence the separation of those who are brought from Africa, since it is claimed that there they have no family. I continue to set aside all *abuses;* but can it be denied that separation is a necessary consequence, — 1st, of partitions after death; 2d, of sales for debt; 3d, in fine, and above all, of the *raising* of negroes, of which we have just spoken, now a flourishing trade in several States, and which leads to sale at every age, in every direction, according to the exigencies of the buyers? *

The husband is thus wrested from his wife, the mother from her infant, the aged father from his son! This monstrous, daily, inevitable consequence, the separation of the family, is in itself alone, to every man of heart, the condemnation beyond appeal of slavery. Ah! our hearts are rent with the thought that death may suddenly snatch from us our wife or child! What would it be, if it were necessary every morning to ask, Is my child sold? has my wife been carried away? The stories of Mrs. Stowe are only the skilful and touching delineation of these separations, the threat of which, always suspended, weighs on all the joys of the unhappy negro.

* Some have even gone so far as to ask whether this forced separation dissolved the marriage, and gave the right to marry a wife to another husband, and an assembly of Protestant ministers have been found to declare categorically that such a marriage was dissolved and a new one authorized.

Listen to the simple tale of an eyewitness,* more touching in its reality than the most pathetic scene that the imagination could invent.

"The cars were coming down from the country to the city. I was sitting by the window, conversing with a wealthy, gentlemanly slaveholder, when our train stopped. Looking out, I saw a group of twenty-four slaves near the car, — some of them crying, — some weeping silently, — others running to and fro, as if in the excitement of incipient mania or approaching delirium, — while *one* sat mute in despair. The whole scene was so wild and unnatural that I did not comprehend it, and asked the slaveholder what was going on there.

"'Nothing, only some of these niggers are sold, I suppose, and the others are making a fuss about it,' he replied, in a cold, formal manner, as he raised his chin and gave a stoical, stupid look, then attempted to resume his conversation with me.

"Three generations of slaves were there. This family consisted of the old grandparents, with their six children, and eighteen grandchildren. None had been lost by death, and until now none had been sold; and had I visited them at any former period of their lives, and proposed to offer them the boon of freedom, they would probably have refused to accept it, if by so doing they would have been compelled to leave their kind master, whom the afflicted grandparents said they had always loved, as well as his father before him, 'in whose house they were born.' But their young master had become intemperate, and a gambler. After losing all his money in the game, a few nights previous, he had staked six slaves — two boys and four girls — on a game of billiards, and they were won by a New Orleans gambler. The latter was putting them into

* Inside View of Slavery, by C. G. Parsons. Boston, 1855. The Parting Scene, Chap. XI.

our train of cars to carry them to S., forty miles below, where they were to be shipped for his own city, as I was informed.

"I first noticed the old grandmother, seated near the car, sitting on a short, round pine log, that had been cut off for shingles. Her emaciated form, curved spine, and snow-white hair gave her the appearance of being a very old woman. Her head was bent forward and downward, rising and falling as she inhaled the slow, full breath and breathed out the deep, long sigh, followed by neither words nor tears. I likened her at once to an aged mother in a sick-room, where a beloved daughter was lying upon a dying bed!

"Her daughter was uttering the last words of affectionate, fond farewell to that devoted mother, — but she did not seem to hear the last words of her child. She was *beyond tears*, — as physicians say, — mute in despair! Or, in the thrilling words of *Ida May*, 'her sorrow was too stern and crushing for outward demonstration. The iron hand of slavery had seized her heart, and she seemed as if it were wringing the last drop of her life-blood.'

"Next in order was the grandfather, an old man, bent down with toil, and bowed down with years, standing with the left hand resting on a long staff that ran above his head, and the right arm on the shoulder of one of his sons, who was just to be removed forever from his sight. It was a vivid, life-like picture of an aged father, standing by the death-bed of an only, idol son, on whom he had leaned for support and comfort in his old age, and upon whom he had depended to smooth his dying pillow!

"A kind-hearted slave girl in the neighborhood had taken the grandchildren out a little way from the cars, where she was playing with them on the grass, — just as I have seen a kind neighbor's wife visit the house of sick and dying parents, and take the children home, or to a remote room, to soothe and caress them, and thus divert their attention from the agonizing parent, and the death-bed scene.

"The doomed fathers and mothers were standing with their arms around the necks of their wives and husbands, from whom they were the next moment to be torn! These mothers were, perhaps, to become the mothers of yet more unfortunate children in New Orleans. The wives and husbands of those that were leaving belonged on other plantations, and to different masters, who had kindly allowed them to come and take the final leave of their bosom companions.

"Slaves usually have wives on other plantations. If you ask the slave the reason, he gives you this answer: 'If I marry one of my master's girls here at home, I may never be permitted to leave the plantation while I live; but if I go off ten or fifteen miles and take a wife, every Saturday night my master will let me go to see her, and pass the Sabbath. In doing this I shall pass by other plantations, and become acquainted with other slaves, and thus there will be a little novelty, a little more variety to life.' This is one very good reason, and the only one the slave dare give, why he prefers not to have his wife at home, where he can be constantly present with her and his children, and where he can sympathize with them in their afflictions and sufferings.

"But the true reason for this fact, which has few exceptions, is that the masters think it unwise to have slave families together, where they can witness the punishments inflicted on each other. It has a tendency to make them discontended. And the same reason induces the slaves to conform to this custom. Their feelings are very strong, and if their relatives are to be punished, they shrink from the sight. And besides, they fear that, if they should be present on such an occasion, they might interfere, and thus expose themselves to the same fate. *Very few slaves can stand by, and look on passively, and see a mother, or wife, or daughter, or sister brutally treated by a lawless woman-whipper!*

"But the bell rings, and the slaves are ordered on board the cars. They break away from their wives and husbands at the sound of the whip, and start for the 'nigger' car. One of them, whose name was Friday, bounded back and gave his wife the last kiss of affection. Then the husband was pushed on board and the wife was left! Friday's wife had a present tied up in an old cotton handkerchief, which she designed to give her husband as her last token of love for him. But in the more than mortal agony of parting, she had forgotten the present until the cars started, when she ran, screaming, as she tossed the bundle towards the car, 'O, here Friday! I meant to give you this!' But instead of reaching the car, it fell to the ground through the space between the cars, and *such a shriek* as that woman gave, when she saw that solitary emblem of the fidelity of her early vow and constant affection for her devoted husband fail to reach him, I never heard uttered by human voice. It thrilled my soul, leaving impressions that will never be effaced till my dying day. Her heart was breaking! She could no longer suppress her grief; and for some distance after the cars started, the air was rent with her bitter lamentations, bursting forth with the most frantic wails ever uttered in despair.

"There were thirty-five passengers in that car, but no sympathy was expressed for the wretched victims of the billiard-table. Young ladies, daughters of slaveholders, well educated, connected with refined families, were in that car but they did not seem to pity the poor, despairing slaves. They laughed at them, and ridiculed their expressions of grief. 'Look out here!' said one of the young ladies at a window to a schoolmate opposite, 'just see those niggers! What a rumpus they are making! Just as if niggers cared anything about their babies! See Cuffee kiss Dinah! What a taking on! Likely as not he will have another wife next week!'

"These ladies were returning from one of the female colleges in the interior to their homes in the city. But sympathy for the slave is not taught in these colleges. I felt indignant, and so much did I pity the slaves, and so highly were my feelings wrought up, that I would have sacrificed my life, if that would have prevented the separation of those husbands and wives, and parents and children. I had remained silent for some time after the cars started, when the slaveholder said to me, 'What are you thinking about, — those niggers?'

"'I will thank you not to refer to that scene,' I replied, 'lest I may say something that will endanger my own liberty.'"

This is very different from all the testimony in praise of the happiness of the slaves.

We will grant, notwithstanding, that many slaves are happy; habit is so powerful and God so good! The poor girl has in her garret a holy image or her mother's ring, the lonely orphan tending goats or swine on the slope of the mountain knows of unknown springs and bird's-nests hidden in the rock, which belong to him and to him alone; and even in the dungeon's depths the prisoner at length creates to himself a little world apart, peopled by an insect, a flower, a sunbeam, a name cut in the wall. God does not suffer a blade of grass to lack a drop of water, nor a human being to lack a gleam of happiness. The poor slave, if he does not divert his thoughts from life, ends by becoming accustomed to it, consoled for it; he thinks of death, then of heaven! But he is happy *in spite of* slavery, not *on account of* it; his happiness he finds in the little liberty of which he dreams, or which he gives himself. The master knows it well. What recompense does he promise the slave at the end of a life of devotion? Liberty.

Besides, is there not veritable confusion in all this discussion? Do we rightly comprehend ourselves, and are we speaking of the same thing? *To be happy, to be free,* — are these things synonymous? I tell you that the slave should be free, and you reply to me that he eats, that he drinks, that he sleeps, that he dances, that he is happy. I speak to you of liberty, which is the happiness of the soul, and you tell me of enjoyment, which is the servitude of the senses. I speak to you of a birthright, and you answer me with a dish of pottage! Let us have done with this misunderstanding. Ah! let not the slave expect, if he become free, to be rich, to be indolent; liberty is effort, pain, and struggle; if he chooses rather to be groomed like an ox, let him stay in the stable. Or rather let us not degrade that glorious name, happiness. All of the French peasants are not fed like the slaves; many among them suffer and complain: are they then less happy? Let us compare them.

Poor Jacques goes to the field; he toils and sweats, and earns forty sous; on the morrow work ceases, taxes fall due, sickness threatens him, and old age draws nigh. Yes; but work returns, his neighbor lends a little aid; then poor Jacques has a hovel of his own, which he hopes to enlarge for his children; for he has children whom he cherishes, he has a wife whom he has the right to love and the happiness to respect; his toil is not sterile, his sweats are fruitful, and his tears of pain are mingled with tears of joy.

Uncle Ned goes to the field; he toils and sweats, and receives no wages; but he eats, drinks, is cared for, and has no thought for the future. Yes, but every day brings the same pittance, the same lot; if the sky is without a cloud, it is without a sunbeam, — gloomy, pitiless. Ned has children, — they are sold ; a wife, — is she his alone ? How can he be happy ? he cannot render any other person happy ! If he complains, he is whipped ; if he dances, it is because he has lost the secret of tears ; if he believes in heaven, it is in the hope of meeting no whites there ; if he does not believe in it, what is his life ! His sole resource is to be a saint or a drunkard ; a horrible fate if he reflects, an abject one if he succeeds in not reflecting.

The sultana of the harem is, also, more happy than the peasant-woman ; she sleeps, she is waited upon, she reposes without care, and is luxuriously lodged. The poor woman suffers, toils, gives birth in a manger, watches, and often weeps. What a distance between this couch of shame and this bed of honor, — this ignoble repose and this holy toil !

Happiness is duty, pure love, and liberty ; it is wholly within our soul, and the happiness of dining well is nothing but the felicity of the belly and the pleasure of swine.

Is it alleged to us, that all these reasonings are good for a French citizen, who goes to school and reads the papers, but by no means suited to a miserable negro ? that it is absurd to pity him who does not himself complain ? He does not complain ! Are you quite sure of listening to his complaints with attentive good-will ? What the ear of man hears not, that of God receives. Let us serve for an instant as an echo of what the blacks themselves think of their fate.

Every prisoner dreams of escaping, every slave dreams of fleeing ; a number succeed, and Canada thus contains from forty to fifty thousand negroes, nearly all fugitives from the United States, who have settled at St. Catherine, Toronto, and other towns.

A very curious book * has been composed of tales written

* The Refugees, or Narratives of Fugitive Slaves in Canada, related by themselves to Benjamin Drew. Boston, 1856. A few of these narratives, full of interest, which would demand too much room here, will be found in the Appendix.

from the dictation of these fugitive blacks of Canada, — a few of which I transcribe.

"29. WILLIAM JOHNSON: —

"I look on slavery as a deadly poison. The slaves are not satisfied with their lot. On the farm where I worked, in Virginia, and in all the neighborhood, no one was contented. The man to whom I belonged did not give us enough to eat. My feet were frozen in my flight, but I would rather have died on the road than have turned back. . . . . I have never seen a single fugitive that wished to return; I have never even heard of one.

"One of my companions was tied by a violent overseer, and whipped unmercifully. He died shortly after, and there was no doubt that his death was caused by the whipping. His master was told of it, but he would not discharge the overseer. This sin will find him out on the judgment-day.

"The fear of being sold South urged me to escape more than anything else. Our master was in the habit of telling us that, if we did not suit him, he would *soon put us in his pocket*, meaning that he would sell us and pocket the price.

"His son had a child by a negress, and the master wished to sell this child, his own grandson, but was prevented from doing it."

"32. REV. ALEXANDER HELMSLEY: —

"My master was not in the habit of buying and selling, but this was common in his neighborhood. The atrocity of separating husbands and wives, parents and children, seemed to me a crime that cried to heaven. . . . . It was pitiable to hear their shrieks, as they were huddled by force into the carts. . . . . The masters sometimes had regard for certain slaves. But I have never seen any mercy shown in the infliction of punishment; this regard was due in general to the most tyrannical feelings. I have seen a pregnant woman tied up and whipped.

"At first, my thoughts constantly wandered back to my native soil. Now I find potatoes and salt in Canada better than chicken and pudding in the United States, with eternal anxiety. I am an Englishman. My American blood has left my veins. I hate tyranny. I had rather meet snakes than some men whom I know in the United States. . . . . I am not a writer, but if any one would correct my style, I could write a story of slavery which would show how tyranny acts on the mind of slaves. . . . . Once I dreamed that I was retaken. . . . . I waked in inexpressible anguish! It was horrible! . . . . . I am now sixty years old. I have for twenty years performed the duties of a Methodist minister, ... poorly paid, because I preached the Gospel, but I have always put my trust in the Lord, never praying for fortune or renown, but always that his name might be blessed and his will be done."

"41. James Seward: —

"I had a niece married and the mother of two children, one at the breast. My master was in debt, and I was put in prison as security. My niece had been hired; it was resolved that she should be sold. She was separated from her children, and put, handcuffed, into the prison where I was. The irons were taken off, but she cried constantly, in despair, 'O my children, my poor children!' She was sold, and carried far from her children."

"44. Mrs. Ellis: —

"I was a slave in Delaware thirty-two years. I was treated tolerably well in comparison with many others. I was brought up in ignorance, and felt my mind debased, and I have been beaten with a cart-whip. I shall carry to my grave a scar on my forehead from a blow my master gave me. I have had four children; two are dead, and two fled with me when my master threatened to sell me and keep my children. Slavery is a bad institution. I think that, if the whites should free the slaves, they would run no danger. Laboring men would go on with their labor without rebelling."

"DAN JOSIAH LOCKHART: —

"My master threatened to whip me till I was striped like a zebra." *

We might add other narratives; but the picture is always the same, — the whip, separation, ignorance, contempt, threats, — this is what men dare call the happiness of the slaves.

Are all of these features exaggerations or exceptions? Admit, if you will, that no slaves flee but those who are ill-treated, but do not forget that to this bad treatment, to which several thousand slaves are really subjected, several millions are daily exposed.

"Damocles † is seated at a king's table, covered with gold and silver plate, loaded with exquisite viands. 'What a lucky fellow that Damocles is,' exclaims Mr. South, 'at such a glorious wedding-feast!'

"'Yes,' replies Mr. North; 'but tell me, do you not see that sword suspended over his head by but a single hair?'

"'What matters the sword? You confound the grave and the gay; you are wrong; leave us now at our ease to contemplate the dinner. Judging by the vessels of gold and silver, the bouquets of roses, the mingled odors of roast and boiled, and the vigorous appetite of Damocles himself, every one must greet him as a very lucky fellow.'

"'If he be happy, it is because he knows nothing of his condition, or, knowing that the hour of trial is nigh, has adopted the philosophic maxim quoted by the prophet, "Let us eat and drink, for to-morrow we die." However

* This atrocious jest of the ancients reappears, after nineteen centuries of Christianity, like an ignoble echo from the pagan world: "Caprigenum hominem non placet mihi neque pantherinum." (Wallon, Tom. II. p. 240, Epid. Lib. I. Chap. I. 15.) The Latin poet compared the slaves to a race of goats or panthers, on account of the lashes from which their bodies were scarred.

† Introduction to "The Refugees."

happy he may be, the sword is still over his head. Who would accept a good dinner with such an accompaniment?'

"'You are wrong: the dinner is good, let us enjoy it! Damocles is well enough; it is a pity that the hungry, dirty, ragged, and quarrelsome Irishman could not have as good a dinner every day at King Dionysius's table; by and by we will look into the matter of the sword; but for the moment, admit that this Damocles is a lucky fellow!'"

We will terminate by this pleasant, bitter, and, alas! too exact allegory, this long discussion upon the pretended happiness of slaves, — the happiest of men under the best of masters. But who would consent to be for a single day the slave of even his most loving friend?

"It is absurd," says Bentham, "to reason upon the happiness of men otherwise than by their own sensations, and to declare a man happy who finds himself unhappy.

"That slavery is pleasant to masters, is a fact of which there is no doubt, since it depends on their will to put an end to it at any moment. That it is unpleasant to slaves, is a fact which is no less certain, since they are retained in this condition only by constraint. No one finding himself free would wish to become a slave; no one finding himself a slave but would wish to become free."

This settles the question.

CHAPTER IV.

WHAT ARE THE LEGAL MEANS OF ABOLISHING SLAVERY?

§ 1. The Powers of Congress in Accordance with the Constitution.

To the most urgent entreaties, the politicians of the United States have, for forty years, opposed this sole answer : —

Slavery is a terrible scourge ; but there is no remedy. In England and France, indeed, the form of government permits the question to be settled by law. In America, the central power is naught ; it has not the right to abolish slavery in the individual States, and if it had, it could not exercise this right, on one hand, without the concurrence of a majority in Congress, which is becoming more and more favorable to slavery, and, on the other, without violating the Constitution by which it is authorized.

Is not this to calumniate the power of the Constitution? Is it not to diminish the authority of Congress?

I.

The question *de facto* admits of no doubt.

Yes, even before the Secession crisis occurred, the majority in Congress would not have been in favor of emancipation ; and if this violent crisis should end amicably, the same obstacle will again be found.

Lamentable confession ! Could there be a more manifest proof of the ravages of this scourge, than this predominance of a monstrous opinion in a government, the founders of which have deserved, before God and man, the name of Fathers of Liberty, as we say, the Fathers of the Church? But upon what is based this majority in favor of slavery? In great part, strange as it may seem, upon slavery itself. It is known that the Constitution accords to the Free States a number of representatives proportioned to the number of inhabitants, in which latter number it includes all persons other than citizens, that is to say, slaves, in the proportion of four slaves to three freemen. This singular measure, by the successive increase of the slave population, has had the following result. From 1789 to 1798, the South gained 7 representatives; from 1795 to 1813, 14; from 1813 to 1823, 19; from 1823 to 1833, 22; and from 1833 to 1843, 24. By the terms of the last electoral bill (Apportionment Bill), one representative has been accorded for 70,680 freemen, or a proportionate number of slaves; thanks to this arrangement, the South has gained, in a house of 225 members, 20 representatives, or more than one twelfth of the whole number, by reason of its slaves. In 1848, the North had 138 representatives for 9,727,893 inhabitants, or one for 70,492 inhabitants; the South, 87 representatives for 4,848,105 freemen, or one for 55,725 free inhabitants. In the following elections, the South had 117 votes, or one for 41,436 freemen; the North, 166, or one for 52,576 freemen. The unhappy slaves thus contribute increasingly, despite themselves, to send to Congress interested representatives, who are pledged to the maintenance of slavery.

The same calculation serves in the apportionment of the general taxes levied at various times, of which, thanks to its slaves, the South has paid the least, and in the apportionment among the States of the surplus revenues, of which, thanks to its slaves, the South has received the most.*

Removed from letters, arts, and sciences by slavery, the

* Theodore Parker's Letter, 1848, pp. 101, 102.

men of the South have devoted themselves with ardor to politics, because their interests depended on their influence; this, as we have seen,* has become preponderant, and thus the same contagion which infects Congress has invaded the whole administrative hierarchy, — the high places most of all.

It is the fashion in the United States to say: "If a majority for freedom cannot be formed in Congress, if emancipation is not decreed, it is the fault of the *Abolitionists.*" We are accustomed in France to this way of reasoning; it is admitted that causes are always better than their partisans; that the Republic would have endured, but for the Republicans; Legitimacy, but for the Legitimists; and that all reforms are hindered by the Revolutionists. Such assertions are always at once true and false: true, because party excesses are everywhere blamable; false, because resistance to legitimate grievances forms the pretext of these excesses. The wise man does not trouble himself with these external obstacles; without submitting to any constraint, without sharing in any fear, he seeks what is just; if he be in a position to effect it, if he be a legislator, it is his duty to vote for justice, even where it is demanded with unjust violence, even where it is refused by interested influences. In such a case, every public man should call to mind the noble saying of Hamilton, cited by M. de Tocqueville: † "It has more than once happened that a nation, which has been saved from the fatal consequences of its own errors, has delighted in raising monuments of its gratitude to the men who had the magnanimous courage to risk displeasing it in order to serve it."

Should it please God to inspire the conscience of the majority in Congress, what right will it have to act?

Before all things, Congress may undo what it has done. It has intervened by right to permit the pursuit of fugitive

* Chap. II. of this work. † Vol. I. p. 247, note.

slaves; it may by right prohibit it. It has admitted Territories with slavery; it may refuse to admit new ones. It has prohibited the slave-trade, in conformity with the Constitution; it may punish it more severely, it may even interdict it between the States. In this manner the positions occupied by slavery may be one by one regained; it will recede as many paces as it has advanced. No one can refuse to Congress, should the majority change, the right to say *no* in every case where it had said *yes*.

But may not Congress do more? May it not openly abolish slavery? This is not believed. Could a majority be formed, it is affirmed that it would be powerless, because the Constitution insures the right of slaveholders.

II.

Let us open the Constitution.

Slavery was wellnigh proscribed. Jefferson proposed this measure,—it lacked but a single vote; the bond which held the infant States together was so fragile, that, for fear of breaking it, it was not insisted on,—it was referred to religion, to liberty, to the prohibition of the slave-trade; but being unable to proscribe the thing, the name at least was proscribed; the framer, Madison, did not suffer it to enter a single time into the Constitution. Read the text of the article that treats indirectly of slaves.

Art. I. Sect. II. § 3. "Representatives and direct taxes shall be apportioned among the several States which may be included within this Union, according to their respective numbers, which shall be determined by adding to the whole number of free persons . . . . . three fifths of all other persons."

Art. IV. Sect. II. § 3: "No person held to service or labor in one State, under the laws thereof, escaping into another, shall, in consequence of any law or regulation therein, be discharged from such service or labor, but shall be delivered up on claim of the party to whom such service or labor may be due." *

We see that the name *slave*, the word *slavery*, is not a single time spoken, and the Constitution calls *persons* those whom the legislation of the South calls *things* or cattle, *chattel*.

This silence of the Constitution is an important argument.

A fact of this gravity cannot exist except in virtue of a positive law; it is not self-implied, it is not understood of itself, and doubt, in all legislation in the world, has been always interpreted in favor of liberty.

Two paragraphs are added.

1. The amendment worded thus: —

"No *person* may be deprived of his life, *liberty*, or property, except in conformity with law." North Carolina and Virginia proposed, no *freeman;* this term was rejected.

2. The tenth amendment: —

"The powers *not delegated* to the United States by the Constitution, or *not interdicted* by it to the States, are reserved to these States and to the people."

The powers of the States, therefore, are merely delegated and limited. Now, although the Constitution does not forbid it, have they the right to make a king? No; how then have they the right to make a slave? The one is no more contrary than the other to the spirit of the Constitution.

This spirit is expressed in the Preamble to the Constitution, couched in these memorable terms: —

"We, the people of the United States, in order to form a

* Another article (Art. I. Sect. IX. § 1), relative to the slave-trade, has since become useless: "The migration or importation of such persons as any of the States now existing shall think proper to admit, shall not be prohibited by the Congress prior to the year one thousand eight hundred and eight, but a tax or duty may be imposed on such importation, not exceeding ten dollars for each person."

more perfect union, *establish justice,* insure domestic tranquillity, provide for the common defence, *promote the general welfare, and secure the blessings and benefits of liberty to ourselves and our posterity,* do ordain and establish this Constitution for the United States of America."

"To establish justice! but slavery is injustice," lately exclaimed an eloquent orator; "to secure tranquillity and concord! but slavery produces discord and insurrection; to guarantee the common defence! but slavery is the cause of the common weakness; to increase the general good! but slavery entails general uneasiness; to assure to ourselves and our children the benefits of liberty! but slavery takes away and disturbs every one of our liberties."

In fact, without pretending to bring to the examination of these passages the doctrinal certainty of an American jurisconsult, on reading them with simplicity and sincerity, are we not justified in making the following affirmations?

The principle of slavery is openly and strongly rebuked by the spirit of the American Constitution, inscribed in the Preamble. A fact so radically opposed to this spirit is merely tolerated, but by no means sanctioned. It may be, therefore, directly abolished.

As to the articles cited, if slavery were to be abolished to-morrow, there would be no difficulty in letting them stand as they are. For it will be easily comprehended that men would not dare place the ex-slaves at once upon the same footing with freemen at the ballot-box.* On the other hand, a man may be held to another man *to service or labor,* without being his slave, so that the article relating to extradition would still sometimes find an application.

This article, moreover, only interdicts to separate States

* Thus the Constitution of the State of New York, Arts. 2, 3, etc., exacts that every colored man, to have the right of voting, must have been a citizen for three years, and be possessed of real estate worth $ 250."

the power of making a law securing the right of asylum to fugitives from neighboring States; it is not opposed to a general law made by Congress; and this is so true, that the intervention of Congress was necessary to enact the Fugitive Slave Law of 1850,* since it had power to place the federal forces at the disposal of the masters; therefore, it might, it may still refuse these to them, and leave to the wretched slaves the benefit of flight.

Is this, then, the sole example of the authority of Congress over the States in this matter?

It has the power by the terms of Article I. Sect. VIII. of the Constitution: —

1. To provide for the GENERAL GOOD of the United States; now, is not slavery injurious to this general good?

4. To establish a general rule *for naturalization;* does this infer the right to exclude the naturalization of negroes?

10. To expose and punish piracies and felonies committed on the high seas, and *offences against the law of nations;* therefore, it may not only prohibit the foreign slave-trade, but also the internal slave-trade between the States.

Finally, Art. IV. Sect. III.: —

1. Congress may admit new States, and no new State shall be formed without its consent.

* The discussion of questions relative to slavery had been interdicted by Article XXV. of the Regulations of the House of Representatives, couched as follows: —

"All memorials, petitions, or other documents relating to slavery, the negro slave-trade, or anything concerning these two questions, will be received by the House, and laid upon the table without discussion."

On February 27, 1844, a resolution was offered by a member to strike out this article, which was adopted by a majority of twenty votes; but this vote was reconsidered the next day by the House, and annulled by a majority of one. On December 3, 1844, John Quincy Adams renewed the proposition to suppress Article XXV., and the motion was adopted by 108 against 50. (*Revue Coloniale*, Jan. 1845, p. 65.)

2. Congress has the power to dispose of the Territory and other properties belonging to the United States, and to adopt on this subject all suitable regulations and measures.

If, therefore, Congress had declared, if it should still declare, that no State should in future be admitted into the Union without proscribing slavery, it would be fully within its right, as well as its duty.

If Congress, basing its right upon the article of the Constitution prohibiting the slave-trade, should take earnest measures to prevent its shameless practice, and even go still further, and declare the slave-trade practised between the States infamous and illicit, Congress would again be acting fully within its right, as well as its duty.

Are opportunities awaited? They are continual.

The instigation of the slave-trade in many of the Southern States is flagrant. The formation and admission of new States is presented at every session of Congress. The doctrine of independent sovereignty has been already suffered to make too much way among colonies demanding to be received as distinct States. What! Shall indigent Germans, landed but yesterday, robbers expelled from neighboring States, fortune-hunters and adventurers gathered together from every corner of the world, in a new Territory, in towns of wood and straw, have the right to inscribe in a Constitution, patched up by the most intriguing among them, principles to which the sons of Washington will be forced to submit? What would be said, should the Mormons thus present themselves, with community of goods for their law, and community of wives for their ethics? The answer would be, "Become men before becoming citizens!" Slave-owners deserve the same reply.

We might go so far as to say, "Violate the Constitution, if it violates justice." But its illustrious authors have foreseen the necessity and the manner of its modification. Several amendments have already been introduced into it, according to the terms of Art. V., which permits amendments to be made on the petition of two thirds of Congress, and two thirds of the legislatures of the different States.

Therefore, one of two things is true: either the Constitution does not sanction slavery, in which case Congress may abolish it, if it is injurious to the general good; or the Constitution does sanction slavery, in which case the Constitution may be changed.

It is a question of the majority, consequently of public opinion.

In Europe, public opinion is so strong on this painful subject that we can scarcely imagine among ourselves that there can be in America a philosophy, theology, political economy, and literature in favor of slavery.* Men diversely celebrated have not feared to call slavery † "the surest and most solid basis of free institutions on earth; ..... the corner-stone of the republican edifice; ..... the best form of society; ..... the natural form of government for those incapable of governing themselves. ..... A moral, social, and political blessing to masters and slaves; ..... the normal condition of humanity; ..... the means of establishing a genuine aristocracy; ..... the block of black marble which serves as the keystone to the arch of American society; ..... an institution based on natural and divine laws," &c. It is said that to suppress slavery would be "to put back American civilization two hundred years." These words have been uttered in the Senate and the churches; they have been read in books and newspapers; they have been heard in assemblies, academies, and drawing-rooms. The energy and eloquence of a few men have

* See the writings of Harper, Hammond, Simms, Fletcher, Carey, Brownlow and Pryne, Dew, etc., etc.

† All of these quotations are of the date of 1859. Speech of Hon. Charles Sumner, June 4, 1860.

at length succeeded in making the voice of true Christianity, and the words of the fathers of the independence and religion of the United States, from Washington, Jefferson, Franklin, and Wesley to Channing and Cheever, heard above these sayings. European opinion has crossed the seas. Pitt, Burke, Wilberforce, Adam Smith, Lafayette, De Tocqueville, to speak only of the dead, have become classics in the United States. In all the writings of any value whatever due to the human thought in every language of Europe for the last half-century, not a line has been written in defence of slavery. Against this scourge all our writers have been counsellors, all our travellers, missionaries.

The press has admirably served this movement, which commerce and immigration favor against their will. Equals through the most sublime equality, — that of the conscience, — the sublimest thinker and the poorest laborer, the universal writer and the most commonplace tourist, an Alexander Humboldt and an honest German immigrant, coming from the same country, professing the same opinion, the current of immigration, like the current of thought, turns away from slavery, and the masters of America do not see a book or a man disembark from Europe without counting an argument or an adversary the more against their favorite institution.

It may, therefore, be affirmed, that public opinion favorable to slavery in America is dishonored, if not discouraged, is vanquished, if not disarmed.

We must doubt reason and justice, if the public opinion of the human race does not finally prevail in a country where the Constitution itself, often violated, it is true by the State laws, forbids Congress * *to abridge the freedom of speech or of the press; or the right of the people peaceably to assemble, and to petition Congress for a redress of grievances.*

* Amendments, Art. I.

§ 2. State Legislation and Individual Enfranchisement.

Americans who deny to Congress the right of proscribing slavery, at least agree that individual States possess this power, in so far as it concerns themselves, of which the example of the Northern States is a proof. Another way is thus opened to men of heart; surer, since it is not fettered by any legal objection, shorter, since it does not require the consent of the entire Congress; more pacific, since it does not at once disturb the whole nation.

We may add, that the interests of many States, in default of morality, impel them to this course. From the angry outbreaks and complaints of slave-owners, and still more rarely from their confessions, we discover that this disgraceful species of property is already very onerous; that, except in three or four States, the products of which are a rich monopoly, slavery is not remunerative, — *don't pay,* — and that the masters would willingly give away their slaves. In some States, the number of slaveholders is very small: Delaware numbers but 809; Florida, 3,520; Texas, 7,747; Arkansas, 5,999. Let us hope that many States, prompted by interest as well as morality, will some day voluntarily rid themselves at once of a burden and a crime.

There remains the means of individual enfranchisement. A man always has the right to obey his conscience; it was by appealing to this that early Christianity broke the bonds of servitude. The Roman, the German, every law penetrated by a spark of justice or religion, encouraged voluntary enfranchisement. But in America, the law has taken precautions against virtue, and statutes exist in most of the Slave States prohibiting, or at least imposing taxes on emancipation.

In South Carolina, Georgia, Alabama, and Mississippi the consent of the legislature is required. In other States, no one can be emancipated under thirty years of age. In Georgia, every man who effects emancipation by will is subjected to a fine of 1,000 pounds.*

Lastly, we may cite the laws of Louisiana, to show the progress which evil has made in legislation.

According to the laws of Louisiana, Article 184, any master might emancipate his slave ; since 1852 (statute of March 18) no slave can be emancipated except on condition of being transported, after payment of 150 piasters for the expenses of his voyage, to Africa.

The slaves to whom freedom is due at the expiration of a certain time, shall be transported as soon as they become free (statute of March 16, 1842).

That servitude shall be lawful and emancipation forbidden, is a reversal of morality which one scarcely dare decorate by the name of law! Doubtless, should frequent examples of voluntary emancipation be given, should an entire State decree abolition, such an event would create in the rest of the States, among slaves and slaveholders, a disturbance and agitation that may be easily comprehended; the breaking up of the ice begins with a melted icicle. In this is their fear, and my hope.

Shame to the United States, if laws like these, unknown to ancient Rome, can long endure, and if the historian of the first republic of modern times be doomed again to ask and reply: "Can the common law abolish slavery?" "No." "Can the master, in obedience to his conscience, emancipate his slave, and make him instead his servant or friend?" "No." "Is there hope that liberty will some day be born of virtue?" "There is none."

From law, let us proceed to practice.

* Theodore Parker, p. 93. See the excellent *résumé* of the legal system of servitude of the different States, *Études*, etc., by P. Van Biervliet, pp. 44 - 67.

§ 3. What is the best System of Emancipation.

Who may effect emancipation? I have just shown. But how effect emancipation? If Congress or the legislature of an individual State were to broach this great question of *expropriation for the sake of public morality*, how should it proceed?

It is evident that this question cannot be answered off-hand, without entering into details and circumstances. But the examples of *gradual* emancipation by England and *sudden* emancipation by France prove that both modes are equally practicable. The most important point is the *immediate* proclamation of the principle of freedom; the rest is simply a series of conditions in favor either of the master, the products, or, above all, the slave and his family. Of the two modes, the better will be the speedier.

Is an indemnity due? To whom? It would seem that it should be to the slaves, in return for their gratuitous labor. At least, it is strict justice to impose on the masters the charge of the aged and invalid slaves, who have been worn out in their service; and to exact from them an immediate subsidy for the families who have been precluded by slavery from laying up savings for themselves. Is an indemnity due the masters? In the sight of rigorous justice, none; they restore what they held unjustly. But equity is more accommodating; it considers good faith a valid excuse for most of those who have been born in a land infected by a custom by which they have profited, but which they did not make. The interests of national labor, which are also bound up with those of the former slaves themselves, add powerfully to this motive. If the masters are ruined, where will they find capital to cultivate their lands? how can they employ or pay free laborers? An indemnity appears, then, if not just, at least necessary, as a subsidy designed to defray the expenses of transition.

Raised in part by a tax, and in part from the former slaves, who would be bound to labor for a certain number of days, this subsidy, designed for the support of labor, far from being unproductive, would add to the public wealth.

It is calculated that there are in the United States 347,525 slave-owners, in a total population of 23,047,898 inhabitants. These 347,525 masters possess some 3,200,304 slaves,* divided as follows: —

Owners of a single slave				69,820
"	from	1 to	5	103,683
"	"	5 "	10	80,765
"	"	10 "	20	54,595
"	"	20 "	50	29,733
"	"	50 "	100	6,196
"	"	100 "	200	1,479
"	"	200 "	300	187
"	"	300 "	500	56
"	"	500 "	1,000	9
"	over 1,000			2

If the value of the slaves be estimated at $ 400 per head, the slave property amounts to $ 1,280,121,600, to which corresponds an enormous expense on the part of the owners. The indemnity would be therefore a much smaller sum, to be apportioned in numerous annuities. It assuredly does not exceed the means of the United States, the government of which still possesses, besides the product of imposts, immense territorial wealth.

§ 4. Possible Consequences if Emancipation take place. — Probable Consequences if Emancipation do not take place.

What would be the consequences of the abolition of slavery in America? They are looked upon only with ex-

* According to the census of 1850.

aggerated terror; the examples of France and England, as we have seen, are on record to reassure us. It is true that the number of slaves to be affranchised is larger, the countries to which they may flee are more extensive, the authority to compel them to tranquillity is less concentrated.

I do not deny these difficulties, but the fearful consequences which are made to spring from them are exaggerated.

All the slaves would abandon the country and labor, it is said, and go to people the deserts together with the wrecks of the Indian tribes.

Admitted! room would not be lacking, but the fear of hunger is a motive strong enough to secure us from the danger of a general flight; it would be, besides, a sad but certain means of causing this poor population erelong to diminish and die out, or rather to separate into two parts; the idle, who would soon become extinct, and the industrious, who would gain a livelihood in new lands, or return to their former labor.

It should not be forgotten that there are already 196,116 free blacks in the Free States, and 228,138 free blacks in the Slave States;* in all, 424,254 free blacks, who labor without compulsion when the whites are not cruel enough to banish them.

During this time, the masters will be ruined. Assuredly, a transient loss, compensated insufficiently, I grant, by the indemnity, would weigh upon the Slave States. But in what country is labor so plentiful as in America? Nearly 400,000 immigrants land there every year. The tide of immigration, almost completely turned aside from the South by slavery, would set thither in abundance, and if there be really some limited regions, the climate of which is intoler-

* According to the Nashville Journal, 80,000 inhabit Maryland; 60,000, Virginia; 30,000, North Carolina; 20,000, Delaware; 20,000, Louisiana; 11,500, Kentucky; 11,000, District of Columbia; 10,000, South Carolina; 8,000, Tennessee; the remainder, the other States, in less numbers.

able to the whites, the price of labor there will become high enough to attract and retain the free blacks, who will rightfully enjoy this monopoly which the sun has reserved for them. Perhaps in this manner one or more States may even be formed inhabited exclusively by blacks.* Why not? Who knows whether some of the Antilles may not be destined by Providence to belong exclusively to the blacks, in the latitudes where the black, and not the white, is the necessary man?

This sort of natural partition of the two races on the soil, according to the climate, which may be aided by the idea so much cherished by Jefferson, of the re-exportation, either voluntary or decreed, of the blacks to the African coast,† would be the best method of reassuring those who fear before everything the amalgamation of the two races.

If, moreover, this mixture take place and become an evil, what is to blame? Slavery, which brought to America men destined by the Creator to inhabit Africa. But this original destination, together with the instinct of the preservation of species, which warns every being against unnatural alliances, has raised up an unconquerable repugnance between the two colors which is ample security against this dreaded mixture. This amalgamation has not taken place in the North; it will not take place in the South. Should it be effected, moreover, the predominance of the white race would be certain after a few generations, and lawful marriages at least would take the place of those illicit unions which already criminally mingle the two bloods.

There is another blending, the legitimate triumph of which should overcome all repugnance; namely, social and civil equality, which should be decreed by law. The negro

* This was M. de Tocqueville's opinion.

† Liberia, as it is known, was founded with this design; but this attractive and generous idea, despite notable results, has been far from realizing the hopes of its projectors. From 1847 to 1859 the American Colonization Society had only sent to Liberia 4,813 emigrants, scarcely 400 per year.

should be the equal of the white man, in the church, school, property, courts, and taxes. Shall he be a voter or juror? Nothing can be more equitable than first to impose on him suitable conditions with respect to residence, capacity, and fortune. One is born a man; he becomes a citizen.

These difficulties, the solution of which, doubtlessly perplexing, is nevertheless practicable in the sight of every candid man, have been so often answered, that the partisans of slavery are no longer willing to argue on this ground; assuming a different tone, they offer threats, or profess terror, — excellent reasons for those who have no other!

If this question be touched upon, the South will secede; the plan of separation is all ready.

If it be resolved, the black race will exterminate the white. Separation! extermination! Such are the prophecies of Southern men! *

If it were true that affranchisement would lead to a war of extermination between the blacks and the whites, it would be a sinister demonstration of the treatment endured by the blacks, and the hatred accumulated within their hearts. It would end with the negroes as with the Indians, after fearful horrors, in the repression and disappearance of the inferior race.

But is it not evident that extermination is more to be feared if slavery endures than if it disappears? We are patiently examining the *possible* consequences of affranchisement, pointed out and exaggerated by the interested adversaries of this equitable measure. Is it not more reasonable to return to the *almost necessary* consequences of the maintenance of slavery?

Yes, if slavery be abolished, lands will depreciate, labor will be scarce, order will be difficult to maintain, indemnity will not compensate for the loss; but these are transient evils, doubtful and deserved. Mark the positive and al-

* See Chap. I. § 4.

ready existing results of slavery, if it be maintained: religion profaned and destroyed; the first republic of the world dishonored; in the heart of a great people, decay certain, separation imminent, extermination possible. Justice, religion, and patriotism, holy and divine weapons, your victory is sure in every living conscience! But dead consciences are found, swayed by evil, blinded by interest and benumbed by habit. Of what use is reasoning? What can prayers avail upon merchants who say to themselves: "It matters little to us! We make money; we are the masters, we are the stronger; after us the deluge!"

Of all arguments this is the best, or rather it is the only ruling, irrefutable reply, and all discussion with slaveholders may be reduced to the Italian colloquy, which one of the most generous adversaries of slavery * has taken as the epigraph of his book: —

> "Ricardo. — *Io non posso*, — I cannot.
> "Giorgio. — *Tu non vuoi*, — Thou wilt not."

Yes, the masters *can* abolish slavery, but they *will* not; what do I say? they prefer renouncing their country to their property, and breaking the bond that unites the States to the chain that holds their slaves.

The year 1860 was destined to witness the outbreak of this shameful and dreaded conflict; and it only remains for us to conclude, by recounting this, the history of the ravages of servitude in the heart of a great, free, and Christian people.

* Agénor de Gasparin, *Esclavage et la traité*, 1838.

CHAPTER V.

THE SEPARATION OF THE NORTH AND SOUTH.

§ 1. From the Insurrection at Harper's Ferry (1859) to the Nomination of President Lincoln (1860).

On the 24th of September, 1858, Alexander, Emperor of Russia, addressed these words to the nobility of Moscow and Nishni: —

"I have spoken to you of the necessity of proceeding sooner or later to the reform of the laws which regulate serfdom, — *a reform that must come from the higher powers, that it may not come from the lower ones.*

"I love the nobility, ... I desire the welfare of the people, but I do not mean that this shall be established to your detriment; it belongs to you yourselves, for your own interests, to do your best to ameliorate the condition of the peasants.

"I hear with regret that selfish sentiments are taking root among you. I am sorry, for *selfish sentiments destroy every good thing*; forsake them, act in a manner that may be well for yourselves, and not wrong towards others; *I wish you to think of your own interests, but not to forget those of other people.*"

What would Washington and Franklin have thought of this language? Did they imagine that the republicans of the New World would receive this lesson from the autocrat of all the Russias, and that slaves would be left in Baltimore when there would be no more serfs at Moscow?

Alas! dark forebodings more than once overshadowed the great souls of the founders of the American Union. The republic of the United States had its patriarchs, it had also its prophets.

Washington in dying doubted the future union of his beloved country.

Jefferson openly proclaimed slavery to be the cause of separation and ruin.

We have heard the astonishing previsions of Channing.

Let us listen to the expression of the same fears from a more recent source.

On the occasion of the celebration of the hundredth anniversary of the occupation of Forts Duquesne and Pitt, which was celebrated at Pittsburg, November 25, 1858, the President of the United States wrote the following letter to apologize for not being present at the ceremony.

"WASHINGTON, November 22, 1858.

"GENTLEMEN, —

"I have had the honor to receive your invitation to be present, on the 25th instant, at the centennial anniversary of the capture of Fort Duquesne. I regret that the urgent pressure of public affairs, at a time so near the assembling of Congress, will prevent me from enjoying this privilege.

"Every patriot snould rejoice on reflecting on the unequalled progress made by our country during the century which has just passed. What was at its beginning an obscure fort, far remote from the Western frontier of civilization, has become to-day the centre of a populous, commercial, and manufacturing city, sending its abundant products to the sovereign States which are still farther west, and the territories of which were then a vast unexplored and silent desert.

"At the point which we have reached, the patriot, on surveying the past, cannot fail to cast a glance on the future, and to reflect on what may be the condition of our country when our posterity shall assemble to celebrate the second centennial anniversary.

"Will our country be inhabited by a more populous, more powerful, and freer nation than any other that ever existed; or will the federation be disunited and divided into groups of hostile and jealous states? or else may it not be possible that henceforth all these fragments, worn out by interminable struggles, will finally reunite and seek refuge under the shelter of a powerful despotism?

"I firmly believe that, thanks to Divine Providence, these questions will be decided by the present generation. We have reached a crisis where on its acts depend the preservation of the Union according to the letter and spirit of the Constitution; and this Union once destroyed, all is lost.

"I say it with regret, the present omens are far from favorable. In the past days of the republic, it was regarded as almost treason to utter the word disunion. Times unhappily have changed since then, and now disunion is openly lauded as the remedy for transient evils, real or imaginary, which, left to themselves, would quickly vanish in the march of events.

"Our fathers, who wrought the Revolution, are dead; the generation which succeeded them, and which was inspired by their counsels and examples, has almost wholly passed away. The present generation, deprived of these lights, must, whether it will or no, decide the destiny of its posterity. Let it have in the depths of its heart a tender affection for the Union, let it resist every measure which would tend to loosen or dissolve its bonds, let the citizens of the different States cherish feelings of kindliness and indulgence with respect to each other, and let all resolve to transmit it to their descendants in the form and spirit in which it was bequeathed to them by their fathers, and all will go well for the future of our country.

"I shall take the liberty to anticipate the future with respect to another dangerous evil which is constantly increasing. In past times, although our fathers, like ourselves were divided into political parties which frequently contended with each other, we do not learn that they had recourse to money to effect their elections until a recent date. If this practice continues to increase until the electors, or their representatives in the legislation of the States, and the national legislature, shall be infected thereby, the springs of free government will be found poisoned, and we shall end, as is proved by history, in military despotism.

"Every one agrees in the belief that a democratic republic cannot last long without public virtue. When this is corrupted, and the people becomes venal, a worm is gnawing at the root of the tree of liberty which will soon make it wither and die.

"Entreating the Almighty God that your remote posterity may continue from age to age, in the centuries to come, to celebrate the capture of Fort Duquesne in peace and prosperity, under the protecting banner of the Constitution and the Union, I am,

"Very respectfully, your friend,

"James Buchanan."

The same name that terminates the messages which we have analyzed is read at the bottom of this melancholy letter. There is in the same man a thinker and an adventurer, a patriot and a slave-trader. There is likewise before the United States a double destiny, — brutal conquest or peaceful greatness, ambition or justice, an abyss of degradation or a glorious ideal of moral elevation.

Hear this glorious ideal set forth by a great mind: —

"As a people, we have very generally the conviction that Divine Providence has given us an important mission; and has chosen us to work out for the world a higher order of civilization than has hitherto obtained. We look upon ourselves as a providential people, as a people with a great destiny, and a destiny glorious to ourselves and beneficent to the world. This fact indicates generous instincts and a noble nature, and it will not be without its influence in kindling lofty aspirations in our bosoms, and urging us on in the path of a true and legitimate ambition. We believe ourselves the people of the future, and that belief itself will do much to make us so. There is more than meets the eye in the popular expression 'Manifest Destiny.' We have a manifest destiny, and the world sees and confesses it, some with fear and some with hope; but it is not precisely that supposed by our journalists or pretended by our filibusters, — although these filibusters may be unconsciously and unintentionally preparing the way for its fulfilment. It may be our manifest destiny to extend our government over the whole American continent, but that is in itself alone a small affair, and no worthy object of true American ambition. It is desirable only inasmuch as it benefits the new territories annexed to the Union, and secures our frontiers, and protects us in the peaceful elaboration and extension of the new social order of the world. The manifest destiny of this country is something far higher, nobler, and more spiritual, — the realization, we should say, of the Christian ideal of society for both the Old World and the New." *

This ideal was far distant. The United States saw their honor diminishing in proportion as their territory increased; they saw slavery and license dishonoring freedom more and more; they were becoming at the same time the most powerful and most discreditable people on earth. They grew, yet bearing the weight and shame of that monstrous original sin, — *slavery in the bosom of a Christian republic.*

To the ideal of a Christian community they opposed the lugubrious aspect of a community menaced by the laceration of civil war.

* Brownson's Review, October, 1856, pp. 425, 426.

A war of journals, a war of ballot-boxes, a war of courts of justice!

While the Supreme Court decided that a slaveholder may establish himself with his slaves in a federal territory, the Court of Appeal at Albany, after a suit lasting eight years, proclaimed that every slave, not a fugitive, is free on touching the soil of a Free State.*

* The New York correspondent of the *Gazette des Tribunaux* writes, February 1, 1860:—

"The Court of Appeals at Albany has just rendered a decision in an extremely important affair, which has lasted eight years, and which assumes fresh interest from the agitation which the slavery question is causing in Congress and in public opinion. Whatever efforts may have been made by the advocates of compulsory labor, the magistrates of three different jurisdictions have applied the principles consecrated with respect to affranchisement by French law and legislation.

"In November, 1852, a citizen of Virginia, Jonathan Lemmon, arrived at New York on board a Norfolk steamer, with his wife and eight young slaves, whom he was carrying to Texas, where he designed to settle. While waiting till he should be ready to start for his place of destination, he placed the negroes in an obscure boarding-house. A free colored man discovered them there, and obtained a writ of *habeas corpus* to bring the eight slaves before a judge of the Supreme Court.

"Great agitation prevailed in New York. The Democrats claimed that an inhabitant of the South possessed the right of transit through the Free States with everything that was considered property by the laws of the State where he resided. The Abolitionists, and the various shades which have since formed the Republican party, maintained, on the contrary, that a negro was free from the moment that he touched the soil of a Free State, unless he had fled from the State where he was held in slavery.

"Judge Paine was of the latter opinion; he declared, by a long and elaborate decision, that slaves could under no pretext be introduced into the State of New York, and ordered the eight slaves summoned before him to be immediately set at liberty.

"This verdict produced a profound sensation in the Southern States. The Abolitionists of New York speedily raised a subscription of $300 or $400 to send the freed slaves to Canada. On their side, some merchants who had business relations with the South collected 5,000 piasters by voluntary contributions to indemnify Mr. Lemmon for the loss which he had sustained. Fully satisfied with this pecuniary reparation, the Virginian turned his face towards his State, thinking no more of either Texas or his slaves; but the Southern planters and politicians viewed the matter from a higher stand-point. The Governor of Georgia took it up in his Message of 1855.

"'If it be true,' said he, 'that the citizens of the Slave States, who, by force of circumstances, or for their convenience, seek passage through a Free State,

The law concerning fugitives was far from everywhere obtaining submissive execution. Several Northern States, Massachusetts (Session Acts, 1855, p. 924), Wisconsin (Revised Statutes, 1858, p. 912), and Vermont (Session Acts, 1858, p. 42), opposed it by means of explicit statutes, permitting the slave to demand a trial by jury, punishing arbitrary imprisonment, etc.

Finally the war descended among the people, and the lugubrious affair of Harper's Ferry * filled all the Southern States with mingled rage and dread.

In the State of Virginia, on the confines of Maryland, was a little arsenal called Harper's Ferry, of which, in the beginning of October, 1859, a hundred negroes took forcible possession, headed by a farmer named John Brown, his sons, and a few white men. The band remained two days in the arsenal, in which was deposited a considerable sum of money, without taking anything, with the exception of guns. There was no police; nothing had been foreseen,

accompanied by their slaves, are by this fact alone dispossessed of their property; if it be true that these slaves are thus emancipated, it is time that we knew the reasons of such an assertion. The repetition of such acts of violence would be a *legitimate cause of war* with the State which should originate or suffer them.'

"The Governor of Virginia was still more explicit, and demanded of his legislature to interfere, to appeal, in the name of the State, from the decision of Judge Paine to the Supreme Court of New York.

"On December 12, 1857, the matter was brought before this court, which confirmed the decision of enfranchisement. The State of Virginia appealed anew to the Court of Appeal at Albany, and two years passed before the case was tried and a final decision rendered.

"The slavery interests were sustained with great talent by Charles O'Connor; William Evarts was the no less eloquent defender of the Republican cause. The latter won a complete triumph, and the decision rendered has dispelled all uncertainty in like matters. It declares that the laws of the State of New York neither protect nor tolerate within its limits property consisting in slaves, and cites in particular a statute of 1817, which, combined with the Federal Constitution, gives freedom to every one, not a fugitive, on touching the soil of a Free State."

* The despatches addressed to the Minister of Foreign Affairs concerning this characteristic event have been kindly exhibited to us. All of these statements are therefore authentic.

nothing was known, but everything was conjectured; extended ramifications were imagined, and the wildest terror prevailed at Richmond. There was no militia; three companies of volunteers were armed; two returned, the men wearing a bolder face than on their departure, the other reached its journey's end. Governor Wise demanded troops of President Buchanan. Ninety-three marines, the only troops at the disposition of the government of the United States, were sent from Washington. A few hours sufficed to dislodge, decimate, and disperse the band. Old Brown was made prisoner, wounded by four sword-cuts and two bayonet-thrusts; his two sons were killed by his side. The principal leaders, five in number, Cook, son-in-law of the Governor of Indiana, Copeland, Coppie, Green, and Stevens, were arrested; Douglass fled to Canada, Gerrit Smith became insane. The prisoners were brought to trial.

The arsenal and the troops that guarded it belonged to the Federal government; Harper's Ferry was near the confines of Maryland and Virginia. Notwithstanding, the President eluded the responsibility, well satisfied to wash his hands of the matter. The trial was conducted at Charlestown in all haste, without waiting either for the recovery of Brown, the arrival of his counsel and witnesses, or the return of tranquillity. Brown appeared, half dead, but with a vigorous and lofty mind. Not a confession or regret could be obtained from his lips. He was condemned to be hung.

Public opinion was still more ferocious than the law. This dying, captive, condemned old man, mourning his sons, was insulted by writers in the newspapers, and jeered at by ladies in the drawing-rooms. Pity became a crime, the arbitrary punishment of which met with applause. A man who expressed sympathy was thrown into prison, railway travellers were arrested for having said too much in his favor. A merchant of Savannah for the same crime of inopportune sensibility was arrested, tarred and feathered, and banished. The rumor spread that the slaves would rise and assemble to deliver old Brown. The volunteers were called together, men rose in the night, trembling and agitated, a prey to an absurd panic. The condemned courageously awaited his end; his accusers trembled like criminals pursued by justice. They would not defer it until the opening of the legislature, for fear that there might be question of commuting the penalty. On the 2d of December Brown was hung.

Governor Wise had written to Mr. Wood, ex-Mayor of New York, "Brown will certainly be hung, and his body will be given to the surgeons to be carried beyond the boundaries of the State, so that the carcass shall not pollute the soil of Virginia." *

His accomplices were condemned and executed. Three times more the scaffold was erected.† Their death did not end the agitation. A book against slavery was interdicted, according to the provisions of an article of the Code of Virginia (Chapter CXVIII. Section 24), which requires postmasters as well as federal officers to inform the authorities if any abolition documents are received by them, and condemns the said documents to the flames. The volunteers continued to play the soldier, and to style themselves major or sergeant. The women vowed that they would wear nothing but Virginia cloth; a homespun ball was given; at the second ball, given to the daughter of a citizen of South Carolina,‡ who had been despatched to fraternize with Virginia, the fear of looking ugly prevailed over patriotism. In public gatherings, there was talk of closing the railroads, of opening direct maritime communication with France and England, of raising a militia, of establishing manufactures,

* November 7, 1859.

† The last, Stevens and Hazlitt, were hung March 16, 1860.

‡ Mr. Memminger, who, on his reception by the legislature, made a speech of four hours and a half.

of starving the North by receiving nothing from it and refusing it all supplies. There was talk of commercial and political secession.

The chief magistrate of the United States, encountering this bloody episode in his Message for 1860, recounts it in words, the studied coldness of which adds an additional stroke to this picture of disgraceful morals. He offers up prayers that public attention may be called to some other subject; he exclaims that the Union would be no longer tenable, if fifteen States were to be unceasingly menaced by similar insurrections.

If the peace of the domestic firesides of these States were ever attacked, said he, if the mothers of families could not return home at night without having reason to apprehend the cruel fate which might await them and their children before morning, it would be in vain to speak to this people of the political advantages which would result to it from the Union. Every state of society in which the sword is continually suspended over the head of the people must be intolerable.

Have the slaves no domestic firesides? Are there no slave mothers of families? Are not the whip and stake, if not the sword, continually suspended over the head of this unfortunate people? Is not their situation also intolerable? Do not say that the danger comes from the blacks. The affair at Harper's Ferry proves their almost complete apathy, but it demonstrates no less clearly to what degree of baseness, impotence, wild terror, and vain boasting, the masters were reduced between these two inimical classes; even the shadow of justice had disappeared, peace was no longer anything more than a truce of vengeance; sooner or later, the storm would break forth, and this would be on the day that the slaves should recognize that they were the stronger, and that thus the only right on which their masters relied was transferred to their side.

It was full time to pause on the descent to such an abyss of shame.

Let us cast a sorrowful glance backwards.

Alas! how much progress had been made in half a century! Man thinks that he can eat the forbidden fruit, then brush his hand over his lips and say, "It is finished!" *Quæ abstergens os suum, dixit: Non sum operata malum!* The seed of evil, like that of good, takes speedy root, and grows with fearful and inevitable fertility.

In 1787 the founders of independence refrained from sanctioning slavery by a single word in the Constitution, but designated slaves as *persons*.

On turning from the Constitution to the laws of the Slave States, we find enactments, as we have said, unknown to heathen lawgivers;—affranchisement prohibited or fettered, instruction interdicted, marriage almost impossible, imprisonment of every author or propagator of writings in favor of emancipation, the banishment of free negroes.

In 1820 it was found necessary to draw a line to share the territory of the country between liberty and servitude.

From this date, on both sides of the line, men vied with each other in speedily organizing new Territories in order to cast the weight of their laws and votes in the respective scales of the balance pertaining to the North and South. Invasion become the watchword of politics, adventurers its instruments, the annexation of Texas its masterpiece.

In 1850 the *Compromise* which had appeared a triumph, even to the partisans of slavery, no longer seemed to them sufficient.* The *Fugitive Slave Law* was conceded, the land of liberty ceased to be a place of refuge, the forces of the entire government were subject to the orders of masters hunting their slaves. Slavery was henceforth free to cross

* The Missouri Compromise was proposed by the slaveholders, supported by them, passed by them, and approved by President Monroe and his Cabinet, of which Mr. Calhoun was one. Speech of Charles Sumner.

the borders of a Free State. The Nebraska Bill enabled it to force the doors of the Confederation itself.

What! did not Congress reserve to itself the right to discuss a new State before admitting it, and to refuse entrance to crime or turbulence, hastily embodied by impure hands into the articles of a constitution?

No; in 1859 the Supreme Court recognized, and the President proclaimed, the right of every citizen to transport his property of every kind, *including slaves,* into the common territories belonging to all the States of the Confederation, and to be protected there by the Federal Constitution.*

In this manner, slavery could be planted in a territory where it was unknown; then, when it had grown, could be sanctioned by an article in a local constitution; and no power had the right to pluck up the poisonous weed. Crime was transformed into fact, fact into local law, local law into constitutional right, and Washington's successor wrote at his ease: "It is a striking proof of the sense of justice which is inherent in our people, that the property of slaves has never been disturbed in any of the Territories. Had any such attempt been made, the judiciary would doubtless have afforded an adequate remedy. Should they fail to do this hereafter, it will then be time enough to strengthen their hands by further legislation." †

In 1787 slavery was tolerated by a majority of a single vote. In 1808 the slave-trade was solemnly abolished.

In 1856 we read, in an official message of the Governor of South Carolina, this wish, since repeated by the government of Alabama: —

"To maintain our position, we must have cheap labor. This is only possible through one means, — *the reopening of the slave-trade;* and nothing but a mawkish sentimentality would swoon at the idea of legalizing this trade."

* Message for 1859. † Ibid.

In 1860 the number of Slave States had doubled, the number of slaves had quadrupled, the local business of *raising* human cattle had succeeded the international traffic, the slave-trade still lived ; it was secretly practised, and publicly invoked. In fine, in elections, in the press, in the choice of functionaries, a single question — that of slavery — divided, agitated, decided the contest. The South talked loudly of separating from the North. The Union was rent ; civil war was imminent.

The two fractions of a great people, composed of thirty million Christians, were on the brink of separation or destruction ; yet they staked their honor as a free nation, their destiny as a great power, for the support of a monstrosity repudiated by all Christianity. The Gospel remained buried under bales of cotton, and had Washington returned to earth and been re-elected President of the republic, the South would have refused to acknowledge him, and pronounced the Union dissolved.

Such was the answer given by eight States to the election of President Abraham Lincoln.

It may be said that the threat of disunion preceded the Union.*

In 1787, while the Constitution was under discussion, Georgia and South Carolina declared that they would not enter into the federation unless the slave-trade were tolerated for at least twenty years ; it was suffered to continue until 1808.

In 1794, when the celebrated John Jay, in accordance with Washington's instructions, was negotiating a treaty with England for the indemnities due to English merchants, Virginia, the country of Washington, declared publicly that she would secede if the treaty were ratified ; which, notwithstanding, was done.

In 1820 the Missouri Compromise had for its authors the

* Sumner, speech at Framingham, October 11, 1860.

representatives from Delaware and Maryland, both Slave States, and was only passed because the Union was declared to be in danger.

In 1830, on the occasion of the tariff question, South Carolina threatened openly to withdraw from the confederation.

In 1835 the same clamors were heard when John Quincy Adams laid before Congress petitions against slavery.

From 1840 to 1850, at the time of the project known as the *Wilmot Proviso*, touching the admission of the Territories of Utah, New Mexico, and California ; — on the occasion, in fine, of the *Fugitive Slave Law*, — the cry of disunion was unceasingly preferred.

In 1856 it was opposed to the election of Colonel Fremont. In 1859 the election of a new Speaker,* and in 1860 the publication of an important book against slavery (Helper's *Impending Crisis*), to which sixty-seven members of Congress subscribed, sufficed to raise the threat of separation anew.

We see that the South has always been the one that has sought to break the federal bond. The liberty party has also been the Union party, and in the celebrated speech which commenced his political career, by opposing the Fugitive Slave Law in the Senate, August 26, 1852, a few years before he was caned in the Legislative Chamber by a Congressman from South Carolina, Charles Sumner was right in enunciating the axiom, since become the text of so many writings : *Freedom is national, slavery sectional.*

We see, too, that though the threat was often made, it was not realized. But it became more serious, and was thrown out in advance as a defiance before the election of 1861.

Mark the inaugural message of the Governor of Virginia, in February, 1860. He proposes a plan of a convention or

* For this election, successive ballotings for two months were necessary.

conference concerning the questions which divide the States, then adds : —

"It will perhaps be objected that this plan tends to disunion. I grant it. But is there not imminent danger of disunion, and are not the minds of the people, both in the North and South, deeply agitated by the fear that the days of the Union are numbered ? Speeches in favor of disunion are the order of the day in deliberative bodies, and the press is full of editorials, letters, and quotations on the subject. The legislators of the South are occupied in seeking the best means of protecting the honor and rights of their States, and are taking measures for arming and disciplining the militia, with the sole end to protect and defend themselves, either in or out of the Union. Every one sees and feels the danger that threatens us ; every one regards disunion, not only as a possible, but a highly probable event, and at a not very distant day."

He protests in advance against the election of an Abolition, that is, Republican President. The South ought to resist it ; for, says he, "The idea of suffering such a man to have in his hands the army and navy of the United States, and the appointment of the highest functionaries, cannot for a single instant be endured by the South."

It was in the midst of these noisy threats that the election of the federal electors, whose office it is to choose the President of the United States, took place, November 6, 1860.

Hitherto the North, although possessing more than two million votes against a single million, had never been able to agree upon a candidate ; the constantly compact vote of the South, aided by the support of the intermediate party, had always secured the majority. This time two new facts were exhibited. The formation of a great political party, moderate, skilfully guided, choosing and maintaining its ground with ability, is, in all free countries, the best instrument of rational success. So long as an idea is in the hands of violent men, it fails through the fear which it inspires. The Abolitionists had more than once compromised abolition. The Fugitive Slave Law, the theme of the angry discussions which preceded the election of 1856, was a more contestable ground, with respect to State rights and the rendering of the Constitution, than the Kansas question, that is, of the admission of a new State into the Union, — a federal question of the first importance. The Republican party, having been strongly organized in all the large cities, essayed its powers with success in Congress by numerous successful debates, and outside by local elections and large assemblies or preliminary conventions; and on the decisive day the voters of all the Free States except one,* for the first time, rallied about the candidates of this party.

The South was in some sort taken in the snare of its own devices. To one candidate three had been opposed, representing almost imperceptible differences of opinion on the question of the admission of new States: the first placed the right of the slaveholders above that of Congress; the second, the right of the Territories before their admission into the federal Union; and the third, the right of the States after their admission as such.

These shades of difference did not justify the division, but only served as its pretext; the design was to prevent any person from obtaining a full majority, and thus to send the election to Congress. Now we know, and this mechanism explains the whole combination, that by the provisions of the Constitution (Art. II. Sect. I. 3), though the House of Representatives is chosen according to the *pro rata* of the population, while the Senate is elected by States, the House of Representatives on this occasion only vote *by States.* The forces of the extreme parties being nearly equally balanced, this would have secured the triumph of the inter-

* New Jersey.

mediate party. These tactics were foiled by the triumph of the federal electors. By an immense majority, they were deputed to elect for President, Abraham Lincoln, formerly a workingman, who had attained through his industry to fortune, and through his merit to the honor of representing the State of Illinois in the Senate, — an active and avowed partisan of the abolition of slavery.

§ 2. From the Election to the Installation of President Lincoln.

To the perfectly regular vote cast by the majority of the North, South Carolina replied by raising the cry and giving the signal of an immediate separation. This State, proceeding from threats to deeds, noisily effected secession on the 20th of December, 1860, and four days after the Governor published the following proclamation : —

"His Excellency, Francis W. Pickens, Governor and Commander-in-Chief of the State of South Carolina.

"While waiting until the brave people of this State assembled in Convention, by an ordinance unanimously adopted and ratified on the twentieth day of December, in the year of our Lord 1860, have abrogated an ordinance of the people of this State, adopted on the twentieth day of May, in the year of our Lord 1788, and have thus dissolved the Union between the State of South Carolina and the other States known as the United States of America, I, as Governor and Commander-in-chief of the State of South Carolina, by virtue of the authority with which I am invested, do proclaim by these presents in the face of the world that this State is rightfully a separate State, sovereign, free and independent, and as such has a right to make war, to conclude peace, to negotiate treaties, alliances, or agreements, and to do all acts whatsoever belonging legitimately to a free and independent State.

"Given under my hand, and the seal of this State, at Charleston, on the twenty-fourth day of December, in the year of our Lord 1860, and the eighty-fifth year of the independence of South Carolina.

"F. W. Pickens."

A people dared invoke God at the very moment of sacrificing its country to preserve its slaves!

On the 17th of December, 1787, God was invoked by the great and upright men who inscribed at the head of the Constitution of the United States these memorable words: —

"We, the people of the United States, in order to form a more perfect Union, establish justice, insure domestic tranquillity, provide for the common defence, promote the general welfare, and secure the blessings of liberty to ourselves and our posterity, do ordain and establish this Constitution," etc.

Mark what passed at Charleston on the 20th of December, 1860: —

"The scene was grand and imposing beyond description. The people were there, represented by their highest officials, — almost all patriarchs, dignitaries, priests, and judges. In the midst of profound silence, an old man, the Rev. Dr. Bachman, stepped forward, and, raising his hands, entreated Almighty God to spread his blessings on this people, and smile upon the deed that was about to be accomplished. The whole assembly rose, and with uncovered heads listened to this touching appeal to *the wise Disposer of events.*

"At the end of the prayer the chairman advanced with the hallowed parchment on which was inscribed the decision of the State. He began the reading with slowness and solemnity; but when he uttered the word *dissolution,* the hearers could no longer restrain themselves, and loud acclamations shook the walls and ascended towards the skies.

"The members of the Convention next advanced, and signed the resolution one by one; after which, in the midst of the most tumultuous applause, the chairman declared the State of South Carolina an independent and distinct nationality."

The *wise Disposer of events* has made of the people that implored his blessing in 1787 one of the first nations of earth. Can we imagine, without blaspheming him, that he has a comparable destiny in store for South Carolina?

The plans of this State are gigantic; it wishes to establish an independent confederation, composed of the Southern States, enriched by free trade, peopled by the slave traffic, aggrandized by the invasion of Central America, Mexico, and Cuba, and mistress of that marvellous harbor styled the Gulf of Mexico.

The idea of a separation of the immense nation of the United States has often presented itself to far-seeing minds; it may be welcomed with favor, it may even be desired, since too large states, it is well known, are unfavorable to public liberty: all vast territories give birth to Cæsars. But to separate in order to become freer was not the wish of South Carolina; she seceded to preserve, extend, and perpetuate slavery.

What is this audacious State, and on what does it count?

South Carolina, next to Delaware and Maryland, is the smallest of the Slave States. It occupies 29,385 square miles; and has but 22 inhabitants to a square mile, or a total of 668,507, to wit, —

274,563 whites,
8,960 free blacks,
384,984 slaves.*

Among the *whites* under twenty years of age, one out of eighteen cannot read or write. The imports of the prin-

* According to the census of 1850. The census of 1860 gives 402,406 blacks, to 291,388 whites; in all, 703,708 inhabitants.

cipal city, Charleston, in 1790, reached the value of $2,662,000; it had fallen to $1,750,000 in 1855. South Carolina costs the federation more than it brings in: it is decaying.

Upon what does this little State count for aid? It has instigated and obtained the adhesion of seven of the States, namely, Mississippi, Alabama, Florida, Georgia, North Carolina, then Louisiana, which cannot long obstruct the free navigation of the Mississippi, and Texas,* the fidelity of which is doubtful, since it is for its interest to bring in free immigrants from Mexico, the neighboring States, and Europe to people its immense territories, 237,321 square miles, inhabited in 1860 by only 421,294 whites and 182,566 slaves.

A President has been elected, a flag chosen, a name assumed, and the republic of the *Confederate States* audaciously takes place by the side of the republic of the *United States*.

Of what is the new Union composed?

The first five States would form, with South Carolina, a nation composed of 2,124,698 whites,† with 1,747,186 slaves, and 26,819 free blacks. But, setting aside the two doubtful States, Louisiana and Texas, the eight other Slave States, Tennessee, Virginia, Kentucky, Arkansas, North Carolina, and, above all, Missouri, Delaware, and Maryland, the *tobacco* States, adjoining the North, and known as the Border States, which have scarcely any slaves, comprise a population of 4,055,679 whites, 191,309 free blacks, and 1,453,120 slaves, — a population which

* Surface of Texas	237,321 square miles.
" France	200,000 " "
" England and Wales	57,855 " "

This vast territory ought some day to be divided into four States. The Southern Confederacy cannot defend Texas without dispersing its forces; if it revolts or is attacked, it is lost. (Olmsted, Journey through Texas, 418.)

† Census of 1850. The statistics for 1860 are given in the table.

will remain united with the 13,434,586 inhabitants of the six Northern States. There will be, therefore, on one side, 18,000,000 of free men, possessing the resources necessary to transform erelong into freemen 1,500,000 men more; and, on the other, 2,000,000 of whites in the face of 2,000,000 of blacks, on the surface of a vast territory. Yes, it is said, but it is the country of *cotton!* The Northern States and Europe are tributaries of the privileged land which produces cotton; with cotton, it defies the whole world.

Nature has surrounded with a white soft down, in the heart of the pod, the seeds of a stunted shrub, of the family of the Malvaceæ, which flourishes only within the tenth degrees of latitude north and south of the equator. This down gives employment in the Old and New Worlds to eight million human beings, some in cultivating, some in picking and ginning, some in spinning, and some in manufacturing it into cloths.*

The human intellect has been exercised in a marvellous manner, during the last century, in aiding this double labor by ingenious machinery. In seventy-six years, from 1784 to 1860, the exportation increased from 71 to 4,775,000 bales. In sixty years, the consumption increased from $ 4,000,000 to $ 900,000,000 in value, while the price of cotton cloth decreased from a dollar or a dollar and a half to six or seven cents per yard. The manufacture has progressed in like manner; Europe and the United States number 50,000,000 of spindles, of which England alone has 33,000,000. By one of those contrasts that are so often seen, the immense extension of the cotton manufacture has necessitated in Europe the freedom of trade, the destruction of trade corporations, and the assembling of the working masses in vast manufactories, where three workmen,

* See the admirable essay on the Cotton Manufacture, read before the *Académie des sciences morales*, by M. L. Reybaud. (*Journal des économistes*, Jan. 1861.)

aided by machinery, are sufficient for the task which formerly required five hundred hand-spinners ; it has resulted in the increase of comfort and the diffusion of the use of linen and cotton clothing in the poorest families ; but, on the other hand, in a corresponding extension of slavery in the United States, — on the one side, vast progress, on the other, a fearful scourge. Calico and sugar bring us enjoyment purchased by the sufferings of slaves. Mysterious dispensation of good and evil on earth !

It has long been repeated, "No sugar without slavery !" Facts have demonstrated that, after emancipation in the French and English colonies, sugar continued to be produced by free labor. It is maintained that this will not be the case with cotton. It is affirmed that, in an excessively hot climate, negroes alone can cultivate cotton, and only on condition that they are compelled to do so by slavery. We have already said that this is to calumniate the sun. It will be one day with cotton as it has been with sugar and coffee.

But cotton is now so important an industrial production, and the interests of nations are so deeply involved in it, that the transition is painful and everywhere felt, and the weight of the crisis is even heavier for Europe, which cannot dispense with this raw material, which it receives in exchange for an immense amount of specie, than the United States, which can do without the manufactured articles which Europe sends them in return.

South Carolina counted upon this solidarity ; above all, she divined the embarrassment of England, at once the country of Wilberforce and Arkwright, at once the first abolitionist and cotton manufacturer among all the nations of the world.

The most English of Englishmen, Lord Palmerston, in a curious speech delivered at Southampton on the 8th of January, 1861, contented himself with wishing that "the differences might be amicably settled, *whether for the preservation or dissolution of the Union.*" England has many reasons to rejoice at this secession. The edifice founded on the separation from the mother country is menaced with ruin; the weakening of the United States guarantees the possession of Canada ; the secession of the South will involve free trade and cheap cotton ; the second naval power in the world is about to fall ; and, mistress of the seas, England, should a maritime war break out, will be a tyrannical mistress without a rival. What motives for secret joy! France does not suffer so much from the financial crisis; her political interests are opposed to those of England; she ought to desire the duration of a work in whose birth she gloriously aided, and especially the maintenance of a maritime power which alone can counterbalance the omnipotence of Great Britain on the seas.

But whatever may be the difference of views and positions, whatever may be the difference of counsels, neither England nor France can range itself on the side of slavery, after having the honor of abolishing it in its colonial possessions.

Despite the importance of its cotton, South Carolina cannot entertain the serious idea of forming either an immense federation within, or any alliance without.

Nor are its pretended plans more practical. Should it establish free trade, the North will profit by it like the rest of the world. Should it revive the slave-trade, its slaves will be met on their way by the navies of all civilized nations. Should it seek to extend its territories on the Gulf of Mexico, it will excite the fear of Spain for Cuba, of England for Jamaica, and of France for her West India possessions, and, far from being intimidated, Spain will seize the opportunity to annex the part of St. Domingo formerly held by her.*

* As has already been done.

With what resources, with what soldiers, will the new Confederacy make war? * With what inhabitants will it people its conquests? Its resources and soldiers are scarcely sufficient to maintain peace on its own soil with its present inhabitants, who themselves hardly suffice for its cultivation. To prevent the desertion of the slaves, there will be no more fugitive slave laws; to repress their rebellion, no more aid from the federal forces; to arrest the propaganda, no measure that will be efficient.

On whatever side we look at the position, it seems demonstrated that this terrible crisis, born to the shame of the slaveholders, must sooner or later end to their detriment, but perhaps after fearful misfortunes. They went to extremes, refused the payment of taxes, talked of starving out the Federal troops withdrawn to an island opposite Charleston, threatened to oppose the installation of the President, condemned to the gibbet in advance the soldiers sent against them.

While the North, which had done everything to pacify this violence, and to remain at once impassive and conciliating, hoped for an arrangement or a tardy return of the seceded States to the Union, — while the Central States attempted to intervene as pacificators, and Virginia, the birthplace of Washington, proposed its mediation, — what did the magistrate invested with the sovereign authority, — what did President Buchanan do?

In his Message, December 5, 1860, he attempted to prove that the North was to blame for the acts of violence of the South.

"Why is it that discontent now so extensively prevails,

* The sum total of funds in the coffers of the banks of the American Union was estimated, in 1860, at a little more than $285,000,000. Of this sum, one fourth, or $71,250,000 belonged to the Slave States, the remaining three fourths, or $213,750,000 to the Free States. The State of New York alone had some $117,200,000; South Carolina but $5,000,000. (Extract from the *Economist.*)

and that the Union of the States is threatened with destruction? The long-continued and intemperate interference of the Northern people with the question of slavery in the Southern States has at length produced its natural effects. . . . . . The incessant and violent agitation of the slavery question throughout the North for the last quarter of a century has at length produced its malign influence on the minds of the slaves, and inspired them with vague notions of freedom. Hence a sense of security no longer exists around the family altar. Many a matron throughout the South retires to rest in dread of what may befall herself and her children before morning. . . . . . The agitation has been continued by the public press, by the proceedings of State and county conventions, sermons, lectures, pamphlets, books, etc. All for which the Slave States have ever contended is to be let alone, and permitted to manage their *domestic institutions* in their own way."

If the Union, therefore, be menaced, if the South be agitated, if the sleep of mothers be broken, if the slaves dream of freedom, the fault is the North's, not only through its politics, but its journals, its books, its words!

Does Mr. Buchanan know a secret for arresting human thought? What better could he invent than that law of Maryland (December, 1831), which "condemns to *from ten to twenty years of imprisonment* as guilty of felony, every citizen who may have written, engraved, printed, or circulated, or caused to be written, engraved, printed, or circulated, any picture or pamphlet of a nature to excite the discontent of the colored population"? Vain prohibition! the echoes of speech will cross the frontiers like the breath of the wind or the rays of the sun No power, no prison-wall, can hinder the voice of Liberty from reaching the heart of the captive.

Arrest the propagation of ideas of emancipation! appease the fears of insurrection! For the first, accuse the Gospel and the human soul; for the second, the violence of the South, but by no means the intrigues of the North.

Is it true, that the policy of the North has been a continued and injudicious meddling with the policy of the South?

Who, then, in 1820 obtained through the Missouri Compromise the cession of half the country to slavery? The South, thanks to John C. Calhoun, at that time minister of President Monroe.

Who, then, in 1850 obtained the Fugitive Slave Law, which permits every functionary in every State to be called upon to join in the hunt for fugitive slaves? The South. Who sustained and insured the triumph, with respect to Kansas and Nebraska, of the doctrine of *squatter sovereignty,* which renders a medley of immigrants free to botch up a constitution in which slavery is embodied, and, with this paper in hand, to force the gates of the confederation? The South. Who, then, in fine, has elected twelve Presidents out of eighteen, together with almost all the high functionaries, magistrates, and ambassadors? The South. Who, then, if not the South, triumphed in the election of Mr. Buchanan himself in 1856? The provocation did not come from the North; and the South did not cease to rule until the elections of 1860.

Had the Southern States been endangered by the result of these particular elections, would they have had the power themselves alone to break the federal bond?

The Message of November 5, 1860, clearly proves that no such right exists.

"We cannot recognize the right of an isolated State to throw off its most sacred obligations at will, without the consent of the other States," replied General Jackson to South Carolina in 1833, "and to imperil the liberty and happiness of the millions of men who compose our Union. Such a right is irreconcilable with the principles upon which the federal government is constituted, as well as with the view for which it was organized."

If the separation of the Southern States be a rebellion, the conclusion should have been to oppose it as if it were a rebellion, or at least, while seeking means of pacification, to insure the defence of the federal forts and the recovery of the federal taxes. Nothing energetic was ordered, but a miserable expedient was proposed by President Buchanan.

Calculating that the slavery party, having lost the majority in the country, would still preserve it in Congress, he demanded that Congress should perpetuate slavery by an amendment to the Constitution. If the members of the Senate and House of Representatives had fallen into this snare, they would have conceded what never before had been done, they would have endured a humiliation greater than their triumph, they would have written in their fundamental law a word that had never sullied it, and would have inscribed this word on the stone that covered the remains of its glorious authors. They might, if it were still possible, have granted time, patience, negotiations; but a principle — never. It is better to renounce a State than a truth.

Neither threats nor attempts at assassination were able to intimidate the new President. He took for minister the courageous and eloquent citizen, Mr. Seward, who uttered these admirable words: —

"It would be a source of unbounded shame and sorrow if we, thirty millions of men, Europeans by origin, Americans by birth, Christians in theory, and claiming to be so in practice, if we could not succeed in combining prudence with humanity in this agitating question of slavery, in a manner to save our incomparable free institutions, and to enjoy them in peace and harmony." *

Four ways were open to the new power: —

* Speech delivered February 29, 1860.

To yield, to draw a new Missouri line, to accept amendments to the Constitution, and to give servitude a place and right in it. This would be to lose the whole fruit of a hard-won triumph, shamefully to perpetuate the scourge just condemned by the universal suffrage, and to invalidate the very title by which the President holds office;

To maintain the Union by force, — a perilous, ruinous, lamentable means, difficult in so great a space with so few troops, but after all more injurious to the South than the North, since the first roar of the cannon would give the signal for slave insurrections;

To fix a delay, as was done with the slave-trade in 1794, in order to gain time to restore tranquillity, pave the way for transition and regulate different interests, but on condition of maintaining the Union, — the best and most reasonable means of all, if the South would but listen to reason;

Or to leave the seceded States to themselves, under protest, however, without abandoning the right.

Installed on the 4th of March, 1861, seventy-two years after the illustrious Washington, "the first in peace, the first in war, and the first in the hearts of his countrymen," President Lincoln delivered a conciliating, firm, and sensible inaugural address, which may be summed up as follows.

The Union of the States dates from the Declaration of Independence in 1776; renewed by the Articles of Confederation in 1778, it was consolidated by the Constitution of 1787, which was drawn up for the express purpose of *rendering the Union more perfect.*

Either this Union has formed a *nation,* in which case it is perpetual;

Or this Union is merely a *contract,* in which case it cannot be annulled except by the wish of all the parties;

Therefore, the separation violently decreed by the South is without right.

In the second place, it is without reason. "For," says

the President, "I have no design for interfering, either directly or indirectly, with the institution of slavery in the States where it exists. I believe that I have no right, and I feel no wish, to do so." Then what are the questions under discussion? Shall the search for fugitive slaves, guaranteed by the Constitution, be insured and pursued by the State authorities or the national power? The Constitution does not decide. Shall Congress protect slavery in the Territories? The Constitution does not decide. Who is to settle these questions? *The Supreme Court?* No, for it can only decide between parties in law and in cases submitted to it; if it should render general decisions, the American people would have abdicated in its favor; it would be no longer the interpreter, but the ruler, of the Constitution. The true ruling power is a national convention, summoned according to constitutional forms. The majority must decide. Now the majority is the sole ruling power of a free people, since unanimity is impossible. Whoever rejects the majority falls necessarily into anarchy and despotism.

Secession, which is without right and without reason, is also without efficacy. How long will a confederacy exist which is founded on the right of secession, — a confederacy in the heart of which a minority may demand a new secession? To-morrow the slave-trade will be free, but the flight of slaves will be free also. To-morrow the States will be separated, but they will not be removed from each other; they will be no longer united, but they will be neighbors, obliged to live face to face in peace or war. "Is it possible, then, to make intercourse more advantageous or more satisfactory after separation than before? Can aliens make treaties easier than friends can make laws? Suppose you go to war; you cannot fight always; and when, after much loss on both sides, and no gain on either, you cease fighting, the identical questions as to terms of intercourse are again before you."

There is no reason whatever for acting precipitately.

"Intelligence, patriotism, Christianity, and a firm reliance on Him who has never yet forsaken this favored land, are still competent to adjust, in the best way, all our present difficulties."

President Lincoln, therefore, does not regard the Union as broken. He vows to maintain it peaceably, without having recourse to arms, unless he is constrained to do so. He goes far in the way of concessions, since he declares the *domestic institutions* of the South unassailable, and the law insuring the surrender of fugitive slaves constitutional. He counsels time, and the convocation of a great convention, deputed by the people to amend or maintain the Constitution.

While the President spoke as if the South had not seceded, the South organized itself as if the President had not been inaugurated ; it chose a President, installed him at Montgomery, despatched ambassadors to Europe to demand of England and France whether they would recognize the failure of the great political work which the one has combated and the other seconded ; in fine, it gave the signal for civil war.

Europe will dishonor herself, should she open her arms without inquiry or delay to this strange nation, the offspring of slavery. Let her at least leave time to the wise and patriotic citizens whose efforts and counsels are tending to unite again in the same family, the divided elements of the American people. Let her also leave time to do justice to the mad and culpable attempt of the Southern States, which the North cannot better chastise than by sanctioning. Yes, let them be left to themselves, but without rendering honors to their flag, without opening the doors of Europe to their ambassadors, without adding their name after those of France and Great Britain to the glorious list of illustrious nations.

What! because two or three hundred thousand capitalists work three millions of kidnapped, whipped, degraded beings, because this scandal is advantageous to the culture of cotton, sugar, and tobacco, is this evident crime, this ignoble profit, to be weighed in the balance with the existence of the Constitution, the honor of a great and youthful nation, the love of country and the progress of the human race? "We will secede," repeat a few merchants in human flesh, "and the republic may settle it as it can." I dare affirm, that of all the Christian nations in the whole universe, there is not one, unless it be the United States, where such words could be spoken, or where such words could obtain a hearing. Imagine a Liverpool merchant holding such language in the English Parliament! fancy the blacksmiths of Saint-Étienne, or the farmers of the provinces, addressing such a summons to the French government! But how could one oppose it? Such an hypothesis is an insult. I am well aware that each of the United States is a sovereign; they compose a federation, and the bond is more easily broken. I know, too, that history presents memorable examples of separation; our century offers none more admirable than the emancipation of the United States themselves; interests, fortune, life, were trifles when the companions of Washington fought to repel injustice and secure country, name, rights, and flag. To this magnanimous and disinterested separation, what is sought to be compared? A sort of forced liquidation, after the manner of the fraudulent dissolution of a commercial partnership. The Union separated from England to be free; the South separates from the Union — for what? In order not to diminish the profits of cotton and the revenues of the trade in men.

How can one help being tempted to reply to this absurd threat: —

Do you wish to secede? Secede then! Yes, let there

be henceforth two North Americas; the one, the mother of liberty, — the other, the last refuge of slavery. Recommence the slave-trade, abandon yourselves to your sordid interests without limit or scruple!

The sun will not cease to rise on this fruitful land, the Ohio will not cease to bear its waves to the Mississippi, the Mississippi to the Gulf of Mexico, and the Gulf to become lost in the ocean. The South will have no less need of the capital, intellect, and wheat of the North, nor the North of the cotton, rice, and tobacco of the South. But below a free and flourishing republic, which will have preferred justice to power, a second republic, nameless, branded, blighted, menaced by slavery, having sacrificed greatness to interest, having bartered the Gospel and the Constitution for a bale of cotton, will present itself alone to the contempt of the world, and will erelong behold flight, insurrection, death, or war snatch from it even the profits of servitude.

When you are divided, dishonored, ruined, sunk below the republics of South America, perhaps you will return to solicit re-entrance into the Union which alone makes your honor and your strength. To us, Northern men, the day of separation will be one of new glory; ask of us no more *fugitive slave laws* or share in our votes, functions, and institutions; we will divide our flag, — to us, the stars of independence, to you the bars of servitude.

At the moment that these pages — this ardent but useless protest — are written and finished, the world is in doubt whether this illustrious banner may not be forever rent in twain. We follow with mingled terror and anxiety the increasing struggles which are about, by their inevitable shock, to kindle upon the distant continent the terrible explosion of a civil, complicated with a servile war. We contemplate with a melancholy and disappointed glance the gradual fading out of one of the noblest hopes of an age which has so often witnessed their decay; we are bitterly afflicted at the sight of events which sweep away, with the honor and prosperity of a great nation, a portion of the future of liberty on earth.

Who does not remember the admirable apostrophe of Burke, in his most celebrated speech on America, March 22, 1775?

"Let us reflect that this growth of our national prosperity has happened within the short period of the life of man. My Lord Bathurst might remember all the stages of the progress. He was in 1704 of an age at least to be made to comprehend such things. He was then old enough *acta parentum jam legere, et quæ sit potere cognoscere virtus.* Suppose, sir, that the angel of this auspicious youth had then raised before his eyes the veil of the future, and in the midst of his enthusiasm, in view of the future greatness of England, had pointed out to him a little speck, scarce visible in the mass of the national interest, a small seminal principle rather than a formed body, and had told him: 'Young man, there is America, which at this day serves for little more than to amuse you with stories of savage men and uncouth manners; yet shall, before you taste of death, show itself equal to the whole of that commerce which now attracts the envy of the world. Whatever England has been growing to by a progressive increase of improvement, brought in by varieties of people, by succession of civilizing conquests and civilizing settlements in a series of seventeen hundred years, you shall see as much added to her in the course of a single life!' If this state of his country had been foretold to him, would it not require all the sanguine credulity of youth and all the fervid glow of enthusiasm to make him believe it? Fortunate man, he has lived to see it! Fortunate, indeed, if he lives to see nothing that shall vary the prospect, and cloud the setting of his day." *

Ah! what would the immortal authors of American independence have said, in their turn, — what would Washington have said, if, seeing in spirit with inexpressible admiration the marvellous destiny of the nation which he had just founded, — become in less than a century one of the rulers of the world, — he had sorrowfully perceived at the same time upon its brow a stain that only extended with time? We comprehend the existence of slavery in heathen communities, we explain it also in the small colonial settlements whose place in the world is so limited and exceptional. But that an illustrious, Christian, generous nation, which possesses orators, poets, historians, publicists, economists, and novelists, which knows how to use the language of good sense with Franklin, and of pity with Channing, should contain, tolerate, justify, and authorize men that buy men, fathers that sell their offspring, magistrates that hunt slaves, priests that absolve servitude, women that serve only to reproduce children to be sold, manners that would have blighted, laws that would have been reproved by Pagan antiquity, — ah! I do not believe that there is found in history a more painful contradiction to human wisdom, a harsher disappointment of generous hopes! Less than a century after a revolution which was so fruitful because it was so honest, we are forced to tremble lest this great work should fail, and so young and vigorous a community be about to step beyond the pale of civilization.

To believe in so lamentable a future is to banish from one's mind the sacred hope of the triumph of justice on earth.

A generous spirit, the friend of America and the enemy of slavery, M. Agénor de Gasparin,† fitly reproves the

* Works, Vol. III. p. 249.

† The Uprising of a Great People, or the United States in 1861. By Count Agénor de Gasparin.

premature or interested anxiety with which America inspires Europe. How many on our continent will be made joyous by the shipwreck of a free country! All the liberal sympathy of England, I blush to say, seems stifled by the satisfaction of seeing — pardon me the expression! — a rival cut in twain. I am happy to agree with M. de Gasparin, happy to think, with him, that the separation of the States is better than the perpetuation of servitude, that divorce is preferable to such a household. Yes, a people repenting is a people uprising.

But is the crisis ended? How long will the expiation last?

We are confounded, at every page of history, at the degree which evil is permitted to attain on earth. When an evil has grown, we believe it exhausted, and suppose that it has reached the bottom of the abyss, when, behold, everything becomes envenomed, and to the evil accomplished is added another of which we never dreamed. We have witnessed decay, we witness separation, we witness war, — horrible war. The South, more ardent, more politic, better prepared than the North, has commenced by two adroit acts, — the reform of the Constitution and the reform of tariffs; the North has commenced by two mistakes, — the increase of custom-house duties and the tardiness of preparations. The South may have the first successes, the intermediate States, the slave-sellers, will aid the slave-buyers, Washington may perhaps be taken, insurrection may break forth. . . . . .

It was in vain for Voltaire to say that the war of Spartacus was the nearest just, and perhaps the only just of all wars; the awakening, the explosion of a sleeping rage, the reopening at once, as it were, of the wounds of souls long oppressed, is a perspective which inspires us with horror. We remember St. Domingo. "It happened there," says M. Thiers admirably (Liv. XVI.), "as it happens in every community where a war of classes breaks out, — the first was conquered by the second, and the second by the third. But, differing from what is seen elsewhere, they bore on their face the marks of their divers origins (whites, mulattoes, and blacks); their hatred partook of the violence of physical instincts, and their rage was as brutal as that of wild animals. The horrors of this revolution surpassed everything that was seen in France in 1793." Decay, separation, civil war, insurrection. Such are the threats of the present!

But all these sanguinary follies will have a morrow, and, after the war, the same questions which provoked it will rise up anew.

Either the North will have been the conqueror, and, the triumph of force being added to the victory of right, the Union will be reconstructed, the wishes of the friends of humanity and patriotic hearts will be accomplished, and after more or less concessions and delays, slavery will receive its death-blow.

Or else the South will win; the sole fruit of its victory will be the separation of the States. The North, weakened perhaps, but purified, freed, uplifted in the eyes of all Christendom, will resume the course of its destiny. The South will have all the embarrassment of its shameful victory, the *Confederate* States will live separate from the *United* States; but menaced, involved in debt, blighted, unquiet, condemned to rely on force alone for repose, progress, and aggrandizement, they will feel the terrible problem which they had not the courage to resolve weigh more and more upon their existence. The Border States will abandon them as soon as the revival of the slave-trade threatens their horrible commerce with ruin. The nations which the South has been accustomed to supply, warned by the late events, will seek by every means to rid themselves of the responsibility and consequences of the future solution. Cotton will be demanded of Egypt, Bengal, Senegal, and Dahomey, and Africa, affranchised by commerce, Africa, lying nearer to Europe, will rival the land which holds Africans in bondage. The day will come, the day is near at hand, when the South will atone for its ambition and execrate its violence.

I write in 1861. Before the rapid course of time shall have borne away the last year of the nineteenth century, Europe will celebate the anniversary of 1789, America will have witnessed the dawn of that of 1787. Among the men who have served the cause of justice, equality, Christian fraternity and liberty, in both worlds, more than one perhaps will be sleeping sadly in the tomb, despairing of his work, and prophesying to his country an inevitable descent into those two abysses which follow each other in a never-ending round, anarchy and despotism. I dare believe, I dare affirm, confiding in God, despite so many adverse appearances, that the despondent will be mistaken, and the hopeful in the right. I dare believe, I dare affirm, that, before a quarter of a century shall have passed, there will be no longer in Europe a single despot, in America a single slave.

But even though the hope that I nourish be false, though the gloomiest presages be accomplished, though the first free Christian republic of modern times end its glorious existence after less than a century in discord and degradation, let us not suffer history to accuse liberty of this catastrophe, let us not suffer posterity despairingly to inscribe on the tomb of Washington the words, "His idea was a vision, and his work could not succeed!"

Let us not forget that slavery preceded the Union, and that the republic died of an evil transmitted to it; it bore in its birth a germ of death which its illustrious founders had the weakness not to stifle. It is not liberty that is impossible, but the union of liberty with slavery.

The American Union has been blighted by slavery, debased by slavery, agitated by slavery, rent asunder by slavery: this is the great criminal; if there be ruin, it has caused it; if blood flow, it has been shed by it.

This dangerous scourge is well defined by these four characteristics: —

"The monstrous pretence that one man can be the owner of another, the complete destruction of all relations, of husband and wife, of parents and children, the positive refusal of all instruction, and compulsory labor without wages." *

Slavery had already called forth ardent imprecations from pious souls and just consciences, for the evil it had caused to innocent unfortunates. The history of the United States will henceforth devote it to the execration of all who are not indifferent to the progress of the human race; for this onerous contract not only oppresses the small, but debases the great; it desolated, decimated, and crushed the lowest races of Africa; it has sullied, divided, and imperilled the higher races of the New World; it has blighted the germs which might have taken root, it has withered the fruits which reason, courage, virtue, wealth, and liberty might have matured. If the miserable tyrant of Dahomey slaughters innocent beings, it is by the aid of slavery, and if the great idea of Washington seems about, alas! to be come extinct, it is in consequence of slavery.

Witnesses of these vicissitudes, forget not the lesson! The friends of despotism are about to exclaim, "Cursed be liberty, for with it a great nation cannot live."

But we can reply: "Blessed be God, for he is just; he does not permit liberty to be wedded to servitude, and his

* Speech of Charles Sumner.

sovereign hand, in falling heavily upon the United States, does not smite liberty; it blights, it convulses, it forever condemns slavery.

Europe * has learned with sorrow of the battle fought by the Americans near Richmond, — a formidable and lugubrious conflict, in which, for wellnigh seven consecutive days, 300,000 men of the same nation have been engaged in hand-to-hand combat; 95,000 on the side of the North, 185,000 on the side of the South. The New York despatches which announce this terrible combat come to us dated July 4 and 5, 1862, precisely the same date of the month that the Congress of the United States adopted the memorable Declaration of Independence. Less than a century after the signature of this great charter, signed (these are the very words) with the end *to form a more perfect union, to establish justice, to insure domestic tranquillity, to provide for the common defence, to promote the general welfare, and secure the blessings of liberty to the people of the United States and their posterity,* this people, become one of the first on the globe, is energetic and powerful enough to raise a million men in the space of a few months; but only to make use of its strength for its ruin; and these men, these fellow-citizens, these States so united, have been exterminating each other for more than a year! There is not a generous mind that does not desire, for the interests of humanity, the end of this bloody duel. But humanity also offers up prayers that so much blood shall not be spilt in vain, and that the result of the civil war, whatever it may prove, may at least be turned to the profit of the liberty of the slaves. Can we hope for this?

The friends of the South, more numerous in France and

* *Journal des Débats,* Aug. 9, 1862.

England than one would suppose, continue to affirm that slavery is not the cause of the war; — this is a good way to prevent emancipation from being its consequence. We will not weary of replying a hundred times to this assertion a hundred times repeated; next, we will endeavor to prove that, whatever may be the cause of the war, slavery has received its death-blow.

I have before my eyes a speech delivered at New York on the last anniversary but one of the Declaration of Independence, by a celebrated citizen of the United States, Edward Everett. The speech is published under the title, "The Question of the Day." I know of no more precise refutation of the pretensions of the South. Himself the candidate for the Vice-Presidency on a defeated ticket, Mr. Everett loyally declares that the vote which made Abraham Lincoln the nineteenth successor of Washington was perfectly legal, and in conformity with the Constitution, which expressly declares that the laws and treaties made by a State in opposition to its prescriptions are rightfully null and void. In breaking the Union by a statute of December 20, 1860, South Carolina has, therefore, violated the Constitution adopted by it, May 28, 1788, and to which this State itself caused an amendment to be added, containing the words *forever inseparable.* Now the right to make a contract does not involve the right to dissolve it by one's self alone; on the contrary, each of the parties can force the other party to execute it; while several of the seceded States were not parties in the original contract, as Louisiana and Florida, which were purchased, and Texas, which was conquered. The pretended right of *secession* or *nullification*, which is neither sanctioned nor reserved by the Constitution, is only a theory invented by Mr. Calhoun, in 1830, and which was then refuted and overthrown by Jackson, Livingston, Clay, and Webster, and by the framer of the Constitution himself, the aged Madison, who was still living. The blood spilt rests, therefore, on the head of the South; the right is on the side of the North; the South is purely and simply in revolution.

Doubtless one cannot anathematize revolutions in a country which had a revolution for its origin; yet still it is necessary that the uprising of an indignant people should be justified by the oppression and tyranny of the government. Scarcely any army, no conscription, no impressment of sailors, no burdensome taxes, prosperous finances, churches and schools without number or limit, a cheap free press, free elections, — such are the characteristics of this tyranny! What grievances have been put forward? Georgia has complained of *fishing bounties* levied for the interests of the North; these bounties do not exceed $ 200,000, regularly voted. Complaints have been made of the *navigation laws*, to which the Union owes its navy, and of the *protective tariff*, which was demanded by the South itself, in order to protect its cotton against that of foreign countries, and to call forth the establishment of manufactories in the North, and secure to itself the monopoly of their supply.

Finally, and above all, is alleged the interference of the North in the question of slavery, and especially the non-observance of the Fugitive Slave Law. It is true that several States have not been able to persuade themselves to execute this monstrous law, which transforms their magistrates into kidnappers. But to what is this grievance reduced? There are 3,953,760 slaves in the South; the number of fugitive slaves enumerated during 1860 was 803, and even these did not all take the way to the North; it is much if South Carolina numbers a dozen fugitives a year. It is affirmed that there are 40,000 negroes in Canada; but it is forgotten that the number of slaves annually emancipated exceeds 3,000, and that these unhappy freedmen are obliged by custom, if not by law, to expatriate themselves.

Vain accusations! insufficient pretexts! The present war is a war of predominance. For forty-four years the Southerners have had the rulership of the United States. Thanks to their slaves, — who, without being voters, have counted in the population, the amount of which determined the number of representatives, — the Southern States, less numerous, less populous, less important, have had the superiority in Congress, and they have been unable to resign themselves to see the political influence pass at length to the North. They have risen because they wished to rule. And why do they wish to rule? In order to maintain and extend slavery. The North is fighting to defend the Constitution; the South is violating the Constitution to defend slavery.

The maintenance or destruction of the Constitution, — such is the direct end of the war; the maintenance or the destruction of slavery, — such is the first cause of the war, the cause of this ancient struggle, long rumbling, then bursting forth, which the eminent statesman placed by Mr. Lincoln at the head of his Cabinet, Mr. Seward, defined three years ago, by a memorable expression, *the irrepressible conflict.*

This painful question is really at the bottom of the war, which the administration at Washington, urged, moreover, by the eloquent and logical entreaties of the indefatigable friends of liberty, before all by Charles Sumner, has deemed incumbent upon itself to conduct by slow but important steps towards emancipation. Mr. Lincoln has acted slowly, prudently, legally, refusing and even suppressing all incitements to insurrection, for which he cannot be sufficiently thanked; but he has acted with the loyalty, perseverance, good sense, and conscientiousness which are the distinct characteristics of his individuality. Mark the acts due to his initiative.

An appeal has been made and a subsidy promised to as

many States as are willing to emancipate their slaves. (Message and law of March 8, 1862.)

Slavery has been abolished in the District of Columbia, which still contained 3,185 slaves. (April, 1862.)

Various incompatibilities which still rested on the free negroes, such as exclusion from the office of factor of the port, have been destroyed.

The republics of Hayti and Liberia have been recognized.

All slaves of rebels who have taken refuge in the Federal camps are declared free.

Slavery has been abolished in the Territories of the United States not yet recognized as States.

Finally, a treaty for the suppression of the slave-trade and for the right of visit, always hitherto refused, has been signed with England. (April 7, May 20.)

Since this time, Mr. Sumner has framed a bill to suppress the coast traffic in slaves between the States, while by ardent and practical speeches he has unceasingly moved public opinion to advance the cause of emancipation.

What will be the influence of the war on the great cause of humanity? We see that it has already done more in six months than had been done in sixty years; but what will the end be?

Either the Union will be established, or it will be broken.

In France, all ought to wish that the Union might be re-established. In this great nation, France should see its work, its *protégé*, its ally, the counterpoise to England on the seas. England has other interests; it would joyfully witness the fall of a rebellious scion and growing rival. But will the Union be re-established? Is there a strong Union party in the South? After a discordant family life, is not divorce necessary? We leave the answer to the chances of war and the will of God. We only examine the probable causes in what concerns slavery.

If the Union be maintained, all the laws which we have

indicated will be at least maintained and extended; it is the smallest possible gain that we can expect. Delays, temporizing, will be accorded, but the end of slavery will be only the affair of a little time.

If the Union be destroyed, either France or England will offer the mediation which Lord Palmerston rightly finds still untimely, in which case both nations would dishonor themselves if they did not at least prescribe that the South should directly renounce the barbarous laws which fetter the instruction, marriage, and enfranchisement of the unhappy slaves, by making more ample promises for the future; and that it should adhere to the agreement against the slave-trade.

Or the Union will be divided without mediation, in which case Nature herself will intervene; for an immense frontier will separate the negro republic from the free republic, and there will be no more Fugitive Slave Laws. Beyond this frontier there will be, as it were, a vast Canada within little distance. On the coasts, the surveillance will become costly and troublesome. It will be impossible either to increase or retain the slaves, without maintaining a standing army at ruinous cost, and braving the navies of the world, to say nothing of the universal conscience.

Thus, in both cases, it will be for the interest of the 300,000 masters who hold 4,000,000 men in bondage to soften slavery, then abolish it, with more or less delay, despite more or less resistance, with more or less persecution. After the numberless evils of civil war, I know not what of the Union will remain standing; but I believe that it can be affirmed, that slavery will have received its deathblow, and this will be justice.

BOOK SECOND.

SPANISH COLONIES.*

CUBA. — PORTO RICO.

The cities and temples formerly founded by Spain on the continent of Southern America, the monuments which it raised, the works of art which it had skill to execute, have left imposing ruins. We ask ourselves wherefore so much greatness disappeared. The contempt of a few exclusive minds for the genius of the Latin races explains nothing. For, in North America, the English were deprived of their fairest colonies with a facility which excites no less surprise. We can scarcely believe that the soldiers whom Washington had to fight were of the same blood as those who coped a few years later with the armies of France. Why did the English, why the Spaniards, let fall from their hands these magnificent possessions? Because these hands had become feeble and corrupt.

This corruption, due to very diverse causes, proceeds most of all from this, — over the entire surface of the globe the races who compel others to labor without laboring themselves fall to decay. Wherever the Turk sets foot, the fam-

* *Voyages de Humboldt et de Bonpland*, Part I. *Relation Historique*, Tom. III. Liv. X. Chap. VII. and VIII. Paris, 1825, in fol. — *Description de l'le de Cuba*, by M. Ramon de la Sagra, correspondent of the Institute. — *Cuba, ses ressources*, etc., by Don Vasquez Queipo and Don Jose Antonio Saco; translated by M. d'Avrainville. Imperial Press, 1851. — Spanish and English documents concerning Cuba and Porto Rico, *Revue Coloniale*, 1843 - 1860. — *La Question de Cuba*, Paris. 1859. Dentu. — The West Indies and the Spanish Main, by Anthony Trollope. 1860, etc.

ily disappears, the blood becomes impoverished, the earth grows sterile. It is a general law, and this law is justice's self.

Compare to-day the Northern with the Southern United States, or the Northern United States with Brazil: under different aspects, the same law is manifested.

In the only colony which they have preserved in America, — the island of Cuba, — the Spaniards nevertheless obstinately maintain slavery.

The prosperity of this colony even appears an argument, the chief argument of the partisans of slavery.

Enormous fortunes are made in Cuba, and the city of Havana, with its 200,000 inhabitants, is one of the most wealthy and luxurious capitals on the globe, one of the principal markets of the commercial world. The Spanish government draws a constantly increasing revenue from Cuba. The amount of imports and exports is prodigious.*

* It is the policy of Spain not to make annual statements of the revenue which it derives from its commerce. Nevertheless, from various information collected in the *Balanza general de comercio*, and other documents, we gain the following table of the progress of imports, exports, and revenues, from 1827 to 1847. (*Revue Coloniale*, 1851, No. 7, p. 445, from the Anti-Slavery Reporter, and 1847, No. 13, p. 164, from the Colonial Magazine. *Cuba*, by D'Avrainville, supplementary tables.)

ANNUAL AVERAGE.

	Imports.	Exports.	Revenues.
1828 - 1832	17,000,000 piasters.	11,850,000 piasters.	8,785,000 piasters.
1833 - 1837	20,050,000 "	15,675,000 "	8,945,000 "
1838 - 1842	24,800,000 "	24,275,000 "	11,250,000 "
1843 - 1847	26,300,000 "	33,850,000 "	10,750,000 "

The two following years witnessed a decline, viz.: —

1848	25,434,655 piasters.	26,077,068 piasters.
1849	26,320,160 "	22,436,556 "

The exportation of sugar rose from 6,508,138 arrobas (four to a quintal) in 1826, to 10,166,555 arrobas in 1840; that of coffee from 1,718,865 arrobas to 1,877,646. The exportation of tobacco rose from 5,940,000 lbs. in 1842 to 9,309,000 lbs. in 1847. The statistics of 1848 and 1849 give: —

	1848.	1849.
Leaf tobacco	6,275,630 lbs.	4,017,133 lbs.
Cigars	161,480 "	123,720 "

Lastly, mark the comparative amounts of 1857 and 1858, extracted from the

On the soil of the island, the cane renews itself by its own shoots several years sooner than elsewhere.* The Cuban brown sugars are equal to the second quality English white sugars.†

Cuba represents 22,055,000 pounds in the aggregate production of coffee, and, as rich through her forests as her plantations, her mines as her pasture lands, she furnishes one sixth of the total yield of copper, a great part of the production of tobacco, and her foreign trade equals one fifth that of the whole United States.

Porto Rico is no less progressing; this island defrays its own expenses and sends funds to the mother country; it is, says M. Merivale, the most populous and best cultivated of all the American colonies.

These two West India islands surpass all the rest; yet they alone have preserved slavery.

This relative prosperity is indisputable; but the evil stands side by side with the good. The good is due to two orders of causes, — the one accidental, the other permanent: the evil is due almost solely to one cause, slavery, as we shall speedily demonstrate.

I. An admirable position, at the intersection of several of the great commercial thoroughfares of nations, and destined to become still more marvellous in the future by the cutting through of the Isthmus of Panama; an extent of territory equal in surface to that of England; the incomparable fertility of the soil; the beauty of the climate, —

Balanza general del comercio de la isla de Cuba en 1858, published at Havana in 1860: —

		1857.	1858.
Imports		34,853,338 piastres.	39,063,338 piastres.
Exports		32,668,188 "	33,831,839 "
Custom-house duties		10,547,903 "	11,134,110 "
Vessels entered and cleared,	Spanish	2,106	2,137
	Foreign	6,206	6,382 (of which 4,770 are American.)

* *Revue Coloniale*, 1843, p. 195. † Ibid.

make Cuba a region favored of Heaven. These advantages cannot be ravished from it; before or after, with or without slavery, it will always possess them.

The ruin of St. Domingo enriched Cuba. When the English, French, Danish, and Swedish colonies ceased to receive slaves through the slave-trade, Cuba continued, and still continues, largely to supply her population by this guilty means. The abolition of slavery by England and France brought the weight of a distressing crisis for several years on the colonies, nowhere so grave and so long as at Jamaica, the neighbor of Cuba, which has hitherto been exempt from the same ordeals. While the English and French possessions have been closed to foreign trade, Cuba has enjoyed, since 1809, all the advantages of the free sale of its products, the free purchase of its articles of consumption, the free admittance of all flags.* At the moment when the diminution of the duties on foreign commodities facilitated the competition of foreign sugar in the markets of England, and afterwards in those of France, Cuba, which had been able, having to pass through no shock, to renew its working stock, develop its enterprises, and profit by the experience of others, was the first in a position to bring its products to European consumers.

The position of Cuba is therefore exceptional; it has been so from all time by the gifts of nature; it is still so in our times by all the advantages which we have just enumerated.

But it is always unjust to compare two countries, because God has not made two countries alike. It is no less unjust to draw a parallel between a country which has profited in peace and wealth by all the painful transformations of the neighboring countries, and these countries on the very morrow of these transformations. It should be studied by itself alone.

* About 2,000 Spanish and 4,000 foreign vessels. The commerce with the United States exceeds in importance that with the mother country.

If it be true that the abolition of slavery in the vicinity of Cuba has been fraught with good to this island, does not the maintenance of slavery in Cuba produce all the evils there that elsewhere follow in its train?

If the answer be affirmative, this argument against slavery will be superior to any other. For if there be a spot on earth where slavery might succeed, this is the place. The number of whites is considerable, and consequently the civilizing element is by the side of the laboring element. Free colored persons are numerous, the habit of mixture and the example of liberty facilitates the transition. Slavery is mild; it has always been so in the Spanish colonies. Humane laws insure protection to the African, as formerly to the Indian.* They confer on him four rights; — that of changing one master for another, if the slave finds any one disposed to buy him (the right of *buscar amo*); of marrying; of ransoming himself by degrees by the product of his labor; and of ransoming his wife and children. The exercise of these rights is indeed very difficult, nevertheless they are important, and Don Francisco de Arango justly boasts of them in a Memoir of 1796, at the epoch when the laws of the other West India islands (St. Christopher, 1784) punished with a fine only the crime of having deprived a slave of an eye or an ear. Humboldt, quoting this celebrated Havanese, subsequently praises the laws of Cuba; and he writes (1823) a few years after a sentence rendered in the French West Indies (1815), condemning six young fugitive negroes to be hamstrung.†

* It is common to offer the Indian Legislation (*Recopilacion de leyes de Indias*) as a model of Christian and practical philosophy. Nothing can be more exaggerated than this eulogistic compilation, in nine volumes, of the laws, orders, despatches, and memoranda issued during two centuries. By the side of humane provisions for the Indians are found commercial monopoly, religious intolerance, and despotic penalties. But, above all, Cuba was not the spot to which this collection referred, and its name is hardly mentioned therein. (Don J. A. Saco, pp. 57 - 60.) It is not to these laws, therefore, that we allude.

† *Voyages*, Tom. III. p. 454, note.

The customs are as mild as the laws. This is the testimony of Humboldt, and of all who have visited Cuba, Porto Rico, or the ancient Spanish port of St. Domingo. One and the same religion illumines the consciences of master and slave, — the Catholic faith, so tender to the wretched and obscure. The authority of a European, free, enlightened, Christian government is exercised by high functionaries, invested with unlimited power. Interest renders precious the slaves, whose price is becoming higher and higher, whose labor is growing more and more productive. A military force, larger than in any other colony, maintains peace.* Force, interest, power, religion, customs, laws, seem therefore to concur in the same end, — the alleviation of the evils and dangers of slavery, the tranquillity and prosperity of the Spanish possessions, and the normal and simultaneous development of population, freedom, wealth, and morality. Have these ensued? What of the population? what of the morals?

II. According to Queipo,† the population of Cuba amounted in 1827 to 704,487 souls, viz.: —

Whites	311,051
Free colored	106,494
Slave	286,942
	704,487

And in 1842 to 1,007,624, viz.: —

White	418,291
Free colored	152,838
Slave	436,495
	1,007,624

We give, from a work published in New York under the title "Cuba in 1851," the statistics for 1850. (*Revue Coloniale*, 1851, VII. 448.)

* In 1841, in Jamaica, 1 soldier to 84 blacks and 9 whites; in Cuba, 1 soldier to 45 blacks and 32 whites.

† Page 12. M. Humboldt estimates it in 1823 at 700,000 inhabitants, of whom 256,000 were slaves. *Voyages*, Tom. III. Liv. X. Chap. XVII. p. 334.

Creoles	520,000	605,160 whites.
Spaniards	35,000	
Soldiers and sailors	23,000	
Foreigners	10,160	
Floating population	17,000	
Free mulattoes	118,200	201,470 free colored.
Free negroes	83,270	
Slave mulattoes	11,000	476,000 slave.
Slave negroes	465,000	
	1,282,630	inhabitants.

The same author, M. Queipo, affirms that the ratio of the white to the slave population has not varied much for a century.

	1774.	1792.	1817.	1827.	1842.
White,	68	61	54	52	57
Slave,	32	39	46	48	43
	100	100	100	100	100

He thence concludes that no colony has less favored the slave-trade. But these proportions prove nothing. As has been justly remarked by M. Saco, the black population must not be compared with the white population; if each has increased at the same time almost equally, the ratio between the two is not changed, but the variations of this ratio in no wise indicate the variations of the population. Now we know that at the close of the last century Cuba was an unimportant colony, occupied by small landholders, farming and raising cattle almost without the help of slaves; of 300,000 inhabitants, scarcely one third were slaves.* The white population should be compared with *itself*, and the black population with *itself*, to know what law its increase has followed.

Now, accepting the figures of M. Queipo himself,† the white population from 1827 to 1842 increased about one

* Merivale, quoted by Lechevalier, Introduction, xiv.

† They have been repeated by M. Villaverde in the debate of the law on the slave-trade before the Cortes, Jan. 27, 1845. *Revue Coloniale*, 1845, p. 170.

fourth, the free colored population about one third, and the black population about one half; and if the last be compared with what it was in 1791, it has more than quadrupled.

Again, these figures are far from telling the whole truth. The inhabitants, through fear of taxation, and to hide all traces of the clandestine slave-trade, take care not to acknowledge all their slaves.

At the same epoch when Don Vasquez Queipo wrote, a despatch dated Dec. 31, 1843, from Lord Aberdeen to Mr. Bulwer, Ambassador to Madrid,* says: —

"At this time, according to the report of the most intelligent inhabitants, the number of slaves in the island of Cuba amounts to not less than from 800,000 to 900,000."

If we take into account the statistics of the sugar production, which doubled from 1827 to 1842,† and that of tobacco, which followed the same progress, we must admit that the number of hands which manufactured them has progressed in like proportion.

Now, as M. Saco has demonstrated, this prodigious increase is not due to marriages and births. Doubtless the number of slave marriages and the ratio of legitimate to illegitimate births are much more satisfactory than in any other colony; but the deaths, notwithstanding, exceed the births, and women, despite great efforts made to increase their number, are to men in the proportion of 15 to 28.‡ On the other hand, it results from the custom-house figures that, from 1521 to 1790 only 90,875 negroes were introduced into Havana, but that from 1790 to 1820 this port received more in thirty years than it had done in two centuries and a half; viz. 225,574. If we add what were probably introduced by the way of Trinidad and Santiago, we come to accept the calculation of Humboldt, who esti-

* Speech quoted by M. Villaverde.

† *Revue Coloniale*, 1844, No. 4, p. 492.

‡ Queipo, p. 64.

mates at 413,500 the number of negroes brought through the slave-trade to Cuba from 1521 to 1825. Now they were represented in 1825 by but 256,000 heads.

The slave population, therefore, which seems to have increased, ought to have increased much more; servitude has swallowed up masses of human beings; they constantly come, yet still are lacking.

Prodigious efforts have been made to favor the introduction of colonists of different races. In 1794, the celebrated Havanese, Don Francisco de Arango, obtained funds to encourage the immigration of white laborers.* King Ferdinand VII., by an ordinance dated October 18, 1817, took liberal measures to increase the white population, and attract it by exemption from taxes and other privileges.† The need of these new colonists is, as we see, far anterior to the measures taken to abolish the slave-trade, at least officially. In 1844, under the administration of Captain O'Donnell, the Royal Junta for the Encouragement of Agriculture offered, by a schedule dated August 30, prizes of 6,000 to 12,000, and even 30,000 piasters, for the same object.‡ In 1849 a new plan was addressed to the Queen by Don Domingo de Goicouria, a land-owner of Havana, the only one who responded to the appeal of the Junta, — an intelligent and moral plan, which consisted in introducing *families*, and not mere *day-laborers*, and in separating the raising of the cane from the manufacture of the sugar, so as to diffuse small freeholds.§ All of these endeavors had for their end the immigration of the white race. With one accord, their authors declared that whites were more valuable than negroes, while negroes were more valuable than Indians and Chinese, who created a new element of licentiousness and disorder, and were less laborious and

* *La Question de Cuba*, 1859.

† Supplement to the work of Don V. Queipo.

‡ Ibid.

§ *Revue Coloniale*, New Series, No. II. p. 3.

devoted than the former. But it was all in vain; the white race held aloof. "It is an axiom of political arithmetic," said Don Domingo de Goicouria truly, "sanctioned by experience and the nature of things, that the immigration of free whites into the European colonies of America has been in an inverse ratio to the increase of the slave population. In 1774 the proportion of the whites to the blacks was as 6 to 4; it is now as 4 to 6." *

In 1854 experience and necessity rendered the Cubans less scrupulous. The report of the Minister, Count San Luis, to the Queen, contains cynical confessions and declarations. He attributes the lack of hands to several reasons, — first, to the cessation of the slave-trade, in pursuance of treaties. "*Whatever may be the title these treaties deserve,* honor obliges the government to observe them, although they may be in part the cause of the evil complained of." But we know that the need of laborers dates back far beyond the treaties made to suppress the slave-trade; we know, too, that it is far from being entirely suppressed. The minister points out other causes of the insufficiency of the negro population: —

1. The custom of drawing off slaves from field labor to devote them to domestic service in towns.

2. The little attention given by planters to the reproduction of their slaves, counting, as they did, on keeping up the supply by the clandestine slave-trade.

3. The insecurity of the right of property in slaves, by reason of the difficulties daily called forth by the execution of treaties with a powerful nation. He concludes by recommending the increase of a poll-tax, already established by a royal order, dated July 29, 1844, on domestic slaves, or those residing in towns, and an exemption of six per cent on the duty of *alcabala* on sales of slaves when sold for field labor.

* Memoir cited, p. 5.

† March 22, 1854. See the *Gaceta*, of Madrid, April 13, 1854. *Revue Coloniale*, 1854, No. 13, p. 286.

He proposed to appropriate the product of this poll-tax to the distribution of three annual prizes; the first to the planter whose slaves should have borne the greatest number of children, the second to the one having the greatest proportion of slave women on his plantation, and the third to the one who should have lost the least proportion of slaves within the year. The Minister hoped that the *reproduction of this necessary race* would be thus encouraged, and even that the planters would *devote a large capital especially to this reproduction, as was done in other countries.*

He asked that the immigration of colonists of all races should be largely authorized, and that the agreements between these colonists and the planters should be free, under the surveillance of a special protectorate.

Lastly, he proposed a registration of all the slaves then existing on the island, so that there should be no longer reason to fear investigations of origin in the past, or the registration of slaves introduced illegally in the future.

All of these propositions became royal decrees, March 22, 1854.* They may be summed up in this wise;—to be blind to the slave-trade till 1854; to promise to reform it from that date; to encourage the *raising* of negroes, like that of horses, by premiums; to force the slaveholders, by taxation, to transform the mild yoke of domestic servitude into field-slavery; to summon to the service of sugar-cane and tobacco, Coolies, Chinese, and Yucatanese, with or without family, without fixing any maximum term for their engagement, under the more or less vigilant and disinterested protection of the Captain-General, his delegates, and the municipal syndics.

The promise to put an end to the slave-trade was and continues to be violated. In 1857 the number of negroes seized was 2,704; of those introduced with impunity, 10,436.†

* Text, *Revue Coloniale*, 1854, No. 13, pp. 293, 318.

† Twentieth Report of the Antislavery Society, p. 3.

A treaty, considered an immense benefit, promised to the colony 20,000 Chinese; this treaty is now in process of execution; 5,560 were introduced in 1857; in all, 17,146 since 1847, among whom 7 were women!

Thus, despite the slave-trade, the black population has not followed a normal increase; while its presence arrests all growth of the white population. The island has been reduced to beg Chinese, the offscourings of an ignoble race.

In 1860 a new decree opened the doors of Cuba still more widely to the Chinese,—a decree which called forth the gravest strictures.

"Either," said the journal *El Horizonte* of July 19, 1860,—"either the government wishes to abolish slavery in Cuba, in which case this decree is efficacious, as servile labor, becoming dearer than Chinese labor, will be impossible, but in which case it lacks frankness; or else it wishes, as the preamble declares, *to bring a sufficient number of laborers into the island to insure its prosperity from decreasing,* in which case the decree acts precisely in the contrary direction to its intentions; for the importation of greedy, false, violent, corrupt Chinese, eager to return to their own country, will produce disorder and impoverishment, and diminish prosperity. The basis of the wealth of the island is servitude: it lives by it and for it,—*con ella y por ella vive.*

"If the slaveholders are unable to compete with the rivals who will employ the Chinese, if they see their fortunes disappear in the struggle, it is logical that they will desire independence, or annexation to the United States; and in either case our domination is lost."

But what is to be done? They fear the Chinese; how are they to dispense with them?

The desire of adding new African slaves (*bozales*) to those already living in the island (*ladinos*) is combated, moreover, by the fear which they also inspire.

These slaves, so gentle, so happy, and so well treated, as it is said, have several times rebelled. The Matanzas insurrection * alone (1843 – 1844) cost the lives of four or five hundred men, was stifled by fearfully rigorous measures, and caused the shedding of more blood than was spilt in the sequel of any emancipation. Shortly after, Queipo writes that the island is on *the brink of a volcano*, and that a larger introduction of Africans must be opposed at all costs.

III. Have not these slaves, then, been civilized? Has the pretended conversion of inferior races by the blessings of servitude remained without fruit?

"I cannot place the negroes of Jamaica," says Anthony Trollope,† "on the same footing with those of Cuba, who are left absolutely without religious instruction, and are, in consequence, much more nearly allied to the brutes than any others."

The admissions of Queipo upon this point are extremely valuable. He thinks that for the slaves it suffices for the present to limit the education to religious instruction. He urges the government to facilitate, by every means within its power, instruction so useful; and mark what was the programme of this in his eyes!

"Religious instruction, directed by zealous and learned ecclesiastics, far from influencing the relaxation of discipline, as some perhaps fear, would contribute, on the contrary, to strengthen *the authority of the masters, by accustoming the slaves to submission*, and teaching them to endure the *privations of their transient condition* with the resignation which religion alone can inspire."

To fear the religion which *relaxes discipline*, and to encourage the religion which *accustoms to* submission, — such is, in all places, the embarrassment and the language of the partisans of servitude.

* *Revue Coloniale*, 1844, No. 2, p. 249.

† The West Indies and the Spanish Main, p 47.

But is a convenient clergy found ready to make this ignoble use of its zeal and instruction? What would the clergy be worth who should consent to this disgraceful task?

The same author deplores the constantly increasing aversion and indifference of young men to the ecclesiastical career.

"He would gladly cast a veil over the sorrowful picture presented by the state of religious worship and its ministers."

This clergy is, in fact, one of the most corrupt in the world, despite the zeal of worthy bishops, and the example of decorous and irreproachable Jesuits.

What! you charge religion to strengthen bad kings, bad husbands, and bad masters, by preaching submission to subjects, to women, and to slaves, yet are surprised that priests are not found for this noble vocation, and that those who fulfil it become corrupt and debased!

God be praised that it is so! When the clergy undertakes to excuse the vices which it should combat, it contracts them; and it is just that the physician should take the disease that he would not cure.

We might wager in advance, that justice, which is the next moral power after religion, would be overtaken by the same contagion. The confessions of Queipo, himself Procurer-General, leave no doubt of this.* "Legislation produces a never-failing source of lawsuits; they are the prey of a multitude of business agents (*picaplectos*), barristers (*letrados,*) and attorneys (*causidicos*); they cost enormously dear, and the proceedings are inextricable and endless; in France, England, Spain even, justice is dear; but there is hope of obtaining it in the end. It is not so in Cuba, where the leniency of the superior courts, and the difficulty of bringing to the throne the complaints which may arise against the abuses and injustice of the inferior tribunals and

* The West Indies and the Spanish Main, pp. 240, 243, 256.

their graduate assessors, leave them absolute masters of the fortune and liberty of the inhabitants by favoring impunity." The exorbitant power left to parties to choose and challenge their judges,* the abuse of gratuities (*buscas*) and pilferings (*vistas*, judges' fees), insure ready impunity to the masters of slaves. After a long enumeration of abuses, a magistrate himself concludes by styling legislation and justice *a gnaw-worm which is undermining the island.* †

Above civil justice rises political justice, or government. It is absolute, unlimited. No legislature, as at Jamaica, no General Councils, as in the French West India Islands. To hold the slaves, the colonists desire a rod of iron, and submit to it themselves. We give a few examples of the manner in which it has been exercised during the last few years.

Don José Antonio Saco, for having published some articles against the slave-trade, banished without trial.

Don Domingo Delmonte, a wealthy slave-owner, suspected of having drawn up a petition against the slave-trade, exiled.

Don Benigno Gener, for having written an address against the slave-trade, signed by twenty-three planters of Matanzas, forced to expatriate himself. (1844.)

Don Gaspar Bétancourt Cisneros, a wealthy planter of Puerto Principe, suspected of the same opinions, summoned and severely reprimanded by the Captain-General.

Don José de la Luz Caballero, for the same opinions, indicted before a military commission.

Don Manuel Martinez Serrano, for the same opinions, died in prison.

Thus there might be, or rather there is, an abolitionist sentiment in Cuba. The government does not tolerate it; but it has long tolerated the payment to the Captain-General

* The West Indies and the Spanish Main, p. 304.

† *La Question de Cuba*, 1859, pp. 19, 20.

of an ounce of gold per head for the human cattle introduced. Captains-General still living might be quoted, who have enriched themselves in this manner.

In short, justice, political freedom, and security are falling to decay. But is it at least true, that wealth, the sole object to which everything is sacrificed, is progressing?

If luxury were wealth, if the enormous private fortunes which are seen by Europe, because they are spent in Europe, were a common fact, the island of Cuba might be regarded as the land of opulence, and the city of Havana, so brilliant and animated, — the city of charming prodigality and gilded luxuriousness, — a paradise. But these appearances are veils which we must raise. Let us go to the sources of wealth. More than one is dried up. The commerce being almost entirely in the hands of foreigners, it is the ownership and working of the land which makes the wealth of the island. But the price of slave labor is increasing. If the population had been free, it would have gradually spread over all the most fertile places. Captive, it has been penned up in a single province. In Spain there are 750 inhabitants per square league; at Cuba, 587 per square league in the western part of the island; everywhere else laborers are lacking, and the land remains uncultivated.* To manufacture sugar with the aid of slaves, artificial meadows and the raising of cattle † have been neglected; the forests of centuries have been cut down to cultivate the sugar-cane, and drought and insalubrity have been the result; and the discovery and working of important coal-mines have been

* Land cultivated . . . . 2,188,900 acres.

Natural meadow	3,320,400	"
Artificial "	580,133	"
Land uncleared	13,660,806	"
Land barren	4,642,166	"
	24,392,405	acres.

(*Revue Coloniale*, 1850, No. 5, p. 368.)

† Don V. Queipo, p. 100.

neglected.* The extensive planting necessary for the production of sugar-cane not easily permitting the division of estates; the sugar-works having long enjoyed the privilege of being sold only for a debt equalling their value (Stat. 15, Tit. 16, Book 5 of the Code of the Indies); the apportionment of the lands having been injudiciously made in the beginning, to such a point that a single family (Recios) owns two hundred square leagues; the habit of luxury inducing great improvidence, — the result of all these circumstances is, that real estate is heavily encumbered, and that it "finds itself," says Queipo, "as if lost in an inextricable labyrinth, an inexhaustible source of lawsuits, which disturb the peace of families, endanger and diminish fortunes, ruin honest creditors, and, easily spun out, end for the most part in the sale of the plantations." † The rates of interest are very high, on account of this want of security. Ready money is scarce. Living is very dear. European colonists and capital dare not venture there. Meanwhile sugar, to which everything has been sacrificed, is brought more and more into competition with the sugars from Java, Louisiana, and Brazil. The English and French colonies are resuming their powers. Large fortunes more or less creditably acquired by the side of a general uneasiness concerning property; a prosperity revived by transient causes, the end of which is already beginning to be visible; habits of luxury and prodigality, contrasting with the cruel lot of the slave, and consummating the concealment and consequently precipitation of deeply rooted sources of ruin, — such, then, after reading an official defender of Cuba, is what we are led to think of this material prosperity of which the partisans of slavery make so complacent a display, — a prosperity which might indeed become immense on the day when the efforts of men should correspond with the incomparable gifts of the Creator.‡

* Don V. Queipo, p. 103. † Ibid., p. 105. ‡ Ibid., p. 139.

IV. What has Spain to fear if it abolish slavery?

The expense of indemnifying the slave-owners, a loss of revenues for a few years, and a momentary disturbance.

Without denying the importance of this expense, the weight of this disturbance, we are justified in affirming that both expense and disturbance would be less heavy and less enduring there than elsewhere.

With the precautions whose utility has been revealed by experience, the temporary hiring of the freedmen would be easy. The improved processes of manufacture are already in use, and the combination of small planting with extensive manufacture is no new thing. The military force, schools, and beneficent institutions are ready. The example of free labor has already been set on a large scale.

This has especially been done in the most remarkable manner in the second of the Spanish West India Islands, Porto Rico. A more judicious apportionment of the lands, regulated by an ordinance of Ferdinand VII., August 10, 1815,* which accorded to every foreigner a gratuitous grant of 4½ fanegues (6¼ acres) of land, on condition of cultivating it, and half the quantity to every slave, has attracted colonists, multiplied small freeholds, and facilitated emancipation.

In 1834† Colonel Flinter stated, that among 400,000 inhabitants there was scarcely a single vagrant, and that the whole population was employed in the fields, active and happy. There were not more than 57 towns or villages, containing 6,448 plantations, upon 353 square leagues, while in the country there were 44,295 plantations, occupied by 340,893 inhabitants, on 400,000 leagues. Of 45,000 slaves, 15,000 were domestics, 30,000 only were divided

* Supplement to Queipo's work.

† London, 1834, published by Longman, quoted in a work of Zachary Macaulay, entitled, "Facts and Statements proving the Superiority of Free over Compulsory Labor," translated and published at Paris by Hachette, 1835, Chap. I. pp. 1, 19.

among 300 sugar-works and 148 coffee plantations, independently of 1,277 small plantations. *Three fourths* of the products destined for consumption, or transportation, were the *free* labor of white or colored men, as well as the raising of 100,000 head of cattle.

In 1810 the value of exportations amounted only to 65,672 piasters; in 1832 they exceeded 300,000,000 piasters. Formerly Porto Rico, at first a penal colony, was in the most deplorable condition, and its free blacks were idle and vicious. All the progress is due to the distribution of lands, a liberal legislation, the erection of churches, and good regulations against vagrancy; in other words, to property, religion, and law. In twenty years, according to the testimony of M. Merivale, the population has doubled, the production has quadrupled, the number of slaves, unhappily since augmented, has not increased of itself.* Beside the planters, who usually live on their land and work it themselves, there exists at Porto Rico a very numerous class, almost one third of the population, of small freeholders of the white race, known by the name of *hivaros*, who with their families cultivate their little plantations, — an illiterate but industrious and sturdy race, who live on the best of terms with the colored population. The whites can therefore labor and multiply under the climate of the tropics; tropical products can be cultivated by free labor. The example of Porto Rico establishes these two so much contested facts.

In 1844, by the statement of Don José Saco,† Porto Rico numbered 1,277 small sugar plantations cultivated by their free owners, and the same writer recalls the fact that sugar is also produced by free labor in the East Indies, Java,

* Herman Merivale, Lectures on Colonization, 1841, cited by Jules Lechevalier, *Rapport sur les questions coloniales*, I., Introduction, xx., 1844.

† *De la suppression de la traite des esclaves africains dans l'île de Cubà*, by Don José Saco (*Revue coloniale*, 1845, No. 5, p. 256).

the Moluccas, the Celebes, Sumatra, and Manilla. To these the English and French West India Islands may now be added. But in the Spanish West Indies there are already more freemen than anywhere else, more whites to direct the colored population, more soldiers to maintain order, more capital to weather the crisis, and the experience of others whereby to shun errors and shape the transition. What is lacking, then? Nothing, except will.

But, on the other hand, what has Spain to fear if it does not abolish slavery?

The moral and even material decay of an admirable country; next, the loss of its colony.

Let not luxury, pomp, millions, marriages of Havana Creoles, and incontestable prosperity, due to exceptional and transient causes, delude us.

In short, with a mitigated slavery, constantly renewed by the slave-trade, the island is not peopled; with magnificent elements of wealth, property is in general encumbered with debts and devoured by luxury; the soil has become a vast manufactory; a large military force and unlimited superior power have not prevented insurrections, a state of siege and banishment; religion has become corrupt instead of civilizing; justice is debased, morals dissolute, the whites subjected, deprived of all political freedom, to the absolute power of which they have need to protect themselves against rebellion. It is in vain to say that emancipation will be wrought of itself by degrees; it is in vain to boast of human laws, a serious abolitionist public sentiment, even among the masters, an extended power of redemption, and less prejudices of color than exist in America. The redemption leads to nothing, the public sentiment is not free, no example is given, and men are reduced to repeating that time will destroy slavery. But time rivets more fetters than it wears out. What has it done hitherto? Time has witnessed the growth of marvellous progress in Cuba. This opulent country has writers, scholars, artists, poets, administrators, millionnaires, journals, schools, churches, institutions of all kinds, model manufactories, railroads, plantations managed with superior skill, magnificent harbors, an active commerce; it is what is called to-day a civilized country.

"Wherever," says Humboldt,* "slavery has been of ancient growth, the mere increase of civilization has much less influence on the treatment of slaves than we should like to be able to admit. The civilization rarely extends to many individuals; it does not reach those who are in immediate contact with the negroes on the plantations."

We see at Cuba what was seen at Rome and Athens, — slavery enduring by the side of luxury, extreme abjectness by the side of extreme opulence, the condition of the slaves more miserable in proportion as the requirements of wealth and commerce become more imperious. The same sun ripens the fruit and rots the dunghill. Time increases the wealth of the masters and the wretchedness of the slaves. Forty years have passed since Humboldt visited Cuba, forty years have not changed the condition of the slaves. To count on time is to perpetuate servitude.

It is for the Spanish government to take the initiative. Towards abolishing the slave-trade, it has made, with ill grace, a few tardy efforts; towards abolishing slavery, nothing.

We see it shut its eyes to the continuance of the slave-trade, in contempt of the most solemn treaties. We have seen, and must again repeat, its conduct towards the opinion of the partisans of liberty, who are numerous, to the honor of Cuban society.

In the sequel of the slave insurrections which took place in Cuba at the close of 1843 and the beginning of 1844, a

* Voyages, Tom. III. p. 456.

tendency to emancipation manifested itself in public opinion. Ninety-two of the leading residents of Matanzas signed (Nov. 29, 1843) an address to Captain-General O'Donnell against the slave-trade and indirectly against slavery ; * the Captain-General refused to receive it, and administered to them a severe reprimand. A second address having been signed at Havana, he tore it in pieces before its authors ; to a third address, he replied by written menaces. More than three thousand negroes were executed, and a thousand more banished.† What was their crime ? In the midst of cruel tortures inflicted on these unhappy negroes, to wring from them confessions respecting the origin of the insurrection, they declared, even when bound to the fatal stake, that they had not been impelled to revolt by harsh treatment, but by the love of liberty, of which they had been unjustly deprived; that they were ready to brave for it the keenest sufferings, and death itself; that they could live no longer without it; they saw it escape their grasp, and resigned themselves to death rather than relapse into slavery.

Lord Aberdeen, in recapitulating these facts in a despatch to the Spanish government, May 2, 1844,‡ did not fear to add : "The only persons who lend a hand to the continuance of the slave-trade are the officers of the crown of Spain itself. The cupidity of the government is the real cause of this grievous traffic imposed on the colony, despite its manifest danger and the great discontent of the land-owners, for the sole end of enriching the Captain-General."

Public opinion was moved at Madrid as at Havana. The remonstrances of the English cabinet resulted in the law of 1845 for the suppression of the slave-trade, — a more

* *Revue coloniale*, 1845, No. 7, p. 281.

† Report of the English Commissioner, *Revue coloniale*, 1847, No. 12, p. 104.

‡ *Revue coloniale*, 1845, No. 7, p. 283.

severe but no less violated law than its predecessors. But nothing was done against slavery. Yet this was the cause of the insurrections; it was not enough to say, Bring no more slaves, without adding, Keep them no longer. English emancipation was accomplished; in the same year, 1845, the way was being paved, by important laws, for French emancipation. The Spanish government did not even express a wish or a hope, or announce the design of any initiative. Fifteen years have passed since this measure, without a single step having been taken, without a single word having been uttered, in favor of the abolition of slavery. On the contrary, the report which preceded the decrees of 1854, on *registration, immigration,* etc., opens with these shameful words: * —

"One of the most serious evils from which the island of Cuba now suffers proceeds from the scarcity of laborers. . . . . If haste be not made to provide a remedy, the riches which this island contains will not be long in diminishing, and even becoming completely exhausted. . . . . It will not escape the penetration of your Majesty, that the condition which is deplored is due on the one hand to the *necessary* existence of slavery, and on the other to the treaties in force which suppress the slave-trade. The West Indies appear fated by Providence to show their fruitfulness only by favor of this institution, and *at the expense of the race upon which it weighs.* From this results, as concerns the island of Cuba, an economical and social situation which it is *indispensable to maintain with all its inconveniences,* however exceptional and abnormal it may be; for the mere idea of regulating it by modelling it after European communities, would give rise to still greater damage to the state, and even to the race deprived of civil liberty.

"From the *necessity* of maintaining slavery in these regions *naturally* arose the utility of permitting, in cer-

* *Revue coloniale,* 1854, No. 13, p. 286.

tain cases, the introduction of new slaves; but being prohibited by treaties, this efficacious means of *preservation* fails slavery at the moment when the development and progress of agriculture render it every day more necessary."

Necessary slavery, a *necessary* slave-trade, — these were proclaimed in 1854 by the Spanish government.

But, thank God! it is emancipation that is necessary. What humanity has not inspired, necessity commands. Cuba has not changed masters, but it has changed neighbors. In all the countries which border upon Cuba, from Mexico to Florida, from Panama to Guiana, in all the West Indies, less than a century ago, reigned almost everywhere Spain, everywhere slavery. The centre of Insular America, of North America, and of South America, the Queen of the Antilles, Cuba to-day is without institutions or races about it bearing resemblance to its own. Mexico, Central America, Columbia, St. Domingo, the English, French, Danish, and Swedish West Indies, have ceased to hold slaves. Louisiana and Florida possess them, but these belong to the invading race of Americans. The broad, beautiful, and opulent island of Cuba seems to the Southern slaveholders of the American Union like a territory detached from their continent, which they wish to reconquer from the sea. To augment the number of Slave States by a country divided into two States, is to re-establish the balance of power in both houses of Congress, and to re-establish and strengthen the influence of the South. America is to the Americans what Italy is to the Italians. — Cuba ought to be the prey of the United States; it will be; — the first attempts failed with Lopez; they will be begun anew. The covetousness of the South has become a political scheme. Clad in official language, Cuba shall be bought, given, or taken.

Spain will surrender her last vessel and her last dollar

before losing the only jewel which is left her of her ancient American crown. Already in the Cortes solemn defiances have answered the threats and entreaties of the Cabinet at Washington.* The two hundred thousand free mulattoes, whom the morrow of annexation would hurl back into a rank nearly akin to slavery, will resist with Spain. A powerful party will endeavor to reconquer the independence of the island. Nevertheless, the example of Texas is sufficient proof that America will advance step by step, and that, sooner or later, the usurpation is infallible. For, on the one hand, there is a party in the United States that is paving the way for it; on the other, there are planters in the island who desire it, in order to be relieved from paying so many taxes and the expense of so many functionaries to Spain, and, by uniting themselves to fifteen Slave States, to secure the perpetuity of their own property in slaves. Lord Palmerston once said: "The colonists of Cuba cling to Spain only through fear of an insurrection, and through the privilege of the slave-trade." But America would henceforth better protect their security and traffic. The besiegers, therefore, have allies in the place, and good-will is secured by the complicity of interests.

Unless Europe oppose it, this century is probably destined to see the broad hand of the United States open and shut upon a new conquest, as large as England, richer in the gifts of God than any country on the globe, the Gibraltar of the American Mediterranean, the sentinel posted at the entrance of the Mississippi, the keeper of the future channel of Panama, the Queen of the Antilles, shared by the maritime powers, which the same greed, inflated by its triumphs, will dare menace in turn.

Spain, led by wrong-doing to a false and desperate position, has already attempted to obtain a guaranty from

* See Book I. Chap. I. The United States.

England and France for her possessions. In 1852 a treaty was proposed to the United States, which agreement involved nothing less than an obligatory declaration on the part of the three nations, equivalent to securing to Spain the perpetual possession of the island of Cuba, without any guaranty on its part with respect to the inhabitants of the colony.* The United States refused a treaty which deceived their ambition without satisfying humanity.

Since this epoch, as we have already said, plans have become public, and threats audacious.

Happily for Spain, Providence accords it a respite and an opportunity to uprise. Under cover of the crisis in which the United States are writhing, Spain, by a bold movement, has recovered St. Domingo, and is disposed to intermeddle with the revolutions of Mexico. The owner or protector of two countries without slaves, how will it preserve the third and fairest, how secure to itself the possession of Cuba?

The only means is to emancipate its slaves.

The Southern United States will no longer have the same interest in annexation; should they attempt it, the subjugation of a free country to re-establish slavery there will strike the whole world with horror, and Spain will more easily obtain the support of Europe. Four hundred thousand negroes and two hundred thousand mulattoes will defend the right of Spain with their freedom. Emancipation will take away slaves to give it defenders. The slaveholders will be indemnified, and if they complain over-loudly, the treaties can be brought in opposition to their complaints, which authorize freedom to be granted to every slave to whom they cannot prove a title; — if these treaties were carried out to the letter, how many would be left them?

I repeat, with a distinguished writer: "The abolition of

* *La Question de Cuba*, 1859, p. 57.

slavery is the most infallible means of securing the possession of Cuba to Spain." *

Of all the nations of Europe, Spain was the first to people the world which it conquered with slaves; will it be the last to renounce a crime which has lasted more than three centuries?

* M. Cucheval-Clarigny, *Patrie*, Jan. 17, 1859.

BOOK THIRD.

PORTUGAL.*

Placed at the southwestern extremity of Europe, one of the smallest kingdoms of this part of the world, Portugal had the honor to be chosen by Providence to bring the rest of the globe under the empire of Christian civilization. We know what a brilliant series of discoveries followed the wise initiation, in the beginning of the fifteenth century, of the illustrious prince, Henry the Navigator, one of the sons of King John I., who founded the royal dynasty of Aviz, and transferred the capital of the kingdom from Coimbra to Lisbon. From 1415 to the death of Henry, in 1460, and after him, Madeira, the Cape Verde Islands, the Azores, Guinea, Congo, were so many beacons on the road which was to carry Bartholomew Diaz (1486) beyond the Cape of Good Hope, and Vasco de Gama (1498), then Almeida and Albuquerque, as far as the East Indies. Glorious enterprises were these, which brought to Portugal, with immortal glory, immense possessions, erelong increased by the discovery of Brazil (1500) and the cession of Macao (1557)!

Portugal was for some time the vanguard of Christian civilization in the conquest of the world. The Sovereign Pontiffs encouraged and authorized its undertakings. Sextus IV. declared it master of all the territories situated beyond Cape Bajador (1481), and Alexander VI. (1493) divided the New World by an imaginary line between Spain

* See the interesting work of M. Charles Vogel, entitled *Le Portugal et ses colonies*. Paris, Guillaumin, 1860.

and Portugal. Seconded by admirable missionaries, religion won more souls in these countries, unknown since creation, than Portugal acquired subjects there. The baptism of a queen of Congo was witnessed at Lisbon; and three centuries after, Livingstone found on the coast of Angola and Mozambique the ruins of immense churches built by the Jesuits, the tradition of a monastery of negro Benedictines, and tribes who have handed down from one generation to another the art of reading and writing, which they had acquired from the missionaries.

It is to its conflicts with the Moors that Portugal owes the development of that enterprising, military, and religious genius which raised it so high. But corrupted by contact with the vanquished, it had the misfortune to receive from them a poison destined to endure longer than its victories; it borrowed from them the frightful custom of slavery. The first to give nations to Christianity, it was the first to give it slaves. The port of Lisbon was enriched, the empire of Brazil colonized by the slave-trade, and from all the Portuguese settlements on both coasts of Africa, as from so many convict-prisons, captives in chains were seen to issue for centuries, conducted by force into exile.

The colonial greatness of Portugal is no more; the suppression of the Jesuits by the Marquis de Pombal has destroyed their missions; Christianity has disappeared like commerce; the slave-trade has survived. Suppressed in July, 1842, it still endures in secret. Slavery subsists with it.

The country of Henry the Navigator still possesses settlements in Africa and Asia as so many witnesses of its ancient power; — in Africa, the Cape Verde Islands, Portuguese Senegambia or Upper Guinea, and St. Thomas and Prince's Island, with the governments of Angola and Benguela in the Gulf of Guinea on the western coast, and Mozambique on the eastern coast; in Asia, the province of Goa and the government of Macao.

The Cape Verde Islands in 1852 still had 5,659 slaves out of 86,000 inhabitants. The unimportant stations, Bissao, Cacheo, and Zenguichor, which still remind us on the coast of Upper Guinea of the ancient power of Portugal, now despoiled of Arguin and Elmina, serve as the residences, around ill-defended forts and churches in ruins, of a few thousand Europeans or native Christians, served by about 1,500 slaves. Of the four islands in the Gulf of Guinea, two, Fernando Po and Annabona, belong by right to Spain, in fact, to England; two, St. Thomas and Prince's Island, still bear the Portuguese flag; and a garrison of 160 men are exposed there to the rigors of the seasons, divided between wind and rain, to protect the raising of a handful of cocoa and coffee, and a little pepper, ginger, and cinnamon, the cultivation and sale of which employ 12,253 inhabitants, 139 only of whom are whites, 4,580 slaves.

Lower Guinea, commonly called Congo, is as large as France; 660,000 inhabitants live there more or less submissive to the Portuguese administration, in the districts of Angola and Benguela, amidst nearly 2,000,000 independent natives. This territory was and is still in part Christian. Instruction was diffused there by the Jesuits; twelve of their churches still exist; and it is to the Italian Capuchins that we owe the grammar and dictionary of the *Binda* language. But the same territory was also the greatest centre of the slave-trade, and in its chief town, St. Paul de Loanda, now the seat of a mixed commission charged with passing judgment on the operations of this trade, there might have been seen as lately as 1849 thirty-seven slave-ships at one time awaiting their cargoes under the protection of the same forts which now serve to watch them, and paying a fee for each slave to the government which now condemns them. In 1856 there were still 65,000 slaves under Portuguese dominion.

There were not less than 42,000 out of the 62,000 inhabitants of the opposite coast of Africa in the government of Mozambique, — the last relic of the vast possessions of Portugal in the sixteenth and seventeenth centuries, when, master of the coast of Zanguebar and Mascata, it made Melinda a flourishing colony.

The reason of the decay of these vast possessions must not be sought alone in the obstacles which the climate opposes to the health of Europeans; for several points, especially on the eastern coast, are salubrious, watered by running streams, shaded by forests, and peopled by numerous animals, nourished by a fertile soil. Neither is the disproportion between the resources of a small European kingdom and the extent of the settlements a sufficient explanation: what Holland has made of Java is well known. The two scourges of Portuguese Africa have been bad government and the slave-trade; again, it has been slavery that has, above all, corrupted the government. "By reason of the sale of slaves," says M. Vogel,* "the plantations have been stripped, the laborers frightened away, the native population exasperated, ... and, by the bait of infamous profits, the provinces made the sink of Portuguese society." Who would be willing to sully his name by placing his capital in enterprises so adventurous and disgraceful? If we say that the negroes labor only on compulsion, we calumniate them, for in this part of Africa, says M. Vogel again,† "the method of working by agreement with free, paid blacks is that by which the best results have always been obtained."

We have cited elsewhere the letter of Pope Benedict to John, king of Portugal, in which he represents that the treatment practised by Christians towards the wretched slaves inspires them with abhorrence of Christianity.

The same crime, therefore, destroys at once the three instruments of all civilization, — religion, labor, and capi-

* P. 564, Chap. XXII. † P. 579, *ibid.*

tal. Landing, proud of their race and superior civilization, on these distant shores, it was the mission of Christian Europeans to elevate the miserable tribes who dwelt there above polygamy, idolatry, slave-hunts, and the sale of men. Instead of converting, they have imitated them ; they have practised slavery, the slave-trade, polygamy ; and if they have not been idolaters, if they have not worshipped false gods, it is because they do not worship any. Yet we are astonished that a few poor missionaries, thrown between such believers and such neophytes, have not transformed Africa; and cry out that the negroes oppose Christianity. Yes, when they look at the Christians.

The future prosperity of Portuguese Africa is in evangelization and agriculture. The abolition of the slave-trade, then of slavery, is the indispensable preliminary of both. This is at length understood. After the slave-trade, slavery is beginning to be attacked.

By a decree of December 14, 1854, and by a statute of June 30, 1856,* the slaves *belonging to the state, to the municipalities, and to charitable institutions of the Order of Mercy,* in all the trans-oceanic possessions, were declared free, on condition of a limited service after their liberation.

A statute of July 25, 1856, extends this favor to the slaves *belonging to the churches.*

A statute of July 5, 1856, abolishes slavery in a part of the province of Angola, namely, in the district of Ambriz and the territories of Cabinda and Melinda. A statute of July 24, 1856, declares free all children born of slave mothers subsequently to this date, on condition of serving the masters of their mothers gratuitously until the age of twenty ; the masters remaining charged with their support. The same statute forbids a mother and a child under seven years old to be sold separately.

Two decrees were rendered at the same epoch, declaring

* *Revue coloniale*, 1858, Vol. XX. p. 385.

all slaves free on touching the soil of Portugal, Madeira, or the Azores.

Lastly, August 25, 1856, upon the declaration of the Governor-General of Macao, Timor, Solor, and Goa, that slavery had disappeared in fact in the Portuguese East Indies, the government gave orders to declare it abolished by law.

No law has yet suppressed slavery in the province of Mozambique, the rest of the province of Angola, Upper Guinea, and the islands of the Gulf of Guinea. It is difficult, moreover, to say whether the laws which M. de Sar-da-Bandeira had the honor to countersign have been promulgated and executed on the coast of Africa.

It is evident that, when, at the close of 1857, the Governor-General of Mozambique ordered the arrest by a Portuguese schooner of the French ship *Charles et Georges*, loaded with free immigrants, condemned the captain to two years in irons, seized the ship and kept the negroes, — it is evident that this scrupulous Governor was the agent of a government whose conversion to the great cause of abolition was recent and still incomplete.

Let us hope that the first Christian country which held slaves after the Middle Ages will not be the last entirely to renounce them. Let us hope that Portugal will avail itself of the settlements which are left it on both coasts of Africa to labor at length to convert and civilize a continent which it has held almost alone in its hands for many centuries, without profit either to this unhappy land, to the mother country, or to humanity.

BOOK FOURTH.

BRAZIL.*

Among the Portuguese colonies would have been cited, at the beginning of the present century, as the fairest, the vastest, the richest, Brazil. Independent since 1822, this immense empire is one of the principal centres of slavery at our epoch.

North America possesses the most powerful republic in the world, the United States. South America belongs in great part to Brazil, one of the most flourishing monarchies of the universe, the only monarchical, the only flourishing state in the midst of ten republican states.† The Union is a vigorous branch of the Saxon race, Brazil is a bough full of sap of the Latin race; the first is a Protestant nation, the second a Catholic nation. Both have broken the bond which attached them to the mother country, for the sake of freedom of trade, and the first since 1787, the second since 1822, have not ceased to grow. If we pause in surprise before the gigantic destinies of the United States, how can we help also assigning an incalculable future to Brazil, as large as Europe,‡ already composed of twenty provinces,

* *Brésil*, by M. Charles Reybaud, 1856; *Portugal et ses colonies*, by M. Vogel, 1860; *Le Budget du Brésil*, by Count de Stratten Ponthos; *Brésil*, by Pereira de Silva, *Revue des deux Mondes*, April 15, 1858; *A travers l'Amérique du Sud*, by F. Dabadie, Sartorius, 1859; *Histoire du Brésil*, by Ferdinand Denis.

† It would be unjust not to point out Chili as a flourishing state. See the *Histoire du Chili*, by the Abbé Eyzaguire.

‡ 3,956,800 square miles in area; extending from the 4th to the 33d degree of south latitude, and from the 37th to the 73d degree of west longitude.

sixteen of which have harbors on the Atlantic, — provinces where the vegetation of the tropics and the cultivation of Europe divide the surface of a soil rich in metals, gold, and diamonds, and watered by immense rivers, tributaries or rivals of that Amazon which, after a course of 4,000 miles, reaches the sea, 250 miles broad at the mouth. 8,000,000 of inhabitants dwell on this land, so rich in the gifts of God, and which would support 150,000,000, protected by a free constitution under a popular government. Since the declaration of independence, in 1822, this people has passed through war with the mother country, war with the neighboring countries, and internal wars of parties; yet notwithstanding receipts are progressing, importations have tripled, exportations are yearly increasing,* four lines of steamers run up and down the Amazon, others serve the coasts, others connect Brazil with Europe, railroads are constructed, rivers and roads are improved, and in the city of Rio Janeiro, whose children were forced forty years since to go to Coimbra to take their degrees, to-day 300,000 inhabitants have colleges, an institute, churches, hospitals, Sisters of Charity, journals, writers, poets. This century will have witnessed the birth and growth on the same continent, in the North and South, of two states vaster and erelong more powerful than the most ancient states of Old Europe.

Unfortunately both, again too much alike on this point, hold slaves, — nearly 4,000,000 in the United States, more than 2,000,000 in Brazil. Rio Janeiro alone had, in 1850, 110,599 slaves in 266,466 inhabitants, and, taking into account the free negroes and mulattoes, the African race exceeds in numbers the white and Brazilian races.

Following their appearance on Brazilian territory, the

* We will quote a single fact. Coffee was introduced into Brazil in 1774; in four years, 1834 - 1838, this country exported only 657,575 sacks; in five months, from January to May, 1859, it exported 687,704 sacks. It produces 460,000,000 lbs., — more than half of the total production of coffee (900,000,000 lbs.) on the globe. (Hunt's Merchants' Magazine.)

Europeans enslaved the Indians, and, long after the measures of emancipation decreed by the government, in 1570, 1647, and 1684, these unfortunates remained slaves, until 1755; the Africans were such after them, are still, and will be perhaps for a long time.

The 2,000,000 African slaves in Brazil were brought thither through the slave-trade; no country abandoned itself to this odious traffic more actively or more obstinately.

Portugal pledged itself to England, by a treaty of Jan. 22, 1815, towards the abolition of the slave-trade; Brazil, by another treaty of Nov. 23, 1826, renewed the same pledges. Yet in 1839 Mr. Buxton,* sustained by official documents, estimated at about 80,000 the number of slaves imported annually at Rio, Bahia, Pernambuco, and Para. In 1844 the English consuls declared that the slave-trade had not diminished.† It was at this epoch that England, by a bill of 1845, violating the right of nations in behalf of the right of men, declared Brazilian slave-ships amenable to English authorities; and a long diplomatic contest, backed by forcible demonstrations, threatened the repose of Brazil. A statute bearing date July 17, 1850, which assimilated the slave-trade to piracy, was at length the token of better intentions.‡ The Emperor, in a speech, Sept. 4, 1852, declared that the slave-trade might be regarded as extinct. A society opposed to the slave-trade and in favor of colonization was formed under his patronage, 1853,§ and the same year, May 14, the Minister of Foreign Affairs, M. de Souza, announced that 700 negroes only had been imported in 1852, but added, at the same time, that the importation had amounted

* On the Slave-Trade, 1839, p. 12.

† *Revue coloniale*, 1855, p. 78.

‡ *Ibid.*, 1850, No. 5, p. 213.

§ *Ibid.*, 1832, p. 357; 1853, p. 307.

In 1846 to 50,324,
" 1847 " 56,172,
" 1848 " 60,000,
" 1849 " 54,000.

Since this time, the slave-trade has diminished, yet it still exists ; but one ship out of five reaches its destination, yet the business is still good. Surveillance is difficult on 1,200 leagues of coast. More secret, more cruel, more active, the slave-trade continues therefore to nourish slavery in Brazil, as in Cuba, as in the United States ; slavery and the slave-trade are accomplices which can only be slain at one blow.

What is said in Brazil in justification of slavery ?

That South America is almost entirely destitute of inhabitants, that to people it needs the aid of immigration, that the climate permits none but Africans to labor, and that, to attach them to the cultivation of the soil, it is necessary to constrain them to it by force. It is added, that the Brazilian planters take great care of their slaves, moderate their labor, almost always abstain from corporal punishment, and regulate their dietary and hygienic system with judicious humanity. It is affirmed that the abolition of slavery would dry up all the sources of agricultural wealth, and prove an immense subversion, almost suicide, to the empire.* It is hoped, notwithstanding, that the day will come when Brazil will have none but freemen, and this will be when colonists flow thither. We will briefly review these arguments.

The climate is a bad reason. Brazil presents every species of climate ; let the cultivation of the regions bordering on the equator be confined to Africans, but free Africans, hired for a stated term, as English Guiana and a portion of Porto Rico are cultivated. In three fourths of the empire the white and native races have nothing to

* Charles Reybaud, *Brésil*, Chap. V. p. 187.

fear from the climate. Are slaves employed only under the equator? Are they not employed in agriculture? We have seen that Rio alone contains more than 100,000.

It is hoped to people an uninhabited country by slavery. Everywhere the negro population dies out by degrees in slavery. It is a law of Providence, and this law extends to certain animals, that perpetuation is impossible in captivity.

An overwhelming subversion is feared. If, as is affirmed, the negroes are well treated, if precautions are taken to bind them to the soil by engagements, and also by the threefold bond of property by not disputing to them their cabin and garden, of family by encouraging marriage, of religion by favoring their taste for instruction and religious worship, there is no cause for fear. The example of the French and English colonies proves that the negro race is gentle, domestic, and susceptible of civilization. It flees the plantations only where the memory of a harsh slavery inspires it with dread; only when the transition is not prudently managed.

It is hoped that the influx of European colonists will one day render slavery useless. The day is far off when Brazil will have received 10,000,000 inhabitants by this means. But colonists are little attracted towards slave countries; do not the Northern United States receive more than the Southern? The colonists who come, moreover, make the greatest possible haste to buy slaves in their turn. The French and English themselves, who would blush in their own country to declare themselves partisans of slavery, despite the threat of losing their nationality, do not scruple to own slaves in Brazil. The influx of colonists will, therefore, increase the demand for slaves, unless the abolition of slavery precede their arrival.

We will again invoke here the example of North America. The States which had the courage to abolish slavery when it was of small extent, weathered the momentary crisis without trouble, and are now the most flourishing States of the Union. Where the imprudent insensibility of the legislators suffered the evil to increase, the people know no longer how to uproot it. Let Brazil take warning by the example of the Southern States.

The power being concentrated, the emancipation does not present the difficulties in Brazil which are encountered by the Congress of the United States. Indemnity is not a burden impossible to be borne in a country whose finances and credit are prosperous. It may be satisfied in part by a few years' postponement. Above all, it will be greatly diminished by making literal application, as may rightfully be done, of the statutes and treaties which declare all slaves free who are brought thither by the slave-trade. Should a strict scrutiny be made of the manner in which the slaves came into the hands of their masters, how many would remain whose possession could be justified?

In short, the origin of slavery in Brazil is infamous. Its maintenance is without excuse. Its abolition presents no political difficulty.

Its effects would be a financial burden, an agricultural and commercial crisis, temporary and easily repaired, the gravity of which each day of delay increases, far from bringing the solution.

If the suppression of slavery be a blow dealt to wealth, its continuance is an increasing obstacle to morality; between these two elements of a people, it is necessary to choose, or rather to know that a people without virtue becomes erelong a people without wealth.

It is useless to say that slavery is mild in Brazil; whoever has seen the drunken, gambling, thieving, and licentious negroes at Rio, whoever has visited the *Caza de Correcâo,* whoever has penetrated to the Southern *estancias,* knows what is to be thought of the morality and happiness of the blacks. But to speak only of the whites, they are themselves the victims of slavery. It produces there what it produces elsewhere, — the corruption of the family, the corruption of justice, and the corruption of religion; and when these three sacred things are debased, what remains? I do not pretend that the little communities in the rest of South America are, alas! more virtuous or more upright than Brazilian society. It is, on the contrary, because the latter holds the first rank, because the future of this country is destined, as I believe, to a marked place in history, that I blush to find on its brow a spot which it alone bears on this magnificent yet unhappy continent. To serve God and own slaves, to render justice and own slaves, to be a husband and father and own slaves, — this is what a Christian European of the nineteenth century can no longer comprehend; this is what is witnessed in Brazil.

Happily, a generous movement in ideas, a practical movement in facts, permit us to conceive hopes of better things. Great efforts for European colonization, after a few checks, have fully succeeded. The colony of St. Leopold at Rio Grande do Sul, founded by the government in 1825, has now more than 12,000 inhabitants. Since 1845, the Emperor has founded, a few leagues from Rio, the town of Petropolis, which already has more than 5,000 residents. Private individuals * have established centres where colonists live satisfied and in the enjoyment of abundance, cultivating the land on shares or buying on credit. Lastly, the statute of Sept. 18, 1850, which creates a veritable register of lands, separates the public from the private property, and authorizes the government to institute a *general management of the public lands,* by clearing away from its path all the legal

* Especially Prince de Joinville, on the estates of his wife, the Princess Francisca. See the excellent chapter of M. Reybaud, *Brésil,* Chap. V. p. 198, and the Report of M. Aubé, *Revue coloniale,* 1847, II. p. 332.

difficulties arising from ancient grants or *sesmarias*, opens a vast future to colonization. On the other hand, a society, as we have seen, was formed in 1853 both for colonization and against the slave-trade. In 1856 the English Ambassador, Mr. Scarlet,* wrote to Lord Clarendon that the Minister, Mr. Paranhos, had told him that *the resolution had been taken by the government gradually to abolish slavery in Brazil,* and that he himself was a member of a society called *Ypiranga,* formed in memory of the independence of Brazil, under the protection of the Emperor, which every year solemnly emancipated slaves in open church before the Emperor and Empress.

This generous movement will grow,—let us hope it. Let Brazil leave foolish fears and paltry arguments to petty colonies, where there are so few masters, so few workmen, so little capital, and so few products, that a storm, a blight of vegetation, a bankruptcy, or a change in government, plunges them long into suffering. But a great monarchy of 8,000,000 inhabitants, intelligent, united, and vigorous, should conceive and accomplish the designs commanded by humanity ; and it would be glorious if the Latins of South America, boldly abolishing slavery, should have the honor of setting the example to the Saxons of North America.

* Correspondence with British and Foreign Ministers and Agents relative to the Slave-Trade, 1857, Class B, No. 182, p. 171.

BOOK FIFTH.

COLONIES OF HOLLAND.*

I. THE DUTCH EAST INDIES.

THE Dutch, small in territory, but great in history and character, are among the peoples of Europe that do most honor to the human species. They have wrested their soil from the waves of the ocean, and freed it from foreign dominion. Skilled in navigation, long surnamed the *wagoners of the sea,* daring, ready to go at all times to the ends of the world for wealth or for battle, they have possessed the art, without shedding as much blood as the Spaniards in America or the English in India, by degrees to extend and establish their empire on the vast, fertile, and populous islands of Malasia.†

There, under the authority of the Governor-General, a veritable king, supported by a small army, composed in part of natives, and surrounded by a few thousand inhabitants, twenty million inhabitants ‡ form an empire vaster

* Immediately following the publication of this volume, emancipation throughout the Dutch Colonies was proclaimed by a law bearing date August 8, 1862, to take effect July 1, 1863. M. Cochin's analysis of this law, in the *Journal des Débats*, Sept. 20, 1862, will be found in the "Results of Emancipation," p. 396. — TR.

† *Histoire des établissements hollandais en Asie*, by Capt. Dubouzet, *Revue coloniale*, 1843, p. 137. The last treaty, which guaranteed their possessions to the Dutch, was concluded with England, March 17, 1824.

‡ Java and Madura	9,584,130
Sumatra	3,430,000
Banca	50,000
Riouw	70,000

and more populous than Brazil, and peacefully obey the ascendency of a little nation which scarcely counts three million men. As Baron Dupin has said, the colonizing system of Holland may be summed up in one sentence, — *religious tolerance and commercial intolerance.* They exclude no labor, they leave to others no profit. An ingenious system, improved upon by the celebrated Governors Van der Capellen (1816), De Bus (1826), and, above all, Van den Bosch (1830), to whom Holland owes it that the commerce of Java has doubled in thirty years, imposes a labor tax on all the inhabitants for the benefit of the government, which succeeded the old East India Company in 1795. The native chiefs and princes of each *dessa* are the collectors, and the labor, instead of being regarded as an act of the Dutch, seems to the population to be that of their ancient sovereigns, the proprietors of the soil, in the terms of the Koran. All of the commodities are purchased by the government at a fixed price, then sold to the agents of an association of trade, *Handel-Maatschappy*, founded in 1819, and rechartered in 1849, which, in its turn, transports them to Dutch harbors, in ships built in Holland and

Borneo	1,200,000
Celebes	3,000,000
Moluccas	718,500
Timon	800,000
Bally and Laubock	1,205,000
	20,057,630

These are the statistics of 1849. Of the number, some 200,000 or 300,000 are Chinese. (*Revue coloniale*, 1852, p. 35.)

According to the census of 1855, presented by Baron Dupin,* the population is only 15,500,312; of which 10,916,158 belong to Java and Madura. This difference comes from the fact that the learned writer did not take into account the vast regions of Sumatra and Borneo, which had remained or become independent. Celebes is larger than Java; Sumatra, of greater extent than the British Isles. Borneo equals in surface the empire of Austria. It is well known that an Englishman, by the name of Rajah Brooke, has founded an independent state in Borneo, which England has not yet accepted.

* *Rapport à la commission de l'Exposition universelle*, 1859, p. 280.

manned with Dutch crews, sells them in Dutch markets, and brings back Dutch products to the East Indies.

This series of privileges and monopolies assuredly encounters objections and engenders inconveniences; strongly attacked, the system seems approaching its end.* But, after all, it produces immense results. Lands which would have remained waste have been cultivated. Production has increased in an incredible degree; of the principal product, coffee, 18,000,000 lbs. were exported in 1790, 158,040,000 lbs. in 1840. The profits of all have increased. European civilization has founded magnificent cities. Holland presents the spectacle of colonies that enrich the mother country.† Encountering indolent men on a fruitful soil, it has at length found the secret of subjecting them to labor without subjecting them to slavery. The natives are the debtors of the government, the servants of no one.

The lot of these men is far from enviable; the Hollander regards the native as of an inferior race; he leaves him in the bonds of a gross Mahometanism, nor gives him, like the Spaniard to the Indian of the Philippine Isles, his faith, his customs, municipal franchises. The Javanese is loaded down with taxes, — labor extraordinary, labor ordinary, base labor (*adat* or *heerendienst*), cultivation of the fields, land-tax, patents, duties on the consumption, weighing, and exportation of coffee and pepper, duty on transshipment,

* Condition of the Colonial Question in Holland, by Prof. Ackersdyck, Utrecht, 1861. By a statute of August 8, 1850, the monopoly of navigation was lessened. An ordinance of May 31, 1858, opened sixteen ports to general commerce. *Revue coloniale*, 1859, p. 313, Art. of M. Jonquières.

† M. Dubouzet estimates the net profit of the island of Java in 1838 at 23,000,000 florins. (*Revue Coloniale*, 1843, p. 163.) See also the same *Revue*, 1852, p. 56, and 1859, p. 309. In 1839 Java, by despatch of 23,000,000 florins, saved the mother country from bankruptcy. In 1840 Java produced three times as much sugar as the East Indies. In 1856 the aggregate imports and exports amounted to 300,000,000 florins, and the tonnage to 400,000 tons, — 300,000 under the Dutch flag.

duty on anchorage, duty on storage, duty on registration, duty on wood, on gold, on inheritances, on horses and carriages, on legal proceedings, etc. The government has the monopoly of salt, the monopoly of public sales, the monopoly of Banca tin, the monopoly of edible bird's-nests, the monopoly of Japanese trade, the monopoly of grounds, the monopoly of powder. Tax-payer, taille-payer, base-tenant, the Javanese or Celebese is not a fortunate man; he often rebels; nevertheless, he is not a slave: he never says at night, after his work is done, "I may be sold to-morrow."

He may even quit his village if too much oppressed, and the harshness of the chief is thus tempered by the fear of his removal, — a right which the Russian serf does not possess.*

Nevertheless, if the Dutch have not reduced the natives of their East Indian possessions to slavery, they have until lately held other slaves therein.

Slavery was in the customs of the Indian Archipelago,† before the settlement of Europeans; its violent conversion to Mahometanism had wrought no change in this respect; the population possessed either *domestic* slaves, which were not sold; or *foreign* slaves, prisoners of war or captured on the sea, who were an article of traffic; or, lastly, *debtors*, or *pandelingen*, who put themselves in pledge for the acquittal of their debts. Nevertheless, by degrees free labor gained the ascendency, the inhabitants being numerous enough to render constraint useless, and it is believed that there were no longer any slaves in Java when Europeans settled there.‡ The latter had slaves through luxury and habit,

* Dupin, *loc. cit.*, p. 336.

† The following details are borrowed in part from some extremely curious articles in the *Moniteur des Indes Orientales*, of The Hague, copied into the *Revue coloniale*, 1847, XI. p. 178, and XIII. p. 94.

‡ When the Englishman, William Marsden, visited Sumatra (Voyages, Vol. II. Chap. XIII. p. 34, 1792), he found slavery there, notwithstanding, but very mild, and the king of Achem guarded by armed female slaves.

rather than necessity. With the exception of a few blacks from New Guinea, these slaves were of the same race as the vast majority of the native population: freed, they mingled with it without difficulty; slaves, they were scarcely less dependent than it: they had not to suffer from that inequality stamped on the skin, which weighs on the black, even after emancipation.

Moreover, the founders of the Dutch colonies appear to have been animated by religious and humane sentiments; for ancient documents, which bear the evident reflex of still more ancient rules of the Catholic Church, interdict Christians to sell *Christian* slaves to heathens, Mussulmans, or Jews, — faith thus acting when the feeling of a common origin was effaced. Christian masters are requested, furthermore, to treat unbaptized slaves as *their own children, to convert them to Christianity,** and unchristian masters are obliged to let their slaves be instructed in the faith, and even, if they became converted, to cede them to Christian masters at a rate fixed by the authorities, — a sort of expropriation for the sake of religion decreed at a time when expropriation for public utility was not yet inscribed in the law. Numerous measures (1754, 1777, 1780) protect Christian slaves, prescribe that they shall be well instructed and well treated, and forbid their sale. Considered thus as members of the family, the Christian slaves were gradually raised to liberty under the guardianship of religion; and, long years ago, not a single Christian slave was known in the Dutch East Indies, which proves at once that all the Christians became free, and that good care was taken not to convert the rest, for fear that they might be emancipated through conversion.

At an epoch equally far removed (1688), the slave-trade was interdicted; an enumeration of the slaves was prescribed, sales were no longer to be made except before

* May 4, 1622.

public officers (1669); prisoners taken in war were not to be reduced to bondage (1784).

But, as the good intentions of the first colonists in behalf of *Christian* slaves had ended in keeping all slaves outside the faith, so by that fatal law which condemns servitude to grow worse, far from being ameliorated, so long as it shall endure, the slave-trade, whether negro or Oriental, punished by death in 1710, was only chastised by a fine in 1722; and it became necessary, in 1782, to take measures *against the excessive importation of slaves.* The negro race, in conformity with another law, which dooms servitude to sterility, erelong died out or became lost in the native race, and was no longer to be found. The Oriental slaves diminished in numbers. The government no longer made use of them, except to recruit the army in 1808; not a single one is mentioned in the inventory of the settlements at the time of their delivery to the English in 1811; the latter abolished the slave-trade, and encouraged the formation of a society, the Java Benevolent Institution, at first devoted solely to the suppression of this traffic, but afterwards to the amelioration of the condition of the slaves, and, finally, under a new name, — *Javaansch menschlievend genootschap,* — to the total abolition of slavery. It was upon the initiative of this society that the regulation of December, 1818, was rendered, declaring free all slaves that should not have been registered within a fixed time; and that a bill was prepared, Dec. 24, 1825, freeing all children thenceforth born of slaves, and placing them under the protection of the law. Unfortunately, the difficulty of regulating the question of indemnity caused the postponement of the royal approval. It seemed to have been preferred to leave it to time, which was rapidly diminishing the number of the slaves, and to the good-will of the masters, who indeed regarded their slaves as servants, and usually made them coachmen, cooks, nurses, and chambermaids, and often accorded to them the boon of emancipation, to which they clung so strongly, despite the comparative ease of their lot, that they were often seen to entreat the favor of their masters *to bury them, at least, as free men.*

In thirteen years, from 1830 to 1843, the number of slaves *over eight years old*, according to the revenue of the tax (*Hoofgeld der Slaven*), had diminished nearly one half, viz.: —

1830	20,680
1843	9,907

At Batavia alone there were,*

In 1780	17,000	slaves.
1824	12,419	"
1841	5,040	"

We will add, that the custom of putting one's self in pledge was wholly suppressed by a regulation of 1818 in Java, of 1838 in Sumatra.

In 1846 it was estimated that there were but about 8,000 slaves, and the Governor, M. Rochussen, at this period forbade their employment on the public works. From this time the number doubtless again diminished.

In short, slavery in the Dutch East Indies had become an abused but constantly decreasing domestic service, a matter of luxury; it had nothing in common with the labor of the fields, it was useful in nothing to production. Its history is, however, a proof that, even when useless, slavery is everlasting; even when mitigated, it is unaccompanied with progress: it is like rank weeds, which it is in vain to cut down, but which must be plucked up by the roots, to prevent their springing up anew.

By a law dated Sept. 2, 1854 (Art. 115), the government adopted this generous course. Slavery was abolished from Jan. 1, 1860, in the Dutch East Indies.

If Holland has no slaves in its large colonies, it has them in its smaller ones; it has them in its American and

* M. Dupin, p. 300.

African possessions, in the colony of Surinam or Guiana, in the little islands of Curaçoa, Saba, St. Eustatius, Aruba, and St. Martin, which form part of the West Indies; lastly, in its stations on the west coast of Africa, St. George d'Elmina, Axim-Boutry, etc.

II. GUIANA.

Placed between French Guiana and English Guiana, of greater extent than either, colonized probably by the French (1634), next by the English (1650), then by the Jews expelled from Spain and Portugal, and lastly by the Dutch (1667), who lost and regained it three times (1712, 1801, 1804),* Dutch Guiana contained, at the beginning of 1859, on a space of 2,800 miles, 52,922 inhabitants; namely, 15,959 free white residents, 36,963 slaves, and 236 freed slaves, without speaking of the Indians, whom disease, drunkenness, and want are gradually diminishing, or of about 8,000 runaway negroes, or Bosch, who appear to be also decreasing.

In 1854 the number of slaves was 38,545, of whom 528 belonged to the government.†

In 1845 the number of slaves was 43,285; ‡ of that of freemen, 9,712.

In 1835 the number of slaves was 51,629; § that of freemen, 8,462.

In twenty-five years, therefore, while the white population had doubled, the black had decreased more than one

* M. de Jonquières, *Revue coloniale*, 1859, p. 323.

† M. Vidal de Lingendes, *Revue coloniale*, 1846, p. 36.

‡

Sugar	18,438
Coffee	5,405
Cocoa	837
Cotton	4,742
Domestics and artisans	5,531, etc.

Staats commissie, Part I. p. 95.

§ M. Vidal de Lingendes, article already quoted.

fourth. But this diminution is not due to emancipations, for the statistics of 1859 indicate a number humiliating to humanity, 236 freed slaves.* Neither is it due to the extinction of the slave-trade; for this extinction was anterior to the dates which we have chosen; from the treaty of May 4, 1818, Holland renounced this traffic, and since 1827, at least, she has been faithful to her pledges. According to the testimony of official documents, no fact of the slave-trade under the Dutch flag has been authenticated from this time, and the *mixed commissions*, formed at Paramaribo and Sierra Leone to take cognizance of them, have ceased to act. The diminution of the slave population, lastly, is not due to the climate, for the whites suffer more from it than the blacks; nevertheless, they increase.

It is due wholly and entirely to slavery; it is a law of nature, that in all slave countries the deaths exceed the births. At Surinam, from 1839 to 1843, 5,947 slaves were born, 10,406 died.† A special fact also proves that this grievous mortality is not due to the climate. In the two flourishing districts of Nickerie, where the slaves appear to be better treated than elsewhere, because the masters live on their plantations instead of intrusting them to overseers, *the births exceed the deaths*, — "a remarkable fact in one and the same colony, presenting no difference of climate." ‡

The fact of the decrease of the black population by the constant excess of deaths over births is not disputed. It is proven as well in 1824,§ as in 1843,|| as in 1848, as in

* From 1845 to 1853, 2,158, if we are to believe the Report of 1855, p. 978.

† M. Vidal de Lingendes, p. 25, Supplement, No. 3.

‡ De geboorte overtreft daar de sterfte. Dit is merkwaardig in eene en dezelfde Kolonie, waar het klimaat geene verscheidenheid aanbiedt. *Opmerkingen omtrent de Slaven in de Kolonie Suriname e emancipiren*, The Hague, 1848.

§ Notes of M. Zéni, Naval Engineer, on the Colonies of Surinam and Demerara, March, 1824.

|| *Bydragen tot de kennis der colonie Suriname*, by M. Lans, 1842, quoted in the *Contemporain*, a Dutch journal, Feb. 16, 1843, and in the sequel of a *Note sur la fondation d'une nouvelle colonie dans la Guyane*, Didot, 1844, p. 189.

1860, as well by official documents as by foreign statistics.

Is it, then, because the slaves are maltreated?

It is answered here, as everywhere, that the laws have taken every precaution exacted by humanity. But these laws are not mild, and, moreover, are not executed.

They are not mild.

The *Black Code* of Surinam is an ordinance of Governor Wolphert Jacob Beeldsnyder Matraas, bearing date August 3, 1784.* It enumerates and punishes all offences committed by managers and stewards in such a manner as to give the most unfavorable idea of these deplorable proxies of the Dutch or English, far-off masters, who tranquilly ate and drank at a distance the revenue of the labor imposed on slaves who did not even know their names. It moderates the rigor of the chastisements inflicted on slaves by the following prescriptions: —

"Art. 13. No manager, steward, or superintendent placed in authority, or any white man, whoever he may be, shall suffer himself to use threats or reproaches, accompanied with discouraging words."

A good provision; but where is the sanction? The text continues thus: *They may inflict.* They, — who? Any manager, steward, or superintendent, any white, *whoever he may be,* shall have the right to inflict punishments on whom?

"In case of need, they may inflict punishments not dangerous to the slaves, without being permitted to make use of the stick, or to subject them to the torture called the *spanch-book,* or the punishment of gantlets. They shall only be permitted to use the whip, *in conformity with the custom of the government;* it being provided that the punishments ordered by a steward or other paid white agent for

* The text has been published by M. Vidal de Lingendes, in the sequel of his remarkable report, *Revue coloniale,* 1846, p. 28.

a negro or *negress* shall be applied by a negro overseer, and shall not exceed from twenty-five to fifty lashes in number."

The article continues: —

"*If circumstances require*, the number may be increased to eighty common lashes, applied to the lower part of the body, it being forbidden to bind the slave, *except* standing, to a post or stake, or to strip him of his clothing,* or to hoist him from the ground.

"All *severer* punishments shall be inflicted by the trustees or proprietors themselves, or *on their written order*. It is also forbidden to any white to threaten a slave with fire-arms, a sword, or a sabre, and still more to make use of them, *except absolutely in case of legitimate self-defence*, under penalty of a fine of 300 florins, *for the benefit of whoever the law may direct*."

Is this for the benefit of the slave? Not at all. By the provisions of Art. 1, one half the fine reverts to the fiscal, or magistrate, the other half to the poor.

If a master be guilty of habitual and excessive bad treatment towards the slave, to what is he condemned? To sell him, — that is all.

If the slave has been mutilated or crippled, the fiscal *shall commence legal proceedings in whatever manner he may deem fit*.

"Art. 15. Touching negroes who may come from other plantations, ... any one who surprises them stealing eatables or other things shall summon them to stop, and if they do not stop, and he finds it impossible to overtake or seize them, he may fire on them with large shot, but only at the lower part of their bodies. . . . . . If the slave by *misfortune* be killed, those who have fired, or have

* Has the slave clothing? Art. 17. 2 confines itself to these words: "It is *recommended* to give slaves clothing sufficient to cover their nakedness, and to furnish them with coverings for their beds."

given the order to fire, shall be obliged to *vindicate their conduct,* under penalty, in case the offence be *proven,* of being proceeded against by the fiscal, *according as the facts of the case require,* without prejudice to the action of the civil party."

Doubtless, the ordinance recommends that care should be taken of the slaves when sick (Art. 17. 1), that the food of the slaves should be regarded as a thing of prime importance, that it should be considered as the soul of the plantation (Art. 17. 2), and that, for this end, they should be furnished with salt, pipes, and tobacco, a little fish, or something of the sort, *at least once a year,* and, at least once a fortnight, a basket of fruit or four allowances of bananas, *holding the slaves responsible* if the ground set apart for their support were not cultivated, or the masters, if the slaves should prove that the latter did not give them Sunday in order to cultivate them. . . . . . Care should be taken, moreover, to furnish better food to the whites employed (Art. 18), *in order to inspire the slaves with a salutary respect for servants of the lowest rank.*

At least was this ordinance executed?

It was made, as the preamble indicates, to renew previous provisions which had always remained unobserved, — a proclamation by the same Governor in 1759, an act of 1749, another act of May, 1725, a first act of May 9, 1686. "*Complaints resound as in the past,*" says the ordinance of 1784, " and these *complaints are even daily increasing.*"

In 1799 Governor Fridérici was already obliged to call to mind and reinforce the ordinance, by a proclamation dated January 14, the conduct of the managers *being absolutely contrary to its prescriptions.*

In 1817 Governor Cornelys Rynhard Vaillant published a new ordinance, *considering that the prescriptions of the former were neglected more and more, so that they might be considered as not existing,* . . . . . especially as regarded the obligation of furnishing the slaves ground for their support, "in order to prevent, by the grace of God (Art. 12, § 3), any need of food in the future, *a need which has made itself greatly felt through the forgetfulness of salutary precautions during this year.*"

A new ordinance, January 1, 1826, prescribing the registration of the slaves, was followed by a law, March 23, 1832, on emancipation, and by numerous local ordinances.*

In 1842 the Dutch government framed a regulation, declaring a slave a person, eligible to hold property, to marry, to ransom himself, and to receive instruction.

On May 6, 1851, a new regulation was published, followed by another in 1856.†

In 1860 matters were still at the same point.

How indeed were all these laws to be executed? Where was the surveillance? where the sanction, where, above all, the pity? in what hearts did it still live? Why, here is an honest Governor, the author of the ordinances of 1759 and 1784, full of experience, since he had been in office twenty-five years, full of intelligence and equity, since he heads the second ordinance with the words: "Duty commands us to bring the state of slavery into harmony with the principles of humanity, and to render this state as endurable as possible, and we have a right to expect such sentiments from the masters of slaves, the more, inasmuch as their own interest enjoins it on them." Yet, animated with such good intentions, this M. Beeldsnyder Matraas permits twenty-five lashes, even eighty, even more, and suffers a slave to be fired at with large shot for stealing a banana! Does he concern himself with the garden and cabin of the slave? No. With his ransom? No. With his marriage? No. With his religion? No.

* *Rapport sur la colonie de Surinam*, by Count de Castelnau, Naval Captain, 1847. *Revue coloniale*, XII. pp. 389 – 391.

† *La colonie de Surinam*, by M. Favart, *Revue coloniale*, Nov. 1859, p. 154.

Yet you hope that the voice of humanity will speak more loudly to the conscience of these managers, these overseers, whom the ordinance of 1817 represents to us (Art. 10) as being often discharged for notorious incapacity, or for the indecency, negligence, or immorality of their conduct?

Do you expect more from the pity or the interest of the masters? You are right, and the fact which we have quoted, the diminution of mortality in the districts of Nickerie, arises from the cause that the land-owners more commonly live on their plantations than in the districts of Commewyne, Mattapica, Para, and Cottica, or in the forests of Thorarica and Saramaca. The proverb, "Nothing 's so good as the master's eye," exists in Dutch as in all other tongues: *Het oog van den meester maakt het paard vet.**

But where are the greater part of the masters? At London or at Amsterdam.

Read the admirable study of M. Vitet on the Dutch school of painting,† — a study which is itself one of the finest specimens of the school of French literature, — read in this criticism, in such just, such fine, and such pure taste, the description, or rather the written engraving, of two of the greatest pictures in the Amsterdam Museum. In one, the Banquet, by Van der Helst (1648), "Behold the bold merchants who are destined to cope with Louis XIV.; you see these sea-wolves, you speak to them; they are there in their gala suits, as rough and simple as at their counters, as on their ships. What good sense, what energy, what gravity, and, at the bottom, what pride is under this rubicund gayety!" In the other, the *syndics* of Rembrandt (1661), five Amsterdam merchants in session around a table covered with red cloth, with broad-brimmed felt hats on their heads, dressed in full suits of black cloth, with broad,

* At the end of the note of MM. Zéni, etc. is found the account of two plantations. The one brought in 400 florins per slave, the other 300; the first was managed by the planter, the second by his agents.

† *Revue des Deux-Mondes*, April 15, 1861, p. 790.

shining, turned-down shirt-collars. These sea-wolves, these merchants, who drink or discuss in the corner of a Holland public-house, of the hall of the Staalkof, these are the founders of Guiana, these are the masters of the slaves who were hoisted from the ground to be whipped, of the women who were stripped and made to run the gantlet during a whole century (1667 – 1784), since an ordinance was necessary explicitly to suppress these abuses.

Leap over seventy years. At the Hague, what progress, what prodigies accomplished by these still energetic, sensible, rude, and simple citizens, the able managers of their cities and their fortunes! At Surinam, on the contrary, the same slave system in 1854 as in 1784, as in 1759, as in 1686, and a frightful engraving in an extremely curious book, a sort of Uncle Tom's Cabin of Dutch America, shows us a woman stripped quite naked, and suspended by the arms from two stakes, her feet fastened by a cord from the earth, her extended body lashed by a cat-o'-nine-tails in the hands of a muscular negro, before the face of an elegant and smiling Creole lady.*

I believe, and hasten to say, that acts of excessive violence are rare, but situation is more powerful than legislation. Men would be glad to keep children with their mothers, but embarrassment forces them to separate them.† They would be glad to feed and clothe the slaves well, but avarice, negligence, or poverty leads them to let them suffer, as the ordinance of 1817 attests.‡ They would be glad not to imitate the brutal conduct of the Americans; but when the slaves take flight, they are forced to hunt them, and to employ patrols of other negroes, to track and apprehend the fugitives.§ They would be glad to evangelize

* *Slaven in Vrijen onder de Nederlandsche Wet*, nitgeven door Dr. W. R. Van Hoëvell, 1854, Vol. I. p. 97.

† Ibid., Chap. II., *Moeder en Kind.*

‡ Ibid., Chap. VI., IX.

§ Ibid., Vol. II. Chap. VII., *Wegloopers en Boschpatrouilles.*

these slaves, and the Moravian missionaries occupy themselves with the task. But these Moravians themselves have slaves ; their words without religious worship do little, and their example does more, as well as that of the masters, far from devout in general, in this life which is a continual temptation to harshness and to indolence. Observers, little suspected of sensibility or exaggeration, express themselves likewise.* At Surinam, the negroes are left entirely free on the subject of religion ; may even practise the religion of their country.† They would be glad, in fine, not to beat their slaves, and law, pity, interest, forbid it ; but, write the same witnesses, "there are laws established for the infliction of punishments according to faults, but little attention is paid to executing them ; *each one does nearly as he likes.*"

This continued until the government, wishing at length to act in an effective manner, intervened, fixed the hours of labor, or interdicted transportation and consequently sale from one plantation to another.‡ In this case, the tutelage of the government ends by appearing intolerable ; so that the *régime* of a slave colony always results either in the arbitrariness of the masters over the slaves, or of the ruling power over the masters.

Under this *régime*, is the material prosperity of the colony declining ?

The founders of Surinam have been worthy of their countrymen ; they have conquered this land, by prodigious labors, from the tide and rain, they have rescued from the waters a vast extent of territory, which, stretching from the Maroni to the Demerara, and forming a blue vase,

* Notes of M. Zéni (1824), Soleau, Lagrange (1834), p. 43.

† Van Hoëvell, Vol. II. Chap. II. p. 96, *De Godsdienst.*

‡ M. de Castelnau cites the opposition to this rule, imposed in 1846 by Gov. Van Raders, *loc. cit.*, p. 375. As in all slave countries, the laws are as numerous as fruitless. The Report of the Commission of 1853, Part I. p. 15, quotes *eleven* laws or regulations from 1818 to 1853.

covered over with a thick coating of vegetable compost, produces in abundance sugar-cane and cotton, coffee and cocoa, with almost all the products which the hand of man intrusts to it. It is claimed that, at the close of the last century, 80,000 slaves, distributed over 600 establishments, produced annually $8,000,000 worth of commodities.* In 1845 there were but 102 sugar plantations, 116 coffee plantations, 41 cotton plantations, 2 cocoa plantations, 1 indigo plantation, and 49 forests under cultivation, producing a total value of $1,000,000.† Since French Guiana and English Guiana have passed through the crisis of emancipation, Dutch Guiana has profited little by it. The exportation of sugar, which in 1845 was 29,787,966 lbs., and in 1849, 31,121,202 lbs., was in 1857 but 31,896,993 lbs., nearly the same.‡ In 1824, as in 1834, as in 1845, as in 1849, all observers declared that agriculture was backward, processes imperfect, new machinery almost unknown, and the accounts presented by many of them prove that the net revenue progressed but little. Finally, now as then, the colonists complain, and their dolorous cries may be summed up in this sentence of a writing already quoted: "*Suriname's tœdstand is doodetyk krank.*" §

The history of all slaveholding peoples is therefore always fatally the same; in fact, moral and material wretchedness; in law, arbitrariness; in result, routine or decay,— the same causes, the same effects, the same conduct, we may add, the same arguments.

M. Van Hoëvell has taken pains to notice all the arguments alleged by the partisans of slavery in Holland. They are still reduced to these: —

The negroes are an inferior race. — This is no reason for

* M. Favart, p. 158.

† M. Vidal de Lingendes.

‡ Report of M. Dieudonné, *Revue coloniale*, 1850, p. 296. M. Favart, *Ibid.*, 1859, p. 166.

§ *Opmerkingen*, p. 82.

reducing them to a condition which degrades them still more, and forever opposes their elevation.

They would be slaughtered or oppressed in Africa if they were not slaves in America. — Instead of a crime among heathens, another crime among Christians.

They are brutish. — And the masters? the stewards? the overseers?

They are idle. — What interest have they in working? Idleness is their only gain. All men are indolent, and the hope of possessing and transmitting the fruit of our labors is the only spur which triumphs over our native apathy.

They are happier than they would be in Africa, or than many free laborers are in Holland. — Ameliorate the condition of the Dutch. But consult the slaves upon their happiness.* And why talk of happiness? Freedom is a question of justice.

No slavery, no colony. — In other terms, if 40,000 men receive no lashes, 200 planters will receive no revenues. Are the two evils equal, if we are to choose?

The example of the free and runaway, or *Bosch* negroes, to the number of several thousand, who live in idleness, resist evangelization, do not become civilized, and prefer a savage to an orderly life, is alleged as a special argument in Dutch Guiana. — But what have they in their memory? Slavery. What have they before their eyes? Slavery. Under what form is labor presented to them? Under the image of a negro beaten by a white. Under what form is liberty offered to their sight? Under that of a white who does nothing. What they would like is, not to be free, but to be masters, to have slaves in their turn, and to resemble the whites, who make others labor without laboring themselves. What! are you astonished that the *Bosch* shun towns and remain idle? They fear your company, and follow your example.

* Vol. II. Chap. VIII. p. 210, *Verdedigers der Slavernij.*

To these free blacks in the heart of slavery, fleeing like the Indians, and dreading the whites, under the empire of a secret rancor and instinctive distrust, must be opposed the freed people of English Guiana and French Guiana. We have shown * that in these two colonies a considerable number of laborers have deserted the large plantations; but if the labor of those who still devote themselves to them be compared with the labor of the slaves of Surinam, it is found that where 100 slaves furnish 37 working days, 100 free persons furnish 54; the number of workmen has diminished, the product of the labor of a free workman exceeds by about 17 per cent the product of the labor of a slave.†

Facts and reasons begin to approach this point, when, theory and practice being more and more in harmony, a reform can be wrought without danger. In fact, for several years past, the abolition of slavery has been made a subject of discussion by the Dutch government.

But before indicating wherein lies the question, we will say a few words of the other less important colonies.

III. DUTCH WEST INDIES.

HOLLAND possesses in the Caribbean Sea: —

1. *In the Leeward Islands,* —

Curaçoa, an island 762 square miles in surface, with the city of Willemstadt for its capital, and the little islands of Buen Ayre (450 miles) and Oruba (363 miles) for dependencies. These islands are Catholic.

2. *In the Lesser Antilles,* —

St. Eustatius, which has 3,712 square miles, *Saba,* and a part of *St. Martin,* the other part being owned by France,

* Results of Emancipation, Books I. and II.

† This comparison has been made and supported by official statistics, by Naval Lieutenant Dieudonné, Aug. 1850. *Revue coloniale,* 1850, pp. 299, 300.

which on this part of the globe, as in Europe, has Holland for a neighbor, and has restored to it this territory, after having retaken it in 1794 from the English, by the hand of Victor Hugues.

Curaçoa contains about 16,830 inhabitants, of whom 7,189 were slaves,* January 1, 1854; viz. 3,428 men, 3,761 women; 69 belonged to the government. From 1844 to 1854, 876 slaves were emancipated.

Buen Ayre has 2,339 inhabitants, of whom 769 are slaves (361 men, 468 women), 656 belonging to the government.

Oruba, smaller and more sterile, contains 3,201 souls, of whom 332 are slaves (151 men, and 181 women).

St. Eustatius has 1,856 inhabitants,† of whom 1,071 are slaves (528 men, 543 women).

Saba, the smallest of the Dutch islands, and which is rather a peak than an island, contains 1,709 inhabitants, of whom 649 are slaves (303 men, 346 women).

At St. Martin, the slaves, numbering from 1,000 to 1,200, in 2,790 inhabitants, were freed by the colonists, in the sequel of the French emancipation, with the approbation of the commandant, June 6, 1848, but the masters have not yet been indemnified.

These small islands,† St. Eustatius especially, which Holland has possessed since 1635, have a tolerably active commerce and large production.

The slaves are better treated here than at Guiana. This is generally the case in the islands, where the slave does not desire, nor the master fear flight as much as in extended territories. The planters dwell more on their estates; and, if we are to believe an author already quoted,‡ they treat

* *Tweede Rapport der Staats commissie*, 1856, Part II. p. 6.

† *Les possessions coloniales de la Hollande en* 1859, by M. de Jonquières, *Revue coloniale*, Dec. 1859, p. 326. This author gives St. Eustatius 10,000 inhabitants. The figures which he gives for the surface also disagree with the official statistics.

‡ *Opmerkingen*, etc., p. 72.

their slaves in a cordial and paternal (*aartsvaderlyk*) manner. The morality is lower among them than at Surinam, and, if M. Van Hoëvell * is to be believed, the births exceed the deaths.

	1849. Births.	1849. Deaths.
Surinam	2.82%	3.49%
Curaçoa	3.86	2.77
Buen Ayre	3.22	1.21
Oruba	4.83	1.25

Nevertheless, these little colonies are not what they once were, and they live only by the aid of subsidies from the mother country. It is affirmed that Curaçoa, twenty years ago, possessed more than 10,000 slaves instead of 5,000. Cultivation on a large scale evidently cannot compare there with the sugar of Europe or the cotton of America. Cultivation on a small scale, the nopal or the cochineal, is their destiny. The territory being of small extent, the flight of slaves is not to be feared, and if the masters make themselves beloved, they will not be abandoned. Emancipation, therefore, presents them no serious difficulties.

IV. DUTCH FORTS ON THE COAST OF AFRICA.

Holland, which founded the Colony of the Cape of Good Hope, no longer possesses anything on the western coast of Africa, extending from the Cape of Three Points to Cape St. Paul, under the name of the Gold Coast, over a space of ninety leagues, but a few forts, as Axim-Boutry, Saccoudee, and Chama, maintained in the midst of other forts in ruins, as Akra and Baracoa, and a small town, St. George d'Elmina, built under the shadow of a fort, on the banks of a little river, and composed of a cluster of negro-huts and a European quarter with a garden and promenade.†

* Vol. I. p. 35.

† *Description des côtes de l'Afrique occidentale*, by M. Bouët Willaumez, 1849, p. 207.

Here Holland keeps up a small garrison, and has long recruited soldiers for its East India Colonies ; it reaps thence small quantities of maize, cotton, and spices, and looks forward to resources from gold-washing and the working of vast mineralogical wealth. But it has neither a territory nor population depending on it in a definite manner.

Nevertheless, the Report of the Commission of 1853,* estimates at 136,000 the inhabitants over whom Holland claims to rule, viz. :

Free	34,000
Domestic slave	82,000
Other slave	20,000
	136,000

There is no registration ; but rules for ameliorating the treatment of the slaves have been made, and slave-markets are prohibited.

The commission esteems that Holland possesses over these men and their territory a true sovereignty, and not a simple contract with the inhabitants ; yet considers it very difficult to prescribe liberty in the midst of the universal slavery that reigns in Africa.

V. EMANCIPATION BILLS.

From 1853 to 1855, immediately upon the appointment by government of a commission to pave the way for the abolition of slavery in the Dutch Colonies, it received thirty-two plans for Surinam and seven for the West India Islands.†

An inquiry and profound examination, fully summed up in the two reports of August 26, 1855, for Surinam, and May 26, 1856, for the West India Islands, resulted in a bill,

* P. 74.

† We remark among these plans those of Mgr. Niewindt, Apostolic Vicar of Curaçoa, and M. Putman, ex-Curé of this island.

proposed September 23, 1857.* It is curious to see how so prudent a government, enlightened by the experience of other nations, designs to resolve this great question.

The following are the bases of the bill of 1857 : —

1. Emancipation shall be immediate ; it being recognized that delays cause universal disturbance without securing any preparation.

2. The masters of slaves shall be indemnified. The rate of indemnity shall not be uniform.

At Surinam, the slaves are valued, male or female, —

On sugar plantations at	500	florins.
Coffee and cocoa plantations at . . .	325	"
Woodland " . . .	240	"
Cotton and rice " " . .	200	"
Domestics, according to age, at from 50 to 500, and even	700	"

In the West Indies, slaves are estimated, male or female, according to the age, at from 50 to 500 florins ; from 50 to 405 florins in the little island of Saba.

3. The slaves shall engage to labor for twelve months at least for their former master, or for another whom they shall choose. Those who cannot or will not contract such engagements shall be grouped, to the number of 1,500 at most, in country districts, under the direction of officers of the government, on lands purchased or expropriated for the purpose.

Every member of a district, aged from 20 to 60 years, owes to the district 5 days' labor per week, of 9 hours per day.

Domestic slaves are grouped in societies or guilds, under the direction of officers of the government, having their seat at Paramaribo. They owe to the guild an analogous task, according to their occupation.

* We owe all of these details to the kindness of M. de Frezals, Secretary of the French Legation in Holland, and to an excellent note prepared by M. Lux, one of the most distinguished and honorable citizens of The Hague.

4. Slaves shall take a family name, choose a residence, and make good their claims to it.

5. Children born after the enactment of the law shall be free, but shall remain under the authority of their parents or guardians until the age of twelve.

6. All freed slaves shall contribute to the creation of a fund designed to reimburse the state for the cost of their emancipation.

7. Numerous regulations are prepared besides in detail.

The commission had proposed to expropriate the plantations and slaves at once, for the reason that the soil without the slaves had no value. More generous, the government leaves to the planters the land and buildings, and promises them an indemnity amounting,

For Surinam, to	14,096,760 florins.
" Curaçoa and the islands, to . .	2,292,950 "
" St. Martin, to	250,000 "
	16,639,710 florins.

The receipts of the districts and guilds are estimated at 3,000,000 florins, and their expenditures at 1,288,475 florins.

There will be, therefore, an annual surplus of 1,711,525 florins, serving to reimburse the state.

These bills, presented in the Second Chamber of the States-General, September 24, 1857, were withdrawn, studied, modified, and transformed into a second bill, introduced October 25, 1858. It was thought hard to impose the obligation on the slave to spend long years in paying for his freedom, and thus to remain indefinitely the slave of a debt; the new bill confined itself to subjecting him to a capitation tax, and a right of requisition for the public works. It was judged dangerous to grant an indemnity in ready money, which, as soon as paid, would fall into the hands of the creditors, go out of the colonies, and afford no support to labor ; the foundation of a bank at Paramaribo, and the payment of a part of the indemnity in its stock, provides for this danger. The right is accorded to the planters to choose between indemnity and a total expropriation, which would render the state the owner of their plantations, reserving the right of farming them at a reasonable price. The most minute measures are taken that the slave may be set free with his clothing, tools, and all that is reputed to belong to him; but at the same time the strictest provisions are made that freedom may not exempt the negro from labor; he must be engaged for twelve months at least; he is punished for vagrancy or for simple idleness; he is still a slave, but a slave who is free to choose his master and residence; he has all liberties except that of not working.

After discussions, amendments, and three years' delay, this bill, though so prudent, has not yet been adopted, despite solemn promises which, after having appeased public sentiment, end by wearying it.

It happens in the Dutch Colonies as it happened in France. The lively agitation by the press, books, and petitions, which was manifested especially from 1840 to 1844, has been followed by silence. Then it is from the colonies themselves that the demand for emancipation has come.* Since the French emancipation, preceded by the English emancipation, it is said that Surinam, lying between Demerara and Cayenne, will soon lose all its slaves by insurrection or desertion; and, uneasy about a property thus threatened, the colonists wish at least to assure themselves of the indemnity.

Bills have been heaped upon bills, promises have been added to promises; but it is perceived that the poor negroes remain tranquil; as their faults serve to justify slavery, their virtues serve to retard enfranchisement. The indemnity has been computed, and seems meagre to the slave-

* Condition of the Colonial Question, by M. Ackersdyck. Utrecht, 1861. T. de Bruyn.

holders, heavy to the financiers. Public treasuries do not readily open to acts of virtue that cost dear. It is true that uncertainty will do the colonists more harm than emancipation would do them; but the point is not to wait for the blacks to revolt or the whites to repent, but for the government to resolve the question. The king who has promised to do so will not delay, let us hope, to add this lustre to the honor of his reign and the glory of Holland. Rich, commercial, free, and Christian, this noble nation sees its wealth and commerce, its liberty and religion, polluted by servitude.

Many of the palaces of the Heerengracht or the Keizersgracht have been paid for by the labor of negroes. France, England, Denmark, Sweden, Russia, and the regency of Tunis, have no more slaves; Holland is the only nation of Europe, save Turkey and Spain, which still possesses them. Public opinion is decided, the experiment has been made, the law is prepared, the government is pledged, the colony is resigned, — it waits, it postpones, it hesitates.

In his generous work, M. Van Hoëvell * reminds us of the great fête which took place in the new Church at Amsterdam, May 12, 1849, on the occasion of the advent of William III. Around an escutcheon whose allegories recalled the glory and fortune of Holland, shone the beautiful device, JUSTITIA, PIETAS, FIDES, but an unknown hand had been tempted to write beneath the word SURINAM! Upon this Dutch soil, where rigorous slavery endures, the device is false and the escutcheon sullied.

* *Slaven en vrijen*, Tweede Deel, p. 246; also, Eerste Deel, pp. 1–3.

BOOK SIXTH.

THE SLAVE-TRADE.—IMMIGRATION.—AFRICA.

I.

THE SLAVE-TRADE.

JOHN WESLEY calls slavery *the sum of all villanies.* Canning defines a negro slave-ship as the *greatest collection of crimes in the smallest space.* Sir Robert Peel says that this traffic excites more crimes *than any public act ever committed by any nation, whatever may have been its contempt for human and divine laws.* I think that the history of the traffic in slaves and the abolition of the slave-trade may also be called the summing up of the shame and the greatness of the human race.

I. In the seventeenth and eighteenth centuries, in the age of Louis XIV. and Voltaire, on the eve of the French Revolution, and also on its morrow, all Europe abandoned itself openly to the negro slave-trade. A few men deplored, and, be it said to the honor of the Catholic faith, the Church did not cease to protest against it.* But kings signed treaties, in the name of the Holy Trinity, to or-

* After Robertson (History of America, Book III.), all writers have repeated, and the learned Memoir of M. Charles Giraud reaffirms (*Comptes Rendus de l'Académie des sciences morales*, April, 1861, p. 178), that the slave-trade is due to Las Casas, whose inconsistent charity led him, in order to relieve the Indians whom he defended so energetically, to propose to enslave the Africans. But Doehlinger (*Hist. Eccl.*, Tom. III. Sect. 160, p. 397) demonstrates that this imputation is calumnious, as we have already established. Results of Emancipation, *Religion in the Colonies*, p. 255.

ganize the slave-trade. It was one of the principal financial resources of a great monarchy, — Spain.

The *asientos*, treaties or contracts of the Spanish government with divers private individuals or various foreign companies, to furnish its transoceanic possessions with negro slaves, were very frequent from the beginning of the sixteenth century. As this traffic was surrounded with many guaranties, and as to the monopoly of the sale of negroes was added the profit of fraudulently introducing many other articles of trade, the European governments strove by all imaginable means to secure this privilege to their subjects. Charles VI. granted it in 1517 to his fellow-countrymen, the Flemings. They derived so much gain from it, and multiplied to such a degree in South America, that, in 1522 they came to blows with the Spaniards at St. Domingo, killed the governor of the island, and besieged the fort. From this time the government resolved to limit considerably the *asientos*.* They ceased in 1580, but the needs of the treasury and the necessity of repaying to the Genevese the immense sums which they had furnished for the expedition of the Invincible Armada, led Philip II. to confer the privilege anew. It was bestowed on Gomez Reinel from 1595 to 1600. A treaty was then made for nine years with the Portuguese Jean Rodriguez Continho, governor of Angola, who engaged to furnish the colonies 4,250 slaves yearly, and to pay the king a revenue of 162,000 ducats. His death in 1603 transferred the contract to his brother, Gonzalez Vaez Continho.

On September 26, 1615, a new grant was made to another Portuguese, Antonio Fernandez Delvas, for eight years. He bound himself to introduce 3,500 slaves, and

* *Tratados, Conventos y declaraciones de paz y de comercio que han hecho con las potentias estrangeras los monarcos espanoles de la casa de Borbon desde el ano de* 1700 *hasta el dia, fuestos en orden, etc.*, by Don Alejandro del Cantillo, pp. 32, 35, 58, 72, 78, 800, 857. Madrid, 1843.

pay 115,000 ducats a year. Another Portuguese, Manuel Rodriguez Lamego, negotiated for eight more years, in 1623, and pledged himself to furnish 3,500 slaves, and to pay 120,000 ducats. 2,500 slaves and 95,000 ducats were the conditions stipulated in 1631 for eight new years with the Portuguese Cristobal Mendez de Sossa and Melchior Gomez Anjel.

The war between France and Spain and other unknown causes interrupted the *asientos* until 1662. Domingo Fullo and Ambrosio Lomelin then enjoyed the privilege for nine years, during which they were to furnish 24,500 negroes, and to pay the king 2,100,000 piasters. The lease passed for five years, in 1674, to Antonio Garcia and Don Sebastien de Siliccos, in consideration of 4,000 slaves and 450,000 piasters. The contract was broken for lack of being executed, and another was concluded for five years, in 1676, with the consulate of Seville, offering to pay 1,125,000 piasters, and 1,200,000 premium; then, Jan. 27, 1682, with Don Juan Barrozzo del Pazo and Don Nicolas Porcio, of Cadiz, for 1,125,000 piasters. It was afterwards transferred to the Hollander, Don Balthazar Coimans, then, in 1692, to Don Bernardo Francisco Marin de Guzman, residing at Venezuela, for five years, in consideration of 2,125,000 crowns (*escudos de plato*), lastly to the Portuguese Guinea Company, from 1696 to 1701.

This contract, by which the company bound itself, in proper terms, to furnish *ten thousand tons of negroes* (*dies mil toneladas de negros*), gave rise to so much scandal and difficulty, that the intervention of a compromise to annul it became necessary, July 18, 1701, at Lisbon, between the kings of Spain and Portugal, Philip V. and Don Pedro II., negotiated, as usual, in the name of the Holy Trinity (*el nombre del santisima Trinidad*).*

A treaty with France succeeded the treaty with Por-

* See the text in the Cantillo Collection, p. 32.

tugal. On the 27th of August, 1701, the *Most Catholic* King and the *Most Christian* King stipulated that for ten years (1702 – 1712) the monopoly of the transportation of negroes to the American colonies should belong to the Royal Guinea Company, represented by Major du Casse, governor of St. Domingo. It charged itself with the *asiento*, that is, the introduction of negro slaves into the West Indies of America, belonging to his Catholic Majesty, in order by this means to procure a laudable, pure, mutual, and reciprocal advantage (*una loable, pura, mutua y reciprocad utilidad*) to their Majesties and their subjects ; it was to furnish in ten years 4,800 *pieces of India, piezas de Indias*, of both sexes and all ages, taken from any part whatsoever of Africa, except from Minas and Cape Verde, the negroes of these countries not being fit for the said Indies, or 4,800 negroes per year. (Art. I.)

For each negro, the company was to pay 33⅓ crowns. (Art. II. 55 cents per crown.)

On account of the pressing needs of the crown of Spain, the company was to advance 200,000 crowns (Art. III.) on the 1,585,000 which it owed, in return for which, 800 negroes were released from duties per year. The vessels were to be French or Spanish, the crews of all nations, but exclusively Catholic. (Art. VIII.) The introduction might take place in any port where there were Spanish officers. In the Windward Isles, St. Martha, Cumana, and Maracaybo, negroes could not be sold above 300 piasters, but anywhere else, *as high as the company could.* (Art. IX.) His Catholic Majesty placed the treaty and the operations of the company under the protection of all the functionaries of the Spanish possessions. He pledged "his faith and royal word to the said company, regarding the treaty as his own property, ... and reserving to himself alone the cognizance of all the cases which might arise in its execution." (Arts. IX., XX.) But if the captains landed other merchandise than negroes, "even though they should have been guilty only of negligence in not having watched carefully to hinder the disembarkation of these contraband articles, they were to be condemned to death, and the sentence was to be executed without delay or appeal." (Art. XXII.) The duty was to be the same on negroes who died before they were sold. (Art. XXIV.) The vessels of the *asiento* were empowered to capture those which illegally carried on the same traffic. (Art. XXVII.) *Both kings had one half interest in the business, each one fourth.* His Catholic Majesty pledged himself to invest for his share 300,000 crowns, from the payment of which he was exempted, in consideration of 8 per cent interest, and the company was to "account to his said Majesty from the date of the contract for the profit belonging to him." (Art. XXVII.)

At the end of this treaty, England obtained a grant of the monopoly for thirty years (1713–1734). This was the object of the treaty properly known under the name of the *Asiento* treaty, bearing date March 26, 1713. His Britannic Majesty undertook to introduce into Spanish America 144,000 *pieces of India, piezas de Indias,* of both sexes and all ages, or 4,800 per year, in consideration of 33⅓ piasters escudos per head. (I., II.) The conditions were nearly the same as those of the treaty with France. There was the same obligation to advance 200,000 piasters escudos (III.) on account of the needs of the crown, in consideration of the annual remission of the duty on 800 negroes (IV.), and the same right of importation into all the northern ports and Buenos Ayres. But the English, more adroit, obtained greater commercial advantages. They were at liberty to introduce more than 4,800 slaves a year, during the first twenty-five years, by paying for this supplement only 16⅔ piasters per head. (VI.) They received lands for the establishment of factories in the places of embarkation and disembarkation. (IV.) They obtained the change of the penalty of death for smuggling to fine and imprisonment (XXII.), with fifteen days' respite before paying for negroes landed sick, and an exemption for all who should die within this time. (XXIV.) The two kings had a half interest in the traffic, each one fourth, and the king of Spain was released from the payment of his share of the capital in consideration of the payment of 8 per cent interest, as in the preceding treaty. (XXVIII.) Finally, by an additional article, to testify to his Britannic Majesty *his wish to give him pleasure*, his Catholic Majesty accorded the power of sending a vessel of 500 tons annually to trade with America, on condition of selling the merchandise only at the time of the fairs, not before the arrival of the flotillas and galleons. His Majesty, moreover, also reserved to himself in this operation one fourth of the profits and 5 per cent on the other three fourths. (XLIII.)*

All of these stipulations were sanctioned anew by the preliminary treaty of peace, signed at Madrid, March 27, 1713 (Art. 9), and by Art. 12 of the treaty of Utrecht (July 13, 1703), the same treaty which fixed the succession of Spain and ceded to England the possession of Gibraltar and Minorca.

In 1743 England was near rekindling war in Europe, because Spain refused the renewal of the treaty.†

The soul is filled with horror on being condemned to wade through these sad details. A single government,

* On the 12th of June, 1716, by an interpretative treaty, it was conceded to England that the 500 tons should be increased to 650; that the fairs at Carthagena, Porto Bello, and Vera Cruz should be on a fixed day; that it should be permitted to carry the rest of its merchandise to Buenos Ayres, after trading for negroes in Africa; and, lastly, that the payment of duties should not begin until 1717.

† Speech of M. Dudon. *Moniteur*, May 18, 1825. In France, till 1791, the slave-trade was encouraged by premiums. Among other documents, I have before my eyes a letter from the Minister of the Marine (Sept. 8, 1783) to MM. de Bellecombe and de Bongars, at St. Domingo. "It is most important to maintain commercial confidence, so as not to slacken speculation in the slave-trade." *Archives des colonies.*

Spain, which assumes the name of Catholic, concluded in less than two centuries more than ten treaties to authorize, protect, and profit by the transportation of more than 500,000 human beings. It levied on each of these human heads, counted by the piece or ton, a tax amounting in the aggregate to nearly $ 10,000,000. In all these treaties there was not a provision, not a syllable, designed to defend these unfortunates against abuses and sufferings. But kings shamelessly stipulated for their share of the profit, and one of the most powerful nations of the globe, England, then ruled by a woman, Queen Anne, secured to itself by a celebrated treaty, one of the negotiators of which was a bishop, John, Bishop of Bristol, Dean of Windsor, and Keeper of the Privy Seal, and the other a nobleman, Lord Strafford, a lucrative and disgraceful monopoly, which it continued to enjoy till the middle of the eighteenth century, and which it shared with other nations till its close.

I dare say, to the honor of the nineteenth century, that there could be no longer found in France, in England, scarcely in Spain, a king, a minister, or a clerk ready to put his name at the bottom of such infamous conditions.

II. It is not to the revolution that the abolition of slavery is due. Negroes are found among the colonial commodities enumerated in the balance of trade in 1789, in 1790, in 1791. In the reports of the results of foreign trade made to the Convention, Sept. 17, 1792, and printed by its order in 1793, Minister Roland excuses himself, in consideration of the condition of the colonies, for being unable to give exact information of *the number of African cultivators transported by our privateers to the American islands.** In the table of premiums and encouragements he states that *the gratuities relating to the negro slave-trade have not been paid subsequently to the law of Jan.* 25, 1791, *because of the*

* Note at the bottom of Table No. 23, p. 150.

*silence which the Constituent and Legislative Assemblies have preserved upon the subject.** At the end of this emphatic and ridiculous report, Roland exclaims, *apropos* of the colonies, "May the genius of liberty purify *without destroying them* from relations which, *in more than one respect*, do no honor to humanity." He concludes by showing "the territory of the Republic, shut in by a double chain of mountains, and bathed by two oceans, become the CENTRAL CLUB where men of all nations shall repair to draw lessons of fraternity."

What all Europe had made, what the French Revolution had not unmade, what absolute power remade, the honor of destroying belonged to the Gospel, served by liberty. A handful of Christians, by acting on public opinion, acted on the world; they obtained — an almost unheard-of spectacle on earth — the peaceful triumph of justice.

These men, it is well known, were Wilberforce, Clarkson, Granville Sharp, and Buxton; a few obscure but persevering pastors and Christians.

Seven times they proposed the bill for the abolition of the slave-trade, seven times it failed.† When they at length succeeded, they had to struggle against the most powerful personages of their country, — Lord Eldon, who still affirmed in Parliament in 1807 that "the slave-trade had been sanctioned by Parliaments where sat the wisest jurisconsults, the most enlightened theologians, the most eminent statesmen"; Lord Hawkesbury, since Earl Liverpool, who proposed to strike out of the preamble the words, "*incompatible with the principles of justice and humanity*," and Earl Westmoreland, who declared that, even though he should "see all the Presbyterians and the prelates, the Methodists and the preachers, the Jacobins and the assassins, united in

* Observations on Table No. 25, p. 156.

† P. 13. It is known that, in 1802, the Consulate placed the slave-trade anew under the protection of the law.

favor of the abolition of the slave-trade, he would none the less raise his voice in Parliament against this measure." *

Thank God, the generous impulse which inspired the law of 1807 thenceforth animated all the ministers whose duty it was to apply it, and for more than half a century this flame has not been for a single day extinct.

Men have accused England of having acted through interest, they have even fancied that the end which it had in view was to ruin all the colonies worked by African laborers, including its own, in order to secure the monopoly of agriculture and commerce to its vast East Indian possessions.† They have pretended that it sought, under the pretext of humanity, to conquer the surveillance of all the navies on the globe, the high police of the seas.

Its efforts, its expenditures, the difficulties which it risked, the language of its statesmen, place the complete disinterestedness of England beyond doubt. It is possible that it may have found its interest in its duty, and that, among its statesmen, some may have been more sensible to utility, others to humanity. Let us wisely congratulate nations whose interests accord so well with those of the human race, without always seeking small motives for great actions. The abolition of the slave-trade throughout the globe has become as it were an article of faith of English policy.

In the Congress of Vienna, February 8, 1815, a declaration against the slave-trade was signed in behalf of England, Austria, France, Portugal, Prussia, Russia, Spain, and Sweden. England had already obtained of France, in the treaty of Paris, May 30, 1814, an article with this end.‡

In 1818 at the Congress of Aix-la-Chapelle, and in 1822

* Quoted in the protest of the Minister from Brazil, M. de Abreu, Oct. 22, 1845. *Revue coloniale*, 1846, VIII. 62.

† Opinion of M. Dejean de la Bâtie. *Précis de l'abolition de l'esclavage.*

‡ Additional Articles, Art. I.

at the Congress of Verona, the five great powers repeated the same declarations.

Since 1814 England has unremittingly employed every effort of her diplomacy to obtain individual treaties from the different powers.

Twenty-seven years were needed to persuade Portugal.

By an agreement, January 21, 1815, followed by a treaty signed January 22,* England promised the remission of an old debt and £ 300,000 to indemnify the owners of Portuguese vessels captured before this time by English cruisers, while Portugal interdicted the slave-trade under the Portuguese flag, except to supply its own possessions. By another agreement, July 28, 1817, both nations accorded to each other the reciprocal right of *search*, detention of slave-ships, and judgment by mixed commissions. Portugal promised a special penalty against all Portuguese subjects who should engage in the slave-trade. Despite these agreements, nearly 60,000 slaves † were transported to Brazil in 1822, the year that this vast empire separated from the mother country. Notes, remonstrances, and threats remained without effect till December, 1836. A decree then forbade Portuguese subjects to engage in the slave-trade, but it was nowhere executed, and not even proclaimed at Mozambique. The slave-trade continued to be carried on under the Portuguese flag, with the connivance of Portuguese functionaries, to the profit of America and of adventurers from the colonies of Europe. On August 24, 1839, both Houses of Parliament passed a bill authorizing British cruisers to stop Portuguese slavers and bring them before the Vice-Admiralty Courts for judgment.

This was to punish one violation of the rights of nations by another. Conquered, Portugal conceded, by a treaty

* Some Account of the Trade in Slaves, by James Bandinel, 1842. *Revue coloniale*, 1844, II. pp. 154-214. On the Slave-Trade, by Sir J. Fowell Buxton, 1849.

† *Revue coloniale*, *loc. cit*, 160.

dated July 3, 1842, the right of visit and search, judgment by mixed commissions, the obligation to demolish or sell the vessels condemned, the assimilation of the slave-trade to piracy, the application to the condemned of the penalty of death instead of the lesser penalty, and the freedom of the slaves seized.

It was necessary to adopt the same conduct, in 1845, with Brazil, although the treaty of 1817 with Portugal had been followed by a new agreement, November 23, 1826. More than 50,000 slaves were imported in 1849. A law dated July 17, 1850, at length suppressed this odious traffic.

With Spain, the struggle lasted twenty-one years. The treaty of August 28, 1814, that of September 23, 1817, by which England promised £400,000, the decree of December 19, 1819, and the additional agreement of December 10, 1822, remained without effect. At Madrid, the government prohibited the slave-trade; at Havana, its agents encouraged it and turned it to their profit. All of the most forcible representations were useless until June 28, 1835. At this date, after the death of King Ferdinand, the constitutional government concluded a treaty with England, effective at least so far as regarded the slave-trade *under the Spanish flag.*

We have said that France promised, by the treaty of Paris (1814), the abolition of the slave-trade. On March 29, 1815, Napoleon, on his return from the Isle of Elba, declared the slave-trade abolished. An ordinance of January 8, 1817, repeated this interdiction. Nevertheless, the government of the Restoration refused to enter into a league proposed by England to the great powers to assimilate the slave-trade to piracy, to withdraw from the traffickers the protection of their national flag, and to prohibit admission to the products of slave colonies. It limited itself to pronouncing, by a law dated April 25, 1825, the penalty of fine, imprisonment, and deportation against Frenchmen engaged in the slave-trade. The treaties of November 30, 1831, and March 22, 1833, which conceded the reciprocal right of search, are well known, together with the debates to which they gave rise, the refusal to ratify the treaty of November 20, 1841, between the great powers, and, lastly, the agreement of May 28, 1845, the term of which has now expired, without having been renewed. The proof, moreover, of the last act of the slave-trade committed under the French flag dates back to 1830.

The abolition of the slave-trade is one of the articles of the Constitution of the United States, but this article postponed its cessation until 1807. All the propositions of the treaty proposed to the government of the United States by England in 1819, 1820, 1823, 1824, 1831, 1834, 1839, and 1841, and the resolutions of Congress in 1821 and 1822 ended only in an agreement. The United States have always refused the right of visit. Only by a treaty of August 9, 1842, the two powers are bound to keep up separately a naval force of at least 80 guns, in surveillance, on the coast of Africa.

England had less difficulty in negotiating with Holland,* Sweden,† Denmark,‡ the first state that abolished the slave-trade, Russia, Austria, whose vessels transported negroes from Barbary to Turkey, Prussia,§ the kingdom of Naples,|| Tuscany,¶ Sardinia,** the Hanse towns,†† Hayti,‡‡ Texas,§§ Mexico,|||| Columbia,¶¶ New Grenada,*** Vene-

* March 4, 1818; Dec. 31, 1822; Jan. 25, 1823; Feb. 7, 1837.

† Nov. 6, 1824; June 15, 1835.

‡ July 26, 1835.

§ Feb. 19, 1842, Russia, Austria, and Prussia.

|| Feb. 14, 1838.

¶ Nov. 24, 1837.

** Aug. 8, 1834.

†† June 9, 1837.

‡‡ Dec. 23, 1839.

§§ June 18, 1842.

|||| Dec. 26, 1826; July 29, 1841.

¶¶ April 18, 1825.

*** 1841.

zuela,* Ecuador,† Uruguay,‡ Buenos Ayres,§ Chili,|| Peru, and Bolivia.¶

By twenty-three treaties, obtained in less than thirty years, England has thus succeeded in determining almost all the Christian nations, according to the admirable expression of Lord Aberdeen, "to rank themselves among the great powers of Christianity, united together by a common sentiment of commiseration and justice.**

The greater part of these nations, and a few others, Greece, for instance (1840), before or since these treaties, have devoted special laws to the interdiction of the slave traffic, while, by a memorable bull, dated December 3, 1839, the sovereign pontiff, Gregory XVI., fulminated, in behalf of all Catholicism, a sentence of condemnation against this odious traffic, in the name of the Law of laws, the Gospel, the Lawgiver of lawgivers, God.

The work would have been incomplete, if it had acted only on the buyers without affecting the sellers of slaves. To the treaties with the great powers of Europe and America succeeded treaties with the petty sovereigns of Africa. One might have been tempted to lord it with a strong hand over these contemptible monarchs, ruling by brute force over ill-defined territories and wretched subjects. England thought it worthy of itself to treat them according to the right of nations, a science in which it found them little advanced. Her Britannic Majesty signed treaties in the strictest forms of governmental etiquette with Nama Comba, Chief of Cartabar, in Gambia,†† Obi Osai, Chief of

* March 15, 1839.

† 1841.

‡ June 13, 1839.

§ Feb., 1825; May 24, 1839.

|| Jan. 19, 1839; Aug. 7, 1841.

¶ June 5, 1837; Sept. 25, 1840. See the list of these treaties, *Revue coloniale*, 1844, IV. 253.

** Despatch of 1841 to the United States.

†† Ibid., 1849, p. 236.

the territory of Abok, on the banks of the Niger ; Eyamba, Chief of Calabar, and Radama, King of Madagascar, in 1841; then, in 1847, with nearly all the chiefs of the Bissagos Islands, Sierra Leone, the Grain Coast, the Ivory Coast, Congo, Gaboon, and Loango. To give an idea of this sort of agreements, we will quote the shortest, made March 7, 1841.*

"William Simpson Blount, Lieutenant commanding her Majesty's steamship the Pluto, in the name of her Majesty, the Queen of England, and King Bell, of the village of Bell, at Cameroons,

"Do hereby agree to the following articles and conditions : —

"Art. I. The two contracting parties, from the date of this treaty, shall wholly cease upon the territory of the said King Bell, and wherever his influence may extend, all sale and transportation of slaves or of any other persons, whoever they may be ; and the said persons shall not be transported from any point whatever of the territory of the said King Bell into any other country, island, or possession of any prince or potentate whatsoever. The said King Bell shall issue a proclamation and a law forbidding his subjects and all persons dependent on him, either to sell any slave to be transported beyond the territory, or to aid or encourage any sale of this kind, under pain of severe punishment.

"Art. II. The said King Bell doth bind himself to inform the cruisers of her Britannic Majesty of the arrival of all slave-ships that may enter the river.

"Art. III. In consideration of this concession of the said King Bell, and to indemnify him for the loss of revenues that may be thereby occasioned him, the said Lieutenant W. S. Blount doth bind himself, in the name of her Britannic Majesty, to remit annually for five years to the said King Bell, the following articles, viz. :

* Despatch of 1844 to the United States, III. p. 536.

"Sixty muskets, one hundred pieces of cloth, two barrels of powder, two puncheons of rum, one scarlet coat with epaulets, and one sword.

"The said presents shall be delivered in exchange for a certificate, signed by the said King Bell, attesting that the conditions herein stated have been put into execution."

In other treaties more serious conditions are introduced. Thus, in the treaty with the chiefs of Malimba, 1847, it is agreed that no house, warehouse, or *barracoon* whatsoever shall be erected for the slave-trade, that the chiefs shall destroy all those which shall be or are already built, and that if they fail to do so, the English shall demolish them themselves, and shall give practical proof to the chiefs of Malimba of the serious displeasure of the Queen of England. It is also agreed that the negroes already held for exportation shall be delivered up to the English to be carried to their colonies and liberated. Lastly, entire freedom of trade is accorded to the English.

Agreements were signed in 1822 and 1839, then renewed in 1845, with a more powerful sovereign, the Imam of Mascata, who rules over a great part of the eastern coast of Africa, from the Persian Gulf to the Portuguese possessions, comprising the islands of Zanzibar, Pemba, and Monfia. His states are the theatre of the detestable slave-trade carried on by the Arabs, for which slaves are brought from along the coast and from Madagascar. Negroes, laden with commodities, are led to the coast, then sold with their burdens to boot; from which traffic the Imam receives annually more than £20,000. In 1844, on the authority of Captain Hammerton, a child brought from $5 to $15; a man, from $15 to $30; and a woman as high as $35, only to be sold again, Heaven knows in what condition, on the frontiers of Arabia or Persia, for from $3 to $6; dead slaves are thrown to the dogs. The Imam Seïd Saïd promised to renounce the slave-trade, and to interdict it to his subjects.

A consul was established at Zanzibar, and the English cruisers were authorized to seize the vessels and subjects of his highness.

A number of treaties were concluded with the Arab sheiks on the western coast of the Persian Gulf.

Subsequently to the agreement of 1845, France was associated in several of these treaties, and directly concluded some others.

A committee of inquiry, appointed in 1853 by the House of Commons, ascertained that there were at this epoch twenty-three treaties in force between Great Britain and the other civilized powers for the suppression of the slave-trade, and sixty-five treaties concluded with the African chiefs.*

We have seen the stipulations contained in the latter. Among the first, ten treaties established the reciprocal right of visit and the jurisdiction of mixed commissions; fourteen, the right of visit, but with the jurisdiction of the national tribunals; two (with France and the United States) without guaranteeing the right of visit, contain the reciprocal obligation to maintain squadrons on the coast of Africa.

England has neglected nothing to insure the success of all these complicated means. While the government has established cruisers, consulates, commissions, and correspondences which yearly fill two folio volumes,† submitted to both Houses, abolitionist opinion has organized missions, voyages, inquiries, societies, meetings, and journals.‡

In France, a lesser yet notable agitation was kept up during the whole duration of the constitutional government, and this government, with the sincerest zeal, executed treaties, demanded appropriations, negotiated agreements, multi-

* *Revue coloniale*, 1853, XI. 317.

† Correspondence Relating to the Slave-Trade.

‡ Anti-Slavery Reporter, etc.

plied instructions, and finally ordered the translation of all the documents in the *Revue coloniale*, the thirty-three volumes of which (1843 – 1857) contain the history from day to day of this prodigious effort of two great nations in the service of the most degraded members of the human race.

III. What has been, in brief, the result of so much pains and perseverance?

This is greatly contested. In England, the leading organ of public opinion, the London *Times*, has undertaken the task of denying the good effects of the policy followed for the suppression of the slave-trade. We have spent enormous sums, it is often repeated, $ 80,000,000 or $ 100,000,000, and for what? to pay higher for sugar and negroes.

The *Society for the Abolition of Slavery*, contrary to the opinion of its oldest and most illustrious founders, has warmly attacked the cruiser system,* and members of Parliament have, by successive motions, demanded its suppression, on the pretence that £ 650,000 were annually expended in endangering the lives of sailors and rendering more cruel the condition of the slaves, on account of the embarrassment in concealing and clandestinely transporting them.

Finally, the susceptibilities and violent discussions to which the *right of visit* has given rise are well known.

That the abolition of the slave-trade has aggravated the sufferings of the negroes can with difficulty be admitted. — Before the slave-trade, the native kings sacrificed their prisoners; thanks to the slave-trade, they sold them to charitable Europeans; since the abolition of the slave-trade, they are led anew to slay them. The slave-ships render them more wretched by being obliged to conceal them. This is what is affirmed, but how prove it? how know precisely what the petty sovereigns do with their prisoners, how, to lessen the doubtful crime of these sovereigns, toler-

* The Slave-Trade, by Sir Fowell Buxton.

† This was the opinion of the traveller Raffenel. *Revue coloniale*, 1846, VIII. 496.

ate the certain crime of negro slave-ships? If the latter are obliged to conceal their cargoes, it is because the cruising system is efficient. We are assured that they treat the negroes worse than before, — this is impossible. Read the horrible descriptions of the witnesses of the slave-trade in former times, especially the English reports, which picture to us, in such strong language, the sufferings of these unfortunates, wedged in, spoon-wise, in technical language, stowed in bulk like figs or raisins.

I make it a point to exaggerate nothing, I do violence to myself by excluding the pictures which might seem too dramatic, yet I may be permitted to quote two imposing witnesses, the one on the slave-trade by Christians, the other on the slave-trade by Mahometans.

We will first hear Lord Palmerston address the House of Lords, July 26, 1844 (*Revue coloniale*, 1844, p. 537): —

"According to the report of Messrs. Venderwelt and Buxton, from 120,000 to 150,000 slaves are landed annually in America. It is calculated that of three negroes seized in the interior of Africa, to be sent into slavery, but one reaches his destination, the two others die in the course of the operations of the slave-trade. Whatever may be the number transported, therefore, we must triple it to obtain the true number of human beings whom this detestable traffic kidnaps every year from Africa.

"Indeed, the negroes destined for the slave-trade are not taken from the neighborhood where they are embarked. A great number come from the interior. Many are captives made in wars excited by thirst for the gain procured by the sale of the prisoners. But the greatest number arise from kidnapping expeditions, and an organized system of man-stealing in the interior of Africa. When the time approaches to set out with the slave caravans for the coast, the kidnappers surround a peaceful village at night, set it on fire, and seize on the inhabitants, killing all who resist.

If the village attacked is situated on a mountain, offering greater facilities for flight, and the inhabitants take refuge in the caverns, the kidnappers kindle large fires at the entrance, and those who are sheltered there, placed between death by suffocation and slavery, are forced to give themselves up. If the fugitives take refuge on the heights, the assailants render themselves masters of all the springs and wells, and the unfortunates, devoured by thirst, return to truckle their liberty for life. The prisoners made, they proceed to the choice. The robust individuals of both sexes, and the children from six to seven years old, are set aside to form part of the caravan which is to be driven to the sea-shore. They rid themselves of the children under six years of age by killing them on the spot, and abandon the aged and infirm, thus condemning them to die of hunger. The caravan sets out; men, women, and children traverse the burning sands and rocky defiles of the mountains of Africa, barefoot and almost naked. The feeble are stimulated by the whip, the strong are secured by chaining them together or by placing them under a yoke. Many fall from exhaustion on the road, and die or become the prey of wild beasts. On reaching the sea-shore, they are penned up and crowded together in buildings called barracoons, where they fall a prey to epidemics. Death has often cruelly thinned their ranks before the arrival of a slave-trader. The first who appears takes his choice, setting aside the sick and feeble, and taking care always to take one third or at least one fourth more than his vessel can hold, and this according to a mathematical calculation, for the same reason that casks are put into a vessel loaded with wine, designed to compensate for the loss which will result from evaporation or leakage; for the captain knows perfectly well that a large number of the negroes of his cargo will perish, some from grief, others from the change of diet, and many from asphyxia.

"They do not always wait until the dying are dead to cast them into the sea, but sometimes throw them overboard as soon as they are hopeless." The orator quotes an incident of this kind which happened in 1783. A man named Collingwood was carrying slaves to Jamaica; the ship took a wrong course, and water and provisions became scanty. Knowing that if the negroes died of famine, the owners would lose the insurance upon them, while they would be entitled to this premium if it were proved that he had been compelled by the perils of the sea to sacrifice the cargo, the captain did not hesitate to precipitate 132 living beings into the waves.

Lord Palmerston then draws a description of a negro slave-ship, and quotes the words of a man who had seen one of these vessels: "A negro has not as much room in them as a corpse in a coffin." For all these reasons, the noble lord thinks that if 150,000 slaves land annually in America, the slave-trade carries away from Africa 300,000 or 400,000 souls. According to him, all the crimes of the human race, from the creation of the world to our days, do not exceed those which have been caused by the slave trade.

See now an episode of the Mahometan slave-trade, recounted by an eyewitness.

"On the 10th of February, 1843, I quitted Farrec, the last town of the kingdom of Shoa. Our caravan was composed of the employees and domestics of the embassy, and about 130 or 140 slaves, a part of whom belonged to the drivers of the camels designed for the service of the embassy, and the rest to some slave-traders who profited by the escort of the embassy to escape the brigandage of the Bedouins of the county of Adal.

"More than two thirds of these slaves were young girls under fourteen. Several among them had not yet reached their eighth year. The rest were young lads from ten to fourteen years of age. One of them had been recently the victim of a barbarous custom in accordance with which the Abyssinians mutilate all men killed in battle, and all the children of their enemies under six years old, who are usually spared, while those who exceed this age are slaughtered without mercy. Independently of the cruel operation which he had suffered, this child, named Affrano, had been grieviously wounded in the thigh by a sabre cut. He was scarcely seven years old, and it was at this age and in such a condition that he was about to commence a journey of 350 miles on foot, by long stages. He was to be carried, indeed, to the market of Mocha, Cairo, or Constantinople, to be sold as a eunuch to some wealthy Mahometan.

"His wretched condition filled us with compassion. Captain Harris obtained permission to place him on one of his mules. Without this aid, he would never have reached the journey's end alive.

"I noticed, during the course of the journey, that the young girls whose beauty promised the most considerable profits, received permission every other day to mount their masters' mules or camels. This interested humanity was only practised, however, with respect to five or six. The others, with the exception of one alone, who had fallen sick and was placed upon a camel, walked with surprising gayety to the very end of the journey.

"The boys, on the contrary, literally watered the road with their tears; they dragged themselves along the way, urged on by their driver, a young lad who, by his brutality, had earned the surname of *sheitan* (demon), a title of which he was very proud, and which he strove to make good by redoubling his harshness.

"The difference of the state of mind in the two sexes must be attributed to the different state of their moral and physical condition at the beginning of the journey. The girls were bought in consideration of their beauty and good constitution. In the purchase of the boys, on the contrary, the merchants were guided only by their cheapness.

"I say nothing of the violations publicly committed on the youngest girls by the slave-traders or their friends, in the journey from Abyssinia to Tadjourah. It is one of the most infamous circumstances of this infamous traffic.

"More than half the slaves were Christians. A few wore the *matab*, a sort of blue or white silk drawers, in this country the distinctive mark of Christianity.

"We reached the coast on the 15th of March, having traversed in 36 days a distance of 350 miles, making an average of 10 miles a day. But our day's marches had often been longer. One can scarcely comprehend how children could have accomplished so long and painful a route. The young girls were worn out with fatigue, and the boys half dead, yet not one had sunk beneath it. This was great cause for rejoicing to the slave-traders and their friends. They never remembered to have accomplished the journey so successfully, and declared, in consequence, that we had brought them good luck, and that we possessed a high degree of heavenly favor."

How can it be affirmed, in the presence of such pictures, that it is possible still to exceed these horrors, and that they could have been aggravated by the measures taken to abolish the slave-trade? I challenge any one to go further in the contempt of man and the excess of brutality.

Nevertheless, the traveller Vogel, that hero of twenty years, since slain himself by the Sultan Wadai, has recounted that, in 1854, the Sheik of Bornon, having taken 4,000 negroes, slew all the men, and only kept 500 women and children. Dr. Barth also thinks that massacres have increased since the chiefs have no longer the outlet of their markets.

But Livingstone, on the contrary, writes to Lord Clarendon, March 19, 1856, from the river Zambesi: "A certain

Dr. Brysson has written that the measures taken to suppress the slave-trade have done nothing but increase its horrors. It has also been gravely affirmed that the Maravi now kill their captives, whereas formerly they kept them to sell to the whites. I can assure your Lordship that such an assertion could not come from a man mixed up, as I am, with slave-traders, in the very country where the traffic is carried on ; it is spread by those who have an interest in the slave-trade. In the extensive portion of Africa with which I am acquainted wars are now very rare : *they were evidently provoked by the slave-trade.* It is rare now to see a *cafilah* of slaves on its way to the sea-shore, and the traffickers know that they risk more than in venturing their money at play. By taking away all possibility of industry, the commerce in slaves is the cause of the complete ruin of East and West Africa."

Even though the abolition of the slave-trade were the occasion of a few new crimes, does not every penal law result sometimes in impelling the criminal to a second crime to hide the first ? It might also be said that thieves would never kill those whom they plunder, if theft were permitted.

Let us have done with this reasoning, nor suffer the suppression of the slave-trade to be accused of aggravating its horrors.

Yet it must be granted that, of all the means employed, there is not one that may not be contested, not one that may not be eluded.

The right of reciprocal visit, the assimilation of the slave-trade to piracy, the surveillance of the coast by cruisers, the establishment of mixed commissions, — these are the means which have proved truly efficient.

But the *right of visit* is repugnant to the honor of nations. On the high seas, in time of peace, nations are independent as regards each other. There is, notwithstanding, an international police, which originates in the right of nations; every ship has a right to verify the identity of the flag which it meets. There are other rights, resulting from treaties. Such is the right of *visit,* in consequence of the negro slave-trade, to which England has added the right of *search,* — the right to demand the papers, the right to explore the ship. We comprehend that to a feeble power this right is oppressive; to a strong one, humiliating.

When the July government thought it incumbent upon it to accept the treaties of 1831 and 1833, the scheme of which had been rejected by the government of 1815, public opinion and the marine protested.* When a new treaty was signed in 1842, the ratification was refused. Finally, when M. de Broglie and Mr. Lushington had signed the very reasonable agreement of May 29, 1845, by the terms of which France and England pledged themselves, each for ten years, to keep at least twenty-six cruisers upon the Western coast of Africa, and England an additional cruiser upon the Eastern coast, without any right of visiting the papers or cargo, unless the vessel were *suspicious,* it was exclaimed that this right was exorbitant, and well-known addresses loudly demanded *that French commerce should be placed again under the exclusive surveillance of the French flag.*† Finally, when the agreement came to an end, in 1855, it was suffered to fall in silence. Who would dare propose to take it up again?

The United States have always positively refused the right of search, and the discussions with England on this subject did not end until 1858.

The same resistance has been made to the establishment of mixed commissions. France has always refused to sub-

* Despatches of MM. de Polignac and de Laval.

† Discussions of the two Chambers, Jan. 1846, Speeches of MM. de la Redorte and Billault. (*Revue coloniale,* 1846, VIII. 136.)

mit its national affairs to any other jurisdiction than that of its national tribunals. England maintains Anglo-Spanish commissions at Sierra Leone, St. Paul de Loanda, the Cape, and Havana.

France has alike refused to assimilate the slave-trade to piracy in its laws. Two conditions united constitute a *pirate,* — having no regular papers, and being armed.* A negro slave-ship, if it be not armed, even though it have no papers, is not a pirate, except though special laws. England, Portugal, Spain, the United States, and finally Brazil, have declared the slave-trade *piracy.* The assimilation is perfectly just; but in 1825 the slave-trade still continued, and no one dared inflict on it such severe penalties. I believe that this will come; the progress of morality on this question is slow but sure. A hundred years ago, the slave-trade was encouraged; fifty years ago, it was tolerated; forty years ago, it was a misdemeanor: it is time that it passed to the rank of a crime.

The surveillance of the coasts by cruisers is assuredly a costly and incomplete means; it is impossible to watch over the observance of order on the ocean as in a village. But the cruisers have done much for the service of humanity; they have delivered an immense number of victims; at the same time that they prevent the slave-trade, they protect commerce, and extend over the missions the protecting shadow of the French flag. Let us add, that they have also done much for the honor of humanity. Who would refuse the tribute of grateful admiration to those noble officers, those daring sailors, who brave exile, the sea, the sun and death, and stand two years as sentinels without glory or repose to pounce upon the oppressor and set free his obscure victims.

* Law of April 12, 1825; *Moniteur*, April 25; Reported by Baron Portal. Simple *piracy* is punished by compulsory labor; when accompanied by depredation, it is punishable by death. *Barratry* is the crime committed by a captain or pilot, in stealing, losing, or selling the vessel which he is charged to conduct.

Whatever may be the inconveniences, whatever the imperfections of all these means, that their results have been very considerable cannot be doubted. The most experienced and best informed men — Lord Palmerston, Lord Aberdeen, Lord Clarendon, Sir Robert Peel, and Lord John Russell — have not ceased to affirm in England, and M. Guizot, M. de Broglie, Admiral Duperré, and M. de Mackau in France, that the number of slaves taken from Africa has largely diminished. The calculations produced before the Committee of Inquiry of 1848 place the number of slaves exported from 1788 to 1840 at from 100,000 to 140,000 per year, and from 1840 to 1848 * at from 50,000 to 80,000. There is, therefore, a diminution of about one half.

There are flags under which the slave-trade no longer appears, as the French, English, Dutch, Swedish, and Austrian. Of all Christian lands, America alone, and in America the Southern States, Cuba, and Brazil alone, receive slaves.

Since this time, special laws have been obtained in these countries; of Spain in 1835, of Portugal in 1842, of Brazil in 1850. At Cuba, an upright governor, General Valdès, has sufficed almost completely to check the slave-trade during the past few years. The law of 1850 in Brazil has caused the number of slaves imported to fall from more than 50,000 to 700 or 800 per year.†

From 1837 to 1847, the English cruisers captured 634 slave-ships, destined for Brazil or Cuba. If the French cruisers ‡ make fewer prizes, it is because, having no special treaties with the different nations, they can only seize the slave-ships in case of *piracy*.

The destructions of numerous slave barracoons by the system of shore blockade has struck the merchants with

* *Revue coloniale*, 1848, p. 148.

† 1846 54,000
1847 59,000

‡ The African Squadron Avenged, by Lieut. Henry Yule, Colonial Magazine, March, 1850; *Revue coloniale*, 1850, IV. 277.

terror, and substituted the traffic in ivory and gum for that in slaves. Matters have been carried so far as to besiege towns, as at Lagos in 1852, and to replace one chief therein by another.*

"When we compare what took place a few years ago," said Lord John Russell, June 8, 1860,† "when we remember that 140,000 slaves were yearly carried away from Africa, while this year the number has not reached 30,000, we should neither deny the progress nor abandon the hope of a complete suppression of this traffic."

In short, this commerce, which was the appanage of kings, is considered as a crime; all the nations of Europe have promised by treaties the suppression of the slave-trade, and interdicted by laws its practice to their subjects; this odious traffic has been driven to bay, circumscribed, punished, and diminished, at an epoch when the immense increase of the consumption of colonial products would have infallibly augmented it. Have the colonies been ruined? Has their production decreased? Not at all! ‡ The slave has only become more costly, and consequently has been better treated; servile labor increasing in price, emancipation has encountered fewer obstacles. The crime dishonored, the slave-trade rarer, the slave happier, freedom easier, — these are immense and satisfactory results.

Another result I style very important, — the conviction that the entire abolition of the slave-trade will never be wrought except by the entire abolition of slavery.

So long as men are sure of selling a kind of merchandise

* *Revue coloniale*, 1852, VIII. 270, 360.

† Papers relating to the Slave-Trade. Barclay, London, 1861.

‡ Exportation of Sugar from the English West India Colonies:

Before the abolition of the slave-trade,	1801 - 1806 . .	1,138,390,736 kil.
After the abolition of the slave-trade,	1817 - 1822 . .	1,141,197,628
" " "	1823 - 1828 . .	1,171,881,526
" " "	1829 - 1834 . .	1,190,990,566

(*Revue coloniale*, March, 1848, p. 262.)

at a high price they always find the means of procuring it. The risk increases the gain.*

But slavery is not everywhere abolished, and the nations who have abolished it, in order to procure additional laborers for their colonies, engage in the importation of free Africans, known under the name of "immigration," which is accused of being a return to the slave-trade. What are we to think of this?

* The surveillance of Cuba is easy. The navigable passes are not broad. The wind almost always blows in one direction, and for about four hours in the morning there is a dead calm, which gives steamers a great advantage over sailing-vessels; yet, notwithstanding, at least 30,000 slaves are annually imported into Cuba. (Mr. Cave's Speech in the House of Commons, June 8, 1860.)

II.

IMMIGRATION, OR THE IMPORTATION OF FREE NEGROES FROM THE COAST OF AFRICA.

SINCE the French have taken the liberty of contracting for free negroes on the coast of Africa, despatches have poured in from every post where an English flag floats over a consular house, which seem to have been copied one after the other.

Thus Mr. Sunley, Consul at the Island of Mauritius, wrote in 1857 to Commodore Trotter, commanding the station of the eastern coast of Africa, to inform him of the arrival at the Comoros, Oibo, and Johanna of ships bound from the Isle of Bourbon, with permissions and agents of the French government* to hire ransomed or freed negroes. He pointed out no abuses. He even declared that Capt. Durand of the *Aurélie* had refused to anchor at Maroni, in the Comoro Isles, to give the sultan time, as he proposed, to form slave depôts on the coast, *because he was expressly forbidden it by the instructions of the government.* Notwithstanding, he added that he could not hinder the native sultans, despite the treaties which bound them to England, from seeking to profit by the ransom of negroes effected by France. Upon this, Commodore Trotter wrote to the admiralty: "There is no attempt to transport slaves around the Cape of Good Hope. But it is greatly to be regretted that the French government persists in its system of the emigration of negroes from the eastern coast of Africa to the Isle of Bourbon, a sys-

* New York Journal of Commerce, April 6, 1858.

tem which naturally leads the chiefs, in order to supply the market on the coast with laborers, to bring slaves from the interior, instead of the products of the soil."

We find the same complaints arise from the western coast of Africa. The unique little republic of Liberia, founded in 1822, on the old *Grain Coast*, between Cape Palmas and Sierra Leone, by the American abolitionists, in order to re-export thither free negroes to their native soil, is well known. This republic, where negroes alone are citizens, is far from being a model.* Nevertheless, it endures and grows; has a constitution, elective president, senate, and parliament, property qualification and irremovable judiciary body, and numbers 11 towns, nearly 400,000 souls, 50 churches, 30 schools, and a college. It treats with the European nations, who keep up the friendship by small gifts; as for instance, England has presented it with a steamboat, and France, it is said, has given it a thousand Zouave uniforms. Finally, it seeks to aggrandize itself, and sends explorers into the interior. In a letter, dated February, 1858, from one of these explorers, George Seymour, despatched to the territory of Pessay on the eastern coast, I read: "The French system of seeking emigrants from this coast for its Indian colonies leads the native chiefs in the neighborhood of Cape Mount to resume their old practice of kidnapping, and to make wars of pillage upon each other in order to supply themselves with emigrants."

* As an attempt gradually to abolish slavery in the United States, and to remove the colored race, according to the hopes of Mr. Clay, the Republic of Liberia is only an illusion. The most idle and turbulent negroes are thus got rid of, and men born in America are sent to Africa. Liberia costs as much to those who desire abolition as to those who repel it, and are not sorry to have free negroes out of the sight of their slaves. Finally, there is no doubt that President Roberts, as well as several other high functionaries, was paid to second the slave-trade. Liberia is interesting only as an experiment as to how negroes can govern themselves and labor, even in detestable conditions. See the Edinburgh Review, 1859, pp. 550 - 565.

Less than this would have sufficed to cause France to be openly accused in England of resuscitating the slave-trade, and to reawaken all the echoes of Exeter Hall, all the fervor of the old abolitionists of both Houses of Parliament.

On July 17, 1857, Lord Brougham questioned the French government concerning the importation of negroes into the French colonies. He believed that the Emperor was deceived; he hoped that the religious influences which surrounded him would demonstrate to him that this importation would resuscitate the slave-trade, that the negroes were incapable of comprehending the contract proposed to them, that, in bringing them to the coast, the chiefs abandoned themselves to all imaginable horrors. He proposed an address to the Queen. This was sustained by Lord Malmesbury and Lord Harrowby. Lord Clarendon responded, that he was greatly concerned about these facts, that he had written to the French government, that he was watching. The address was adopted.

Nevertheless, public opinion was not yet greatly moved, for the Times of July 18, in giving an account of the meeting, adduced several arguments, *pro* and *con*, and ended by declaring that each country ought to act in the matter as it thought fit.

But two events, occurring in 1858, inflamed public opinion and revived the discussion.

The first was the mutiny of the negro emigrants and massacre of the crew of the *Regina Cœli* of Nantes, afterwards captured by an English ship and carried to Monrovia. The journals of June, 1858, have all recapitulated the thrilling details written by a witness of the massacre, M. de Brulais, the ship's surgeon, who saw the captain hacked to pieces and all the sailors killed, and only survived by force of courage, and as it were by a miracle, after passing two days and nights in the midst of the mutinous negroes, true wild beasts.

The second event was that of the *Charles Georges*, captured on the coast of Mozambique, beyond the legal bounds and despite the regularity of its papers, by the Portuguese authorities, — an event which forced the French government to send two men-of-war to Lisbon, and was at last terminated by a just satisfaction rendered to our right and flag, but after many difficulties, and amid the unbridled clamors and insults of the English and Portuguese journals, who accused France anew of engaging in the slave-trade.

Is this so? Is the system of the importation of free negroes an involuntary return to the slave-trade?

If this be false, the system should be persevered in, in spite of appearances. If it be true, it is right to renounce it, in spite of its advantages. We have said enough of immigration elsewhere to be brief here.*

We have proved that the necessity of immigration was not born of the necessity of the emancipation of slaves. It is the means of peopling lands insufficiently inhabited, of cultivating lands insufficiently cultivated. But the abolition of slavery adds to this necessity in two ways: first, because a part of the former slaves become freeholders, artisans, or vagrants; second, because, a part of the former masters becoming more active and industrious, labor is in greater demand.

We have also proved, that after having tried all races, no better substitutes are found for Africans than other Africans.

We have shown, lastly, that at the West Indies as at Bourbon, at Jamaica as at Cuba, at Charleston as at Surinam, at Rio de Janeiro as at New Orleans, the unanimous cry of all the planters has been for a large immigration of laborers as the only means of safety or progress, and that all the governments, English, French, Spanish, Dutch,

* Results of Emancipation, p. 202.

American, and Brazilian, have authorized, encouraged, and regulated this operation.

It is true that this imperative want necessarily involves the resuscitation of the slave-trade?

It is said, on the contrary,* that the engagement of free negroes is a means of annihilating the slave-trade, because the native chiefs, having the choice, prefer delivering their slaves to honorable merchants to be freed, instead of to cruel slave-traders. This is to attribute great refinement of feeling to these frightful petty sovereigns. It is to forget, most of all that the slave-traders pay higher for a slave to sell again than the emigration agents can pay for a hired man whose contract will soon expire. If this be so, emigration will never prevail over the slave-trade. It offers besides in many points the same dangers.

What is the slave-trade?

A drama in five acts, — the capture, the caravan, the sale, the passage, the slavery. Immigration is a drama which ends differently, but begins the same. The negro is captured, carried to the coast, sold, and transported, only instead of going to slavery, he goes to freedom, — to the freedom which begins with exile and a contract to labor.

Like the slave-trade, immigration brings buyers to horrible sellers, who, to satisfy their demands, engage in kidnapping and war, lash their captives onwards in droves, slay all useless mouths, and truckle the remainder for goods or gold. It leads wretches to freedom on a strange land, who do not rightly know what is asked them, and who in general abhor quitting the soil where they have always suffered. Finally, intrusted to honest hands under vigilant eyes for a few years, by degrees it will become the trade of merchants of doubtful honesty or unfaithful agents, and will lapse erelong, in proportion as surveillance and public

* See the remarkable article of M. J. Delarbre, *L'immigration africaine et la traite des noirs.*

opinion are lulled to sleep, into the old ways of the slave-trade. No regulation is minute enough, no protection strong enough, no intervention of the state sure enough, when the point in question is a contract entered into under the equator, far from courts of law and notaries, — a contract which consists of a few words addressed in a few minutes by an interested interpreter to an ignorant and terrified captive, which decide the life of a wretch who does not even suspect that in changing hands he changes his fate.

In short, —

1. The engagement of negroes in a *preliminary state of freedom* seems to me perfectly legitimate; but this way is slow and insufficient.

2. The engagement *by preliminary redemption* is free from all reproach on the part of those who hire the negroes after having freed them; but on the part of those who capture and sell them, it precisely resembles the slave-trade; the immigrant is hired free, but he is not brought free to the sea-shore.

3. The surveillance organized to suppress abuses is loyal and laborious, but inefficient. Numerous and horrible facts prove this.

I have confidence in those who *ransom;* I honor and admire those who *watch;* but I distrust those who *transport;* I am convinced of the barbarity of those who *sell;* I have doubts as to the consent of those who *are sold;* I have little belief in the reconciliation.

These serious motives, and too well founded scruples, inspired the letter addressed by the Emperor, in 1858, to the prince, charged with the direction of the colonies: —

"SAINT CLOUD, October 30, 1858.

"MY DEAR COUSIN: —

"I ardently desire that, at the moment when the difference

with Portugal respecting the *Charles-Georges* has just terminated, the question of contracting for free laborers on the coast of Africa should be definitively examined, and resolved in accordance with the true principles of justice and humanity. I have earnestly demanded of Portugal the restitution of the *Charles-Georges*, because I shall always maintain intact the independence of the national flag; and in this circumstance, the profound conviction of its right alone could have induced me to risk the disruption of the friendly relations which I take pleasure in sustaining with the King of Portugal.

"But as to the principle involved in contracts for negroes, my ideas are far from fixed. If, indeed, the laborers hired on the coast of Africa have no free will, and *if this contracting be nothing more than a disguised slave-trade, I will not have it at any price.* For I will not be the one to protect enterprises anywhere that are contrary to progress, humanity, and civilization.

"I entreat you, therefore, to investigate the truth with the zeal and intelligence which you bring to all matters to which you apply yourself, and, as the best manner of putting an end to the continual causes of conflict would be to substitute the free labor of East Indian coolies for that of negroes, I invite you to join with the Minister of Foreign Affairs in resuming the negotiations with the English government which were entered upon a few months ago. Upon which, my dear cousin, I pray God to have you in his holy keeping.

"NAPOLEON."

A commission was appointed, and at the close of its labors, the engagement of negroes on the western coast of Africa was suspended, but without annulling anterior treaties. Negotiations have been resumed with England for the engagement of coolies, and, thanks to the address of one of the delegates from the Isle of Bourbon,* a treaty concluded at London, July 25, 1860, in spite of vehement and unjust criticism,† secures to this colony 6,000 East Indians. One of the stipulations of the treaty of 1860 with China secures the liberty to import Chinese.

China and India, — here are two immense territories where the colonies can find free laborers, *officina gentium*; and these reservoirs are vast enough for none to have the right to complain, if forbidden to draw elsewhere. Nevertheless, no laborer is as good as the African. How procure him? How render justifiable a most natural operation?

It is criminal on two sides, — slavery in the colonies, barbarism in Africa. Slavery in the colonies is destroyed; nothing more remains but to destroy barbarism in Africa. Such is the reply of the illustrious traveller, David Livingstone, and this great name will quickly check the derisive smile or saddened sigh of those who denounce this reply as chimerical.

God be praised! After so many centuries of remorseless iniquity, after a lamentable series of guilty operations which have sunk Africa in brutishness, without carrying to the possessions of Europe either lasting wealth or even sufficient population, humanity is brought back by experience to justice, interest itself preaches duty; what the exploitation of Africa has not produced, may be expected of the exploration and evangelization of Africa.

This point deserves to arrest attention.

* M. Imhaus.

† See the debate in the House of Commons, March 8, 1860, and the speech of Mr. Cave. "Las Casas delivered up the negroes to save the Indians; this was at least to deliver up the strong to spare the weak; you do the contrary. Will the loyalty of our subjects be insured by their sojourn in a foreign nation, which may become hostile?" etc.

III.

THE EXPLORATION AND EVANGELIZATION OF AFRICA.

AFRICAN CIVILIZATION.

I repeat it, these words will call forth on many lips a smile of sadness or incredulity. If Africa be not civilized, it will be said it is not Europe that should be blamed for it, but the Creator, — He who placed on an inhabitable territory a population unsusceptible of civilization. Is it our fault if the climate of Africa is fatal to the whites, if the negroes, with their great, soft, simple eyes, their ridiculous features, and their gross instincts, have not grown, have not changed, since the beginning of the world? Have you not remarked, as it were, a mysterious irony in the distribution of the gifts of God over the globe? See the Hollanders, — those men so intelligent and proud, who do honor to our species and its Author, — their soil is a heap of mud. The African, on the contrary, on whose brow, of all beings, the stamp of the Divine workman seems the most effaced, is the lord of a domain where everything is grand and colossal; large animals, the lion, the elephant, and the tiger, the largest fish that exist, the largest vegetation, the baobab and mimosa, large rivers, large mountains, and large lakes, — man alone is grovelling and diminished. Four thousand years have passed, four thousand years will again pass, over this species with the name of man and the rank of the beast. What can we do in the presence of this mystery? Scarcely comprehend, by no means modify it.

We Frenchmen should be willing to do what is beyond our power.*

How arrive at the heart of Africa?

Through Algeria?

The four countries of less imperfect civilization which occupy the north of Africa compose, as it were, an island between the ocean, the Mediterranean, the Red Sea, and that other ocean called the desert. The rare commodities of Europe which make their way to Soudan or Nigritia land at Mogadore or Tripoli. From Tripoli they reach Mourzouk or Gadams, and from Mourzouk to Bornou, on the shores of Lake Tchad, needs forty more days' hard march. From Mogadore to Timbuctoo requires fifty days. The caravans, provided with animals endowed, like the negroes, with the *painful faculty of always suffering*, advance under scorching rays, through the wind and sand, hoping to fall in at distant intervals with a little water at the bottom of a well, sometimes dried up, and threatened at every step with meeting dangerous animals or men more dangerous than nature. Gadams is at least near the Mediterranean, but Constantinople or Tuggurt is far to the north, separated from Soudan by the Moors and Touaregs no less than by the desert.

Would we penetrate by the eastern or western coast?

There is scarcely a spot on these coasts where, attracted at first by a beautiful sky, smiling shades, or severe landscapes, Europeans do not encounter fever, dysentery, exhaustion, and death.

Why expose one's self to so many fatigues? no longer to barter slaves, as formerly, but a little gum or ivory, inferior cotton, peanuts, indigo, ostrich-feathers and gold-dust for cloths, guns, glass beads, and bracelets.

* *Note sur le commerce du Soudan avec le nord de l'Afrique*, by M. Jules de Lasteyrie, in the sequel of the report of Gen. de Bellonet on the supplementary appropriations for Algeria, May 26, 1844; *Moniteur*, p. 1525. See, on the other side, the speech of M. de Corcelle, Ibid., p. 1635.

Is it worth while, for these doubtful or paltry results, to give the life of a European, more precious than that of a hundred negroes?

To these discouraging words I oppose the instincts of faith and the lessons of experience.

That God has made so numerous a population in so beautiful a land without design I cannot believe, without outraging him. We are accustomed to a lofty ideal of civilization, we have listened to M. Guizot's admirable definitions of the twofold individual and social movement which constitutes the progress of nations, and, placed ourselves so high, raising our ideas even far above our customs, we let fall on the inhabitants of Darfour or Congo a look of disdainful pity. But, in the humble reality of facts, do not all the smaller members of the human family strongly resemble each other? The peasant of Sologne, the wood-cutter of the Alps, the Laplander among his snows, the miner of Siberia, the Baskir of the Ural, the Coolie of the mountains of India, the Chinese boatman, the Mexican Indian, the Brazilian diamond-seeker,—in what does their condition differ from that of the Makololo visited by Livingstone or the Toukouleur of Senegal? Have you ever thought on the condition of the great majority of human beings? Of the twenty-four hours of the day, one half is spent by all mankind in reposing, feeding, and clothing themselves; that is, in preserving themselves from death. Of a million men, nine hundred thousand at least are occupied in preparing the food, clothing, or dwellings of themselves or others, and the heavy labor which the necessity of preserving life thus imposes upon almost all men, holds them curbed in the same manner under the weight of the same destiny. The condition of the inhabitants of the African continent is neither higher nor lower, and their origin was the same; the antiquities of Egypt are worth as much as the Peruvian antiquities, and in the beginning all the races seem on the same level. It is true, that almost all peoples have elevated themselves, were it but for a moment, from their native nothingness; a few were more intelligent; they have aided the others and improved themselves; on the soil of Africa, on the contrary, we meet a population, but no communities.

But the incomparable advantage of the Sologne peasant over his fellows in misery throughout the human race, is that he belongs to a regular community. In the most wretched village of Europe I find (yet this is not everywhere, nor has it been common long) a church, a school, a road, a market or tradesmen. To what does the inhabitant owe all this? To civilization; and from what proceeds civilization? Three fundamental causes, — reason, education, and revelation.

I grant that the European surpasses all the races in reason, and I directly conclude from it that it is destined by God to be the preceptor of the rest. I see climates which can neither be inhabited by the whites alone, for they do not labor there, nor from the blacks alone, for they do not progress there; and I perceive a mixed race, sprung from the fusion of their blood, which, more vigorous than the one, more intelligent than the other, might people and civilize the tropical lands. I conclude from this that the conjunction and blending of these races were in the views of Providence. I see, finally, that God has confided the torch of the Christian faith to the race which he charged with civilizing the others; and I again conclude from this that the propagation of the Gospel is the mission of Europe, the medium of civilization between the Creator and his creatures on earth. What the superior classes are to the inferior in a regulated community, Europe is to the human race in the world.

But which of its duties has Europe ever fulfilled towards Africa? What good has she carried it? What harm has she not wrought it? What interest does Europe take in Africa?

Apart from the annals of the countries which border on Europe, what do we know of the history of Africa? Nothing. Herodotus made mention of it in a few words. *Twenty-three centuries* after him, we have learned a little more; in this immense interval, a few half-fabulous relations, a few letters from Portuguese navigators, a few abandoned attempts at missions or stations have brought us only some trifling incorrect or incomplete details, which may still be summed up as follows, — wretchedness, pillage, slavery, ferocity, fetichism, and brutishness.

What do we know of its geography? Until very lately, the maps of Africa have been covered with two sentences, — *a vast desert, — unknown countries,* — and many honest men remain persuaded, with Sallust,* that this part of the world is an accursed region, where the earth is sterile sands, and the sun a devouring caldron, and where the animal kingdom is represented by tigers and serpents, and the human species by ferocious and stupid varieties of the species of apes.

What have we done for this people? We have made it an article of traffic. During many centuries, we have drawn these negro masses from their unknown retreats to devote them to furnishing our breakfasts with coffee and sugar, as we extricate charcoal from the bowels of the earth, to heap it up, sell it, and consume it.

What have we done to carry into this darkness the torch of Jesus Christ? Thus answers a learned and pious writer: † —

"Africa seems to recall to religion naught but funereal

* After a few words concerning the Getulians, Numidians, Persians, Medes, and Phœnicians in Africa, Sallust adds: "Super Numidiam Gætulos accepimus partim in tuguriis, alios incultius vagos, agitare; post eos Æthiopos esse, *dein loca exusta solis ardoribus.*" (*Jugurtha,* XVIII. p. 19.)

† *Vie du Père Libermann,* by Don Pitra, 1855, Chap. VII. p. 432.

memories, — five centuries of efforts to plant the cross at a few points, the rapidity with which flourishing Christian communities have disappeared by unheard-of catastrophes, the ruins everywhere accumulated from the Thebaids of Egypt to the last of the five hundred churches of Christian Africa, so many scourges which barbarism causes to weigh upon a people, and which civilization has only augmented by all the miseries of slavery. One would say, from the general aspect, that a predestination of misfortune hovers mysteriously over this vast continent. . . . . .

"On the western coast, during more than fifteen centuries, none of those apostles came hither who followed all the routes of the ancient mariners, none of those Irish missionaries who searched out the islands and seas, and landed on every shore. It appears that the Normans opened stations there at an early date, without announcing the good news of faith, before the arrival of the Portuguese, at the end of the fifteenth century. The Franciscans and Dominicans shared this new field with great emulation of zeal; numerous churches, a bishop of Congo, and a dynasty of Christian kings were seen; then all disappeared in a civil war, under the invasion of ferocious tribes. In 1547, four Jesuits attempted unsuccessfully to upraise the Church. At successive times, the Company of Jesus, the French Capuchins, and the Spanish Franciscans made new efforts. The desolation was consummated by the fanaticism of the Dutch, at the close of the seventeenth century, and the conquests of the English, during the last century."

How could Christianity have become established?

"The slave-trade carried away yearly by hundreds of thousands the very tribes evangelized by the missionaries. Fourteen million souls could not disappear from these coasts without exasperating all the interior tribes, without fomenting abominable wars among them, without attaching to the Christian name an ineffaceable odium. It is not necessary to add to this scourge the scandalous spectacle of European morals, the cupidity and ambition of Christian nations."

Mark what a bishop writes to the Propaganda, in 1819, after a visit to the Angola Mission: —

"Illam aspexi, mœrorem concepi, lacrymas effudi, quia omnia, si fas est dicere, sine duce, sine luce, sine cruce inveni. Omnia desunt; desunt sacerdoces, ob defectum illos instruendi, et qui existunt sunt omnino ignari; desunt ecclesiæ, quia omnes vel dirutæ sunt, vel quasi dirutæ apparent. Religio est pene extincta." *

While Christianity has become extinct, Islamism has been rekindled. Africa had white races; they have received from Europe the Islamism which sterilizes them: Africa had black races; they have received from Europe the slave-trade which devotes them to war and brutishness. By an odious exchange between the inhabitants of the two continents, they give us diseases, we carry them vices, and Africa has unceasingly received from Europe the abhorrence of all that could civilize it, — religion, labor, commerce, contact with the white race.

Ah! if we could do it no good, at least why do it so much harm?

But is it true that the good is impossible?

Thank Heaven, the dawn of better days seems breaking. Wherever, indeed, any serious attempt has been essayed, it has succeeded.

On looking at the map, which we should always have before our eyes in all these questions, for God himself has drawn the map of the world, we cannot help foreseeing that, if a new division of the earth among the children of Christ is drawing near, like the ancient division among the

* "I have seen, I have groaned, I have wept, finding everything almost without light, without faith, without the cross. Everything is lacking, — priests, because they cannot be instructed, and those who exist are wholly ignorant; churches, destroyed or in ruins. Religion is wellnigh extinct."

sons of Noah, Asia appears designed for the influence of Russia, America and Australia for the invading industry of the Anglo-Saxon race, and Africa for the genius of the Latin races, headed by France.

This great movement has commenced.

Bold expeditions of our officers have proved that communication can be established between Algeria and Soudan.* In 1843, it was denied that this communication was practicable or desirable. In 1851, another official commission feared that the incursions of the Mahometans would oppose an insurmountable obstacle.† In 1860, the Minister of the Colonies asked the Emperor to throw down a third barrier, which was neither the Arabs nor the desert, but the custom-house; and the frontier of Algeria was opened to the importation, free of duties, of natural and manufactured products from Sahara and Soudan. The report which preceded the decree of 1860 was couched as follows: * —

"SIRE: —

"Before the conquest by France of Algeria, the caravans which brought the products of Sahara and Soudan to the markets of Northern Africa bent their course, according to their needs or preferences, towards Algiers, Tunis, or Morocco.

"Doubtless, when we had to fight the Arabs to extend and enforce the acceptance of our rule; when the country could not present the security indispensable to trade; when

* *Sahara*, by Gen. Daumas; *Le Sahara et le Soudan*, Arabic documents translated by the Abbé Bargès, *Revue de l'Orient*, February and June, 1853; *Voyage du commandant Bonnemain à R'damès*, 1856, 1857; *Explorations de M. de Colomb*, 1858, 1860; *Route de Tuggurt à Tombouctou*, by M. Cherbonneau, 1860; *Du commerce de l'Algérie avec l'Afrique centrale*, by M. Carette, 1843; Report to the Chamber of Commerce of Algiers on the same subject, 1860, etc. I am indebted for these documents to M. Jules Delarbre.

† Report of M. Benoist d'Azy, p. 5.

‡ *Bulletin officiel des colonies*, No. 85, p. 440, Decree, No. 1023.

finally, we had before us people who comprehended neither our designs nor the advantages of our civilization, the current of trade which formerly existed between Central Africa and the countries which we occupy was forced to turn aside and flow towards Tunis, Tripoli, or the kingdom of Fez.

"But now that peace is re-established, that the safest routes are those which traverse the territory subject to our authority, finally, that the renown of our arms and of the benefits of our power has penetrated beyond the desert, there would be nothing to hinder caravans laden with the productions of Soudan from coming, as formerly, to enrich the Algerian markets, and to demand in exchange all that our industry can offer them, had not the custom-house legislation of 1843 opposed an insuperable barrier by laying an absolute prohibition on everything that they might bring us.

"It is this barrier, Sire, that I come to entreat your Majesty to destroy.

"The moment has come to form close commercial relations with these countries, the mysteries of which a few of our intrepid travellers have more than once sought to penetrate. The chiefs of the Touaregs have already come as far as Algiers, where they have been able to form an idea of our civilization; they have loudly expressed their admiration of the abundance and variety of the merchandise which our warehouses displayed to their eyes; finally, these Touaregs, whose trade consists, above all, in serving as intermediums between the traders of Northern Africa and the producers of Soudan, and transporting articles of barter, have shown themselves fully disposed to bring back part of their caravans to Algeria.

"To second a movement which can only be profitable to all our interests, the first thing to be done, Sire, is to authorize on the southern frontier of Algeria the introduction, free of duties, of all productions of Soudan and Sahara.

"My colleagues of the departments of the finances and trade think, with me, that nothing opposes this measure, and have given their full assent to the bill of a decree which, while maintaining the provisions of anterior legislation as to the introduction, under certain duties, of products arriving by the eastern and western frontiers, and destined to encounter similar products in Algeria, removes all prohibitions laid upon the products of Central Africa, and frees them from all taxation.

"Inspired by the liberal views of the Emperor, this decree, which I have the honor to submit to the approbation of your Majesty, is destined to procure new markets for our arts and manufactures, to extend its relations with countries until now almost unknown, and thus to open vast horizons to the beneficent influence of our civilization."

"Despite the incontestable superiority of Mahometan nations over those which are still subject to the superstitions of Fetichism, it is not probable that civilization can penetrate by this means into the interior of Africa.

"The Mahometan religion stagnates everything that it touches; it is the enemy of all progress, of all action, of more enlightened Christian nations. . . . . . Relations with the coasts are more easy."

In the report which contains these words, — a report which is a veritable masterpiece of precision, knowledge, and humanity, the president of the commission of the trade and stations of Africa, M. Benoist d'Azy,* has fully established that almost all of our settlements of any importance on the coasts have, or might have, succeeded.

He already attached a high importance to the possession of Senegal, a possession more valuable than Guiana, which secures to us, with the monopoly of the gum trade, the

* We formerly possessed twenty-one forts or stations on the western coast. (*Notices*, by M. Roy, p. 77.)

navigation of a large river, navigable 240 leagues from its mouth, and with an active and numerous population on either shore. Nevertheless, at this epoch, the French settled at St. Louis, near the mouth of the Senegal, with a station at Bakel, at the head of the river, and a branch at Senovdeboo, in Falama, were traders rather than owners, and the Moors on the right bank tormented them unceasingly. From 1854, after the glorious struggles headed by Colonel Faidherbe, we became masters of the Senegal, from the cataracts of Feloo to St. Louis, that is, a distance of more than sixty miles. The government no longer pays tribute, has signed treaties, and peacefully possesses vast territories. Trade is increasing, agriculture is developing. There are no more slaves.

At the extremity of Cape Verde, the island of Gorea is becoming a free entrepot of more and more importance, from which arise the stations of Portendick, Sedhiou, and Caravan Island.*

On the great coast of 800 leagues which extends below Senegambia, Grand Bassam and Assynia support each other, and trade with the Gold Coast,† almost entirely occupied by the English and Dutch, and the country of the Ashantees whose capital, Coomassie, has not less than 60,000 or 80,000 inhabitants; farther south, Gaboon ‡ is a military post indispensable to our cruisers, and a promising station, with an admirable harbor, in the midst of a populous and fertile country. These stations cost little; cultivation on a small scale is increasing there, as well as commerce. The trade in peanuts alone represented, in 1851, 30,000 tons,

* Upon which is the principal establishment of M. Bocandé, who has kindly given me information which fully confirms all that I affirm respecting the progress of commerce and free labor.

† *Commerce et mœurs de la côte d' Or*, by Capt. Peuchgaric, Sen. Paris, Rouvier, 1857.

‡ *Revue coloniale*, New Series, XI. p. 382; XII. p. 126; XIII. p. 468; XIV. p. 245.

employing 150 ships and 1,500 sailors, half the production of the sugar of the colonies.

On the eastern coast, almost divided, from the Red Sea to the Cape, between the possessions of the Imam of Muscat and the magnificent regions nominally and uselessly held by Portugal, we possess nothing except the little island of Mayotte, where we have abolished slavery since 1846, and whose rapid progress will still increase when regular communication shall have been established with Bourbon.

We speak only of the settlements of France; that is, of the nation which has the least taste for distant settlements. It would be to make a parade of a sterile erudition, for erudition is not experience, to enumerate the stations of England, whose flag floats, not only at the Cape and Sierra Leone, but over almost all the western coasts,* at the same time that its captains obtain treaties from numerous chiefs which English diplomacy carefully locks up in its portfolios as so many claims to be one day enforced on this as yet valueless portion of the patrimony of mankind. The stations succeed with little expense; the trade with the coasts, and also with the interior, is already enormous.

Holland, America, Denmark, Spain, and Portugal are represented on the same coasts, and Africa is cognizant of all the flags of Europe. Commerce increases in exact proportion to the diminution of the slave-trade. In 1848 Admiral Bouet † prepared an ingenious map, the lines of which, following the western coast of Africa, indicate, by the difference of their colors and breadths, the importance on each point of the trade in gold (*yellow*, Gold Coast and

* *Description nautique des côtes de l'Afrique occidentale*, by M. E. Bouet-Willaumez, 1849; *Voyage du capitaine Guillain;* Map of M. Brossard de Corbigny, 1861. From Cape Verde to the Gulf of Biafra, England has twelve stations, and France two.

† *Commerce et traite des noirs aux côtes occidentales d'Afrique*, by M. Bouet-Willaumez, Jan. 1, 1848.

coast of the Bissagots), gum (*pale-yellow*, Senegal), palm-oil (*green*, Grain Coast, Sierra Leone, Ivory Coast, Calabar), hides (*light green*, coast of Senegambia), rice, maize, and peanuts (*blue*, Grain Coast), wood (*red*, coast of Gaboon), wax (*red*, coasts of Congo and Angola), ivory (*white*, coasts of Benin, Gaboon, etc.), lastly, men (*black*, Bissagot, Grain Coast, Benin, Loango, Congo, Angola, and Benguela). Were this map to be revised to-day, the *black* would be seen to diminish and the *red* or *blue* to increase in a reciprocal proportion. Since this epoch, Senegal, which had, in 1837, a commerce amounting to $ 2,500,000, saw it rise to $ 4,600,000 in 1847, and to $ 4,000,000 in 1856, and Gorea, which had lived only *by* and *for* the slave-trade during two centuries, until our repossession in 1818, in ten years more than tripled its commerce,* and figured in the preceding statistics at $ 1,157,341 in 1845, and $ 1,719,495 in 1856.

Before the stations, I should have named the missionaries.

The population of Africa is divided between a senseless Fetichism and a gross Mahometanism.

Mahometanism, which is in its death-throes in Europe, is growing in Africa; it shows itself there as in the days of its birth, invading, warlike, implacable. Before a century, if Africa be not Jesus Christ's, it will be Mahomet's, and Europe will be forced to cope for new centuries with this rude enemy, easy as yet to anticipate or suppress.

Animated by apostolic zeal, sustained by the alms of the *Work for the Propagation of the Faith*, religion has established in this unhappy land courageous missions, beacons in the darkness, oases in the moral desert.

In a few houses built of boards, aided by paltry subsidies, under an unhealthy sky, in the midst of natives who are ignorant of the faith, and Europeans who dishonor it, a handful of priests relieve each other through the whole

* *Notices*, by M. Roy, pp. 73, 79. Gorea and its dependencies have been separated administratively from Senegal by a decree of November 21, 1854.

length of the coast, and, despite these ungrateful conditions, they build churches, open schools, form blacksmiths, tailors, weavers, and gardeners, evangelize in six tongues, prevent human sacrifices, and all repeat that the black race is most accessible to Christianity when not estranged from it by Christians themselves.*

It is needless to say, that wherever England and America have entered, Protestantism has entered in their train. Catholics may deplore this; but let us be wise enough to recognize frankly that it is a great honor to these nations always thus to carry their religion with them. Let the Catholics also endeavor always to plant the cross in every place where they set foot. Let us add, that Protestantism is assuredly great progress for people devoted to the worship of the serpent, to bloody sacrifices, or to Mahometanism; it takes them from complete Paganism and leaves them halfway to the perfect truth.

To nations that have awaited the Son of God for six thousand years, we bear, alas! a divided truth, and I know of no more grievous obstacle to the propagation of the Gospel. But the men who have the courage to spread it in the centre of Africa, whatever be their communion, are men who honor humanity and serve it. It is impossible to read their narratives † without emotion. Livingstone admirably remarks, that "all classes of Christians find that sectarian rancor soon dies out when they are working together among and for the real heathen."

It was, moreover, the zeal of the Protestant missions which attracted the Catholic missions. Alarmed for the

* In the greater part of the Portuguese churches religion is not only dead, but corrupted, which is much worse. Livingstone remarks (Missionary Travels, p. 644), that there is not a single bookseller's shop on either the eastern or western coast of Africa. At Loanda, a town of 10,000 or 12,000 inhabitants, there is not a library.

† *Les Bassoutos*, by M. Cazalis, Paris, 1860; Twenty-Three Years in the South of Africa, by Robert Moffat, 1846, etc.

salvation of the negroes re-exported from America to Africa, the American bishops loudly demanded the attention of the Propaganda, and an Apostolic Vicar was despatched thither in 1840. Since, in 1843, Upper and Lower Guinea have received the heroic missionaries of that holy father, Libermann, who, when questioned on the condition of his establishments by a parliamentary commission, replied humbly, "We can do but one thing, — to die." And, indeed, of the first seven missionaries, at the end of two months a single one survived, who passed two years for dead, struggling at once against the negroes and the Methodists, and was discovered, in 1845, to be living; — this was M. Bessieux, since bishop and founder of the mission of Upper and Lower Guinea. Seventy-five missionaries followed each other on this field of battle; twenty are dead, nineteen have renounced it, twenty-six persevere in the midst of 3,500 Catholics and 50,000,000 heathen, disseminated in Nigritia and over 1,500 leagues of coast.

The same zeal animates the missionaries who are evangelizing Tripoli, Tunis, Upper and Lower Egypt, the Gallas, Abyssinia, the Seychelles, the Cape, and Madagascar. It equally animates the priests of Algeria and Senegal, unfortunately fettered by the habits of a law which contents itself with suffering the different creeds to live in peace, thinking to avoid their disputes by arresting their progress, as if, for truth, it were living not to grow.

In 1859 the Holy See founded a bishopric at Sierra Leone. In 1860 a vicar-general of the Isle of Bourbon, the Abbé Fava, went to the island of Zanzibar to establish a sisterhood, then to found on the eastern shore a mission full of promise, the only point where an altar is erected to Jesus Christ on a thousand leagues of coast inhabited by myriads of human beings, and enriched with all the gifts of God.

Rivals, precursors of missionaries or missionaries themselves, ambassadors of civilization, heralds announcing to the world the coming of truth, and preparing the way for it, heroic travellers, Barth, Vogel, Richardson, Overweg, Baikie, Livingstone, Burton, Speke, Guillain, the brothers d'Abbadie, and Raffenel, intrepid successors of Mungo Park, Anderson, Caillé, Denham, and Clapperton, are exploring Central Africa, Soudan, Abyssinia, the course of the Niger, the shores of Lake Tchad, in every direction; from Bernghazi to the Cape of Good Hope, they march from one coast to the other, teaching Africa the worth of Europeans, and Europe what is contained in Africa.*

While we read the journals, or go on 'Change or to the theatre, eight or ten intrepid men, differing in nation, bold representatives of the whole human race, go thus one by one to face death through love of science. The ones are the martyrs, the others the heroes of science and humanity.

Richardson set out in 1850, touched at Tripoli, gained Mourzouk, then advanced to the country of Bornou, explored Lake Tchad, and died, March 4, 1851, at forty-one years of age, alone, six days' journey from Kouka. A few days before, he dreamed that a bird descended from heaven, and alighted on the branch of a tree, when the branch broke and the bird fell to the ground; this dream gave him a presentiment of his death. His companion, Overweg, succumbed, Sept. 27, 1852, at thirty years of age. Barth survived them, undertook alone the journey to Timbuctoo, entered it, Sept. 7, 1853, twenty-five years after René Caillé (April 20, 1828), sojourned there six months, and, returning to Kouka, had the happiness to meet, in the midst of a vast forest, Dr. Vogel (Dec. 1, 1854), who was destined, after admirable labors, to die in Waday, while Barth, more fortunate, brought back to Europe the scientific trophies of their common enterprise.

* I know of nothing more interesting than the short, complete, and graphic *résumés* of M. Malte-Brun concerning the greater part of these travels.

† Letter of Dr. Barth (*Revue coloniale*, 1855, p. 109).

Livingstone set out from the Cape on his first journey, which conducted him in 1849 from Kolobeng, 187 miles north of the Kuruman mission, 1,000 miles from the Cape, to Lake N'gami, 504 miles north of Kolobeng; he returned thither in 1850 with Mrs. Livingstone, then returned a third time in 1851, attained Linyanti, and then the Zambesi, a magnificent river, which, pursuing its course to the Mozambique Channel, is destined to become the highway of travellers and missionaries to the unknown centre of Africa. He set out, June 8, 1852, on his fourth voyage, traversed all Africa from the Cape to Loanda, on the western coast, which he reached March 31, 1854, after having a thousand times escaped the jaws of death; then set out again eastward, following the course of the Zambesi, the beautiful river which he calls the companion of his travels, and, May 26, 1855, reached Quilimane, on the eastern coast, having for the first time explored Southern Africa from coast to coast. On the 11th of December, 1856, he embraced his wife and children at London. What is he doing at this moment? Making a new exploration of Africa.

These martyrs, these heroes, these great men, have brought back from their travels a threefold harvest, for the benefit of geography, commerce, and humanity.

Where the map, in the place of the countries visited by Livingstone, bore the words, *Great, elevated, and desert plateaus,* must now be read, *Great, deep, and populous valleys.* Where history, with respect to the regions explored by Barth, gave the definition, *Savage and dispersed nomadic tribes,* must be now read, *Agglomerate populations in towns considerably advanced in civilization.* Below and above the equator, Livingstone and Barth, to use the expression of Malte-Brun, have discovered a *New Africa.* In the one, traders; in the other, admirable products. Botany is too modest a science; it might, as does ethnography, for basins and climates, found a theory of the influence of vegetation on mankind; there would be the peoples of the grass, changing place with their flocks, or pitching and striking their tent-pole according as the seed falls into the furrow or the ear into the sheaf; the people of the palm and the olive, forced to become sedentary, because the shrub which rules them demands years of care; the people of wheat, the people of cotton, the people of tobacco, the people of the forest. Africa presents a thousand arguments in favor of this theory; God has sown upon its territory the most admirable variety of vegetation, its peoples are nomadic or sedentary, pastoral, agricultural, or even industrial, according to the plant which is born in their midst; the people follow in some sort the manners of the plants, but there is need that commerce should teach them to multiply cultivation by exchange. But great travellers have brought proofs that products for exchange are innumerable; cotton, to mention but one, grows in a native state throughout almost all Central Africa, and the quality is easily improved by better seeds. An intelligent society, founded at Manchester, in anticipation of the crisis which threatens the cotton of the United States, the *Cotton Supply Society*, has already carefully pointed out several points of Africa, especially our Senegal, as being as well suited as Egypt to the cultivation of this precious shrub.* It is a whole future of wealth, and also of liberty; for all travellers attest that we no longer sell men when it is to our interest to sell things.

The discovery of great rivers, which are the natural routes towards the centre, is rendered more valuable by

* See an exact summary of the report made to this society (March, 1861) in the useful *Journal d'agriculture coloniale*, by M. Paul Madinier. See also the *Crise américaine au point de vue de l'industrie du coton*, by M. John Ninet (*Revue des Deux-Mondes*, March, 1861), and by M. Justin Améro (*Correspondant*, May, 1861).

the verification of the important fact that the central regions are more salubrious than the coasts.*

Maritime expeditions, scientific explorations, and religious missions thus vie with each other in bringing us testimony that Africa is not inaccessible to the European, that the African refuses neither religion, nor agriculture, nor commerce.

With a common voice, scholars, mariners, and missionaries repeat to us that slavery and the slave-trade have been fatal to religion, agriculture, and commerce, but that commerce, agriculture, and religion are fatal to the slave-trade and slavery.†

With a common voice, they affirm to us finally, that, to light the torch in this darkness, but two or three European settlements are needed, extended, substantial, provided with the means of navigation, comprising a vast, well-defined territory, — places of refuge, as it were, where population ‡ will be seen to flow in, cultivation to prosper, and civilization to grow by degrees.

To these centres of civilization, warmly recommended by Livingstone, we might have recourse, after a few years, without danger, to supply our colonies with free immigrants, who might already be readily engaged, if, for the last three centuries, Europe had done Africa as much good as it has done it harm. We also perceive too late that evil is always a bad speculation, and continually return by a long circuit to seek, even through interest, the good which we despised.

* Gov. Faidherbe also attests the great diminution of mortality among Europeans at Bakel, in Upper Senegal. (Senegal in 1859, *Correspondant*, 1860, p. 310).

† Richardson had for the end of his journey the abolition of slavery. It was also the passion of Livingstone, and he was often protected in his journey because it was learned that he was of *the nation friendly to negroes*.

‡ It is known that since slavery has disappeared from the region of Tunis, numerous slaves have taken refuge there, in order to become free.

I close with these distant but consoling prospects, this incomplete chapter.

On January 31, 1848, Père Libermann wrote to Eliman, king of Dakar: —

"Jesus Christ, the Son of God, the God of the Christians, the God of all the universe, loves all men alike; blacks as well as whites, all are his well-beloved brethren. . . . . I am a servant of Jesus Christ; he wishes me to love all men as he loves them; but he inspires me with a much warmer and tenderer love for his dear brethren, the black men."

On February 15, 1856, David Livingstone wrote to Mr. Maclear: —

"I am not so puffed up as might be expected with having accomplished the journey over the continent. The end of the exploration of the geographer is only the beginning of the enterprise of the missionary. That I may have the honor of doing some little good to this poor degraded and oppressed Africa is a wish in which, I doubt not, you will cordially join."

We read in another letter: —

"I hope to live long enough to see the twofold influence of the spirit of Christianity and of commerce dry up the bitter source of African misery."

We are no longer to despair of the transformation of Africa, since God has given it such friends.

BOOK SEVENTH.

CHRISTIANITY AND SLAVERY.

Christianity has destroyed slavery.

Yes, He who is pre-eminently the Redeemer, he who has ransomed woman from degradation, children from abandonment, subjects from tyranny, the poor from contempt, reason from error, the will from evil, the human race from punishment, Jesus Christ has restored fraternity to mankind and liberty to man, Jesus Christ has destroyed slavery.

I find this fact established or affirmed by the most impartial, the most severe, the most renowned writers ; it is written in a long series of laws, decisions, and canons, in an uninterrupted train of historical monuments. This imposing unanimity of testimony confirms the presentiments of universal instinct. Before all demonstration, we comprehend, we divine that Christianity must abolish slavery, as daylight abolishes darkness, because they are incompatible.

It is hackneyed, therefore, to attribute this magnificent boon to Christianity, and those even who contest it everything do not usually dispute this.

This is true, at least, on this side of the ocean ; but in America and Spain, the need of justifying what is practised leaves still some credit to the contrary assertion. In France and England, emancipation has thrown analogous dissertations into the shade. The time is not far off, however, when a well-known publicist * dared write : "*Chris-*

* M. Granier de Cassagnac, *Voyage aux Antilles,* Tom. II. p. 409.

tianity has always justified and maintained slavery." And, more recently, not to justify slavery, but to blacken Christianity, it has maintained, with a great show of erudition, that reason and philosophy can alone pretend to the honor of emancipating the slaves.*

The question of the influence of Christianity on emancipation is not so simple as is supposed, and the objections are worth the trouble of refuting anew, since they are of a nature to mislead many minds.

Consult the Old Testament, it is said : it sanctions slavery.

Open the New Testament : it is silent.

Read the writings of the Apostles : they counsel the slaves patience, far from promising them liberty.

The councils, the fathers, the popes, the modern theologians, hold the same language.

Consult history : slavery is maintained after Christianity ; destroyed, it springs up anew ; and, in fine, has been so far from abolished, that it still endures.

Against slavery, therefore, Christianity has said nothing, Christianity has done nothing.

We will take up this theory, word by word, preceding it by a brief summary of the history of slavery before Christianity.

* *Revue de Paris*, Article of M. Larroque, January, 1856.

CHAPTER I.

SLAVERY BEFORE CHRISTIANITY.

After admirable labors, devoted to this painful history by scholars of the first rank, after the patient researches of M. Édouard Biot and M. Yanoski,* after the writings, unhappily unfinished, of Moehler † and Mgr. England,‡ and the works of Guizot, Ozanam, Albert de Broglie, Troplong, Champagny, Wilberforce, Buxton, Balmès, and so many other eminent writers, and above all, after the great, scholarly, conscientious, and complete work of M. Wallon,§ it seems as if nothing remains to be added to the united erudition of France, Germany, England, America, and Spain.

I shall be proud and satisfied if I succeed but in summing up these excellent works, and communicating all their substance, and, as far as in me, all their enlightenment.

A cursory view of the history of slavery in the days of antiquity, and a special glance at slavery among the Jews, will conduct us, by an indispensable but brief road to the study of the means employed by Christianity to inaugurate liberty and equality into the world.

* *Abolition de l'esclavage ancien en Occident*, by M. Édouard Biot; *Abolition de l'esclavage ancien au moyen âge*, by M. J. Yanoski.

† *L'Abolition de l'esclavage par le christianisme dans les quinze premiers siècles*, by Moehler, translated by Abbé S. de Latreiche, and preceded by the *Dissertation sur les christianisme et l'esclavage*, by Abbé Thérou.

‡ Letters to John Forsyth on Domestic Slavery, by Dr. England, First Bishop of Charleston. Baltimore, 1849.

§ *Histoire de l'esclavage dans l'antiquité.*

I.

SLAVERY IN ANTIQUITY.

We must have the pain of repeating once more, to the shame of the human family, that, if all the greatest minds agree to-day in condemning slavery, all the greatest minds formerly agreed in justifying and practising it.* In Greece, Plato has sanctioned it in the name of politics; Aristotle, in the name of natural history; Epicurus, in the name of pleasure; Zeno, in the name of stoical indifference; Thucydides, in the name of history; Xenophon, in the name of social economy. Once himself a slave, Epictetus remains almost insensible to the ills of his fellows. Euripides does not experience the most transient emotion at the sight of these unfortunates; Aristophanes thinks it a good jest to show us Charon refusing them his bark; and old Hesiod coldly writes that the slave is to the rich what the ox is to the poor. At Rome, Cato likens the slaves to the worn-out cattle in his stable; Varro enumerates them among the implements of labor; † Cicero apologizes for too deeply regretting a slave; Pliny compares them to hornets; Lucretius troubles himself little about them; Horace derides them; Plautus calls them a race good for chains, *ferratile genus;* Seneca and Marcus Aurelius offer them barren consolations.

* See the original in the learned works of Wallon and Moehler. The little that I give belongs to them, — above all, to M. Wallon, whose book is, in my eyes, a veritable masterpiece.

† The text of Varro (Wallon, II. 189, note) is cynical indeed: "Instrumenti genus *vocale*, et *semivocale*, et *mutum;* vocale *in quo sunt servi;* semivocale, in quo sunt boves; mutum, in quo sunt plaustra." (*De re rustica,* I. xvii. 1.)

‡ The extent of the estates, and the difficulty of watching over numbers of slaves at a distance, resulted in causing the slaves to be put in irons. Cato, Varro, and Columella relate this without surprise, and Seneca contents himself with the phrase, *Necessitas fortiter ferre docet, consuetudo facile.* (Wallon, II. 217.)

I know that we lessen what we exaggerate. I have no intention of vilifying beyond measure the baseness of man in order to exalt the greatness of God: it is a mistaken philosophy to glorify the workman by depreciating his works. Christians have no need to be taught that man is capable by his own strength of a certain amount of goodness, since Christians profess that humanity, at the lowest degree of degradation, is still too noble to be unworthy the intervention of God.

I delight, therefore, in seeking and finding some traces of better sentiments in the Pagan authors. Aristotle quotes unknown philosophers who combated his doctrine; Plato hesitates; Plutarch censures the rigor of Cato; Seneca writes passages on equality so noble that they have been supposed secretly inspired by Christianity.* Some emperors, the Antonines, Claudius, and Diocletian, who was himself a freed slave, enacted the most human measures. Religion inspired some salutary customs, and established a few places of refuge, at the foot of the statues of Hercules and Theseus, liberating spirits, or of the emperors in the temples; so true is it that, as soon as the thought of God intervenes, the instinct of the equality of men in his sight becomes manifest. We should be glad also to find some examples of the gentleness of woman; all were not Messallinas; I believe without proof that the heart of woman was more than once, like the altar of the gods, a place of refuge for the unhappy slaves.

But what are these feeble vestiges, these conjectures, these shreds of phrases, by the side of the unanimity of doctrines, the universality of customs? These philosophers with sympathizing words, — were they *practising* philosophers, as is forcibly said of Christians who conform their

* 1 Ep. xlvii. Vol. II. p. 196, etc. "Servi sunt? Immo homines. . . . . . Hæc præcepti mei summa est: sic cum inferiore vivas, quemadmodum tecum superiorem belles vivere."

life to their faith? Did they love, did they free their slaves? Did they change the laws? Did they attack the institution as a crime?

No, all were persuaded of the doctrine of Aristotle: "The slave is the property of the master, without limit or restriction; not to belong to one's self, but fully to another, yet notwithstanding, not to cease to be a man, — this is slavery. . . . . . Whoever also is inferior to other men, the soul having the ascendency over the body, is a slave *by nature*." *

The slave is therefore of an inferior species.

But what? the slave Mycithus was the wise lawgiver of the Rhegians; Phædon, the friend of Plato, was a slave. How many other slaves were superior to their masters and to all the freemen? How many times, in the day of need, was it necessary to believe in equality! After the battle of Cannæ, it was thought good to free 8,000 slaves, and arm them.

It matters little. The animal engenders an animal, and the slave a slave.

Read books! Open the laws, especially those of Rome, which are most familiar to us.

In the most ancient times, under the republic, the slave was classed among things, *res mancipi;* he even received by preference the name *mancipium.*

A document recently discovered reveals to us to what degree this odious assimilation had reached, and how long it endured in practice. As Si Moktar, Cadi of Ouled Sellam, in the subdivision of Bathna, was constructing a water-mill in the spring of 1858, there was discovered in the excavation a *tariff of duties,* dated in the third consulate of Septimius Severus; that is, in the year 202 of our era, coming from the ruins of Zaraï, the ancient *Colonia Julia Zaraï.*

This is the first and only document of the kind that has

* Moehler, Chap. II.

been found throughout the whole extent of the Roman Empire.

Mark the rate of duties per head : —

A slave, ...	1½ denarii.
A horse or mare, . . .	"
A mule, ...	"
An ass or ox, ...	1 denarius.
A hog, ...	"
A sucking pig, . . .	"
A sheep, a goat, . . .	"

Two quotations from Papinianus, who wrote under Septimius Severus, inform us that the legal price of slaves was then fixed at 20 gold pieces, or 500 denarii.*

What was the valuation fixed by government upon a human being, endowed with an immortal soul? The same as a horse or a mule, a little more than an ass or a hog! This man, our brother and our fellow, might be given, pledged, let, bequeathed, ceded, sold, seized, lastly killed, *nullum caput habet.* For him, there was no civil state, no marriage, no paternity, no property, no right, no obligation, no claim in law, *servitus morti adsimilatur.* He was a witness only with torture, he did not acquire, he stipulated only for his masters. On holidays, the oxen were permitted to stand still, but not the slave. He was insulted, he was beaten; there was no recourse, unless it were damages due his master. What was the indemnity if he were killed? The same as for an ox or a mule, replies the Aquilian law.† But if he were guilty of faults, the rod, the whip, hard labor, chains, handcuffs, fetters, the fork, death by the sword, the axe, the precipice, the gibbet, the stake, the *cross.*

If the law permitted these horrors, how did the masters

* Report of M. Regnier, of the Institute, to the Prime Minister of Algeria. *Moniteur*, Dec. 6, 1858.

† "Idem juris est, si quis ex pari mularum unam occiderit." (Gaius, Inst. III. 211, 218.)

use the law? If such was the law, what were the customs? Save rare exceptions, where everything is permitted, everything is practised, human perversity goes even beyond what is permitted. The proofs superabound. The abominations described by the poets and satirists are affirmed by grave historians, demonstrated by the laws made to put an end to them. Disgust prevents us from making quotations. Picture to yourself, in the heart of paganism, a man given up to the anger of an idler, a woman abandoned to the luxury of a voluptuary, an old man intrusted to the generosity of a miser! What atrocities and vexations, from the wretch who fed his fishes on the flesh of his slaves, to the women who painted their faces while their bondwomen were lashed, or amused themselves by sticking pins into them for pastime. To cite but one incident, it is not generally enough known that the so much quoted line of Juvenal, *sic volo, sic jubeo*, refers to a slave condemned to crucifixion:—

> "Pone crucem servo. Meruit quo crimine servus
> Supplicium? Quis testis adest? Quis detulit? Audi!
> Nulla unquam de morte hominis cunctatio longa est.
> — O demens! ità servus homo est! Nil fecerit, esto!
> Sic volo, sic jubeo, sit pro ratione voluntas." *

Such was, for many centuries, the condition of human beings to be counted by hundreds of millions.

Greece and Rome — the whole world — quit their vast domain, consult the most ancient documents of the history of Germany or Scythia, search out the antique texts of India, pass over the then known portions of Africa, traverse Asia; in all places, in all latitudes, under the shelter of all religions, is the same spectacle of one half of humanity held in bondage by the other; slavery as ancient as

* Juv. II. 219-223. "To the cross with this slave!" "But has he deserved it by a crime! Where are the witnesses? What is the complaint? Listen; a man's life is well worth a moment's delay." "Fool! is a slave a man? He has done nothing; what matters it! I wish it, — I command it, — there is no reason but my will!"

war, is as ancient as human nature. What need of insisting further? These facts, like polytheism and human sacrifices, are among those which may be affirmed without dispute, while they cannot be dwelt upon without shame. They are the hereditary maladies of poor humanity.

Upon a single point the glance rests with a little more complaisance. Did the Jewish nation, the marvellous guardian of the true religion, sanction and practise slavery?

II.

SLAVERY AMONG THE JEWS.

It is in some sort hackneyed to repeat that Noah cursed Ham and condemned all his race to servitude, that Abraham and the patriarchs held slaves, that the Old Testament contains numerous texts in favor of this guilty institution, and that it rests, therefore, after all, upon one half of the Bible, admitting even that the New Testament condemns it. American dissertations especially are full of these assertions and of tiresome quotations which, were they correct, would still leave it to be demonstrated that the negroes are the direct descendants of Canaan, that the planters are like the patriarchs in everything,* and that

* Among all the replies which have been made to this kind of argument, much employed by the school of the apologists of slavery, which M. de Gasparin so well styles *cottony theology* (Barnes, Fletcher, etc.), I will cite a brief and precise article, published at Philadelphia in 1847, by W. H. Brisbane, under the title, "Slaveholding examined in the Light of the Holy Scriptures." I cannot resist the pleasure of quoting the opening passage: —

"Once a slaveholder myself, — born, reared, and educated in midst of masters and slaves, — I studied the subject at first with the zeal and energy of the warmest partisan of what is called the *peculiar institution*. I soon found myself embarrassed by the result of my own researches. I discovered my error; I became persuaded that slaveholding was iniquitous; I abandoned it, and my conscience made it a duty for me to free more than forty slaves. I have had to sacrifice the largest portion of my patrimony, to exile myself from the State where I was born, to break all my ties of family, friendship, and fellowship. I feel, consequently, that I have a right to a hearing." (Preface.)

all the historical facts related by the Bible are examples recommended by God himself!

We will take up each of these allegations.

I. We read in Genesis ix. 18,* that Ham was the father of Canaan. We know the irreverence of which Ham was guilty towards his father. To punish him, Noah said: —

"Cursed be Canaan; a servant of servants shall he be unto his brethren.

"Blessed be the Lord God of Shem; and Canaan shall be his servant.

"God shall enlarge Japheth, and he shall dwell in the tents of Shem; and Canaan shall be his servant."

It is concluded, from this passage, that the whole race of Ham, that is to say, the Africans, is accursed, and consequently condemned to serve the race of Shem and that of Japheth.

Canaan alone was cursed, and not the whole race of Ham. Where is the parish register which verifies the progeny of Ham? Where is the proof that these words had the meaning, and were destined to involve the effect, that it is chosen to attribute to them? I read, on the contrary, in history, that Canaan, doubtless the favorite child or the accomplice of Ham, is the first *mighty man* of whom mention is made in the annals of the human family; that the children of Ham, civilized before the other races, invented the earliest arts, founded the kingdom of Egypt, built Thebes and Babylon, and, in the land of Canaan, Sodom, Gomorrah, and that Sidon from which Inachus went to found the first city of Greece; that the posterity of Abraham, descending from Shem, served that of Ham in Egypt, before subjugating, in turn, after a long struggle, the land of Canaan, to fall again

* The Scriptural quotations are made in the original from the Catholic Bible. As the difference is chiefly in the form of expression, involving no essential point or sectarian distinction, I have thought it best, for convenience's sake, to use the Protestant version. The references being similar, the curious can compare the two. — Tr.

under the dominion of the sons of Ham at Babylon; that the Assyrians, the children of Shem, subjugated the Medes, the children of Japheth, and the Babylonians, the children of Ham; that Japheth (the Medes) in turn seized upon Shem (Nineveh); that Shem (the Persians), united with Japheth (the Medes), took Ham (Babylon).

But these were enslavements of nations by nations, and this it was that was predicted by Noah, who had not in view the slavery properly called of man to man. In fact, he said that Canaan should be *a servant of servants* to his brethren. Can any one be *the slave of another slave?* We comprehend, on the contrary, that one nation may be enslaved by another, which in its turn is subjugated by a third; and, indeed, the children of Ham were enslaved by the children of Shem, who fell under the dominion of the children of Japheth, since the Jews were reduced to servitude by the Persians, then with the latter by the Greeks under Alexander. In this sense, but in this sense alone, the prophecy of Noah has been realized.

Had it referred to a veritable slavery, is to predict slavery to justify it? In this case, adultery and war are justified, for they have been predicted. (Deuteronomy xxviii. 30, 68, 43; Jeremiah, Joel, etc.) Is to punish the wicked by predicting that they will be enslaved, to grant an amnesty to other wicked who will enslave them? In this case, the Jews are absolved for having crucified Jesus Christ, for it had been foretold.

Noah, Ham, and Canaan have nothing, therefore, to do with the planters of South Carolina.

II. No more can I recognize in their habits an image of the patriarchal life of Abraham or Laban.

It is true that there were slaves among the Israelites, and this was almost inevitable; for how, as Bergier remarks, at this epoch, and under the *régime* of tribes, how could a man quit his master without changing his country? How could the master have been free to discharge a slave without separating a family? Thence arose voluntary but permanent and hereditary engagements. Subjected to these engagements, were the servants true slaves? It is permissible to doubt it. Abraham sent away Hagar, but did not sell her. Genesis (xiii. 2) informs us that he was rich *in cattle, in silver, and in gold;* he does not number slaves among his riches; it shows them to us (xvii. 12, 13) treated like his family; they were armed and sent away on distant expeditions.* (Genesis xix. 14, 15.) One of them, in default of children, was destined to be his heir. (Genesis xv. 3.) His niece calls the first among them *my Lord.* (xxiv. 18.) Under the same name, the Bible assuredly comprises officers, subjects, servants, and, lastly, true slaves, those, which he had *bought for money of strangers.* The latter even appear to have been treated like the servants which he had with Lot, in the country of Nachor, or in Egypt, those given him by Abimelech, or those born in his house. Had he treated them more harshly, what would it matter? Are all of Abraham's examples law to Christians?

It is said of Isaac (Gen. xxvi. 14), that he *had possession of flocks, and possession of herds, and great store of servants.* The text does not indicate that he *possessed* the latter.

Doubtless it was written that Esau should serve Jacob, that Jacob had been made the lord, and that all his brethren had been given him for servants. (Genesis xxv. 23, xxvii. 37.) But history demonstrates that this subjection was wholly national; for the Edomites, the descendants of Esau, were none the less considered the brethren

* Compare this fact with the American laws. In *Virginia* slaves are forbidden to keep or carry arms. For this offence the laws of *Missouri* condemn a slave to thirty lashes; those of North Carolina and Tennessee to twenty lashes. By another provision of the laws of *Virginia,* a slave cannot leave the plantation of his master without a passport from him or his agents. (Barnes, p. 77.)

of the Jews (Deut. xxiii. 7), and Esau received from Isaac himself the promise that he should break the yoke of Jacob. (Gen. xxvii. 40.) The subjection by Joshua of the Gibeonites, condemned to have their lives spared, despite their fraud, but to be hewers of wood and drawers of water for the house of God (Joshua ix. 21, 23), a subjection, moreover, upon which *the Lord was not consulted* (Ibid. 14), and other subjections in question in the books of Samuel, Kings, and Job, are evidently in the same manner momentary reductions to servitude of a people conquered by a victorious people, and not examples of slavery, properly so called.

What inference is to be drawn from other texts which tell us that Laban *gave his servants* to his daughters for handmaids (Gen. xxix. 24, 29), or that Jacob had much cattle, and maid-servants, and men-servants, and camels, and asses? (Gen. xxx. 43.) Were real slaves in question? what proves it? who can affirm it?

III. By the side of the picture of patriarchal life, the Bible presents to us another picture, that of the captivity in Egypt. This is indeed true slavery, and the Nile has looked on the sufferings of which the Mississippi to-day is the witness.

Doubtless, the entire nation was subjected to another nation, without any one individual appearing to have been separately owned by another; there is reason to believe that the Hebrews, settled in the fertile land of Goshen, enjoyed a certain amount of comfort; they had preserved their division of tribes, their family life, and their mode of worship; in many respects their captivity was milder than that of the Africans. But, like them, strangers, enslaved by the race of Ham, without being descended from it, taken and sold, retained by force, after Joseph, sold by his brethren to Ishmaelites, with their camels, bearing spicery, and balm, and myrrh (Gen. xxxvii. 25), subjected to rude labors, without wages, multiplying despite the most cruel measures, the Israelites were veritable slaves. In numbers, three million (Jer. xi. 4), they were almost equal to the four million slaves enumerated in America. We may, therefore, rigorously, despite these differences, compare these two servitudes; that of the Africans in the United States and of the Hebrews in Egypt. But this oppression was abominable in the sight of God; no expression seems strong enough to blight, to stigmatize, to devote it to perpetual execration. Sad remembrances of the absent country mingle in the sublime poetry of the Psalms with anathemas hurled from Heaven upon the oppressors, and with the Hebrews' song of deliverance. Freedom and servitude will remain forever in the memory of the people of God as the greatest of calamities and the chiefest of blessings. God himself intervened.

"For he hath looked down from the height of his sanctuary; from heaven did the Lord behold the earth;

"To learn the groaning of the prisoners; to loose those that are appointed to death." (Ps. cii. 19, 20.)

"For the oppression of the poor, for the sighing of the needy, now will I arise, saith the Lord; I will set him in safety from him that puffeth at him." (Ps. xii. 5.)

God delivered his people, and this blessing was so great that it was henceforth the great object of the public gratitude. "I am the Lord your God, which have brought thee out of the land of Egypt, out of the house of bondage." (Ex. viii. 20, xx. 2; Deut. v. 6, etc.)

To those who ask of the Old Testament what God thinks of slavery, behold the true answer!

IV. But, it is said, How was it that Moses, himself the child of a slave, saved miraculously from death, — that Moses, the liberator of the people of God, inscribed slavery in its institutions?

We will analyze the Mosaic law on this point.

Of one Hebrew to another, there existed no slavery proper. He could, nevertheless, be bound to forced service in four cases :

1. In case of the redemption of a captive Jew from a stranger (Ex. xii. 43, 44, 45), a redemption which might always be effected (Lev. xxv. 47, 48, 49, 53) by the captive or his parents ; any one who had redeemed him had not the right to sell him again (Ibid. 42) ; the price was considered as a sort of advance of wages, in exchange for which the person redeemed owed a certain number of years' labor ; but the slavery of the Hebrew was temporary, every seven years, in the Sabbatic year, or year of release (Deut. xv. 12), he was free, and also in the year of Jubilee, a year in which *every man was to be returned unto his possession and every man unto his family* (Lev. xxv. 10), if redeemed before, his master reckoned with him for the years he had been in service. (Ibid. 50.)

2. In case of voluntary sale, either on account of poverty * (Ex. xxi. 2, Lev. xxv. 39) or because of debt. (Lev. xxv. 10.) The same provisions for redemption, and freedom by law and without ransom in the year of release and the year of jubilee; the same prohibition to sell again.

3. In case of condemnation by the judge for theft or other misdeed (Ex. xxii. 3), the culprit became the slave of him whom he had injured ; this was domiciliary imprisonment, as in Egypt, in Greece till the days of Solon, in Rome according to the law of the Twelve Tables. The same limit as in the two preceding cases.

Deuteronomy (xv. 12, 18) prescribes that the Hebrew slave shall be sent away on the seventh year, not only free, but furnished liberally with flocks and corn and wine. If the slave be contented in his master's house, if he love him,

* As in Rome, Greece, Germany, and Gaul. See Grotius, Dion, Tacitus, and Cæsar.

if having married during the course of his bondage, he finish his time before his wife and children, and will not consent to be separated from them by freedom, he has a right to present himself before the judges; in whose presence his ear is bored through with an awl, and his master is obliged to keep him as a slave forever. (Ex. xxi. 2–6; Deut., *loc. cit.*)

4. A daughter could be sold as a slave by her father, on condition of being betrothed; in this case, she did not become free in the year of jubilee, like a man, because she could not be abandoned before being espoused. But if the master failed to take her to wife or to marry her to his son, and thus *to set her at liberty*, he could not sell her to a stranger; if she espoused the son, she was free; if her master took him another wife, her right to food, raiment, and kind treatment did not diminish; if she did not receive these, she was free without ransom. (Ex. xxi. 7–11.)

Thus in no case was there perpetual and compulsory slavery of one Israelite by another; in a single case, perpetual but voluntary slavery.

It was not the same with strangers. They could become perpetual and hereditary slaves. (Lev. xxv. 44–46.) But even in this case:

1. Contrary to the universal usage of all nations, it was forbidden the Hebrews to reduce prisoners of war to slavery. Moses does not say so expressly; nevertheless, the texts from Leviticus which we have just quoted always speak of stranger slaves *bought with money*. Besides, we read in 2 Chron. xxviii. 8, 15, that, in a war against King Achaz, the children of Israel made captive of their brethren two hundred thousand men, women, and children, of whom they wished to make bondmen and bondwomen. But the prophet Oded said unto them that they should not do this; that it would be *to sin against the Lord*, that *this sin was great*, and that *the fierce wrath of God was upon Israel.* And

they sent away the captives, after having clothed, fed, and carefully tended them.

A stranger could only become a slave, therefore, by means of purchase.

2. The purchase must be by private agreement. Exodus (xxi. 16) declares that "he who stealeth a man and selleth him, or if he be found on his hand, he shall surely be put to death"; there was no slave-trade, therefore, but a contract which the purchased assuredly did not accept without conditions.

It was forbidden not only to buy, but even to covet the man-servant or maid-servant of one's neighbor. (Deut. v. 21.) Once bought, the stranger could not again be sold.

3. If the stranger became a Hebrew by submitting to circumcision, the rules and limits of slavery among Israelites became applicable to him; if he remained a stranger, he became free, at least in the year of jubilee.* (Lev. xxv. 10.)

4. The fugitive slave could not be pursued. (Deut. xxiii. 15, 16.) Lastly, as well in favor of stranger as of Hebrew slaves, numerous tutelary rules were written in the law.

1. The slave was free, if his master smote out his eye or struck out his tooth. (Ex. xxi. 26, 27.)

2. If a master abused his slave, he was scourged, and made to offer a trespass-offering in the face of the congregation. (Lev. xix. 20, 22.)

3. The slave could have recourse to the law for all wrongs; his testimony was received; he could hold property and redeem himself; he was instructed; his rights were respected. If he were killed, the master was severely punished; if the survival of the slave proved that he had had no intention to kill him (which was moreover to lose his

* This important but nevertheless contested point is attested by several learned Hebrew commentators of the Bible. See Barnes, p. 147.

money), he was not punished in the same manner.* (Ex. xxi. 20, 21.)

4. He should do no labor on the Sabbath day (Ex. xx. 10, 17; Deut. v. 14); and should participate in three great yearly feasts, Easter, Pentecost, and the Feast of the Tabernacles (Ex. xxxiv. 23), and in all family festivals, (Ex. xii. 44; Deut. xii. 11, 12.)

Lastly, Moses everywhere repeats to the Hebrews that men are brethren, and says again and again:

But the stranger that dwelleth among you shall be unto you as one born among you, and thou shalt love him as thyself; for ye were strangers in the land of Egypt. (Lev. xix. 34, Ex. xxii. 21.)

Such is Hebrew slavery. Doubtless it is far from Christian liberty. But how much above all it differs from Grecian or Roman servitude! How much it is superior to American slavery! No slave-trade, no fugitive slave law, no slavery among natives; a year of jubilee; the purity of woman, the weakness of childhood, the rights of manhood, placed under the provident protection of the law; equality professed, fraternity preached. Let the partisans of modern slavery cease to seek arguments from it, let them rather take examples. On the day that the law of the Jews shall become the law of one of the self-styled Christian Southern States of the American Union, immense progress will be accomplished, and the unhappy slaves may await and catch a glimpse of full liberty.

The manner in which men find in the Bible all that their interest desires fills me with astonishment, and I thank God once more for having caused me to be born in the bosom of a Church which does not abandon the Holy Books to the interpretations of caprice and selfishness. What! do seven or eight sentences extracted, put together and

* The text seems to say that he is not at all, but verses 26-30 leave no doubt of the meaning.

turned over in favor of slavery, transform the entire Old Testament into a law of servitude? To me, every page of this venerable text exhales as it were a perfume of liberty.

I see, in the earliest days of the world, God bless man and give him dominion over the fish of the sea, and over the fowl of the air, and over every living thing that moveth upon the earth, and every herb bearing seed, and every tree (Gen. i. 28, 29); I do not read that he is to have dominion over other beings. The deluge inundated creation; it was because *the earth was filled with violence through men.* (Gen. vi. 13.) Why was the captivity of Judah, of Egypt, of Babylon, inflicted upon the Hebrews? In chastisement of the oppression of their brethren. All the maledictions, all the wrath of God, all the thunderbolts of Heaven, fall on the oppressors, and God thus shows the strongest that he is stronger than they.

Open the prophecies, lend an ear to these marvellous words which still resound after the lapse of four thousand years like peals of thunder. "Thus saith the Lord; ye have not hearkened to me, in proclaiming liberty, every one to his brother, and every man to his neighbor; behold, I proclaim a liberty for you, saith the Lord, to the sword, to the pestilence, and to the famine; and I will make you to be removed into all the kingdoms of the earth." (Jer. xxxiv. 17.)

"To crush under his feet all the prisoners of the earth,

"To turn aside the right of a man before the face of the Most High,

"To subvert a man in his cause, the Lord approveth not." (Lam. iii. 34 – 36.)

"The children also of Judah and the children of Jerusalem have ye sold unto the Grecians, that ye might remove them far from their border.

"Behold, I will raise them out of the place whither ye have sold them, and will return your recompense upon your own head." (Joel iii. 6, 7; Jer. xxii. 13; Amos vii. 7-17; Prov. xiv. 31.)

At the very moment that I re-peruse these great words, the Catholic Church is celebrating the solemnities of the times which preceded the nativity of the Lord. Like a distant echo which becomes gradually more intense, like a gleam of light arising in the south with the dawn, the marvellous liturgy carries us back through the ages to the impressions and words of the Old Testament. The expectation of the Messiah is about to be followed by his coming, the days grow shorter, realities come to crown the promises. What does humanity await? What does the Saviour bring? Listen:

"Look down from heaven, and behold from the habitation of thy holiness and of thy glory; for thou art our Father and our Redeemer. . . . . . O that thou wouldest rend the heavens, and come down. Where is thy zeal and thy strength, the sounding of thy bowels and thy mercies? Display thy power, and come to save us." (Isa. lxiii., lxiv. 1st S. in Advent, Procession.)

"Look up, and lift up your heads, for your redemption draweth nigh." (Luke xxi. 28. 1st S. in Advent.)

"The Lord has sent me *to preach the Gospel to the poor, to preach deliverance to the captives.*" (Luke iv. 18. 2d S. in Advent, Tierce.)

"Drop down, ye heavens, from above, and let the skies pour down righteousness; let the earth open, and let them bring forth salvation, and let righteousness spring up together." (Isa. xlv. 8. Ibid., Procession.)

"Say to them that have a fearful heart, Be strong, fear not: behold, your God will come with vengeance, even God with a recompense; he will come and save you." (Isa. xxxv. 4. 3d S. in Advent, Communion.)

"Though I have afflicted thee, I will afflict thee no more, and *will burst thy bonds in sunder.* Behold upon the mountains the feet of him that bringeth good tidings, that publisheth peace." (Nahum i. 13 – 15. Ember Wednesday, Introit.)

"Fear no more, O Jacob, my servant; have no fear, O Israel; behold, I come to save thee." (Jer. iii. Ember Friday, Communion.)

"The Lord *raiseth up all that be bowed down;* but all the wicked will he destroy." (Ps. cxlv. Ember Saturday, Gradual.)

"Keep ye judgment, and do justice; for my salvation is near to come, and my righteousness to be revealed." (Isa. lvi. 4th S. Advent, Introit.)

"I will break thy captivity; rejoice, I am with thee, and I will save thee."

"O Lord, *break our captivity.*" (Isa. lvi. Ibid., Vespers.)

"Master, what shall we do? Do violence to no man, neither accuse any falsely; and be content with your wages." (Luke iii. Monday after 1st S. in Advent.)

"O key of David, *open to the captive the door of his prison!* Sun of justice arise! arise, that iniquity may be destroyed, and that justice may reign!" (Grand Anthems, 15, 19, 20.)

"I will remove iniquity from the land." (Zech. iii. Christmas Eve, Off.)

"The Lord hath said unto me: Thou art my son; this day have I begotten thee." (Ps. ii.)

"Glory to God in the highest, and on the earth peace, good-will to men." (Luke ii. Christmas Eve, Mass, Introit.)

"For the Son of God has put on human nature to reconcile it with its Creator. He who has the nature of God has annihilated himself, *taking the form of a slave* to render himself like unto men." (St. Leon, Sermon. Gradual. St. Paul to Philip. ii.)

It is by this marvellous portico, to the memory of these ancient predictions, to the sound of these sublime chants, among the soothing strophes of this dialogue of the prophets and apostles, through these solemn promises of freedom and salvation, that the Old Testament prepares us for the New, that the Church conducts us to the cradle of Jesus Christ.

It is time to open the Gospel, in order to witness the triumph of peace, justice, and liberty, and to show once more that the slaves, like the shepherds, received the glad tidings announced by the angels.

CHAPTER II.

SLAVERY IN THE SIGHT OF CHRISTIANITY.*

I.

THE GOSPEL.

In general, those who dispute to Christianity the honor of having abolished slavery pass lightly over the Gospel.

There is, I grant, little question in it of slavery, at least directly.

Learned commentators have essayed to demonstrate, by the aid of somewhat grave proofs, that our Lord came at a time when there were no longer slaves in Judæa; they affirm that he was never brought face to face with a single slave-owner; † they observe that, always choosing examples placed before the eyes of his listeners, he said nothing of the temple of Delphos, or the groves of Dodona or Bacchus, in the same manner, he would have made no allusion to the slavery that did not pollute his sight, and would have employed the word *servant* only in the sense of *domestic.*‡

I think this proof contestable, and moreover superfluous.

* I need hardly say, that, distrusting my own knowledge, I have consulted learned theologians on all the texts quoted. I disown in advance anything that, without my knowledge, may be incorrect or audacious.

† We know that the servant or the centurion is called by Luke παῖς, *puer*, and that nothing proves that this servant was a slave.

‡ The word *servus* introduces into all arguments drawn from texts a lamentable confusion, of which it is important to be forewarned. *Servus* signifies *servant* as well as *slave.* All the words of the Gospel and Epistles apply exactly in countries where the servants are *domestics;* nevertheless, they were uttered in countries and at a time when slavery was universal; it is evident that they apply no less exactly to *slaves.* When does *servus* mean *slave;* and when does it signify *domestic?*

The Greek language, more affluent, has as many different terms as the expression admits of shades; the general, indistinct term is δοῦλος, δουλεύω; λατρεύω, λάτρις, to serve as a soldier or to serve God; οἰκετεύω, οἰκέτης,

The words and looks of the Saviour, issuing from the narrow categories invented by men, as well as from the petty frontiers of Judæa, took flight to the extremities of time, of space, and of the created world. There are precise texts in the Gospel concerning slavery.

What is true is, that the Divine Master, striking to the root of the evil, as a chemist (pardon me the comparison), taking no account of compounds, acts directly upon simple bodies, does not point out by name the varied results of human corruption, but goes straight to the capital sins, pride, idleness, theft, and homicide, and in condemning them condemns in the same breath the homicidal yoke which pride and idleness impose on a being robbed of his chief blessing, which is liberty. Do not say, therefore, that the Gospel comprises few texts against slavery, for it comprises

domestic; μισθόω, μίσθιος, person receiving a salary; ὑπακούω, ὑπήκοος, follower, *attaché*; — ἀνδράποδον, slave properly called. In all of the cases where δοῦλος is employed, to which of its synonymes does it correspond?

The Hebrew makes no distinction, it always employs the general expressions *ebedh*, *abodha*, *abudda*, servant, service, to serve, which come from *abadh*, to labor, — and sometimes only *sakir*, person receiving wages. The two words are found in the same verse, Job vii. 2, 3.

The only conclusion to be drawn from these linguistic difficulties is, that it is not sufficient that the words *ebedh*, δοῦλος, *servus*, *servant*, *knecht*, *serviteur*, are employed in the different translations of the Scriptures to conclude thencefrom that *slaves* are in question. The facts must control the meaning. It has been calculated (Barnes, p. 64, etc.) that the word *doulos* or *servus* is encountered 122 times throughout the New Testament, of which number it signifies

Servants of God and of Christ, . .	29	times,
Servants of sin or of the world, . . .	6	"
Servants of each other through charity,	2	"
Servants of the Jews, ...	47	"
Servants in general, ...	38	"

Is it possible to affirm that in these last examples veritable slaves were once in question? No; the Greek language does not *a single* time contain the word *andrapodon*, although the correlative word *andrapodistes*, dealer in men, *plagiarius*, is read in St. Paul (1 Tim. i. 10). We do not cling to the words, therefore, but only to the sense and the circumstances in which these words are employed.

In the French translation of the New Testament the word *slave* is often used instead of the word *servant*, employed both in the Protestant and Catholic English versions. — Tr.

numerous and withering texts against the vices which are its cause and result. But you can affirm that it does not contain a sentence nor a word *in favor of* slavery.

Nevertheless, this text is brought forward : —

"Ille autem *servus* qui cognovit voluntatem Domini sui et non præparavit, et non fecit secundum voluntatem ejus, *vapulabit multis;*

"Qui autem non cognovit et fecit *digna plagis, vapulabit paucis.*"

"And that *servant,* or *slave,* which knew his lord's will, and prepared not himself, neither did according to his will, shall be beaten with many stripes;

"But he that knew not, and did commit things worthy of stripes, shall be beaten with few stripes." (Luke xii. 47, 48.)

It is inferred from this text that our Lord himself authorized slavery and corporal punishment.

I might content myself with remarking, that the Divine Master drew an example from the every-day life of the Jews; and that he acted thus in all his parables, without transforming the alleged examples into laws.

But read the parable entire, then read it again in Matthew (xxiv. 42 – 51). It admonishes us to hold ourselves in readiness, in view of the rewards and punishments of eternal life. It tells of the "chastisement of a steward, *dispensator*" (Luke 42), who "had authority over the other servants" (Matt. 45), a "wicked steward who beat the men-servants and maid-servants, and ate, and drank, and was drunken" (Luke 45; Matt. 49), and "did things worthy of stripes, *digna plagis*" (Luke 48). These stripes he was to receive, or, according to Matthew:

"The lord of that servant shall come in a day when he looketh not for him, and *shall cut him asunder, and appoint him his portion with the hypocrites; there shall be weeping and gnashing of teeth.*"

Let it be remarked, that it is not to slaves alone that this sermon on vigilance is addressed, but to all mankind. "Ye yourselves, like unto *men* that wait for their lord, —*hominibus* expectantibus dominorum" (36); such is the beginning. In the midst of the parable, Peter interrupts Christ to ask (41): "Lord, *speakest thou this parable unto us, or even to all?*" But the Lord continues in a manner to leave no doubt, and thus concludes (48): "For *unto whomsoever*, much is given, of him shall be much required; and to whom men have committed much, of him they will ask the more."

But who is this man, then, to whom much has been committed, — this man who has been set over the other servants? Is it the master? Is it the slave? The divine and terrifying words of Jesus Christ fall upon the slave-owner; he it is that eats, drinks, is drunken, beats the men-servants and maid-servants, and forgets the day of judgment. He it is of whom much will be again required, and not the poor slave to whom so little has been given Here, then, the master is God, the slave the planter!

This is indeed a text happily chosen!

Let us continue.

From what chapter is this parable taken to make it the sanction of property in slaves? Precisely the chapter in which our Lord refuses to decide questions of property (14): "*Who made me a judge or a divider over you?*" — in which he lays down this admirable rule (31): "*Seek first the kingdom of God and his righteousness*"; — in which he exhorts to renunciation (33): "*Sell that ye have, and give alms*"; — in which he reproaches men for being unjust (57): "*And why even of yourselves judge ye not what is right?*" — in which he recommends reconciliation, under penalty of hell (58, 59).*

* See, too, Matt. vi. 25, etc.; vii. 25, 26.

What remains of this unlucky quotation? Chosen to justify slavery, it forcibly condemns it.

Are, moreover, precise texts against slavery desired? Open the same Gospel according to St. Luke. In the first chapters, St. John the Baptist announces our Saviour in these terms. Chap. iii. 16: "*One mightier than I cometh*" (17); "*Whose fan is in his hand, and he will thoroughly purge his floor.*"

In chap. iv. Jesus, baptized, begins his ministry by triumphing over the Devil, then, returning to Nazareth, what are his first words?

16: "*As his custom was, he went into the synagogue on the Sabbath day, and stood up for to read.*"

17: "*And there was delivered to him the book of the Prophet Esaias. And when he had opened the book, he found the place where it was written,*

18: "*The Spirit of the Lord is upon me, because he hath anointed me to* PREACH THE GOSPEL TO THE POOR; he hath sent me TO HEAL THE BROKEN-HEARTED, TO PREACH DELIVERANCE TO THE CAPTIVES (the Vulgate and the Hebrew read: *Captivis libertatem et clausis apertionem*) TO SET AT LIBERTY THEM THAT ARE BRUISED.

21: "TO PREACH THE ACCEPTABLE YEAR OF THE LORD (according to all interpreters, the year of jubilee wherein all the slaves were free), 'THIS DAY *is the Scripture fulfilled in your ears.*'"

This text appears to me decisive. It is impossible to maintain that it is figurative; for verse 18 is certainly not figurative, and verse 21 leaves no doubt. Wherefore, then, was our Lord sent? Was it not to *preach deliverance to the captives, to set at liberty them that were bruised, and to preach the jubilee that freed the slaves?*

It has not been sufficiently remarked, in my opinion, on the other hand, how often our Lord makes use of the word *servant* in a sense assuredly quite new. He who came, taking upon himself the form of a servant, *formam servi accipiens*,* destined to die the death of a slave, and to lead captivity captive, *captivam duxit captivitatem*, transfigures the word: *servus* becomes the name of those who give themselves to God, *servi Dei;* the Holy Virgin is the first to employ it: *Ecce ancilla Domini.* Far more, this word expresses the duty of those who command: —

"And whosoever will be chief among you, let him be your *servant.*" (Matt. xx. 27.)

"The disciple is not above his master, nor the *servant* above his lord. It is enough for the disciple, that he be as his master, *and the servant as his lord.*" (Matt. x. 24, 25.)

"Blessed are those servants whom the lord, when he cometh, shall find watching; verily, I say unto you, that he shall gird himself, *and make them to sit down to meat, and will come forth and serve them.*" (Luke xii. 37.)

This word, transfigured, passes into the language of faith and honor. We read on the tombs of Christians, "*Ingenuus natu servus autem Christi.*" We read on the tombs of knights, "*I serve.*" The abandoned race of bond-servants will be freed. The great family of voluntary servants of Christianity is about to appear on earth.

But let us cease to seek, with somewhat too narrow minutiæ, the texts where figures the word *servant* or *slave.* We must read the whole Gospel. I abhor those who divide it, those who, careful to repeat to men what it takes from them, never tell them of what it brings them; who speak of submission, never of liberty; of fear, never of love; of repentance, never of gladness. I love the whole Gospel, and I do not separate its rigor from its tenderness.

Let us follow Jesus, therefore, upon the blessed mount whence fell those adorable and marvellous words: "Blessed are the poor! Blessed are they that mourn! Woe unto the rich!" Lend an attentive ear to the persuasive words

* St. Paul, Philip. ii. 5.

of the Master, addressed, after just reproaches to his country, to the rest of mankind: —

"Come unto me, all ye that labor and are heavy laden, and I will give you rest." (Matt. xi. 28.)

Listen and tremble to the sentence of the last judgment: "I was in prison, and ye came to me. Inasmuch as ye have done it unto one of the least of these, my brethren, ye have done it unto me." (Matt. xxv. 36 – 40.)

Let us gather from the lips of the King of the world himself this new doctrine of authority on earth: —

"Whosoever will be great among you, let him be your minister. (Matt. xx. 26.)

"For even the Son of Man came not to be ministered unto, but to minister." (Mark. x. 42 – 45.)

"Whether is greater, he that sitteth at meat, or he that serveth? is not he that sitteth at meat? but I am among you as he that serveth." (Luke xxii. 25 – 27.)

"Be not ye called master; for one is your Master, even Christ; and all ye are brethren. . . . . He that is greatest among you shall be your servant. . . . . Woe unto you, hypocrites! for ye pay tithe of mint and anise and cummin, and have neglected the weightier matters of the law, *judgment, mercy, and faith: these ought ye to have done,* and not leave the other undone." (Matt. xxiii. 8, 11, 23.)

Let us remember all these divine and powerful words which laid the foundation of the dignity and moral liberty of the conscience, paved the way for new men and modern society, rehabilitated labor and poverty, condemned idleness, covetousness, and anger, communicated a hitherto unknown tone to the word justice, oftener repeated in the Gospel than even the word charity, finally gave for the first time a true meaning to the name brethren, before that of derision and mockery; for, according to the strong expression of a woman, fraternity was only the romance of the human race, fratricide was its history. Man is the equal of his fellow-man; labor is noble, it is the duty of all; these two ideas more in the world are the condemnation and end of slavery.

We will conclude and sum up the subject by repeating to the slaveholder these noblest of sentences, the pillars of morality: —

"Thou shalt worship the Lord thy God, *and him only shalt thou serve.*

"And as ye would that men should do to you, *do ye also to them likewise.*" * (Luke vi. 31.)

"Therefore all things whatsoever that ye would that men should do to you, do ye even so to them; for this is the law and the prophets." (Matt. vii. 12.)

"Thou shalt love thy neighbor as thyself."

I defy the most unfeeling planter to go, immediately after hearing these words, to the slave-market to buy slaves, and I defy the most resolute critic to maintain, after having read them, that the Gospel does not condemn slavery.

After the Master, let us listen to the disciples.

II.

THE ACTS OF THE APOSTLES AND THE EPISTLES.

It is known that the Acts of the Apostles, written by St. Luke, present the picture of the primitive Church. Do they make mention of slaves? † not a single time. We

* Some have dared turn this Divine command to jest. The beggar might say to the king, "Give me your crown, for you would wish it in my place." They forget this other command, Thou shalt desire nothing that is unjust. But is it not just to desire to be free?

† We read only that Paul and Silas, being at Philippi, a Roman colony, met a damsel possessed by a devil, who brought her masters much gain by soothsaying; but, without care for the interest of the masters, the apostles drove out the devil; whereupon the masters, deprived of their profit, caused the apostles to be seized, scourged, and imprisoned. (Acts xvi. 16-23.)

see from them that the chief of the apostles labored with their own hands; we do not see that they were ministered to by slaves.

Will any pretend that the apostles and early Christians practised communism, and that they could not speak of slaves, since they did not admit the right of private property?

This we may say, in passing, is a gratuitous absurdity, often repeated on the score of this text: —

Acts iv. 32: "The multitude of them that believed were of one heart and one soul: *Neither said any of them that aught of the things which he possessed was his own; but they had all things in common.*"

But the following verses evidently demonstrate that the believers lived thus to practise charity, by no means to practise communism. Indeed: —

34: "Neither was there any among them that lacked; for as many as were possessors of lands or houses sold them, and brought the prices of the things that were sold;

35: "And laid them down at the apostles' feet; and distribution was made to every man according as he had need."

Verses 36 and 37 show us Barnabas setting an example; then, in chap. v. 1 – 12, we see Ananias and Sapphira struck dead, wherefore? not because they had not brought their goods in common, but because they had lied, declaring that they had given them, while they had kept back a part. In fact, Peter says to Ananias, —

3: "Why hath Satan filled thine heart to lie to the Holy Ghost, and to keep back part of the price of the land?

4: "*While it remained, was it not thine own? and after it was sold, was it not in thine own power?* Thou hast not lied to men, but unto God."

These texts, therefore, fully sanction the right of private

property, far from abolishing it; and the silence of the apostles concerning slave property cannot be attributed to their pretended opinion on the right of property in itself.

Another trait, another saying, another detail, reveals in the apostles and the early believers the purest and most practical conviction of the fraternity of men, so clearly professed by St. Paul before the Areopagus (Acts xvii. 23, 26): "Whom, therefore, ye ignorantly worship, him declare I unto you, ... *He hath made of one blood all nations of men* for to dwell on all the face of the earth, and hath determined the times before appointed, and the bounds of their habitation." We know, moreover, that a slave, to be admitted to the priesthood, must be set at liberty; the slave Onesimus was freed before becoming deacon, after which he became priest, although once a slave.

The Epistles were composed both to unfold to the faithful the rules of faith and morality, and to resist the earliest tendencies that impelled them towards agitation or error. The admonitions contained in the Epistles denote, therefore, the points on which the authority of the Church was obliged already to manifest itself; and the counsels to patience given the slaves may prove that the new law inclined them to impatience under a yoke whose injustice they felt more deeply.

But, be this as it may, these counsels are positive. It is necessary to analyze, and first of all to understand them.

All the texts of St. Paul and St. Peter which bear reference to slaves may be divided into two categories: the one forcibly enjoins the duty of labor and the equality of mankind; the other recommends to slaves, submission, to masters, kindness and justice.

In general, these texts are only quoted by extracts, and all are not quoted. I have made it my business to seek them out with the greatest care, and ask permission to reproduce entire these venerable articles of the charter of Christian equality.

I shall follow, with respect to the Epistles of St. Paul, the chronological order indicated by Dom Calmet : —

First Epistle to the Thessalonians, A. D. 52.

Chap. iv. 10 – 12 : "We beseech you, brethren, to work with your own hands, as we commanded you ; that ye may walk honestly toward them that are without, and that ye may have lack of nothing."

Second Epistle.

Chap. iii. 10 : "This we commanded you, that if any would not work, neither should he eat.

11 : "For we hear that there are some which walk among you disorderly, working not at all.

12 : "Now them that are such we command and exhort by our Lord Jesus Christ, that with quietness they work, and eat their own bread."

Epistle to the Galatians, A. D. 55.

Chap. iii. 28 : "There is neither Jew nor Greek, there is neither bond nor free, there is neither male nor female ; for ye are all one in Christ Jesus." *

Chap. iv. 7 : "Wherefore thou art no more a servant, but a son."

31 : "So then, brethren, we are not children of the bond-woman, but of the free, and Christ Jesus has gained us this liberty."

Chap. v. 13 : "For, brethren, ye have been called unto

* The Jews regarded with disdainful contempt all those who were not Jews ; the Greeks, all those who were not Greeks ; they estimated them as slaves by nature, and of an inferior race. . . . . . The intelligence of this saying of St. Paul supposes acquaintance with the sentiment of Aristotle. (Moehler, Chap. III.)

liberty; only use not liberty for an occasion to the flesh, but by love serve one another.

14: "For all the law is fulfilled in one word, even in this, thou shalt love thy neighbor as thyself.

15: "But if ye bite and devour one another, take heed that ye be not consumed one of another."

First Epistle to the Corinthians, A. D. 56.

Chap. vii. 20: "Let every man abide in the same calling wherein he was called.

21: "Art thou called, being a servant? Care not for it; but if thou mayest be made free, use it rather.*

22: "For he that is called in the Lord, being a servant, is the Lord's freeman: likewise, also, he that is called, being free, is Christ's servant.

23: "Ye are bought with a price; be not ye the servants of men."

35: "And this I speak for your own profit; not that I may cast a shame upon you, but for that which is comely, and that ye may attend upon the Lord without distraction."

Chap. xii. 13: "For by one Spirit we are all baptized into one body, whether we be Jews or Gentiles, whether we be bond or free; and have all been made to drink into one Spirit.

14: "For the body is not one member, but many."

22: "Nay, much more those members of the body, which seem to be more feeble, are necessary.

23: "And those members of the body, which we think to be less honorable, upon these we bestow more abundant honor."

27: "Now ye are the body of Christ, and the members in particular."

* Can any one comprehend how M Granier de Cassagnac could have translated this remarkable text, *If thou canst have thy liberty, remain so much the more in bondage?*

Second Epistle to the Corinthians.

Chap. xi. 20: "For ye suffer, if a man bring you into bondage, if a man devour you, if a man take of you, if a man exalt himself, if a man smite you on the face."

Epistle to the Romans, A. D. 58.

Chap. ii. 11: "For there is no respect of persons with God."

We may add, from the same Epistle: —

Chap. vi. 16: "Know ye not, that to whom ye yield yourselves servants to obey, his servants ye are to whom ye obey; whether of sin unto death, or of obedience unto righteousness?"

18: "Being then made free from sin, ye became the servants of righteousness."

21: "What fruit had ye, then, in those things whereof ye are now ashamed?

22: "But now being made free from sin, and become servants to God, ye have yeur fruit unto holiness, and the end everlasting life.

23: "For the wages of sin is death; but the gift of God is eternal life through Jesus Christ our Lord."

Throughout the whole of this passage, St. Paul addresses himself to the Romans who practised slavery, and he speaks figuratively of the subjection to sin or to the law. But who will find in these words the sanction of slavery? Read *servant* for bondman everywhere, and the meaning remains the same. Furthermore, closely scrutinize the words, and you will remark, — 1. That a *voluntary* subjection is in question; 2. That the bondman can free himself; 3. That *wages* are allowed. But slavery is not voluntary, has no limit, is not paid. The figure itself, therefore, of which St. Paul makes use can only mean *service* properly so called.

The same Epistle.

Chap. xiv. 1: "Him that is weak in the faith receive ye, but not to doubtful disputations."

4: "Who art thou that judgeth another man's servant? to his own master he standeth or falleth. Yea, he shall be holden up; for God is able to make him stand."

It is more than evident that the Master here is God, and that the *servant* is not consequently a *slave.* This is again an allusion to the manners and customs of the Romans.

All of the other Epistles to the churches are of the same date, A. D. 62.

Epistle to the Ephesians, A. D. 62.

Chap. vi. 5: "Servants, be obedient to them that are your masters according to the flesh, with fear and trembling, in singleness of your heart, as unto Christ;

6: "Not with eye-service, as men-pleasers; but as the servants of Christ, doing the will of God from the heart;

7: "With good-will doing service, as to the Lord, and not to men;

8: "Knowing that whatsoever good thing any man doeth, the same shall he receive of the Lord, whether he be bond or free.

9: "And, ye masters, do the same things unto them, forbearing threatening: knowing that your Master also is in heaven; neither is there respect of persons with him."

Thus ends this beautiful and tender Epistle, Chap. iv. of which commences with these sublime words:

1: "I, therefore, the prisoner of the Lord, beseech you that ye walk worthy of the vocation wherewith ye are called,

2: "With all lowliness and meekness," etc.

4: "There is one body, and one spirit, even as ye are called in one hope of your calling;

5: "One Lord, one faith, one baptism,

6: "One God and Father of all, who is above all, and through all, and in you all.

7: "But unto every one of us is given grace according to the measure of the gift of Christ.

8: "Wherefore he saith, When he ascended upon high, he led captivity captive, and gave gifts unto men."

25: "We are members one of another."

Epistle to the Philippians, A. D. 62.

Chap. ii. 7: "He made himself of no reputation, and took upon him the form of a servant."

Epistle to the Colossians, A. D. 62.

Chap. iii. 10: "Put on the new man.

11: "Where there is neither Greek nor Jew, circumcision nor uncircumcision, barbarian, Scythian, bond nor free: but Christ is all, and in all."

22: "Servants, obey in all things your masters according to the flesh; not with eye-service, as men-pleasers; but in singleness of heart, fearing God:

23: "And whatsoever ye do, do it heartily, as to the Lord, and not unto men:

24: "Knowing that of the Lord ye shall receive the reward of the inheritance; for ye serve the Lord Christ.

25: "But he that doeth wrong shall receive for the wrong which he hath done: and there is no respect of persons."

Chap. iv. 1: "Masters, give unto your servants that which is just and equal: knowing that ye also have a Master in heaven."

Epistle to the Hebrews.

Chap. ii. 16: "For verily he (Christ) took not on him the nature of angels; but he took on him the seed of Abraham."

Chap. xiii. 3: "Remember them that are in bonds, as bound with them."

After the Epistles to the churches, come the Epistles of

St. Paul to the companions of his labors, Timothy, Titus, and Philemon; the recommendations are more confidential, and the Apostle gives to his confidants the motives of his conduct.

First Epistle to Timothy, A. D. 64.

Chap. i. 9: "The law is not made for a righteous man, but for the lawless and disobedient, the ungodly, etc.

10: "Whoremongers, them that defile themselves with mankind, them that steal freemen to make them slaves, etc." *

Chap. vi. 1: "Let as many servants as are under the

* Dom Calmet and the Abbe de Vence translate it thus. Some French translations read, *stealers of slaves;* the English translations say, *men-stealers*; the Latin says, *plagiarii;* the Greek, ἀνδραποδιστής. But the dictionaries (see Facciolati, Freund, Quicherat) translate it like Dom Calmet. The word *plagiarius*, admitted in one language to denote the literary pilferer of another's works, does not come from *plaga*, blow, but from *plaga*, thread. It is a judicial term, which must be interpreted by definitions of law. But these definitions tell us clearly that the *plagiarist* was *he who stole a freeman to make him a slave.* It is only lately and by sufferance that the stealer of slaves has been designated by the same word. The following definitions are taken from the *Pandectes*, Lib. XLVIII. Tit. XV. *De lege Fabia, de plagiariis* (Pothier, Tom. III. p. 424). This Fabian or Favian law appears anterior to Cicero, *Or. pro Rabirio*, no. 3.

D. Ulpian, Lib. I. *Regul. Si liberum hominem emptor sciens emerit, capitale crimen adversus eum ex lege Fabia de plagio nascitur, quo venditor quoque fit obnoxius, si sciens liberum esse vendiderit.*

Likewise Diocletian and Maximian, Lib. XV. Cod. 20, h. tit. *Liberum sciens conditionem ejus, invitum venumdando, plagii criminis pœna tenetur.*

The same law extends the penalty to slave-stealers; a rescript of Adrian testifies that this analogy is not admitted without dispute. *Plane autem scire debet (judex) posse aliquem furti crimine ob servos alienos interceptos teneri, nec idcirco tamen statem plagiarium esse existimari.* (Callistr. Lib. VI., *De Cognition.*)

Later, the penalty became pecuniary. But Constantine maintained it capital against stealers of children, *plagiarii, qui viventium filiorum miserandas infligunt parentibus orbitates* (Lib. XVI. Cod. 9, 20, h. tit.)

It appears to us of use to establish the true meaning of this very curious text of St. Paul, by which, likening those who reduce a freeman to servitude to the most abominable criminals, he condemns the origin itself of all slavery, the one who takes the slave, the one who sells him, and the one who buys him. Such, moreover, is the explicit prescript of the Old Testament: "And he that stealeth a man, and selleth him, or if he be found in his hand, he shall be surely put to death." Ex. xxi. 16. The same law is found, Deut. xxiv. 7.

yoke count their own masters worthy of all honor, *that the name of God and his doctrine be not blasphemed.*

2: "And they that have believing masters,* let them not despise them, because they are brethren; but rather do them service, because they are faithful and beloved, partakers of the benefit."

Epistle to Titus, A. D. 64.

Chap. ii. 9: "Exhort servants to be obedient to their own masters, and to please them well in all things; not answering again;

10: "Not purloining, but showing all good fidelity; *that they may adorn the doctrine of God our Saviour in all things.*

11: "For the grace of God that bringeth salvation hath appeared to all men."

We intentionally omit the Epistle to Philemon, to revert to it presently, after having quoted the texts of St. Peter.

First Epistle.

Chap. ii. 13: "Submit yourselves to every ordinance of man for the Lord's sake;

15: "For so is the will of God, that with well-doing ye may put to silence the ignorance of foolish men.

16: "*As free,* and not using your liberty for a cloak of maliciousness, but as the servants of God.

18: "Servants, be subject to your masters with all fear; not only to the good and gentle, but also to the froward.†

19: "For this is thankworthy, if a man for conscience toward God endure grief, suffering *wrongfully.*"

The Epistles of St. James and St. John contain nothing special concerning servitude, yet notwithstanding, how can we help recalling, with respect to this iniquity, these admirable words: —

* This word indicates clearly that verse 1 is addressed to servants with heathen masters; verse 2, to those with Christian masters.

† This text is always quoted, but without accompanying it with what precedes and follows it: *As free . . . . . suffering wrongfully.*

Epistle of St. James.

Chap. ii. 8: "If ye fulfil the royal law according to the Scripture, *Thou shalt love thy neighbor as thyself,* ye shall do well.

9: "But if ye have respect to persons, ye commit sin."

Chap. v. 1: "Go to now, ye rich men, weep and howl for your miseries that shall come upon you."

4: "Behold the hire of the laborers who have reaped down your fields, which is of you kept back by fraud, crieth: and the cries of them which have reaped are entered into the ears of the Lord of Sabaoth."

9: "Behold, the Judge standeth before the door."

First Epistle of St. John.

Chap. iii. 18: "My little children, let us not love in word, neither in tongue; but in deed and in truth."

I have not feared to quote these so numerous texts. Who would grow weary of reading the Gospel and Epistles? Who does not feel himself, on the contrary, edified, strengthened, and refreshed by listening to all these words, so tender, but so wise, these positive doctrines of liberty, equality, and fraternity, mingled with these counsels of submission and patience, — words, doctrines, and counsels equally distant from the distorted Gospel of subversionists, and the no less false doctrine of despots? In these words, a hundred times reread, we discover at each new reading new riches and surprise, and we find ourselves repeating with enthusiasm, "I rejoice at the word, as one that findeth great spoil." (Ps. cxviii. 162.)

Shall we animadvert and attempt subtle interpretations? No, no, these texts should be taken respectfully by the letter. The partisans of emancipation, we will not allege that all the texts which preach submission are addressed to servants, to domestics, *servi*, and not to slaves. It is perfectly true that, applicable to both, they are employed without modification, in our modern communities, as the code of duties for all in service. But it is no less true that the Apostles, surrounded by slaves, spoke for slaves. The text, *sive servus sive laber*, as well as tradition, leaves no doubt of this, and does not permit us to take refuge behind this argument; moreover, useless.

It would be another subtlety to pretend, on the other hand, that all the sayings in favor of liberty are figurative, and should be understood to mean only the moral enfranchisement of souls, not the real emancipation of individuals.

Ah! I am not ignorant that the true Christian is free in chains, free in the hands of the executioner; violence is powerless to force the impenetrable intrenchment of the liberty of a heart that believes in God,—the sublime liberty that makes martyrs, and also sustains the unknown heroism of so many obscure victims of a life of suffering. But let us abuse nothing, not even virtue. Without material liberty, moral liberty, often faltering, is always imperfect. The martyr is free to detest the torture, but not to shrink from enduring it. For fifty years, the slave has internally abhorred what he has been compelled to do, but he has nevertheless done it for fifty years. Say that he is a martyr, but do not say that he is a free man. Only, this is true, the more he is morally free, the more will servitude weigh upon him, the more he will wish, the more we will wish with him, to see it broken; the slavery of a base and servile soul scarcely rouses our abhorrence; the slavery of a free soul is an intolerable spectacle to a lover of justice. To elevate, to transform, to enfranchise the soul of the slave and that of the master, was therefore to crush servitude. The bonds which fettered souls were to be the first to fall; but Jesus Christ freed the whole man, the soul and also the body. His words, and the acts with which they directly inspired his first disciples, then the Church, demonstrate it clearly.

If any one asks to see a slave actually freed by the hand of an Apostle, he shall be satisfied! This memorable example has been preserved to us in the Epistle of St. Paul to Philemon, which we have wished to analyze by itself, and last, because, unceasingly presented as an objection, it appears to us, on the contrary, a proof as touching as decisive.

Philemon was a rich citizen of the city of Colossus; converted with his wife Apphia, by St. Paul, he became the model and stay of the Christians of the country. One of his slaves, Onesimus, robbed his master and fled, and, reaching Rome, where St. Paul was a prisoner, sought him out. St. Paul received him with charity; converted him, and wished to make use of him to preach the faith. But, first of all, he sent him back to Philemon, charging him to carry to his former justly irritated master an epistle which it is fitting to quote entire: —

"Paul, a *prisoner* of Jesus Christ, and Timothy our brother, unto Philemon our dearly beloved, and fellow-laborer,

"And to our beloved Apphia, and Archippus our fellow-soldier, and *to the church in thy house:*

"Grace to you, and peace, from God our Father and the Lord Jesus Christ.

"I thank my God, making mention of thee always in my prayers,

"Hearing of thy love and faith, which thou hast toward the Lord Jesus, *and toward all saints;*

"That the communication of thy faith may become effectual by the acknowledging of every good thing which is in you in Christ Jesus.

"For we have great joy and consolation in thy love, because the bowels of the saints are refreshed by thee, brother.

"Wherefore, *though I might be much bold in Christ to enjoin thee that which is convenient,*

"Yet for love's sake *I rather beseech thee, being such an one as Paul the aged, and now also a prisoner of Jesus Christ.*

"I beseech thee *for my son Onesimus, whom I have begotten in my bonds:*

"Which in time past was to thee unprofitable, but now profitable to thee and to me:

"Whom I have sent again: thou therefore receive him, *that is mine own bowels:*

"Whom I would have retained with me, that in thy stead he might have ministered unto me in the bonds of the Gospel:

"*But without thy mind would I do nothing, that thy benefit should not be as it were of necessity, but willingly.*

"For perhaps he therefore departed for a season, that thou shouldest receive him forever;

"*Not now as a servant, but above a servant, a brother beloved,* specially to me, but how much more unto thee, both in the flesh and in the Lord?

"If thou count me therefore a partner, receive him *as myself.*

"*If he hath wronged thee, or oweth thee aught, put that on my account;*

"I, Paul, have written it with *mine own hand,* I will repay it: albeit I do not say to thee how thou owest unto me even thine own self besides.

"Yea, brother, let me have joy of thee in the Lord: refresh my bowels in the Lord.

"Having confidence in thy obedience, I wrote unto thee, *knowing that thou wilt also do more than I say.*

"But withal prepare me also a lodging; for I trust that through your prayers I shall be given unto you.

"There salute thee, Epaphras, my fellow-prisoner in Christ Jesus;

"Marcus, Aristarchus, Demas, Lucas, my fellow-laborers.

"The grace of our Lord Jesus Christ be with your spirit.

"Amen."

St. Jerome tells us that this Epistle has been thought unworthy of being placed among the canonical writings, as too familiar, and devoted to too special and trifling an object. But the Church has always maintained it, for which we should bless it, and millions of unhappy slaves will bless it with us, — it is a letter addressed by the hand of St. Paul, in the name of Jesus Christ, to all their Christian masters. Men have dared say that this letter sanctions slavery, since St. Paul sends back a fugitive slave to his master. Doubtless, he sends him back, but, first, the Apostle of nations has the goodness to teach and convert this slave, this fugitive, this robber; become the brother of Onesimus, but remembering also that he is the brother of Philemon, in what terms, with what art so charming in its tenderness, with what a mingling of authority and entreaty, he commends his new friend! He calls Philemon his fellow-laborer, Apphia his beloved sister, their household a *church*;* he praises them, and thanks God for their faith, and, above all, for their charity, liberality, and good works. He associates in his demand Timothy, Epaphras, Mark, Aristarchus, Demas, Luke, all his companions, all the saints of the infant Church. He, Paul, *already aged, a prisoner of Jesus Christ,* as he twice repeats, writes *with his own hand* for Onesimus, *his son,* whom he has begotten in his bonds. But, above all, it is in the name of "*God our Father and the Lord Jesus Christ*" that he salutes, entreats, and blesses them. And what does he ask?

* St. John Chrysostom (1st Sermon on the Ep. to Philemon, 1) says that under this name *church* St. Paul also comprises the other slaves of Philemon, and adds: "This word *church* should not give pain to masters, in seeing themselves thus confounded with their domestics. The Church knows no difference between masters and servants. It is only between good and bad actions that it makes discernment, ... for in Jesus Christ there is no difference between master and slave."

"*Though I might be much bold in Christ to enjoin thee that which is convenient, ... without thy mind would I do nothing; that thy benefit should not be as it were of necessity, but willingly.*" What is this *benefit*, what is this *thing which is convenient?* "THAT THOU SHOULDEST RECEIVE ONESIMUS FOREVER; NOT NOW AS A SERVANT, BUT ABOVE A SERVANT, A BROTHER BELOVED. . . . . Receive him *as myself!* * . . . . . If he oweth thee aught, I will repay it. . . . . . Yea, brother, let me have joy of thee in the Lord. Having confidence in thy obedience, I wrote unto thee, *knowing that thou wilt also do more than I say.*"

Does not this tenderness suffice? what more is needed? Some would prefer the six words: "I command you to free him!"

St. Paul might, as he says, have *enjoined* on Philemon *a thing which was his duty;* he did not wish it; like his Divine Master, he did not govern the affairs of men, but wrought internally on their soul, the seat of their will. He acted like a mother, who might say, "My son, I command you"; but is her voice less irresistible when she says, "My son, I love and entreat you!"

Philemon comprehended. Onesimus was freed; St. Ignatius of Antioch informs us that he died Bishop of Ephesus. The Church honors him, the 16th of February, as a martyr.

III.

SLAVERY IN THE SIGHT OF THE CHURCH.

THE word of the Master and the language of the disciples are now known to us.

It remains for us to see what were the effects of this divine word and this inspired language in the history of the world.

* St. John Chrysostom, *loc. cit.* He does not say simply, "Do not quarrel with him, do not be angry with him, let him quietly return to your house, *but receive him with the honor which he merits, since he has become the son of Paul.*"

But let us not forget that, even though the evangelical prediction should not yet have wholly triumphed in our day, it will be none the less the truth and law of the future. Jesus Christ was in advance of all that preceded him, but he is also in advance of all that will follow him. The end of the world will arrive before all the treasures of his holy law shall be understood, applied, and exhausted by mankind.

Some few of these treasures are blessings now acquired; this will be true, I firmly hope, before the close of this century, of the abolition of slavery. The struggle will have been long, and, as we shall see, formidable.

§ 1. Abolition of Ancient Slavery.

Two reasons permit us to be brief in this part of our study.

The first is, that the same work has been admirably done by the authors before cited. I shall confine myself, therefore, to an abstract, or rather selection of scattered traits in the history of Europe for twelve centuries, — an incomplete sheaf, as it were, gleaned at random from rich harvests.

The second reason is, that we may be certain in advance of finding again in the conduct of the Church the exact reproduction of the language of the Apostles. The water of a stream, whatever impurities it may gather in its tortuous flow, retains all the elements of the pure ripples of its source.

As we have seen, the Holy Scriptures lay down as absolute principles, the equality of men before God, the lawfulness of wages, the unity and brotherhood of the human race, the duty of loving one another, and of loving the smallest most of any, the obligation to do to our neighbor as we would have him do by us. . . . . . But they preach at the same time submission, the voluntary acceptance of the conditions inflicted on each one in the transient exile on earth. They radically change the title of authority and the spirit of servitude. They do not detach the slave from being a slave, they detach the master from being a master. Occupied, moreover, before everything with the enfranchisement of souls, they seek to make of the master and the slave two brethren on earth, and of these brethren two saints in heaven. To those who suffer, they say, "Wait!" to those who inflict suffering, "Tremble!"

1. The Church has not for a single instant deviated from this conduct. We might draw up a long list of opinions of the fathers, decisions of the councils, prescripts and letters of the popes. Some recommend patience, others recommend kindness; some punish revolt, others punish oppression. All reiterate the doctrine of the Lord on the equality of men. Thus the Church destroys slavery, yet notwithstanding appeases the slave.

It is easy to abuse this persistent system of tactics. To prove that the Church has favored slavery, it suffices to quote,* passing lightly over the rest, all the acts which preach submission or reduce rebellion to order.

But the Church does not confine itself to maintaining equilibrium.

As far as it can permit itself to act indirectly on the temporal domain of peoples and kings, more energetic in proportion as it becomes more powerful, it tempers, restrains, guards, and by degrees shakes, slavery. In the early ages, Christianity had no public power; it was, as it were, a family religion, often proscribed, concealed, and persecuted; it converted by thousands the lowest classes of society,—the laborers, the wretched, and the slaves; the glad tidings were first announced to the poor, as they were first witnessed by the shepherds. It calmed, and at the same time

* Opinions of St. Augustine, St. Jerome, etc., Council of Langres, 324; Council of Carthage, 419; Council of Seville, 619, etc.; cited by M. Larroque, *Revue de Paris*, December, 1856.

elevated and prepared them. What was there to do, except to preach to them dignity in patience ? Two men die a century apart, the one before, the other after Jesus Christ, the one named Spartacus (71), the other St. Peter (65). The slave Spartacus exclaims to his fellows, "Arise, revenge yourselves !." The fisherman, Peter, repeats to the wretched the words of the Master, "Blessed are the poor, for they shall be comforted."

In the third century, the pride of the philosophers reproached the Christians with their predilection for the unlearned and wretched : "If they meet an ignorant boor," exclaims Celsus, "they greet it as a good omen, and open wide their doors to him. Avowing that the dregs of the human race are worthy of their God, they show clearly enough that they will not, that they cannot, persuade any but idiots, men of no account, slaves, women and children. . . . . . They flock into gatherings of young lads, slaves and ignoramuses, to take advantage of their simplicity ; their houses overflow with weavers, shoemakers, and tanners. . . . . . Slaves teach children to throw off the yoke of their parents and their masters." Origen replied to Celsus by glorifying this divine love of the poor. More than one gross and brutish slave remained insensible, as St. Jerome informs us, to this touching tenderness. Others kissed the liberating cross ; women resisted the brutal passions of their masters in the name of Christ, as a St. Potamiana, of whom Eusebius speaks ; other slaves gained by the same blow, freedom, death, and heaven. The slaves Victorinus, Nereus, and Achilleus were among the number of martyrs. Before the third century, servitude in Christian families was completely transformed, although the Church had as yet no public power.*

A little later, the religion of the cottages invaded the palaces ; the executioners could not efface from their swords

* Moehler, Chap. IV.

the stain of the blood of the martyrs, nor from their souls the imprint of the faith of those they had immolated. The Church made use of its new power. It acted by the voice of doctors, it acted by the examples of saints, it acted by the rules of monasteries, it acted by the orders of popes, it acted by the decisions of councils.

The Greek and Latin Fathers gloriously established the native equality of men, lost by sin, restored by redemption. "The slave, like his master, glorifies Jesus Christ," says St. John Chrysostom (Hom. XIX. on the First Epistle to the Corinthians), "and the master acknowledges himself the servant of Jesus Christ; both submissive, yet free, both in this common obedience equal both as freemen and as slaves." St. John the Almoner, St. Augustine, St. Ambrose, St. Peter Chrysologus, elaborated the same doctrine.

Open, with Moehler, the *Acts of the Martyrs*, and admire, in the early ages of the Church, Hermes, Prefect of Rome, who was destined to become a martyr, converted, with his family, by the fifth successor of St. Peter, St. Alexander (109 – 119), and presenting for baptism, at Easter, twelve hundred and fifty slaves, whom he freed; Chromacius, another Roman Prefect under Diocletian (284 – 309), converted by St. Sebastian, restoring to liberty, after baptism, fourteen hundred slaves, exclaiming, "Those who begin to be children of God should no longer be slaves of men"; St. Melanie (417), the illustrious daughter of St. Albina, the granddaughter of St. Melanie,* the ancient, noble, pious, and powerful woman who affranchised several thousand slaves; St. Cantius and his family, less wealthy but no less virtuous, setting at liberty seventy-three slaves; St. Samson, the contemporary of St. Justinian, giving the same example.

These individual acts became a written law in the most ancient constitutions of monastic orders. St. Plato and St.

* Montalembert, *Les Moines d' Occident.*

Theodore (795), two of the leading saints of the Eastern Church, imposed this principle on their monasteries. "You should never employ slaves," writes St. Theodore, in his second testament, "either for personal service, or for conventual affairs, or for the cultivation of the land; *the slave is a man created in the image of God.*" In the West, the Council of Epaone (517) was forced to impose a limit on the zeal of monks for the abolition of slavery in their convents, in order not to risk becoming absorbed in an exclusive work. The son of Count de Maguelone, once the courtier of Pepin *le Bref* and Charlemagne, — St. Benedict of Anian (780), — would not suffer his convents to be served by a single slave; if he received them as a gift, he set them at liberty. In the bosom of the monastery, in the ranks of the priesthood, the former slave was confounded with the former master; he rose without obstacle to the episcopal dignity, and when haughty monarchs, like Bela, king of Hungary, were found to complain that a bishop was of servile condition, popes like Clement IV. (1265 – 1268) replied, that before God all men are equal. Several centuries before, St. Gregory the Great (590 – 604) had given the example of emancipation, with its reasons, and Gregory III. (745) had attached to the traffic in Christian slaves the same penalty as to homicide.

We find, again, in the councils the same inspiration and the same influence. From the third to the twelfth centuries, the Protestant Blakey * cites thirty-seven councils which rendered decisions in favor of slaves. Masters who maltreated their slaves were condemned (305), those who killed them were excommunicated (517). The right of asylum in churches was sanctioned (549). Bishops and priests who maltreated their slaves were severely punished (666 – 675). Manumission of slaves was protected and encouraged (441). Slaves freed by the Church were protected (549); and the

* The Temporal Benefit of Christianity.

Church took it upon itself to defend the liberty of all those who are freed, in whatever manner it may be (585). The Church instituted the redemption of captives (506); it permitted the ecclesiastical property (585), even to the sacred vessels (625), to be sold to ransom them. It interdicted the enslavement of a free man (566). It forbade a slave to be sold outside the limits of France (650). It forbade one Christian to hold another in slavery (922). It released Christians from the hands of Jews or heathens (538, 625, 633). It multiplied the causes for emancipation, so far as to declare the slave free who has been forced to work on Sunday, and also he who had been held at the baptismal font by his masters or their children,— a touching custom, by which the slave was born at the same moment to liberty and religion. It punished, before all, the bishops and priests who transgressed its decisions (656). It freed slaves who wished to enter religion or the orders (597, 655).* It interdicted the traffic in slaves (743).

To these decisions of the councils we might add others concerning marriage, the right of asylum, etc. We will confine ourselves to remarking, that this slow but persistent action extended from one end of Europe to the other. The councils, the dates and decisions of which we have just cited, were held at Orleans and at Toledo, at Rome and at Rheims, at Lyons and at Lerida, at Chalons and at Lateran.

The influence of the Church was exercised also in another manner. It acted on the law; by degrees the Gospel penetrated the learned statutes of the Empire and the sanguinary codes of the barbarians.† But here it did not act directly,

* The two most common modes of enfranchisement, became emancipation before the Church, and emancipation *by charter*. The greater part of these charters set forth as their reason, *the salvation of the soul.*

† *Influence du Christianisme sur le droit civil des Romains*, by M. Troplong. *L'Église et l'Empire au quatrième siècle*, by Albert de Broglie. See the works of Augustin Thierry, Guizot, Ozanam, Naudet, Mgr. Gerbet, Balmès, Rohrbacher, Bonald, etc.

and we must not be surprised that the sovereigns, so weak yet so cruel, so cowardly yet so passionate, with which it had to do, did not always obey it. We find in their laws that counter current, already pointed out in the conduct of the Church, of prescriptions to secure property and prescriptions to temper servitude and facilitate emancipation, with relapses into cruelties, inconsistencies, and delays; for which it is sought to render the Church responsible, as if it had in all times and all countries inspired those crowned idiots and monsters to whom it had had such difficulty to communicate only a little gentleness or religion.

It is forgotten that to the legislative reform was to correspond one of the most complicated of economical reforms. The substitution of machinery for manual labor in a few arts and manufactures, a transformation so distressing, is nothing compared to the substitution of paid for servile labor, as well in domestic service as in the practice of agriculture and manufactures.

In regard to this vast and salutary influence, we may cite and rightfully blame individual decisions, stamped with cruelty or covetousness; we may cite and rightfully stigmatize the conduct of unworthy prelates; we may justly deplore the guilty indifference of numerous popes, bishops, and members of the clergy, accomplices or insensible witnesses, from the earliest ages, of the customs of their times contrary to human liberty. It is not enough to answer, that the clergy at that time acted like all the world, for it was their duty to act better than the rest of mankind.

But it is unjust not to admit that, from century to century, the tide of good rose, prevailed, and gained the mastery over the tide of evil. The Church, severe as it was towards heretics, never permitted them to be regarded as new heathen and reduced to slavery. Slaves were better treated in the ecclesiastical domains than elsewhere. "Unter dem Krummstabe es ist gut zu leben," *It is good to* *live under the cross,* is a familiar proverb in Germany, and the German law (tit. ix.) contains the words, "*Colonum ecclesiæ, quem liberum vocant.*" We gladly complete the gallery of the saints, who may be styled the patrons of the abolition of slavery, by quoting Eptadius (500), St. Cesarus (512), St. Eubicius (531), St. Bathilda, once herself a slave (665), St. Aloysius (659), St. Bercharius, St. Bavon, and St. Gregory, ransoming and liberating slaves by thousands; Smaragdus counselling Charlemagne to emancipate his slaves (790), after the example of Queen Bathilda; bishops in France, Germany, and England preaching the same cause; the great bishop of Paris, St. Germain, exclaiming, on receiving an alms, "Return thanks to divine clemency, for we can ransom a slave"; * other bishops, as Acacius, St. Remberg, and Wilfrid, selling the sacred vessels to redeem and liberate slaves; St. John of Matha (1199) and St. Peter Nolasco (1215) founding special orders to dispute with Saracens and Africans the soul and freedom of Christian slaves.

II. The Church profited by every occasion in which its spiritual action was demanded by men, to suggest to them counsels of liberty. The birth of a prince was a cause for enfranchisement throughout the kingdom (in order that God may be pleased to grant life to the new-born child), reads the Formula 39, Book I. of Marculfus (7th century). The right of asylum, so ancient, and so much respected, especially in the West, had the same origin and the same end. We see, under the like influence, external signs become effaced; the monks wearing cropped hair, a usage hitherto regarded as servile, but which by degrees passed into custom. Finally, the numerous testaments emancipat-

* *Vie de St. Germain,* by Fortunat, Tom. I. p. 324: "All the Spanish, Scotch, Breton, Gascon, Saxon, and Burgundian slaves flocked thither in crowds at the name of the blessed St. Germain, quite sure that he would free them." — See Yanoski, Chap. II. p. 45.

ing slaves all bear the mention of a thought of salvation, and consequently the trace of Christian influence at the moment of death.

The Church had at its disposal, moreover, two powerful means of obtaining from the Christian master more than the law exacted of him, and of loudly and daily proclaiming equality.

The first was the confessional. The master who went to confession could no longer corrupt, maltreat, or afflict his slave; he could no longer revile him; it was his duty to care for, to convert, to instruct, in a word, to love him. If the fact of possessing him was not yet imputed to him as a sin, this possession at least became *a proximate cause*, an almost inevitable occasion of sin, and this was sufficient to disgust sincere souls by degrees with this dangerous advantage.

What human institution preaches equality, compared to the Catholic sacraments! The same water falls on the brow of the shepherd and the king; both are amenable to the same tribunal; on the same day they approach the same holy table; their souls at the last moment are weighed in the same balance, and over the same altars the monarch St. Louis and the slave St. Blandina obtain the same worship.

Words, those medallions which bear the chronological stamp of the variations of thought, themselves changed meaning, though they did not change sound. *To serve* was no longer to be a slave, the wife was no longer a concubine, to die was no longer to end. Doubtless, centuries were to roll away before these great lessons would pass into human laws. Neither princes nor legislators showed themselves in haste; the clergy itself was long in comprehending how far the light cast its rays which they had in their keeping. There were slaves long, therefore, in the sight of the Gaiuses and Papinians, there were no more slaves in the sight of Jesus Christ.

Little by little the chain of slavery was broken, or rather it fell apart and was soldered anew; but it was worn out, filed away, reduced to dust; the net ravelled out mesh by mesh.

In the sixth century, *field* slavery began to become transformed into *serfhood*,* *domestic* slavery subsisted, but was greatly softened, and, thanks to the number of manumissions, and the influence of the doctrine of the equality of men, servitude, which had progressed from the birth of human communities, commenced at last to decline.

III. Let us pause a moment before a remarkable monument of the precise point which this great work had reached at this distant epoch, the sixth century, — the letters of St. Gregory the Great, who occupied the pontifical throne from 590 to 604.†

It is known that the conversion of England was due to his sympathy for slaves. Touched by the youth and physiognomy of some English children exposed for sale in the market at Rome,‡ Gregory, before becoming Pope, ransomed and instructed § them, and prepared them to become the apostles of their country. On becoming sovereign pontiff, he did more; "their progress was slow and his zeal impatient," says Lingard; || he sent St. Augustine and his companions to convert this island, where the Saxons, more ferocious than the savages of Africa, who sell their captives taken in war, trafficked even in their fellow-countrymen and their own children.

* See the works of M. Edouard Biot and M. Yanoski.

† The text of those of the letters of this great pontiff which treat on the question of slavery has been published and fully commented upon by the learned Bishop of Charleston, in the Letters on Domestic Slavery, addressed in 1841, to Mr. Forsyth, then Secretary of State and of the Public Works. See Letters X.-XIII., Vol. III. of the Complete Works, published by Mgr. Reynolds, Baltimore, 1849. See also the great work of M. Montalembert, *Les Moines d' Occident.*

‡ Bede, *Hist. eccl. gent. Anglor.*, Lib. II. Cap. I. See the text, Results of Emancipation, Appendix, p. 412.

§ Letter to Candide, a priest sent into Gaul, Lib. V. Epist. X.

|| Lingard's Antiq. Anglo-Sax., Chap. C. 1.

The analysis of the numerous letters of St. Gregory the Great establishes the following points : —

The traffic in slaves was in his eyes abominable and forbidden.

Domestic slavery was permitted, but on condition that the slave really made part of the master's family.

Consequently, Jews and heathen were absolutely forbidden to hold Christian slaves. This interdiction was embodied in the law. (Cod., Lib. I. Tit. X. and Statute of Valentinian III. 425, to Cod. Theod.) St. Gregory rigorously maintained it, at the same time that he wrote other admirable letters to protect the Jews against excess of zeal and injustice.*

Furthermore, the slave was not to be separated from his wife and children, even in case of the division of an inheritance. (Lib. X. Epist. XXVIII.) † I take pleasure in quoting entire an indignant letter from St. Gregory to Maximian, Bishop of Syracuse (Lib. III. Epist. XII.) : —

"I hear of so much evil committed in this province, that I believe (may God avert the presage!) that its sins erelong will lead it to destruction. The bearer of these presents came to me in tears to complain that, several years ago, a man whom I do not know, of the church of Messina, had caused him to be baptized, and had forced him to marry one of his slaves, by whom he confessed to have had children, and that now he has violently separated this woman from him, and sold her to another. If this be true, it is, my friend, a cruel and unheard-of crime ; we, therefore, enjoin

* Lib. VII. Epist. LIX. *Fantino defensori Panormitano.* The Jews having complained that their synagogues had been unjustly wrested from them, he replies: "Ipsa sine ambiguitate aliqua volumus restitui ; quia sicut illis quidquam in synagogis suis facere ultraquam lege decretum est, non debet esse licentia; ita eis contra justitiam et æquitatem nec præjudicium nec aliquod debet inferre dispendium."

† See also Novelli, 163, 63; Justinian, 539. *De Rusticis qui in alienis prædiis nuptias contrahunt.*

it upon you to employ all the activity which you display in religious matters to make a thorough inquiry into this great and heinous offence (*tantum nefas*). And if the denunciation that has been made to me be true, you shall not only take care to repair the wrong, but shall hasten to exact an expiation which may appease God. As to the bishop who neglects to correct and punish men who commit such acts in his diocese, rebuke him severely ; letting him know that if such a complaint from one of his diocesans reach us again, we shall not only rigorously punish the culprit canonically, but himself also."

Add the continual preaching of the duties of masters, and the punishment of anger and lewdness. Add, also, the restriction of the causes which produce servitude ; thus, a son could not be held for the debts of his father, nor a wife reduced to servitude for debt.*

Slavery had become a true domestic service for life ; nevertheless, the domestic was still veritably *possessed ;* he might be *given away ;* St. Gregory gave one to the Bishop of Porto (Lib. X. Epist. LII.) ; another to the Councillor Theodore. (Lib. II. Epist. XVIII.) He could be pursued if he fled. (Lib. VII. Epist. CVII.) Barbarian captives might be bought by Christians. (Letter to Vitalis, Governor of Sardinia.) A free man might sell himself.

But these sales, a species of payment in advance, employed in other contracts, these permanent engagements, although they still implied the right of possession of one man over another, did not introduce *slaves* into the family, as was understood by the Romans, as is understood by the Americans. They were treated as equals. The illustrious St. Gregory scrupulously watched over all the wrongs that were done them. He writes (Lib. II. Epist. XLIV.) to Pantaleon, superintendent of the pontifical domain at Syr-

* Novelli, 134, Chap VII., and Justinian, 541. *Ne quis creditor filium debitoris pro debito retinere præsumat.*

acuse, to congratulate him on having repaired an abuse of his predecessor, who made use of false weights and measures to weigh the wheat owed by the colonists ; he recommends to him to estimate the damage which they had sustained, and not to suffer the Holy See to be an accomplice, but to restore them an indemnity in oxen and sheep, or money. He ends by protesting that he has quite enough, that he does not wish any one to enrich him, and entreats him to act in such a manner that at the great day of judgment neither of them may be deprived of his share in heaven by reason of the wrong done to unhappy servants ; he promises to bless him, himself and his children, if he succeeds in rendering them justice.

Penetrated by this love for his brethren, St. Gregory set a noble example ; he emancipated his slaves ; and nothing equals the beauty of the letter (Lib. VI. Epist. XII.) which he addressed to Montanus and Thomas, on bestowing liberty upon them. It begins by the words : "As our Redeemer, the Author of all beings, has been pleased to put on the human form, to break by the grace of his divinity the bonds which held us captive, and to restore to us our former liberty, it is fitting and salutary that those whom nature has made free, and whom human law has subjected to the yoke of servitude, should be restored by the boon of enfranchisement to the liberty in which they were born."

These documents clearly characterize, if I am not mistaken, the state of the question of slavery at the close of the sixth century ; they prove what Christianity had introduced into the customs and the laws, what it had obtained both of the ancient masters of the world and the barbarians. Was slavery destroyed? No, but it was transformed.

Let a publicist of the nineteenth century be scandalized that he does not read in the texts of the times the doctrine of property, the system of paid labor, the principles of civil liberty ; for my part, I am filled with admiration at so many peaceful victories, won no longer over Constantines or Justinians, in the bosom of civilized empires, but at an epoch when Italy belonged to the Lombards (568 – 778), Gaul to the Franks, Spain to the Goths, Portugal to the Suevi, Germany and the North to nameless hordes, evangelized by St. Boniface, to whom Pope Gregory III., in 735, wrote to strive to put an end to *the sale of slaves destined for human sacrifices;* England to the Britons, Picts, and Scots; Africa to the Visigoths, Vandals, and Moors; the East to Phocas (602 – 610) and Chosroes (531 – 579) while awaiting Mahomet.

What! the Council-General of Algiers still expressed the fear, at the close of 1858, that French tribunals could not be made applicable to Mussulmans; in English India, the rulers dare not thwart the usages of those they govern; yet we demand that the Church, the only moral force that struggled against heathenism and barbarism should, after scarce two centuries of systematic influence, have wrested servitude from hordes that hardly knew the meaning of property or family, and whose whole history was limited to subjugating or being subjugated.

Wherever it could do more, the Church went further; and, to its glory as well as to the honor of France, it is glorious to cite this Canon of the Council of Chalons-sur-Saone, held in 650, under the reign of Clovis II.

"Pietatis est maximæ et religionis intuitus, ut captivitatis vinculum omnino a christianis redimatur. Unde sancta synodus noscitur censuisse, ut nullus mancipium extra fines vel terminos qui ad regnum domini Clodovei regis pertinent, penitus debeat venumdare; ne quod absit per tale commercium aut captivitatis vinculo, vel quod pejus est, Judaica servitute mancipia Christiana teneantur implicita."

In the religious statutes of Ina, king of Wessex, about 692, we find: —

"III. Servus si quid operis patrarit die dominico ex præcepto domini sui, *liber esto.*"

In the statutes of Withred, King of Kent, about 697, rendered after the Council of Berghamstead, near Canterbury, we read again: —

"*Ninth Canon.* Si quis servum ad altare manumiserit, liber esto."

"*Fifteenth Canon.* Si quis servo carnem in jejunio dederit comedendam, servus liber exeat."

At the same epoch, Theodore, Archbishop of Canterbury (deceased in 690), who summed up in his person the East and the West, since he was born at Tarsus in Cilicia, like St. Paul, writes in his canonical rules, 117, "Servo pecuniam per laborem comparatam nulli licet auferre."

It would be as easy to multiply these quotations, borrowed from the sixth and seventh centuries, as difficult to find anything similar in the entire repertory of the laws of the Southern United States in the nineteenth century.

IV. But, alas! the march of humanity is not like the flow of a peaceful river, but that of a torrent, — to-day dried up, to-morrow swollen anew by the storm and overflowing the dikes raised to restrain it. Mahomet appeared. A new invasion of barbarians overrun the world like a deluge. The Saracens, Danes, Normans, and Moors filled Europe with their depredations; their victims, their captives, their slaves, were counted by thousands; the work of the Church was to be recommenced; it was recommenced. This it was that baptized Rollo, arrested Genseric and Attila, softened the manners of so many savage oppressors; its bishops protected the slaves and set the example of emancipation; new councils promulgated new decrees of gentleness and justice, and even at London, in 1102, seven centuries before the laws of Parliament, a council, assembled by St. Anselm, interdicted the traffic in slaves, tolerated during the whole of the Anglo-Saxon period (Lib. I. cap. xxvii.): "Ne quis illud nefarium negotium quo hactenus in Anglia solebant homines sicut bruta animalia venumdari, deinceps ulla tenus præsumat." * In 1167, Pope Alexander III. (1159–1181) declared that *all Christians should be exempt from servitude.*† In 1171, a council assembled at Armagh, in Ireland, declared all English slaves free.

The revolution was thus accomplished and completed in ideas ; why be astonished that it was slower in facts ? Create individual liberty in the midst of these stormy times ! Apply to the workman the system of paid labor ! Make his existence dependent on what is called to-day the quantity of labor and the abundance of capital ! All of these exigencies are anachronisms. The reed, in the midst of perpetual storms, can do nothing better than to take refuge at the foot of the oak. It was less important at that time to extricate beings without enlightenment and resources from servitude than to change the chain into a light bond, to soften the master, to upraise the servant, to proscribe oppression, to organize protection, and to pave the way for liberty by unceasingly teaching it to minds and introducing it into customs. This transformation was wrought in the bosom of the barbarous peoples successively converted, as it had been a first time accomplished by the influence of Christianity on the Roman world.

The researches of scholars agree in regarding slavery as almost extinct in France, Germany, and England from the eleventh to the thirteenth century.‡ The foundation of cities, the organization of trades, the fraternity of military service, the enthusiasm of the Crusades, the depopulation resulting from frequent famines, the amelioration of the laws, and various other causes, were so many influences, which united with the constant preaching of Christian equality to effect this great and slow work.§

* Moehler, note 53.

† Voltaire, *Essai sur l'histoire générale*, Tom. II. Chap. LXXXIII.

‡ Moehler, Biot, Naudet, Yanoski. It is well known that Bohemia and Denmark were not converted until the ninth century, Sweden in the twelfth.

§ As to serfhood, traces of it were prolonged to the beginning of our century.

It seemed accomplished before the outbreak of Protestantism, and it is just to leave the glory of this first part of the task to that which had had the trouble of it, — the Catholic Church. In Italy and Spain, slavery among Christians had disappeared; but that of heathens by Christians showed itself here and there after this epoch, both on account of the proud and indolent character of these nations, and, above all, of their relations with Africa and the East, where slavery and the slave-trade with all their horrors, were freely let loose.

Shall we measure by words the revolution which Christianity had wrought in ideas? What was a slave in the eyes of Cato? A thing. What was a slave in the eyes of Varro? An animal. What was a slave in the eyes of Seneca? A man. What was a slave in the eyes of St. Paul? A soul.

If Cato thought thus 234 years before Christ, if Varro thought thus 116 – 26 years before Christ, what must have been thought by the common herd of slaveholders before them and around them? If Seneca thought thus a century after Varro, — Seneca, born and died 3 – 65 after Christ, almost at the same moment with St. Paul, 2 – 66 after Christ, — how did he live, — this rich and luxurious advocate of the poor? How did his contemporaries act? St. Paul conformed his life to his doctrine; what he thought, the most obscure Christian thought with him; for both *believed* in the divine word, and not in their own opinion. What the Jews and Romans thought, erelong the Greeks, the Gauls, the Saxons thought also; and at the other end of Europe, in a land which Seneca and Varro despised as barbarous, almost savage, and which a monk sent by a Pope went to conquer for Jesus Christ, we read in a statute these

Louis XVI. abolished it in the domains of the crown, Aug. 8, 1779; and in the preamble of this edict his noble soul deplores "the remains of servitude which exist in several of the provinces." These remnants were consumed by the great conflagration of 1789.

words: "We forbid Christian slaves to be transported to foreign, and above all to heathen countries, *that souls may not be slain whom Jesus Christ has ransomed with his own blood*." Who, then, thus called these despised slaves *souls?* Was it a Roman, a Greek, a saint, a writer, a philosopher, a modern? No; it was a barbarian, living scarcely two hundred years after the conversion of his country by St. Anscharius (826), — the Dane, Canute the Great, in the beginning of the eleventh century.

It was at this moment, as we have already said, according to the most learned authorities, that ancient slavery may be considered as disappearing in almost all Europe.

Let it not be said, therefore, that Christianity has not abolished slavery; for before the thirteenth century it had abolished it twice, — abolished it in the Roman world, abolished it in the barbarian world, without speaking as yet of the modern world.

V. Let us sum up this long history.

The era of the emancipation of the slaves commenced on the day when it was recognized that, in the sight of God, there is neither bond nor free; and this principle was laid down by Christianity.

It did not write it in a book of philosophy, it did not insert it in a code; it engraved it on the human conscience. It was the opinion of but a few; it has become the opinion of all.

After having laid down the principle, it set the example; it admitted the slave into the Christian community; it elevated him, become free, to the rank of priest or bishop; it founded his family, it ransomed him, it enfranchised him, it ameliorated his lot even when it did not change it. A triple revolution, first moral, then social, then finally legal.

In the first century, the principle was laid down; the idea by degrees became virtue, virtue became usage, usage well-nigh became law.

In the third century, the general condition of the slaves was ameliorated and their number diminished.

In the sixth century, field slavery was transformed into *actual serfhood; domestic slavery* died out and became modified.

From the tenth to the thirteenth century, slavery, which disappeared from the Roman world, was resuscitated in the barbarian world; but Christianity rushed to encounter the barbarians, won them over, then ruled to the profit of the weak and oppressed ; slavery receded and disappeared throughout almost all Europe.

At the end of the Byzantine Empire (1453), the immemorial right of making a slave of a prisoner, the right of war, the chief source and reason of slavery, no longer existed between Christians.

Nothing is more confused in history than this slow transformation of the inferior classes; patient and admirable researches have been devoted to the study of the condition of persons in the different ages. It is impossible to read these learned writings without making two reflections : —

All of this work of transformation is due much less to the external changes of governments, institutions, and laws than to an internal change in souls. Sentiments of equality are born, and this suffices, before the laws sanction progress, before words express it. Reciprocally, laws change in vain; the relations between men are what their sentiments make them. My servant is my equal, although he still bears the same name as a slave ; yet, notwithstanding, I would not give him my daughter, although he be my equal. It is not, therefore, in the law, but in the heart, that are written both the title and the measure of equality.

This is the second reflection : —

It is very necessary that a higher doctrine should preach this true sentiment of equality to men, for all history reveals the frightful disposition which inclines them to put other men under their feet ; on the morrow of the birth of man, servitude is born ; twelve centuries after the birth of the Redeemer, it has scarcely yet expired.

Again, it is difficult to fix a precise date. Slavery seems at this epoch to have disappeared from Christian laws and customs ; yet isolated cases still break out, as after the disappearance of an epidemic. It is not only in slavery that we will again find vestiges of the enmity and ferocity of men, as piracy, the pillage of wrecked vessels, the right of *aubaine* over the property of foreigners, the atrocity of penal laws, etc. When a vast conflagration devours a city, the water does not gain the mastery over it at once ; sometimes those who extinguish the fire are themselves consumed ; sometimes they profit by the disorder to satisfy their cupidity. At length, the scourge is appeased ; but half-extinguished fires blaze up here and there ; or it seems as if the invisible hand of an enemy rekindled the conflagration at the other end of the city, where no watch had been kept.

We have seen servitude driven from the Roman world ; it springs up with the invasion of the barbarians ; barbarism is scarcely transformed, when new irruptions submerge the infant civilization ; the reign of Christ scarcely begins to extend when Mahomet rises to declare war against it ; slavery decreases, then springs up anew, the dike is carried away, then raised again ; the waves redouble their efforts. The slaves become Christians ; it will be the turn of the Christians to relapse into slavery. But, at least, O God ! may the Christians never consent again to become masters !

Alas ! alas ! we shall also witness this spectacle, and we shall have the grief of seeing slavery, expelled from the Old World, win and ravage the New.

§ 2. Abolition of Modern Slavery.

Schiller was right in saying that the history of the world is the condemnation of the world, "Die Weltgeschichte ist das Weltgericht." How many shameful maladies ravage proud humanity! What frightful rapidity in their progress, what lamentable slowness in their cure! But there is a still more despairing spectacle than the progress of evil, — the relapse.

I know not that history offers anything more glorious than the infuriated struggle of a feeble doctrine against a universal scourge, anything more discouraging than its rout after its victory, anything more glorious than the triumph of Christian brotherhood over slavery, anything more shameful than the revival in the sixteenth century of pagan slavery in true Christianity.

I. On the 12th of October, 1492, Christopher Columbus landed at San Salvador. He kissed the ground three times, planted the cross on it, then exclaimed: —

"O Lord, eternal and all-powerful God, who by thy sacred word hast created the firmament, earth, and sea, may thy name be blessed and glorified everywhere; may thy majesty be exalted which hath deigned to permit that, by thy humble servant, thy sacred name shalt be known and preached in this other half of the globe!"*

And on this magnificent land, the unexpected gift of God, who offered, as a present to the Old World, a new world and new brethren, all nations flocked speedily, thirsty for gold, bringing thither, under the Christian banner, slaves captured like game, bought like oxen, treated like dogs.

No nation has the right to reproach another with this infamy, or to cast the first stone. All sinned. Catholicism, which had destroyed ancient slavery, Protestantism, which it has been sought to make the parent of modern liberty,

* *Christophe Colomb*, by M. Roselly de Lorgues, I. 278.

both suffered themselves to be infected by the example of a new paganism, the religion of Mahomet.

Portugal and Spain are supposed to have been the first. Who knows whether the weight of such a crime does not still weigh upon their destinies?

The Mahometans of Africa brought negroes to Lisbon to exchange for the prisoners that the Portuguese had made from among them. Upon this, the latter conceived the idea of going themselves to buy negroes in Africa, at their station at Arguin. On the 8th of August, 1444, before the birth of Columbus, a certain Captain Lanzarote landed for the first time at Lagos, in the kingdom of Algarve, 235 negro slaves whom he sold. This commerce continued, and in 1539 the sale amounted in Lisbon to 12,000 heads.

The Spaniards imitated this example; Seville became the entrepôt of the traffic in slaves, and the trade developed itself at Madeira and the Canaries. The introduction of slaves at St. Domingo dates from 1510, at Cuba from 1521. They were brought successively into all the Spanish and Portuguese colonies, and it is known that the Indians owe it to Las Casas that they were not also reduced to slavery.

After the foundation of the United States, a Dutch ship was the first, in 1620, to land twenty negroes at Jamestown, Virginia.

The first slaves of the French West Indies were brought thither in 1650. There were none as yet in Guiana in 1688.

The increase of the number of slaves was not rapid, the *hired whites* or immigrants at first sufficed for labor. At St. Domingo, slaves were dispensed with for eighteen years, at Cuba for ten years. There were in Cuba, in 1763, only about 32,000 negroes.

But two causes rapidly increased these figures, — the development of the consumption of sugar, coffee, and cotton, and the profits of the *slave-trade.*

All of the maritime nations * have carried on the slave-trade; next to Spain, to England belongs the shame of abandoning itself with the most impudence and avidity to this odious traffic. A treaty, in 1763, secured it the monopoly, and the very name of the slave-trade (*traite*, trade) is a stigma imposed on the English tongue.

Disgust prevents our tracing the remembrance of these horrible scenes, of which happily the peoples of Europe, save Spain and Turkey, are no longer the witnesses or accomplices. For two centuries the Father of the earth and of mankind has looked down from heaven upon three continents polluted by Christian hands, — Africa, desolated by savage wars, and traversed by droves of robust men, young women and little children, captured by the sword or musket, driven onward by the lash, marching through burning sands, decimated by death, and leaving after them by hundreds those decaying corpses and dry bones which the unfortunate Mungo Park and the intrepid Caillé encountered on their route; Europe sharing with America this living merchandise, and truckling gold for human blood; the ocean furrowed by floating prisons, loaded with these *ebony logs*, heaped up in the bottom of the hold, the waters serving as a silent tomb to all those whom death, less cruel than men, delivered from their execrable hands.

It is calculated that a proportion of from one seventh to one tenth of the human beings who were the victims of this traffic lost their lives during the voyage; how many died in Africa before reaching the coast, no one knows. More than one hundred million Africans were thus apportioned among the Spaniards, English, French, Portuguese, Dutch, Danes, Swedes, North Americans, Brazilians, — in a word, all Christian peoples that possessed colonies.

I need not repeat here what I have said respecting all these slave countries; I need not ask myself whether these

* See *The Slave-Trade*, Book Sixth.

Christians treated their slaves better than the heathens treated theirs. I should be glad to believe it; but it is permissible to doubt that the heathens possessed them in greater numbers, and to add that they did not owe them to so odious means. War is a bad reason, but it is at least a pretext; purchase for the love of gain is an abomination without excuse.

II. When a criminal usage introduces itself into facts, we are certain to find the demonstration of it in books. Man likes to justify what he practises. A war of demonstrations and protestations then becomes established on the ground of ideas, the issue of which decides the triumph of evil or of good on the disputed ground.

The revival of slavery in fact resulted, therefore, in the revival of doctrines in favor of slavery.

The illustrious Dominican Las Casas saw his fervid writings against slavery arrested by the royal censorship, and theologians prefer to his protestations the erudite subtilties of Sepulveda on races born for slavery.

In the seventeenth century, at the moment when the human thought attained an incomparable height, the greatest minds seemed indifferent. The founder of the right of nations, Grotius, coldly disserted on the lawful causes of slavery; Puffendorf imitated him. Bossuet himself only said a word, in passing, on the origin of slavery by war;* his lofty reason did not pause. Happily, his heart was moved, and in the admirable *Panegyrique sur Saint Pierre Nolasque,*† he extols this hero of sanctity, and shows him to us "content to give everything, to sacrifice everything, provided he procure the liberty of his brethren, ... preferring the liberty of the meanest slave to his own."

In the eighteenth century, so justly proud of its passion for humanity, slavery was attacked, but almost laughingly.

* Preface to the Letters of Jurieu, Art. 50.

† Tom. VII., Versailles edition, p. 48.

Voltaire scoffed at slavery, and also at the slave; he took interests in a colonial society. Montesquieu, profounder and graver, devoted an entire book, composed of nineteen chapters,* to slavery. But he jested, he hesitated, he concluded but weakly, to such a point that learned minds † have found it possible to regard him as a partisan of slavery. I believe, on the contrary, that he was its adversary, and I know nothing more decisive than his Chapter XV., which terminates with these admirable words: —

"It is impossible that we should suppose that these people are men; for, if we supposed them to be men, we should begin to believe that we ourselves are not Christians.

"Small minds too much exaggerate the injustice done the Africans, for, if it were as they say, would it not enter the heads of the princes of Europe, who make so many useless agreements among themselves to make a general one in favor of mercy and pity?"

It is to the closing years of the eighteenth century, it is, above all, to the beginning of the nineteenth century, that belongs the generous movement of minds which called forth that *general agreement* of the sovereigns, signed in 1814, which Montesquieu was not wise enough to prophesy.

III. What had the Church done during this time. Nothing, it is said. Alienated from the charity of its founders by a long use of power, rent by the Reformation, everywhere enfeoffed by the governments, it permitted kings to sign agreements for the slave-trade in the name of the Holy Trinity, it lulled their scruples by representing servitude as a means of conversion, it had bishops, priests, and monks the owners and sellers of slaves, it still has theologians who defend slavery.

I do not deny some few of these misfortunes, — God has not rendered his ministers inaccessible to the vices of their

* Lib. XV. Chap. I.-XIX.

† Ch. Giraud, Memoir to the *Académie des sciences morales*, on negro slavery.

times, — but I deny that these faults were without counterpoise, I seek the voice of the Church elsewhere than in the example of its vilest members. What was said by. the Popes? What was done by the saints?

In four centuries, four times the Holy See solemnly protested.*

On the 7th of October, 1482, Pius II., at the time of the first discoveries of the Portuguese in Africa, vehemently censured the Portuguese, who dared hold in bondage men like unto themselves.

After the discovery of the New World, May 29, 1557, Paul III. declared that it was "an invention of the Devil to affirm that the Indians might be reduced to servitude," stigmatized the cupidity of the Spaniards, and decreed "that the Indians, *like all other peoples, even those that have not been baptized*, shall enjoy their natural liberty and the ownership of their property; that no one has the right to trouble or disquiet them in what they hold from the liberal hand of God. All that shall be done in a contrary direction will be unjust, and condemned by divine and natural law."

On the 22d of April, 1639, Urban VIII. forbade any "to deprive the slaves of their liberty, to sell them, to buy them, to carry off themselves, their wives, or their children from their country, and to despoil them of their property."

In 1741, Benedict XIV. repeated to the bishops of Brazil the same prohibitions.†

If bishops, priests, and laymen were seen to have slaves, others were seen to sell themselves in order to free them. There might have been read, with incomparable sorrow, on the doors of churches, placards which cannot be cited with-

* See Balmès, Wallon, and Van Biervliet.

† See the text in Appendix.

‡ In the primitive ages, St. Gregory of Armenia (whom the Church honors, Oct. 1), whose father had slain King Pusaron, to expiate the fault constituted himself the slave of the son of this king, and endured, without a murmur, the most terrible tortures.

out weeping and blushing: "ON LEAVING MASS, *the sale of the negress — enciente, with her children,* etc., *will be proceeded with.*" But there were also to be seen the Las Casases, the Clavers, the Libermanns, the Jean de la Mennaises, devoting themselves to the defence, conversion, and instruction of these poor creatures. The Christian doctrine was viewed in a distorted light, and preachers and monarchs congratulated themselves on wresting from tyranny, and restoring to the faith, the Africans passing from the bloodthirsty sultan of their country to the hands of the slave-trader, as if one crime could excuse another. But it was impossible to stifle the pure voice of the Gospel beneath these guilty sophisms; they did not cease for a single day to repeat in all the churches the little text that knows no change: "Thou shalt love thy neighbor as thyself."

Finally, by a sort of compensation, while sovereigns organized the sale of men, the Church perpetuated and developed the ransom of captives.

Too little is known of this sublime undertaking.

On this earth, the transient sojourn of good and evil, the same sun of spring germinates the wheat and the tares, the same progress of the art of navigation lends the same facilities to commerce and discoveries as to piracy, and by another harmony of the moral world, the same epoch witnesses the birth of the crime and its expiation. At the end of the thirteenth century, the Christians renounced slavery everywhere, but they fell captives in their turn to the merchants of Genoa and Venice, the Moors of Spain, and the pirates of Algiers, Tunis, and Morocco. At this moment, an ancient and sublime custom of the Church resumed new developments. It had always been forbidden to sell the sacred vessels, *except for the redemption of captives.* St. Ambrose had legitimized this touching exception in eloquent words: "What! you will not sell vessels of gold, and you will suffer the living vessels of the Lord to be sold! The true adornment of the sacraments is the redemption of captives, *ornatus sacramentorum redemptio captivorum est.* . . . . Let the chalice ransom from the enemy him whom blood has ransomed from sin. . . . . This blood has not only tinged the metal, but, by an impression of the divine operation, has in some sort transmitted to it a redeeming virtue." (Book II., Off. Chap. XXVIII.) St. Paulinus of Nola gave himself as a hostage for the son of a poor widow. Two saints, both Frenchmen, both born on the shores of the Mediterranean, which were desolated by pirates, John of Matha and Peter Nolasco, conceived at the same epoch the idea of consecrating themselves and founding a special order devoted with them to the redemption of Christian slaves. The one, in concert with Felix de Valois, founded in 1199 the order of *Trinitarians,* which the people called by the name of its first father, *Mathurins.* The other,* aided by Raymond de Pegnafort, instituted in Spain the order of our Lady of Mercy (1218).

* Nothing equals the beauty and simplicity of the life of St. Peter Nolasco, as it is recounted in the Roman breviary. He was a French nobleman, from the environs of Carcassonne. From childhood, his heart was full of the most tender charity, and it is related that, one day, while he was sleeping, the bees deposited their honey on his lips. Having withdrawn to Spain to shun the heresy of the Albigenses, the Holy Virgin appeared to him, and manifested to him how agreeable it would be to her divine son that Christians should devote themselves more to the redemption of their brethren, the slaves of infidels. Peter, who had already expended all that he possessed for the ransom of slaves, devoted himself to the foundation of an order, with the co-operation of Raymond de Pegnafort, and King James of Aragon, who had had at the same moment an inspiration from above. Gregory IX. approved the new order. James of Aragon permitted it to bear his royal arms on its costume. The members added to the three habitual vows, the vow to give themselves as hostages to the heathen, if necessary, for the redemption of their brethren. All Christianity associated itself by alms with this admirable apostleship. It is affirmed that the blessed founder, full of works and days, asked, when, after having received the last sacraments, he felt death approaching, to have the psalm read to him, *Confitebor tibi, Domine in toto corde meo;* at the line, *Redemptionem misit Dominus populo suo,* God has sent redemption to his people, he gave up the ghost.

A number of relations of the Voyages of the Brothers of Mercy and the Trinitarians have been published. I have before my eyes five of these relations, viz :—

Philip Augustus favored the Trinitarians; James, the Brothers of Mercy. These orders received from the bishops

1. *Le Miroir de la charité chrétienne*, or the relation of a voyage made last year (1662) by the brothers of the Order of our Lady of Mercy of the kingdom of France to the city of Algiers, whence they brought back a hundred Christian slaves; by one of the Fathers redeemers of the same order. Aix, 1663.

2. Relation of what happened in the three journeys made by the brothers of the Order of our Lady of Mercy into the States of the King of Morocco, for the redemption of captives in 1704, 1708, and 1712, by one of the Fathers deputed for the redemption by the congregation of Paris, of the same order. Paris, 1724.

3. Voyage for the redemption of captives, to the kingdoms of Algiers and Tunis, made in 1720, by Fathers François Cormelin, Philemon de la Motte, and Joseph Bernard, of the order of the Holy Trinity, called Mathurin, Paris, 1721; followed by conversations on the traditions of the Church for the solace and redemption of captives.

4. Relation, in the form of a journal, of the journey for the redemption of captives in the kingdoms of Morocco and Algiers, during the years 1723, 1724, and 1725, by Fathers Jean de la Faye, Procureur-General, Denis Mackar, Augustin d'Arcisas, and Henry Le Roy, deputies of the order of the Holy Trinity, styled Mathurins. Paris, 1726.

5. Travels in the barbarous States of Morocco, Algiers, Tunis, and Tripoli, or Letters from one of the captives just ransomed by the regular canons of the Holy Trinity. Paris, 1785.

Of these five relations, the most ancient is at once the most curious and the most touching.

It especially makes known the prodigious difficulties of the enterprise of the zealous missionaries. The first trouble was to collect a considerable sum. Instead of freely taking a convenient place on a fixed day in a packet, it was necessary to obtain a permit from the Governor of Provence, then M. de Mercœur, with a safe-conduct from the admiral, then M. de Nuchèze, then to freight a bark, insure its value at the rate of 4 per cent, and pass at least three days and nights on the sea, if the weather were favorable and the pirates not on the watch; at Algiers, to choose between numerous supplicating slaves, and masters who overcharged the buyers, to pay ten per cent to the custom-house for entrance, to pay the governor, to pay the functionaries, to pay the master, to pay the debts of the slave, to disburse thus a sum of which the price of the slave was scarcely one third, to submit to a thousand delays, to avoid a thousand snares, often to remain as hostages; or if able at length to carry away these poor Christians, *who awaited the hour of departure as souls in purgatory await their deliverance* (p. 143), again to pay the custom-house, then to brave once more the sea, and the pirates, more to be feared than the waves. Men were found in the Church to carry on this vocation during six hundred years.

But what task was better fitted to move a charitable and pious heart! Read, in the relation of 1662, the picture of the supplications addressed to the Fathers by the wretched slaves:—

and the Popes especially the most solemn and repeated encouragements. Approved by Innocent III. (1198 – 1216),

" The Fathers, on returning to their house, found there two or three hundred slaves. Some brought letters to show that they were recommended by prelates and other persons of authority. Others alleged their youth, representing that their patrons used sometimes flatteries, at others threats, to make them quit the belief of the Church, and become the followers of Mahomet, and that they solicited them to abominable lewdness. Others showed their white hairs, urging that as long as they were able to endure the fatigues of slavery, they had been patient, but that succumbing under the weight of years, and being unfit for labor, it was a duty to give them repose by releasing them from slavery. You should have seen men of middle age come to ask liberty, not so much for their own comfort as to gain a livelihood for their wives and little children. There were persons of condition, brave officers, who hinted that, their talents being hidden, and their quality unknown, they might then be had cheaply, whereas if it were longer deferred, all would be discovered, and they could only be released by the payment of a fat ransom. Some caused great compassion, weeping because, if not ransomed in three days, they would be forced to go to make war against Christians. Whole families presented themselves, and the husband, speaking in the name of the rest, entreated that his wife or son might be ransomed, or that he might be set at liberty to go to Christian lands to procure alms for the two others. Some disinterested Christians gave or loaned money for a portion of the ransom of others whom they knew to be most maltreated. Finally, some charitable captives came to ask nothing for themselves, but rendered themselves solicitors for others, accompanied by the blind, the deaf, the lame, and the maimed, praying that since they could be bought cheaply, they should not be left to perish in their misery. Others made complaints that they had to do with masters possessed of devils, who did not leave them an instant's repose, but sometimes stunned them with blows; at others, worked them to death; at others, did not give them wherewith to live, contenting themselves with loading them with insults. Others affirmed that, being unceasingly employed in working in the mountains, they mixed only with men plunged into the most shameful vices; that no one ever spoke to them of God; that for six months they had not had an opportunity to hear mass, and that to their great regret four or five years had elapsed without their being able to go a single time to confession. O God, is it not true that these poor slaves will stand up in condemnation against many Christians who abuse so many fine opportunities of so easily advancing the affairs of their salvation!" These pious sentiments of the redeemers did not always inspire the redeemed. Nothing can be more absurd than the letters of a ransomed captive, a century after, in 1785. He had been separated, before espousing her, from *an adorable Eugenie.* He writes to his future father-in-law. The editor publishes these letters *to interest feeling souls by teaching them the misfortunes of a brave young soldier, deprived of all the joys which marriage and love promised him, and to satisfy philosophy by acquainting it with a country whose peculiarities, often singular and bizarre, may rightfully pique its curiosity.* It is much if, after more or less serious narratives, the captive renders thanks

and by his nephew Gregory IX. (1227 – 1241), in the beginning, they were unceasingly loaded with benefactions by almost all their successors, Alexander IV. (1254), Clement IV. (1265), Nicholas III. (1277), Nicholas IV. (1288), Calixtus III. (1457), Leo X. (1513), Clement VII. (1523), Clement VIII. (1601), Urban VIII. (1623), Alexander VII. (1655), and numerous others beside. This protection was destined to last as long as the work itself of the two orders, which acted during two centuries, in the midst of incredible difficulties. The Order of Mercy had, in 1655, ransomed from Algiers alone more than 12,000 slaves, and left a great number of its members hostages, faithful to the fourth solemn vow, added to the three vows of religion : *In Saracenorum potestate in pignus, si necesse fuerit ad redemptionem Christi fidelium detentus manebo.* The ransomed slaves were brought back to France, and carried in procession through the cities where their redeemers had collected their ransom, then restored to their own families and their native land. The two orders several times attempted together, especially in 1704, a general redemption of all the captives held in Algiers and Morocco ; but it was not until the reign of Louis XVI. that this noble work was accomplished by the ransom of the last Christian slaves, numbering 314, at the epoch when this great but unfortunate monarch abolished the last remnants of slavery in the royal domains (1779).

to " the *paternal cares* shown him by the canons of the Holy Trinity, *who obtained of our king permission to ransom us. What joy will be felt by these virtuous brothers when they see the distracted bride fly to meet her husband! So true is it that man is good, and that the sensibility of his heart never appears better than in these great spectacles.*" This jargon savors of its epoch; it has its marked place between Rousseau and Robespierre. I wish to draw from it a single conclusion, namely, that to devote themselves to the redemption of captives, the children of Peter Nolasco and John of Matha had need of another attraction than gratitude, — of another permission than that of the king; — to ransom slaves was to please God; such charity has no other explanation nor other recompense.

Strange contrast! At this moment, in Africa, the redemption of the slaves was completed; in America, slavery was on the point of assuming a lamentable growth; in Europe, God raised up a movement of public opinion which was about to win the cause of the slaves forever in the sight of the conscience, and to arm for its abolition the two first nations of the world. The spirit of the French Revolution, on this subject at least, was wise enough to remain Christian; and this is why it was conqueror. Who commenced, who kindled this generous flame? In England, a pious Christian, William Wilberforce; in France, a priest whose political and religious faults should not efface his good actions, Henry Gregory, since Bishop of Tours, then Curate of Embermesnil. In England, in France, it was the *saints*, as they were called, who did violence to politics. Philosophers, literary men, poets, journalists, diplomatists, orators, all who spoke or wrote, had their part in this crusade. Pius VII. associated in the proceedings which, in 1814, brought about the abolition of the slave-trade. Gregory XVI. wrote the memorable bull of Dec. 3, 1839, which stigmatized, condemned, and, going still further, forbade any one, in fitting terms, to *despoil, torment, and reduce to servitude human beings.*

In America, Holland, and Spain the movement against slavery was, again, is becoming more and more a wholly Christian movement.

Doubtless neither Protestants nor Catholics are irreproachable. There are curates in Brazil who have children and slaves. There are ministers in the United States who practise the most odious slavery. There are, lastly, theologians, both Catholic and Protestant, who still teach the lawfulness of slavery.* Others, more numerous, are silent,

* These theologians take a purely abstract and theoretic stand-point; the greater part, in practice, abhor slavery, and tolerate it only in doctrine.

Theologians in general have their tendencies, — they love the absolute, tradi-

not believing in the mission of attacking, in the countries which they are evangelizing, a system established by law.

But the great majority of the clergy, followed by the great majority of believers in the Catholic Church and the dissenting communions,* belong to the cause of emancipation. In 1853 the Council of the province of Bordeaux assembled at Rochelle, and, receiving for the first time into its bosom the bishops of the colonies, publicly thanked God "for the blessing of liberty, accorded to so many men, who, although of a different color, are our brethren in Adam and in Jesus Christ, and who were held in hard slavery, *to the destruction of their souls,*" — a solemn declaration, by which the Church of France, gathering up the links of the past, closes the list of the ancient councils of the early ages, and prolongs to our hearing the echo of their holy voice.

Another council, as it were, might be formed of men

tion, and indulgence. Indulgent, they hesitate much, make distinctions and comment before declaring that such an action is a sin; I thank them for this disposition, so favorable to poor, feeble humanity. Absolute, they examine each thing in itself, *in se*, before regarding it in a practical point of view; and thus it very often happens to them to lay down a general rule followed directly by a universal exception. It is in this manner that they declare slavery allowable when its origin is legitimate, its practice irreproachable, its end pure and religious, the slavery of one saint in the house of another, in the bonds of the tenderest and most Christian love; but as these conditions are never encountered, this ideal slavery figures in books, and real slavery falls under all the censures deserved by the faults which it involves. Finally, given up to the worship of tradition, theologians are especially anxious to connect themselves with the chain of the past, and to rest their doctrines on those which were professed before them; a valuable, or rather indispensable, tendency when points of faith are in question, — a dangerous tendency when it regards open questions, the solution of which changes and is susceptible of progress. They teach concerning slavery what was taught yesterday and the day before, what no priest or layman believes longer to-day. They teach that slavery is not unlawful, — 1st. When it proceeds from a legitimate war or voluntary sale; 2d. When it respects the soul, body, family, and instruction of the slave. But I challenge any one to show me to-day, throughout all Christianity, a single slave who has become such as a prisoner of war or through voluntary sale, to say nothing of the manner in which he is treated.

* The Uprising of a Great People, by Count Agenor de Gasparin.

who do not belong to our faith, and who, notwithstanding, declare, with a common voice, that the abolition of slavery is the work of Christianity. Listen to the men, so different in opinion, whom this cause has had the happiness to unite, — a radical democrat like M. Schœlcher, an ardent Protestant like M. de Gasparin, a fervent Catholic like M. de Montalembert, a sincere liberal like the Duc de Broglie; listen to Burke and Pitt, to Canning and Stanley, to Parker and Channing, — all invoke the Gospel. The Gospel is the terror of masters, the hope of slaves, the argument of their friends, the support of legislators, the source, the light of public opinion.

It is necessary, above all, to hear the appeals that are made to religion as soon as speech-making is abandoned to begin to act. It is not named in decrees, it is not invoked in assemblies, but it is charged with success. Whether we will or not, we return directly or circuitously to Christianity, as the institution of human liberty. The legislators who do not say at first, "Enlighten us!" are forced to say erelong, "Aid us!"

Thus Christianity explains to the philosopher the cause of the evil, it inspires the writer with the desire to combat it, it furnishes the statesman with the means to destroy it without danger. Slavery was not abolished before it, it is not abolished outside of it, it will not be abolished without it. Before the suppression of slavery, it rehabilitates labor, it affirms equality, it prescribes charity and justice, it softens the master, it elevates the slave, it moves the law After the abolition of slavery, it corrects the slave of idleness and envy, it founds for him the church, it founds the school, it founds the hospital, and, if it establishes neither prison nor court of justice, it visits the prisoner, and inspires the judge.

The history of the present and that of the past unite their enlightenment. Men have to choose.

Their eyes on America, they are at the moment of contemplating the abolition of slavery, committed to the bloody hands of violence.

Their eyes on history, it is given them to follow the peaceful and gradual extinction of this scourge, by the gentle but strong hand of Him who has ransomed sinners, upraised the weak, and delivered captives, — our Lord Jesus Christ.

CHAPTER III.

THE THEORY OF SLAVERY.

It is fitting that, before summing up and concluding, I pause to ask the question, If Jesus Christ did not abolish slavery, who then destroyed it? who then will suppress it?

Is it philosophy? is it human reason?

I ask philosophy, I ask human reason, to explain to me, if this be true, what is slavery? what is the nature, what the origin of this scourge?

Interrogate conscience, — it answers that liberty is the most precious of possessions, the clearest, the most sacred of rights.*

But interrogate history, — it teaches that half the human race has lived in slavery, is still groaning in it, relapses into it unceasingly, and that tyrants and victims are eternal.

How comprehend, how explain, this lamentable contradiction? how resolve this enigma?

This is a monstrous fact, yet it is the most ancient preserved in the memory of man. As soon as two men, as soon as two peoples, have been face to face with each other, the stronger has subjugated the weaker, and as

* "I have no need to reason to know that my liberty is inviolable. It is my right, like life itself. No one can take away my life without crime; and no one can mutilate, vitiate, or degrade my being without crime. I hold from the same God existence and the faculties which render it possible to me. It cannot be that Divine and human laws condemn the assassin and absolve the liberticide. . . . . . Not only is my liberty mine, like my life, and no one can dispose of it in my place, but I am not master to dispose of it myself. It is not enough to say that liberty is a right; liberty is a duty. . . . . . It does not depend on me to throw off the responsibility which God has imposed on me; it is not permitted me to desert the post where I have been placed by the Creator." — Jules Simon, *Liberté*, Tom. I. pp. 25, 26.

soon as there has been a law, it has decided in favor of the stronger.

The most ancient of facts is also the most universal. Slavery was an institution of the Greeks and Romans, the Germans, the Scythians, the Ethiopians, the Persians, the Indians, the barbarians, more refined among some, more brutal among others, everywhere pitiless, incontestable. All exercised or endured it ; sometimes it was shaken, never destroyed ; and rebel or freed slaves held slaves in their turn.

This is a fact immemorial, obstinate, everywhere rising and springing up anew, indestructible, universal, at once natural and contrary to nature. Man, to exempt himself from labor, condemns another man to it ; if he resist, he beats him ; if he become useless, he sells him ; if he be fruitful, he disposes of his progeny ; — in a word, over this being, his fellow, who has the same form, the same language, the same soul, and the same face, he exercises in every point the empire of the Arab over his steed.

This pretended right philosophers do not condemn, but demonstrate ; laws do not reprove, but organize.

Once more, how comprehend and how explain it ? Who will dare answer coldly, Since this fact is universal and immemorial, it is, therefore, legitimate ?

We might reply by the witticism of Voltaire : "For some thirty or forty centuries, the weasels have been in the habit of eating our chickens, yet we take the liberty of destroying them when we meet them."

The universality of slavery proves nothing more against the equality of men, than the universality of polytheism proves against the unity of God.

Let us seek again the secret of this enigma.

Is the theory of Aristotle on the inequality of *souls* found worthy of refutation ? Would we lose ourselves with the Hindoos in the clouds of the doctrine of pre-existence ?

Do we prefer to believe in the differences of races, and do we hope to find in the color of the skin or the inclination of the facial angle the title-deed of one brother over another?

Are we to listen to the false economists who laud the organization of forced labor, the false jurisconsults who deduce servitude from a contract which lacks at once a lawful object and the consent of the parties, the false philanthropists and false Christians who make of slavery a happy system of moralization and a convenient catechumenate, the false liberals who found on the subjection of the greater number the political existence of the ruling minority?

To all these vain or cruel systems, whether founded on nature or utility, the human heart and history return a loud denial.

The Creator is ignorant of the inequalities invented by science. To all men, it has pleased him to give a soul; to all souls, liberty.

No, no, labor, morality, religion, politics, do not accept the odious services of the slavery which dishonors without seconding them.

Were it true, moreover, these explanations would need, in their turn, to be explained. If labor, morality, religion, and politics derived a real benefit from servitude, how could we comprehend this monstrous amalgam, how justify God for having thus rendered evil necessary and inherent to good? This would be a second enigma to resolve.

It is repeated readily enough, that servitude is among the imperfections which mark the first steps of humanity on earth; that it will gradually disappear through the influence of progress and in the course of time.

If humanity had been fated to pass through slavery as it passes through infancy, the law would have been common to all men without exception; who, therefore, would have had a right to be *master?*

If it had been an evil destined to disappear by degrees and according to the laws of a continued progress, slavery would doubtless have been more cruel and more universal in the earliest days of humanity; after a few centuries it would have been seen to grow lighter, then finally to disappear. But this was not the case. In the beginning, it was confounded with domestic service in the bosom of patriarchal life. In proportion as society became enlightened and organized, slavery became organized also; the longer it endured, the heavier grew its weight, and the heathen tribes of Africa and the heathen slave-traders of the New World invented cruelties and forged chains which the ancients never knew. The moderns have possessed more slaves than the ancients, they have invented the *slave-trade, slave-trading,* the prohibition of emancipation, — odious refinements unknown to antiquity. Far from decreasing, then, the evil is growing, as the movement of a falling body accelerates through the invisible law of gravity.

Slavery is not, therefore, an inferior condition, which will disappear through the lapse of time alone. What, in fine, is its nature, what its origin?

Shall we, like almost all writers, return to the old theory, which derives slavery from the right of war, — that is, from the right of the stronger?

This theory is revolting to us. At our epoch, amidst formidable wars, the Christian powers hasten to restore prisoners without exchange or ransom, after treating them humanely.* This theory is, however, the most common and most plausible; for anger sometimes hurries away justice, and vengeance is the criminal punishment of another crime; we cannot pardon, but can nevertheless comprehend them.

Historically, war has indeed often been the origin of slavery; but it has proceeded from a thousand other causes,

* *Moniteur*, May 28, 1859.

— from destitution, debt, voluntary alienation, — lastly, and above all, inheritance. How, moreover, justify the one by the other?

Instead of killing an enemy, it is said, the victor preserves him; he does a deed of power and goodness; he exchanges one right for another. — Touching beneficence!

Does war give the right to kill? Yes, during the conflict; after the battle has ceased, can you cut off the head of a disarmed foe? No, this would be infamous. Where, then, do you draw the right to enslave him, since you have no longer the right to kill him? This right is born with the necessity of defending yourself, and expires with it.

And the children of the enemy, his wife, his race to perpetuity, — you have the right therefore to immolate them, since they become your possessions and your chattels! Fragile and shameful argument, crime justified by another crime, explanation perpetuated by favor of a play of words! *Servus* comes, it is said, from *servatus;* and why not from *servire;* or else from the name of the *Servii*, the slaves of the Greeks, as slave comes from the *Slavii?*

If slavery be often born of war, war is still oftener born of slavery. It is made to take captives, and captives are taken to sell.

Let us admit this explanation, notwithstanding; it explains nothing, for it is itself inexplicable. Why, then, for what end, under the empire of what inclination, does the warrior reduce his captive, his fellow, to servitude?

In order that he may labor for him. Does man, then, abhor labor? is labor a punishment? a punishment, for what? Man is not only tempted, then, but conquered, by this inclination to reject labor? What is this creature, vanquished by evil and chastised? Has God made man thus, unhappy and wicked?

To all these formidable mysteries I know but a single answer. To ask what is the origin of slavery is to propound the most redoubtable question in existence, — What is the origin of evil? This is the answer.

Yes, the brother knows not his brother; the same blood flows, yet struggles, in their veins; an evident dissension betrays itself between the members of the human race; because the very cradle of the family has been the scene of a secret, profound, incontestable disorder, which is transmitted from generation to generation, and extends from people to people. Nothing escapes this disorder; it explains, it produces at once the crime and the suffering, — the crime of those called masters, and the sufferings of those called slaves.* Instruments of a higher justice, living proofs

* The first of the Four Unpublished Chapters on Russia, by Count Joseph de Maistre, published in 1859, by his son, is devoted to liberty, and an analogous question to that which I am examining is thus propounded by this great mind: —

"How does it happen that, *before Christianity*, slavery was always considered as a necessary part of the government and political state of nations, and that it never occurred to any legislator to attack it by fundamental laws or circumstance?"

If M. de Maistre confined himself to replying, "*History proves by evidence that the human race, in general, is susceptible of civil liberty only in proportion as it is penetrated and led by Christianity*," (p. 10,) I should take care not to dispute it. But he resolves the problem by this sweeping formula: "*Man, in general, if reduced to himself, is too wicked to be free.*"

He then adds: —

"*If civil liberty belonged to every one, there would no longer be means of governing men in a body as a nation.* This is why slavery was always the *natural* condition of the greater part of mankind until the establishment of Christianity. And as *universal good sense felt the necessity of this order of things*, it was never combated either by the laws or reasoning." (pp. 4, 5.)

He concludes from this, that, "Russia being abstracted from the general movement of civilization and enfranchisement which came from Rome, *slavery exists in Russia because it is necessary there, and because the Emperor cannot reign without it.*" (pp. 13, 14.)

Thus, either the Catholic religion or slavery.

It is true that M. de Maistre, repeating his formula under another less contestable form, "*A great people can never be governed by the government alone*" (pp 23, 24), adds: "How is Turkey governed? By the Koran. How is China governed? By the maxims, laws, and religion of Confucius." He admits, therefore that Catholicism is not the only supplement of civil law.

Moreover, he writes further: —

of an antique decay, both compose a violent, fatal, inhuman society, where the absence of liberty seems the vengeance for the abuse which has been done it. In other terms, order was originally disturbed at the birth of humanity; slavery is one of the proofs and the consequences of this fact which

"If emancipation should take place in Russia, it will be wrought by what is called *nature*. Circumstances wholly unforeseen will cause it to be desired on both sides All will be executed without noise or injury." (p. 28.)

Finally, the last part of the chapter of M. de Maistre concludes by considerations on the necessity of rendering the higher classes stronger and better before emancipating the lower classes, thus presenting the nobility, and not religion, as the counterpoise of liberty.

These contradictions, these breaks, this lack of harmony between the opening and the conclusion, lead me to believe that this posthumous chapter is one of those too hasty inspirations common to this great man; he did not design these incomplete pages for posterity, which, I know not why, are brought to light at the very moment when the emancipation of the serfs is *being wrought by what is termed nature.*

If it were necessary to take the first formulas of this chapter literally, I should not hesitate to combat them, in the name of the only two voices which superiority of talent cannot stifle, — history and conscience.

Yes, historical truth raises two pleas: —

1. Philosophers and legislators have not remained mute; they have openly approved slavery; neither their opinion nor their silence has been *the effect of the universal good sense;* but, on the contrary, the result and proof of the universal darkness and error which held souls in bondage before Christianity.

2. Slavery has been attacked and destroyed only *since* and *by* Christianity, this is certain; yet outside the Catholic Unity, as well as in its bosom; our Saviour died for the Russians, as well as the rest of mankind, and the philosophers and law-makers at London, St. Petersburg, and Tripoli have been enlightened by the reflection of this light.

Conscience joins with history in protesting against this absolute theory, *Men being too wicked to be free*, therefore a part of mankind must be slaves. Why then a part? The wicked is the master, and not the slave. In the countries without religion, are all men slaves? in the countries without slaves, are all men religious? If religion be one curb replacing another, who then, master or slave, would accept it? What! faith or chains, — is such the alternative? These odious consequences were assuredly far from the thought of the illustrious writer; that they are deduced from it is that the thought is too absolute; no one attains oftener than he to the sublime, but this summit borders on the precipice of paradox.

Why did slavery rule before Christ? Because error, suffering, and vice are universal. Why does it disappear since Christ? Because Christ brings truth, redemption, and virtue, and thus restores man to his true nature; now the nature of man is liberty.

rules the history of the human race. Save this explanation, it is inexplicable.

Who will re-establish the order profoundly, originally disturbed? He alone who established it, — God.

A primitive disorder, a necessary restorer.

I challenge any one otherwise to explain and cure the inconceivable and ancient maladies of humanity on earth. In this problem, as in many others, the reason is insensibly but forcibly conducted to a sort of instinctive Christianity. Up to this point, like a man groping in the darkness and striking against every wall, the spirit ends only in enigmas and discouraging impossibilities. As soon as it has laid hands on this key, the sole outlet by which it could penetrate, the light appears also, and everything is revealed in its place and its true light.

But these instincts, these presentiments, these involuntary acts of faith of the mind, history, veracious history, controls and ratifies. The primitive fall? The annals of the universe and the voice of the conscience, — these two witnesses attest it. The Redeemer? It is wellnigh two thousand years since humanity received him in the arms which it had extended towards him since the beginning of the world. What my reason demonstrates to me, therefore, history shows me, — facts serve as the counter-proof of ideas. Is it possible to rise to a higher degree of certainty?

Strange spectacle! The light is dazzling. When man receives the proof of what he forebodes, it is then that he hesitates; when it is necessary to pass from an internal intuition to a positive faith, he trembles and draws back. Man believes in a hidden God; God reveals himself, and man takes flight. Our conscience is in harmony with an invisible Christianity; before the Christ incarnate, it dares no longer confess aloud what it contemplated in silence. It is no longer Thomas crying, "Unless I see, I will not believe." We, on the contrary, seem to say, "If I see, I will no longer believe." A new demonstration of that strange weakness of the reason and the will which cannot, without aid from on high, upraise itself from doubt and soar to faith.

Let us seize with a firm hand the proofs so abundant and clear of the better solution. What do I say? there are not two, there is but one.

"It was a fault that created this word, and not nature," says St. Augustine. "The first cause of slavery was sin."

This universal and immemorial fact comes from another universal and immemorial fact, — the fall of man.

Yes, slavery is a positive evil, a disorder born, like all others, from the fall, communicated to all men by the fault of their first father. It is only one of the forms of that lamentable servitude of the soul ruled by the body, and the body ruled by the rebellious nature, — a servitude in the bonds of which mankind, in the fleeting sojourn on earth, struggled during the centuries which preceded Jesus Christ, and from which it has been emancipating itself with his aid during the last eighteen hundred years, by turns ungrateful or faithful, victorious or cast down, ashamed or full of glory, on the way to its true country.

Christianity has been well styled *the joint of the leaves of history*. Let us open and read.

Before Jesus Christ, in all the countries where his coming was not expected, slavery prevailed and grew; there only where he was expected, slavery was restricted and decreased. Since Jesus Christ, in the part of the globe where he is adored, slavery is dead or dying; there only where he is ignored, slavery rules harshly and endures. The day that Christ was born witnessed the breaking of the dawn of liberty. The same hour strikes their appearance in history, the same tint on the map of the world marks their progress.

CHAPTER IV.

RÉSUMÉ.

WHY THE INFLUENCE OF CHRISTIANITY HAS NOT BEEN PROMPTER AND MORE DECISIVE.

IF we wished to sum up in four sentences this great work of the action of Christianity on slavery, we should do so as follows : —

By its *divine virtue,* Christianity has restored to the reason and will of man the powers which they had lost ; reintegrated in his nature, man has comprehended, desired, and proclaimed liberty ;

By its *doctrines,* Christianity has condemned the principle of slavery ;

By its *counsels,* it has smoothed the transition ;

By its *examples* and influence, it has transformed the practice, and rendered possible what its teachings had demonstrated necessary.

What slowness, how many details, what temporizing, what an embarrassed and heavy march ! What ! you were God, and you did not unchain this thunder ! You were all-powerful, and you did not hurl forth the anathema ! Nineteen centuries have not sufficed to purge the earth of a terrible evil !

Thus reply impatient spirits. For my part, I despair of rendering the picture which I have drawn as graphic to other souls as it is to mine. I confess that this spectacle, instead of leaving me cold and disdainful, ravishes me with admiration. What ! you are not in ecstasies before this triumph of a wholly new doctrine over twenty centuries of learned and refined heathenism, and this combat of a handful of converted Jews struggling against that slough of corruption termed antique society, that powerful colossus, the Roman Empire, that indomitable avalanche of barbarian invasions! These Jews became the Church, you say, and the Church was all powerful; it was its duty to act! But you forget that this power has been a new obstacle and the most fearful of temptations. There was no need of recommending the obscure and weak to the fishermen of Galilee; they were so themselves. But that opulent and ambitious prelates, covered with gold and purple, should not for a single day have forgotten the poor, should not for a single time have mounted the pulpit without uttering, though they blushed thereat themselves, the holy words: "Woe to ye, rich men! God shows no respect to persons; masters, do to your slaves as ye would have them do unto you." This is the miracle.

We reason, moreover, in the bosom of modern, well-constituted society, where authority is strong enough to reform without inciting to insurrection, and public opinion is just enough to call forth the good, instead of combating it. We reason in the midst of a century, the imperishable honor of which is precisely that of witnessing the dawn, perhaps the advent, of an era of reconciliation among the nations of the earth, of amelioration of the condition of the masses, of progress in all directions, — an era wholly characteristic, and so new, that the greatest men of the preceding ages had no presentiment of its coming. We reproach the Church for not having inspired Honorius or Theodosius, Phocas or Clovis, with the decree of April 24, 1848.

A discovery always seems impossible on its eve and easy on its morrow. On the morrow of the discovery of America, his contemporaries thus treated the immortal Columbus. He ought to have taken another route; his companions had had little inclination for the voyage; he attached great importance to a few little islands ; he had wasted much time on the way. It is said, likewise : The Church has been dilatory. How many priests have acted the opposite of rightly ! It has rendered decisions on the most petty details ; it has wasted time.

Christopher Columbus was a man, but you say the Church is divine. Is this the conduct of a God ?

This objection is grave and deserves reply.

It is said truly that the Church did not at once abolish slavery, —

1. Because to condemn it was directly to endanger its doctrine, and to raise up humanity against it ; Christianity would have been stifled in its birth ; this is the reason given by the Apostles themselves.*

2. Because its first mission was to urge men to heaven and harmony, masters as well as slaves ; they would have exterminated each other, had it impelled them to revolt. The subjects of the Emperor of Cochin-China and the King of Dahomey have much reason to complain ; is it the part of missionaries to incite them to insurrection ?

3. Because, instead of abandoning itself to theories, it was the duty of the Church to act with practical wisdom ; to go too fast would have been to endanger the condition of the slave himself ; what would have become of him without bread, without an asylum, without aid, and, above all, without virtue, in the midst of the invasion of the barbarians, in an age when Gregory of Tours and Cantacuzena show us the painful spectacle of freemen offering themselves for sale through destitution ?

4. Because it has always abstained with the greatest care

* It is repeated by the Fathers. St. John Chrysostom's Sermon on the Epistle to Philemon: "The heathens would have said that the Christian religion was introduced into the world only to create general disturbance and excite confusion and disorder, since it wrested servants by violence from the hands of their masters."

from touching questions of human property and civil and political rights.

5. We may add, whether it has fought well or ill, it is certain that it has acted alone, and that the work is done. It is the end that matters, not the mode.

These reasons are excellent, but they do not suffice.

There is a higher reason.

The Church has acted thus because God acts thus, and because Jesus Christ is God.

Men demand of Jesus Christ two things which he will always refuse them ; — *civil and political* laws, because it is for them to make them ; and *revolutions*, because he holds them in abhorrence, being the father of those who make them as well as of those who suffer from them.

What a misfortune, say some, that the Church does not pronounce more loudly in favor of the liberty of peoples ! What a misfortune, say others, that it does not declare the legitimacy of thrones ! Ah ! exclaim scholars, the Church ought to concern itself more with the sciences ! It is most desirable that it should teach the true principles of political economy. Holy Father, raise up Poland, free Italy, reform America !

The Church does not grant these prayers, it is not its mission. In the temporal order it is not the regent, but the conscience, of the human race. It has been told *to go, teach, baptize, forgive,* and *punish;* it goes onward, bearing in its consecrated hands the imperishable deposit of the doctrine and supernatural ministry of the sacraments. It is for men to approach, receive, and voluntarily conform their life and that of society to what they have received.

God might have created things ready made ; it pleased him only to furnish materials to the reason and labor of man. Our Saviour might have repaired everything ; it pleased him to leave to the restored liberty of man the use, abuse, or refusal of his gifts. He lays down principles, it is for men to draw the conclusions; he gives strength, it is for men to adapt the instrument thereto; he converts men, it is for men to convert things.

I dare say that nothing is comprehended of the life of the Church and its action on the heathen world, the barbarians, the family, the penal law, when this is forgotten; but no more is comprehended of the life of the world, and the error is as great on the side of those who pretend that the Church acts in everything, as of those who accuse it of acting in nothing.

The first compose an historical school, very seductive to piety, but very dangerous. It strives to demonstrate that all the progress of the sciences, letters, arts, laws, and charity is due to the *visible* action of the Church. Doubtless, members of the Church have powerfully influenced all this progress. God permits that from time to time there should be encountered on the pontifical throne, in the episcopal seat, or among the lower ranks of the priesthood, a great scholar, a great politician, or a great writer, who acts on the world, and we offer the most fervent prayers that these ornaments may never be lacking our Mother. These benefits have been so numerous, the action of the saints has been so prodigious, the devotion and science of Christians occupy in history a place so vast, that it is easy to suffer ourselves to attribute to the Church wellnigh all progress. This is an error; therein is its human glory, but not its divine mission. To maintain it, is to run the risk of standing speechless before the example of peoples where progress flourishes without the Church, and of other nations where the Church flourishes without progress.

The second historical school, blinder in denying the intervention of Christianity in the temporal order, proves that it understands nothing of the soul, nothing of history so visibly separated into two phases by Calvary, nothing of the action of doctrines on souls, nothing of the power of that moral, internal revolution, which works from within outwards, and attacks the very roots of evil here on earth. The partisans of this school, who do not believe in invisible influence on souls, but demand public, external acts, would be greatly scandalized should their wishes be one day realized. Yes, let a decree signed by a pope come, in the name of God, to-day to interdict all loans on interest, to-morrow to impose a new *régime* of inheritance or property, what would be the indignation of these historians who style *encroachment* a mandate on lewdness or dancing! They ask what they would never consent to accept.

The true doctrine, at once metaphysical, moral, and historical, is this: —

Christianity is the source of all progress without exception, in the sense that it has rendered man capable of progress; his soul was separated from God and sunk in sensuality, a fall of which idolatry, debauchery, and slavery were the results and proof; the coming of Jesus Christ had for its end and aim to save the soul from this evil, and to re-establish its relations with God. But Christians remained free to transfuse or not into their lives and society the human consequences of Christianity. Thus it is said that our Saviour took away from the world but a single thing, — sin, *qui tollis peccata.* This sufficed to take away polygamy, idolatry, war, and slavery. Christianity has not made laws, but it has dictated them. It has said nothing on the contract of marriage, yet it has raised up woman; nothing of gladiators, and nothing of inhuman tortures, yet they have disappeared before it. It has commanded no army, yet it has transformed the heart of the combatants; by degrees, diplomacy has been substituted for war, instead of fighting for subjugation, men have taken up arms for emancipation, and force has been employed to hinder the oppression of weakness. Christianity does not prescribe, therefore, but it influences. It changes man, man changes the world. The true sun of souls, it warms within and enlightens without. The light does not trace his route for man, but illumines each of his steps; thus Christianity intertwines itself with all the events of the world, and projects over every field of history the rays of its divinity.

It follows from this doctrine, that the slowness or abortiveness of progress may be *the fault of Christians without being the fault of Christianity.*

Here, I agree with those who accuse us most warmly.

Yes, if the poor be imperfectly succored, if manners be scandalous, if laws be not ameliorated, if, finally, there be yet slaves and partisans, priests or laymen, of slavery, it is the fault of Christians, and not of Christianity.

Shame Christians for badly observing their law; but do not prove to them that this law is in favor of slavery. You wound and grieve true Christians, but reassure and exculpate bad ones. Fine gain, truly, and great profit! If you exclude the Gospel from all interest in the cause of the slaves, what will be left to gain it?

It follows, in the second place, from the same doctrine, that progress may be *the work of Christianity without being the work of Christians.*

Our Lord has suffered for all mankind, and the Church keeps for all mankind the deposit of doctrine. Protestants profit by the immutable deposit which they mutilate, and philosophers are not at liberty to live outside the Christian atmosphere which surrounds them; all the walls in the world cannot preserve China or Turkey from receiving the rays of light projected by Europe. When Voltaire demanded the reform of criminal laws, he acted out Christianity; when the Bey of Tunis abolished slavery in his states, he acted out Christianity; when the French Revolution established the equality of taxes, it acted out Christianity; when the Emperor of Russia abolished serfdom, he acted out Christianity; when philosophy defends just and generous causes, it acts out Christianity. In a word, Christianity, like God himself, does nothing by itself alone here on earth ; but it has a right to claim as done *by it* all that has not been done *without it.*

I conclude thence that Christians are greatly in the wrong in being unjust towards philosophers, and philosophers in being unjust towards Christians. This ingratitude is especially culpable in the great work of the abolition of slavery.

Men treat Christianity, which has opposed nothing to slavery but *general maxims of charity,* with disdain ; they impute to it as a crime the faults of its disciples ; they expect more from the *active enlightenment of reason and healthy philosophy,* without asking whether Christianity has not contributed some little to render this enlightenment *active,* and this philosophy *healthy ;* they declare, moreover, in advance, *" that the honor of philosophy cannot be called in question even by the gravest aberrations of its disciples,"* * a reservation which is not extended to the Church. Admit all this ; but of what, then, will philosophy avail itself ? Does it hold in reserve a new means of transforming the human race on the spot, as a reagent dissolves a stone ? No, it has itself nothing but *general maxims of equality* to oppose to slavery ; and I do not therefore blame it, for I believe that ideas lead the world ; but why reproach Christianity for not acting differently ? Words for words ; before disdaining those of Christianity, it was fitting that philosophy should have spoken first, but it has been mute. Aristotle, it is said, cites the doctrines of abolitionist philosophers of his times. Doctrines for doctrines ; I ask, what trace is left of the argumentation or name of the abolitionist philosophers contemporary with Aristotle, and I need not open my eyes very wide to contemplate the marvellous effects of that brief saying of the Saviour, *" Thou shalt*

* *Le Christianisme et l'esclavage,* by M. Larroque.

love thy neighbor as thyself." Why has this saying made more impression on souls than the words of the philosophers? Through the same reason which gives to the morality of Jesus Christ an efficiency forever refused to that of Plato or Confucius; because to these words is attached a real and certainly divine virtue; because He who speaks to souls has changed souls; because He who has made the light for the eye has made the Christian truth for man.

How unjust are such discussions! but, above all, how sterile!

Ah! rather let us rejoice to meet a ground whereon all the world is agreed, and to live in an epoch when the questions of humanity inflame all lovers of virtue. The cause of emancipation is won before the conscience of the human race.

To the work, then, sovereigns and statesmen! Complete in deeds the happy revolution accomplished in ideas! To the work, philosophers; instead of humiliating, exhort us! To the work, democrats, too indulgent towards America, which suffers the flag of independence to float over the decks of slave ships, and prefers civil war to Christian justice! To the work, sons of Washington and Franklin, who suffer Russia to give lessons to America! To the work, above all, Christians; pray, write, act, emancipate, give the impulse or the example; let us not be found absent from a crusade to deliver, not the tomb, but the living temples of the Lord!

In my eyes, — and this is the conclusion of this last part of my work, — the enslavement of our fellow-beings, the privation of their liberty, which is their first good, is from this time condemned by the commandment of God: *Thou shalt not take the property of another.* To take this property is theft. I go further. It is pretended that the condemnation of slavery is not one of the principles of Christianity. I maintain that it is a consequence of each of its principles. There is not a single one of the ten commandments, which adults and children recite in their daily prayers, that is not altered by slavery. Try to associate a single one of these commandments with the ownership of your fellow. How can a Christian *worship and love God alone,* and call him *Our Father,* when he regards his brethren as cattle? The oaths which he takes before God, promising to practise justice, — does he not violate them, and *take the name of God in vain,* every moment of a guilty life? What sentiments does he bring to the service of God on holy days, how does he teach his slaves to *keep the Sabbath holy,* to enjoy fraternal equality before God, to believe in his goodness, to love one another? Does he permit them to *honor their father and mother,* if they have ever known them? Is he not guilty, in every respect, of homicide towards the man whom he deprives of the dignity of man, or chastises like a brute? Nothing forbids *lust,* and he finds his interest in exciting it. He lives surrounded by *falsehood;* he lies to himself, he renders *false witness* before God, for his conscience reveals to him the truth of the evil which he commits. He has *coveted the property of others;* he has obtained it *unjustly.* Exposed to the danger of betraying *marriage,* he often violates that of his fellow; he finds in *the works of the flesh* a temptation checked by nothing, and a detestable profit. Lastly, he has *taken the property of others,* he *retains it,* he *knows it,* he *perseveres in it.* I have striven to prove that Christianity has destroyed slavery; but it is still more clear to me that slavery abolishes Christianity.

Which will be conqueror, good or evil? It will be certainly, it will be speedily, good. "The work is advancing. . . . The abolition of slavery is the accomplishment of the Gospel itself. . . . . Despite the resistance of interest, the specious reasons of politics, ... it may be said of the zeal of charity marching in the shadow of the cross, *In hoc signo vinces.*" *

Hope already obtains a glimpse of the breaking of the day when servitude shall have completely disappeared from the bosom of Christian nations.

On this day, there will be great rejoicing in heaven and on earth.

* Villemain, *Essais sur la génie de Pindare et la poésie lyrique*, Part II. Chap. XXV. p. 606.

APPENDIX.

I.

(Book I. Chap. IV. § 2, p. 107.)

Extract from the Civil Code of Louisiana, and the Laws which have amended it from 1825 to 1853.*

Art. 35. A slave is one who is in the power of his master, to whom he belongs. The master may sell him, dispose of his person, his industry, or his labor; he can do nothing, possess nothing, nor acquire anything but what must belong to his master.

Art. 36. Manumitted persons are those who, having been once slaves, are legally made free.

Art. 37. Slaves for a time, or *statu liberi*, are those who have acquired the right of being free at a time to come, or on a condition which is not fulfilled, or in a certain event which has not happened, but who, in the mean time, remain in a state of slavery.

Art. 38. Freemen are those who have preserved their natural liberty, that is to say, who have the right of doing whatever is not forbidden by law.

Chapter III. *Of Slaves.*

Art. 172. The rules prescribing the police and conduct to be observed with respect to slaves in this State, and the punishment of their crimes and offences, are fixed by special laws of the Legislature.

Art. 173. The slave is entirely *subject to the will of his master*, who may correct and chastise him, though not with unusual rigor, nor so as to maim or mutilate him, or to expose him to the danger of loss of life, or to cause his death.

* Edited by Thomas Giles Morgan. New Orleans. 1853.

Art. 174. The slave is incapable of making any kind of contract, except those which relate to his own emancipation.

Art. 175. All that a slave possesses belongs to his master; he possesses nothing of his own except his *peculium*, that is to say, the sum of money, or movable estate, which his master chooses he should possess.

Art. 176. They can transmit nothing by succession, or otherwise; but the succession of free persons related to them, which they would have inherited, had they been free, may pass through them to such of their descendants as may have acquired their liberty before the succession is opened.

Art. 177. The slave is incapable of exercising any public office, or private trust; he cannot be tutor, curator, executor, nor attorney; *he cannot be a witness in either civil or criminal matters*, except in cases provided for by particular laws. He cannot be a party in any civil action, either as plaintiff or defendant, except when he has to claim or prove his freedom.

Art. 178. When slaves are prosecuted in the name of the State, for offences they have committed, notice must be given to their masters.

Art. 179. Masters are bound by the acts of their slaves done by their command, as also by their transactions and dealings with respect to the business in which they have intrusted or employed them; but in case they should not have authorized or intrusted them, they shall be answerable only for so much as they have benefited by the transaction.

Art. 180. The master shall be answerable for all the damages occasioned by an offence or quasi-offence committed by his slave, independent of the punishment inflicted on the slave.

Art. 181. The master, however, may discharge himself from such responsibility *by abandoning his slave to the person injured; in which case such person shall sell such slave at public auction* in the usual form, to obtain payment of the damages and costs; and the balance, if any, shall be returned to the master of the slave, who shall be completely discharged, although the price of the slave should not be sufficient to pay the whole amount of the damages and costs; provided that the master shall make the abandonment within three days after the judgment awarding such damages shall have been rendered; provided, also, that it shall not be proved that the crime or offence was committed by his order; for in case of such proof the master shall be answerable for all damages resulting therefrom, whatever be the amount, without being admitted to the benefit of the abandonment.

ART. 182. *Slaves cannot marry without the consent of their masters, and their marriages do not produce any of the civil effects which result from such contract.*

ART. 183. Children born of a mother then in a state of slavery, whether married or not, follow the condition of their mother; they are consequently slaves, and belong to the master of their mother.

ART. 184. A master may manumit his slave in this State, either by an act *inter vivos*, or by a disposition made in prospect of death, provided such manumission be made with the forms and under the conditions prescribed by law; but an enfranchisement, when made by a last will, must be express and formal and shall not be implied by any other circumstances of the testament, such as a legacy, an institution of heir, testamentary executorship, or other dispositions of this nature, which in such case shall be considered as if they had not been made.

ACT OF MARCH 18, 1852, p. 214.— SEC. 1. *Henceforth no slave or slaves can be manumitted in this State, except under the express condition that, when the said slaves shall have been manumitted, they shall be transported out of the United States.* It shall be the duty of the police juries of the different parishes in this State, and in the Council of New Orleans, before according any act of emancipation of any slave or slaves, to require that the master or masters, person or persons, desiring such emancipation, shall deposit in the treasury of the parish in which the said act shall be made out, or with the Mayor of the City of New Orleans, *the sum of one hundred and fifty piasters* for every slave thus manumitted, which sum shall be applied to the payment of the expenses of his voyage to Africa, and his support after his arrival.

SEC. 2. All slaves whose rights to emancipation shall not yet have been perfected by the proper authorities, shall receive the said emancipation only on the conditions stipulated in Section 1. And on his failure of the said conditions, the said slave shall be let by the master or masters, person or persons having the legal charge of the said slave or slaves; and in case there be no such person, then the district judge shall appoint an agent for this purpose, who shall let the said slave or slaves until the sum of one hundred and fifty piasters shall have been found and deposited as heretofore mentioned, when the act of emancipation may be perfected, and the slave sent to Liberia within a year. Provided that, in case any of the slaves, after having been thus emancipated, shall not be sent to Liberia before the expiration of a year, dating from his emancipation, *or if he return after having been transported, the said slave or slaves shall have forfeited their liberty, and shall again* become slaves to their ci-devant masters or their legal representatives.

SEC. 3. This act shall not be put in force until six months after its passage.

ART. 185. No one can emancipate his slave unless the slave has attained the age of thirty years, and has behaved well at least for four years preceding his emancipation.

ACT OF MARCH 9, 1807, p. 82. — SEC. 1. No one shall be forced, either directly or indirectly, to emancipate his slave or slaves, except only when the said emancipation shall be made in the name and at the expense of the Territory, in virtue of an act of the legislature of the said Territory.

SEC. 2. No master can emancipate any of his slaves unless the said slave has attained the age of thirty years, and has behaved well, and has never been guilty of running away, stealing, or any criminal misdemeanor during the four years preceding the day of his emancipation; provided that the present disposition shall be of no effect in case the slave or slaves set at liberty shall have saved the life of his master, or of his wife, or of any of his children.

SEC. 3. Every master who may wish to emancipate any of his slaves, shall be bound to declare before the judge of his county that the slave to be emancipated is of the age and has led the conduct required above by Section 2, for his emancipation. The judge shall immediately order the following notice in the English and French languages to be placarded in his county: —

"The said A. N. (inhabitant or domiciliary) of the County of —— desiring to manumit his slave (male or female) named ———, aged ——, all persons who may have legal objections to make to the said manumission are warned to present them at the court of the said county within forty days from the date of the present declaration.

"Signed, M. R.,

"Sheriff of the County of ——."

At the expiration of this delay, if there are no objections, or if the judge decides that those which may have been made are not well founded, the said judge shall then authorize the petitioner, by a sentence, to pass the act of emancipation; which emancipation shall have its full and entire effect, unless it shall be afterwards attacked as having been made in fraud of creditors, minors, or persons absent from, or residing out of, the county where the notice shall have been made; and this fraud shall always be presumed if, at the moment of emancipation, the donor had not property sufficient, except the slave or slaves emancipated, to satisfy his creditors.

SEC. 4. Every act of liberty made in contravention of the preceding article shall be null of right, and the master who shall have consented to, and the public officer who shall have passed it, shall be, on conviction, condemned each to a fine of one hundred dollars, to be applied one half to the denouncer, and the other half to the public treasury.

SEC. 5. Every act of emancipation of a slave shall carry with it the tacit but formal obligation, on the part of the donor, to provide for the subsistence and maintenance of the said slave emancipated by him, when this slave shall become unable to earn his own livelihood by reason of sickness, old age, dementia, or any other proved infirmity. And if the said donor shall refuse to perform this obligatory act of humanity, it shall be the duty of every judge before whom such a fact shall be denounced and proved, to condemn the said donor to pay monthly to the freedman thus abandoned by him, such sum as the judge in his discretion shall deem sufficient to secure the subsistence, maintenance, and medical care of the said freedman during all the time that his inability to earn his livelihood shall last.

SEC. 6. When the emancipation of a slave or slaves shall be made by testament or other act of last will, the formalities or conditions prescribed by the third and sixth sections of the present Act shall be fulfilled by the testamentary executors, administrators, heirs, or counsel of the testator.

SEC. 7. All the dispositions of existing laws which are or may be contrary to those of the present Act, are and remain annulled.

SEC. 8. This Act shall begin to take effect on the 1st day of next September, and not before, except its first section, which shall have its full and entire effect from the passage of the said Act.

ACT OF JANUARY 31, 1827, p. 13. — SEC. 1. Any individual, who shall desire to emancipate a slave who shall not have attained the age of thirty years, fixed by Article 185 of the Civil Code, shall be bound to present to the parish judge of the parish where he makes his residence a petition, in which he shall set forth the reasons which lead him to demand the emancipation of the said slave; which petition shall be submitted by the said parish judge to the police jury at its next session, *and if three fourths of the members elected of the said police jury, and the parish judge*, are of the opinion that there is reason to permit the said emancipation (which shall be attested in the manner required for the other deliberations of the police juries), the individual who shall have made the demand shall be authorized to proceed with the formalities required by the Civil Code, although his slave shall not have attained the age of thirty years.

SEC. 2. Nothing contained in the present Act shall be interpreted in a manner to exempt a master from any of the formalities required by the existing laws.

SEC. 3. From the date of the passage of the present Act, *no slave can be emancipated in virtue of these provisions, unless the said slave shall have been born in the State.*

ACT OF MARCH 16, 1842, p. 316. — SEC. 14. All slaves for years now found in the State, as soon as they shall become free, *shall be transported out of the State at the expense of the last owner*, on proceedings instituted *by any citizen*, before the parish judge; and all slaves for years who, after having been deported, shall return to the State, shall be subject to the penalties decreed by the law against free negroes or persons of color who shall come into the State.

ACT OF APRIL 9, 1847, p. 81. — SEC. 1. All the duties hitherto imposed on the parish judges by the laws of the State, in that which relates to police juries, shall be in future performed by the foremen of the said police juries, unless it shall be otherwise prescribed by the law.

ART. 186. The slave who has saved the life of his master, his master's wife, or one of his children, may be emancipated at any age.

ART. 187. The master who wishes to emancipate his slave is bound to make a declaration of his intentions to the judge of the parish where he resides; the judge must order notice of it to be published during forty days by advertisement posted at the door of the court-house; and if, at the expiration of this delay, no opposition be made, he shall authorize the master to pass the act of emancipation.

ART. 188. The act of emancipation imports an obligation on the part of the person granting it, to provide for the subsistence of the slave emancipated, if he should be unable to support himself.

ART. 189. An emancipation once perfected is irrevocable, on the part of the master or his heirs.

ART. 190. Any enfranchisement made in fraud of creditors, or of the portion reserved by law to forced heirs, is null and void; and such fraud shall be considered as proved, when it shall appear that at the moment of executing the enfranchisement, the person granting it had not sufficient property to pay his debts, or to leave to his heirs the portion reserved to them by law; the same rule will apply if the slave thus manumitted was specially mortgaged; but in this case the enfranchisement shall take effect, provided the slave, or any one on his behalf, shall pay the debt for which the mortgage was given.

ART. 191. No master of slaves shall be compelled, either directly or indirectly, to enfranchise any of them, except only in cases where the enfranchisement made shall be for services rendered to the State, by virtue of an act of the Legislature of the same, and on the State satisfying to the master the appraised value of the manumitted slave.

ART. 192. In like manner no master shall be compelled to sell his slave, but in one of two cases, to wit: The first, when being only co-proprietor of the slave, his co-proprietor demands the sale in order to make partition of the property. The second, when the master shall be convicted of cruel treatment of his slave, and the judge shall deem proper to pronounce, besides the penalty established for such cases, that the slave shall be sold at public auction, in order to place him out of the reach of the power which his master has abused.

ART. 193. The slave who has acquired the right of being free at a future time, is from that time capable of receiving by testament or donation. Property given or devised to him must be preserved for him, in order to be delivered to him in kind, when his emancipation shall take place. In the mean time, it must be administered by a curator.

ART. 194. The slave for years cannot be transported out of the State. He can appear in court to claim the protection of the laws, where there are good reasons for believing that it is intended to carry him out of the State.

ART. 195. If the slave for years dies before the time fixed for his enfranchisement, the gifts or legacies made him revert to the donor or the heirs of the donor.

ART. 196. The child born of a woman after she has acquired the right of being free at a future time, follows the condition of the mother, and becomes free at the time fixed for her enfranchisement, even if the mother should die before that time.

Extract from the Code of Virginia.

(Richmond, 1849.)

"*None shall be slaves in this State,*" says the Code of Virginia, admirably (Tit. XXX. Chap. CIII. Sec. 1); but, alas! it adds, "EXCEPT *those who are so when this chapter takes effect, such free negroes as may be sold as slaves pursuant to law, such slaves as may be lawfully brought into this State, and the future descendants of female slaves.*"

As well have said in two words: None shall be slaves except those which have been, are, and shall be such.

What are we to say of a law which thus enunciates the legal motives for arresting a fugitive slave!

"*If there be reasonable cause to suspect that such slave is a runaway.*" Code of Virginia, Tit. XXX. Chap. CV. It is pure and simple despotism.

In nearly all the States the free negroes are rigorously banished, or subjected to hard conditions of registration or authorization, under pain of being sold; yet the authorization given to the mother does not always extend to the children whom she brings into the world. (See especially the Code of Virginia, 1849, Tit. XXX. Chap. CVII.)

II.

(Book I. Chap. III. § 2, p. 78.)

The Happiness of the Slaves. — Divers Facts and Testimony.

I. In the beginning of 1860, a meeting of slaveholders was held in Maryland, for the purpose of proposing a law to compel the free negroes to choose between again becoming slaves or quitting the territory. A Colonel Jacobs attempted to prove the danger of the presence of these free negroes, who number, in Maryland, one to five whites. The meeting resulting in nothing, the Virginia newspapers loaded Maryland with threats and abuse, and I read in one of these journals, *The Southern Argus:* "Henceforth we shall cease practically to regard Maryland as a Slave State. Politically, the State was long since lost to the South." Precious abuse, which is in our eyes a eulogy, and which I would gladly regard as a prophecy.

II. City Court of Brooklyn, before Juge Culver, 1859.

The Hon. E. D. Culver, City Judge of Brooklyn, rendered yesterday the following judgment: —

"The plaintiffs declare and prove that the defendant, who is minister of a colored Episcopalian church in Williamsburgh, is guilty of *bigamy*, having two wives now living.

"The defendant offers in justification the following facts, the proofs of which he has furnished me.

"Warwick (the defendant) and Winnie (the plaintiff) were both slaves in North Carolina, but belonged to different masters. They agreed to marry in 1814, and were united by a colored Methodist minister. It does not appear that any permission was obtained from the County Court, as the laws of the State require, or from their respective masters. However this may be, Warwick and Winnie cohabited, and, in seventeen years, had twelve children. In 1828, Warwick became free, but continued to live with Winnie until 1831, when the law of the State, banishing all free negroes, compelled him to leave. After ten years' absence, he returned to North Carolina, found his wife, and took her again, but was forced by the sheriff to quit the State, in three days, under penalty of again becoming a slave. He departed by the entreaty of Winnie, and came to Williamsburgh, where, in 1843, he regularly espoused his present wife. Winnie remained a slave until 1854, when she reached the North, and found her husband married to another woman. She reclaims her right.

"It is incumbent on the court to recognize that the plaintiff is honest, sincere, and a good Christian, having full confidence in the justice of her complaint. If she had quitted North Carolina with Warwick, or if she had obtained freedom before the second marriage of the latter, he would have been morally bound to regard her as his lawful wife, and this he admits. But hearing nothing from her, and having no reason to count on her being freed, he believed himself able to contract the second marriage in good faith.

"In these circumstances, being called upon to judge whether Warwick is guilty of bigamy, and whether the plaintiffs have proved that he has two wives, I have arrived at the following decision: —

"Considering that marriage is a civil contract, which requires in the contracting parties the capacity to contract it, that *slaves cannot contract a regular marriage, and that cohabitation confers no right on them or their children;* (Laws of Alabama, Maryland, and North Carolina.)

"Whereas the first marriage of Warwick was void in law, he was perfectly free, if he chose, to contract marriage with his present wife, and has violated no law in so doing;

"The plaintiffs, on the contrary, in accusing the defendant unjustly, have acted in violation of the law, and will be subject to damages, should they recommence the suit against the prohibition of the court. They are sentenced at present to pay a fine of $100. Sentence ordered for execution."

(Samuel L. Harris, for plaintiff. D. Parmenter, for defendant.)

Univers, Dec. 28, 1858. "Last month, a negro slave and his family were sold at auction in Washington itself, the Federal Capital of the American Union. Sambo Cuffee was Catholic, as well as his wife, and their three children under twelve years old, and their marriage was solemnized at St. Matthew's Church in Washington. But without heeding this marriage, the wife and three children were sold to a Methodist preacher, and carried to Louisiana, five hundred leagues from Washington. Sambo, who was infirm, found no purchaser in New Orleans, where robust negroes are alone in demand, and was sold cheaply to a Maryland planter. He will never again see his lawful wife and children, and the latter, in the hands of a Methodist preacher, will inevitably lose their faith. The New York *Freeman's Journal*, which cites these facts, says that they are attested by the Mayor of Washington, who has given a similar certificate, rendering testimony to the good conduct and morals of Sambo and his family. There are laws in the United States, then, which authorize such iniquity! There are laws which deprive three million slaves of all authority over their children.

"C. DE LAROCHE-HERON."

The *New Orleans Bee*, Dec. 27, 1858, relates the following details concerning a fact which appears to have caused some sensation in that city.

"On Saturday morning, the Coroner concluded the inquest that he has been holding at the slave depot of R. W. Long, Gravier Street, on the body of the negress Eudora, belonging to Mr. Veau.

"A post-mortem examination of the body was made by Drs. Graham and Deléry, who declared that the woman *had been whipped to death.*

"Dr. Graham deposed, that at five o'clock on Friday morning, he received a call from Mr. John T. Hatcher, who asked him to go to see a negress at the depot, who had gone to bed the night before in good health, and was found dead that morning; and that Hatcher confessed that he had punished her severely.

"R. W. Long deposed, that Mr. Veau had commissioned him to sell the negress; the latter ran away on the 6th instant, and was brought back by some person unknown to the witness. Mr. Long quitted the house early Thursday evening, and did not return until two or three o'clock the next morning. He learned of the death of Eudora before his arrival, and asked Hatcher whether he had whipped her; to which Hatcher made no direct reply.

"The testimony of Mr. R. Harvey proves that a man named Antonio brought the slave back at seven o'clock on Thursday evening. At nine o'clock, the negress went to bed; a few minutes after, Hatcher went up-stairs, and came down again, accompanied by Eudora; he questioned her, then again went up-stairs, telling a boy to follow him. He did not come down again until half past ten o'clock, during which time, the witness on the first floor heard the sound of the whip. Hatcher then went out, and the witness called the boy to shut the doors; receiving no answer, he went up stairs to the third story, and on entering a room, saw the negress stretched on the floor, and asked her why she did not go to bed. She answered that her strength had left her, and asked to drink. Witness gave her some water, and had her carried to bed, in the second story. She added that Hatcher had whipped her. Mr. Harvey deposed that the cracking of the whip was heard during about an hour and a half, with one interruption of five or six minutes.

"The verdict of the jury declared that the negress died under a punishment inflicted upon her while in the immediate charge of John T. Hatcher.

"Hatcher disappeared on Friday evening, and has not yet been arrested. The Coroner declares him guilty of murder."

Extract from a Letter of Mgr. ——, one of the Catholic Bishops of the United States, July 14, 1860.

"There is reason to believe that the activity of this hideous commerce in negro flesh is great. The Island of Cuba, with Florida, and the other Southern States of the American Union, are in need of hands for their vast uncultivated lands, to raise sugar and cotton. It is believed that the negroes alone can resist labor under the burning sun of our climate during the summer. Thence comes this demand for negro slaves, whose price has risen to a degree to stimulate the cupidity of traders. A negro in good condition sells as high as $2,000; young children even sell at from $800 to $1,000, according to their size and strength; at such prices a cargo of these unhappy beings brings an immense sum, and the traders think little of wrecking their vessels on the coasts and losing them, provided they can dispose of their prisoners without being surprised by the officers of government.

"The negroes are to me the subject of the saddest reflections and the most painful anxieties. They form nearly half the population of Florida; and, alas! how few among them are on the way to save their souls! What is my anguish on the subject! They belong to masters who, for the most part, see in them only machines fit to work the land, and gather in sugar and cotton. It is not their physical discomfort in this world which afflicts me and causes my anxiety; many form an exaggerated idea of their bodily sufferings, yet it is doubtless true that in some cases these sufferings are of a nature to move the most pitiless heart; but after all, these cases are tolerably rare, for there are few masters systematically barbarous, and at the bottom they are better off physically as slaves than as freemen. But it is their spiritual misery which grieves me to the utmost. *Marriage is scarcely known among them; the masters attach no importance to it.* We can judge of the disorders which must result from such a state of things in a race greatly addicted to the pleasures of the senses. There is no religion to restrain the unbridled license of earthly desires, and, what is worse, no means, or almost none, of destroying this ignorance. *The masters do not care to have their slaves taught. In general, they consider them more useful in proportion as they are less instructed. In some States, those who teach them to read are punished with death.* In the same manner, many masters do not wish their negroes to hear preaching, for fear of giving them ideas which they are very glad to banish from their minds. We can do nothing at present but pray for the salvation of these negroes, and hope that Divine Providence may shape some circumstance favorable to their instruction and religious amelioration, that the kingdom of heaven may be as near to them as to the other races of the human family."

III.

American Bibliography of Slavery.

I NEED not quote the celebrated works of the historians, political philosophers, economists, travellers, and *littérateurs*, French and English, who, in the steps of M. de Tocqueville, have made the United States known to Europe. I believe it useful only to present a list of some few of the special books written in America, some for, and others against slavery, which I have been able to procure.

BARNES (ALBERT). Inquiry into the Scriptural View of Slavery. 1846.

BRISBANE (W. H.). Slaveholding examined in the Light of the Bible.

BROWNLOW and PRYNE. Ought American Slavery to be Perpetuated? Philadelphia. 1858.

CHANNING. Slavery. Translated into French, with his Letter to Mr. Clay, on the Annexation of Texas. By M. Edouard Laboulaye, of the Institute.

COURCY (H. DE). The Catholic Church in the United States. New York. 1857.

DREW (BENJAMIN). The Refugee, or Narratives of Fugitive Slaves. Boston. 1856.

FLETCHER (J.). Studies on Slavery. Natchez. 1852.

HARPER, HAMMOND, SIMMS, DEW. The Proslavery Arguments of. Philadelphia. 1853.

HELPER (H. ROWAN). The Impending Crisis of the South. New York. 1860.

GODWIN (Rev. BENJAMIN). Lectures on Slavery. 1836.

GRAYSON (W. I.). The Hireling and the Slave. Poems. Charleston. 1856.

GUROWSKI. Slavery in History.

MURAT (ACHILLE). Ex-Royal Prince of the Two Sicilies, Citizen of the United States, *Esquisse morale et politique des États-Unis.* 1832.

(This curious book in favor of slavery has been thoroughly criticised by M. Saint-Marc Girardin, *Essais de littérature et de morale*, Tom. I. p. 309.)

OLMSTED. A Journey in the Seaboard Slave States. 1859.

" A Journey through Texas, or a Saddle Trip on the Southwestern Frontier. 1860.

" A Journey in the Back Country. New York. 1860.

PARKER (THEODORE). A Letter to the People of the United States, touching the Matter of Slavery. 1848.

PARSONS (C. J.). An Inside View of Slavery.

STOWE (Mrs. H. B.). Uncle Tom's Cabin. Dred.

(The first of these celebrated works appeared as a serial in the Washington National Era, in 1851 – 1852; then in two volumes, in Boston, in 1852. It has been translated six times in French, twelve times in German; and in Italian, Spanish, Danish, Swedish, Flemish, Polish, and Magyar.)

STROUD. Law of Slavery.

THORNTON (Rev.). Slavery as it is in the United States. 1841.

TROLLOPE (ANTHONY). The West Indies and the Spanish Main. 1860.

WESTON (G. M.). Progress of Slavery. Washington. 1857.

IV.

(Book II. p. 159.)

Spain to St. Domingo.

By favor of the crisis of the United States, the Spanish government has just accepted the annexation to Spain of the part of St. Domingo, or Hayti, formerly possessed by this monarchy. The President of this Republic, General Santana, by an address of March 18, 1861, transmitted to the Captain-General of Cuba, conveyed the wishes of the people to the Queen, who received and ratified them by a decree of March 19, 1861, thus reincorporating into the monarchy the first island of Central America, of which the immortal Columbus took possession.

This event is a happy one. To the separation, the planters were indebted for the abolition of slavery; but, a prey to continual agitation, they could only find peace and civilization in the union to a great European power. Liberty is not threatened. The statement which preceded the decree declares that slavery, shamefully called by Marshal O'Donnell *the indispensable plague-spot of the colonies*, is in no wise necessary to the working of these fertile territories, and affirms that the government will never dream of re-establishing it. If this be so, the problem of the colonization of the tropics will be resolved on this spot of the globe, — without the white race, no progress; without the black race, no labor; with slavery, the debasement of both, corruption and scandal, then ruin, or war; with the coexistence of the two races, and their free and friendly relations, begin the true foundation of the colonies. Spain will be led to free the slaves at Cuba and Porto Rico, hitherto menaced within and without. Mistress of these three gems of the Gulf of Mexico, the neighbor of Mexico itself, the keeper of the future Panama Canal, Spain will see her colonial grandeur spring up anew, and may become the happy benefactress of some of those magnificent regions bestowed on her by the Creator, and which she corrupted, stained with blood, and then lost, after having discovered them.

(See the curious article of M. Lepelletier Saint-Remy; *Saint-Domingue et les nouveaux intérêts maritimes de l'Espagne*, *Revue des deux Mondes*, June 1, 1861.)

V.

A Concordat between the Holy See and the Republic of Hayti.

There are lands, admirable through climate, soil, and situation, of which history makes mention but once in a century, and then to say little of them, and above all, little good. The great island of Hayti, one of the largest and most fertile on the globe, is among these lands. What was it from creation to the close of the fifteenth century of our era? We are ignorant. Then history teaches us that the immortal Columbus discovered it in 1492, and named it Hispaniola; that the Spaniards by horrible massacres exterminated the natives; that two hundred years after (1697), France settled it; that under the shadow of our flag, a handful of Frenchmen enriched themselves there by the labor of the wretched slaves; that a hundred years later (1791), a new massacre, as if to avenge the first, expelled the French, who persisted in unsuccessfully attempting to retake this land where fever united with hatred to oppose them; that a gross but free government was finally installed; that from a remarkable man, Toussaint l'Ouverture, it fell from generals to presidents, from presidents to an emperor, from an emperor to a president, so that the island of Hayti counts its years by its revolutions, and always independent, never peaceful, it has recently passed into the more intelligent hands of a new president.

In France, where the indemnity due the former colonists is not yet liquidated, where the grandsons of the massacred planters are still living, where the companions in arms of General Leclerc have their heirs, the name of St. Domingo recalls only the saddest memories. These memories have long been turned to account against the abolition of slavery, although this commonplace is a twofold error.

The disturbances at St. Domingo were caused by the refusal of the *free* whites to recognize the rights of the *free* mulattoes; these disturbances broke out in 1791, 1792, and 1793; but it was in 1794 that slavery was abolished by the Convention. What was this prejudice of the whites against the colored men, if not a result of slavery? At what flame, too, was kindled the hatred of the blacks when it burst forth? The memories of slavery, the fear of relapsing into it. Had the whites diffused happiness, love, and enlightenment around them?

After a century, a great deal of sugar and coffee had been sold, enormous fortunes, encumbered with still more enormous debts, had been acquired; fine cultivation had been effected; but what progress had instruction, religion, and morality made, save on a few exceptional plantations? The negroes returned in stabs what their fathers had received in lashes, force avenged itself on force, and all of these horrors denounced slavery by polluting liberty.

It is said, "See what the blacks have made of the land." I answer, "Tell me what the whites had made of the race." I grant that, without the whites, the blacks have profited little by the gifts of the Creator. What would the whites have done with them, had their estates been restored to them without the blacks?

The state of affairs is exaggerated, moreover. Hayti has an indolent, gross, inferior society, nevertheless it is a society, with laws, taxes, an army, a government. Formerly it was an establishment for compulsory labor, recruited by the slave-trade, worked by cupidity, guarded by fear. On the recognition of the island by France, in 1826, M. Humann uttered these noble words: —

"One day, the descendants and heirs of the conquerors of St. Domingo, seeing the conquered population dwindling away and disappearing, bethought themselves to seek for money in distant lands, a savage, but robust race, capable of enduring the fatigues of labor under a tropical sun, and usefully serving the avarice of its masters. The destiny of these slaves was to labor without relaxation, and to die. Prejudice proscribed their color, science disputed to them common reason, men affected to believe them beneath humanity, to excuse the excessive fatigue and pitiless treatment which they lavished upon them. Who did not believe that such a state of things must found a domination without limit or end? Alas! gentlemen, the contrary has happened; and here we must recognize the hand of that higher Power who never suffers human nature to be outraged with impunity, and who, from the wrong itself, knows how to draw the reparation.

"By a remnant of shame, these depraved beings were taught Christianity. Necessity had inured them to labor; and behold, at the end of a few centuries, labor and Christianity has upraised and regenerated them; labor and Christianity has made men where opinion saw none, and when the appointed time has come, from the negro slave-trade arises the republic of Hayti.

* March 10, 1826 (*Moniteur*, p 297), on the Ordinance of April 17, 1825, recognizing the independence of St. Domingo.

"What Providence had made, the king of France has recognized. As a Frenchman and a Christian, I thank the king for it, and congratulate France."

What has labor, what has Christianity become? A curious comparison shows that labor is not, as is pretended, destroyed. It was nearly at the same epoch, under the Restoration, that France consented to the independence of Hayti, and contributed to the independence of Greece. Open the General Table of the Commerce of France for 1858, and we will see that the amount of importations into France,

From Greece (p. 38), amounts to	4,523,069 fr.
From Hayti, ...	12,603,150 fr.

These figures are indeed much below those which represented the products of the island before 1790. We are to labor, therefore, for progress in the future, but without a return to the past. We have before our eyes the vices of the blacks; before, we had equally the vices of the blacks, with the vices of the whites in addition.

Was Christianity widely diffused before 1791? Assuredly not; in all slave countries, imperfectly taught by an inevitably corrupt clergy, it does not profoundly penetrate the soul, but makes a few saints, many hypocrites, and a multitude of superstitious or indifferent persons. Religion desires free souls. How could this religion without root have been maintained during massacres, in the midst of ruins, in a veritable social decomposition, under chiefs like Dessalines, Pétion, or Christophe?

Nevertheless the negroes, whom it had consoled, and who loved the Catholic worship, were never wholly detached from it. At the same time, the Holy See did not for a single day abandon this unhappy land. Pope Leo XII., by a bull, July, 1826, attempted to reorganize religious worship there. In 1834, Mgr. England, Bishop of Charleston, was sent thither as apostolic legate. In 1843, the sovereign pontiff despatched Mgr. Rosati, who laid down the basis of a concordat negotiated with President Boyer. Mgr. Rosati obtained the co-operation of the Congregation of the Sacred Heart of Mary, and the venerable Superior, M. Libermann, sent M. Tisserant thither, a kind communication from whom put me in possession of this touching correspondence.

For twenty years all efforts had stranded upon two insurmountable obstacles, the bad faith of the government, and the corruption of the clergy. There remained, indeed, at St. Domingo, scandalous priests in the heart of a population ignorant, yet well disposed towards religion, if religion had been differently represented. *Corruptio optimi pessima.* What was to be done with priests, one of whom ended a sermon by the words: *Long live the national sovereignty; long live the fair sex!* To dare conceive the thought of converting to the faith such sheep and such shepherds, a saint was needed. Such an one was M. Tisserant, whose touching history seems made to present, in juxtaposition with the horrors to which human nature degrades itself, the spectacle of the sublimity to which it attains.

There were in the Seminary of St. Sulpitius, shortly after 1830, three young men; a creole of Bourbon, a creole of Mauritius, and a creole of St. Domingo. They confided to each other the resolution of devoting themselves to the evangelization of the negroes of their native land. God sent the same vocation to a pious and learned converted Jew by the name of Libermann; he was the first Superior, and they were the first members, of the Communion of the Sacred Heart of Mary (now united to that of the Holy Spirit). "The general end of our society," writes one of these founders, "is to occupy itself with the poorest and most abandoned peoples in the Church of God. The negroes being found at this moment more than any other people in this position, we have offered ourselves to evangelize them."

One of the three missionaries raised up religious worship at Mauritius, another at Bourbon. M. Tisserant was sent to St. Domingo before the concordat, prepared by Mgr. Rosati, had been signed. But this concordat remained without signature, and the young missionary, repulsed from the land to which he wished to consecrate his life, saw himself forced to sojourn at St. Lucia and Grenada, where he did so much good that efforts were made to detain him. But his heart drew him towards St. Domingo, where he finally penetrated. For laborious years, he surmounted incredible obstacles, triumphed over the clergy, the ruling power, and the climate, at length inspired respect and confidence, and came to the point of negotiating with General Hérard the plan of a new concordat. Whence came the obstacle? A letter written from France by M. Isambert denounced the missionaries and the court of Rome as the emissaries of a dangerous policy. The advice of so great *a friend of the negroes* was obeyed; it was no longer doubted that the priests had formed the project of delivering up the island to France, the still more dangerous domination of the Church of Rome was dreaded, it was demanded that the concordat should recognize the *liberties of the Gallican Church.* Behold all our superannuated quarrels revived for the use of St. Domingo, and an old liberal of 1831 sending to Port au Prince his animosities, as one exports thither old fashions and old clothes.

Unhappy people! with faith extinct, corruption overflowing, and ignorance displaying its thick shades, yet persuaded that a missionary thirty years old bore under his cassock the sword of General Leclerc, or the torches of insurrection! It feared French influence, and borrowed from France Gallican liberties. It put aside a Francis Xavier to listen to a diminished descendant of Pithou! There is nothing more frightful than to see our scholastic quarrels, our theses of the Sorbonne, or our parliamentary discussions translated into vulgar language, and aped at the other end of the world.

M. Tisserant, who had already received the co-operation of several French priests, was destined again, after many years of prayers, efforts, and infinite pains, to renounce this third or fourth plan of a concordat; he returned to France hoping for better days, and, in the ardor of his zeal, accepted meanwhile the apostolic prefecture of Guinea. The *Papin*, which bore him to the coast of Africa, was overtaken by a furious tempest. M. Tisserant exhorted his companions, and being unable to save their lives, he strove to save their souls. One of them, a young Israelite, touched by his virtue, fell on his knees, and entreated to be baptized. A few hours after, the priest and neophyte died, ingulfed in the waves, December 7, 1846. M. Tisserant was thirty-one years old.

With him would have been ingulfed the hope of the mission of Hayti, had not his example and merits raised up other devotees. A new attempt was made by Mgr. Spaccapietra to obtain, in the name of the Holy See, a concordat from the ridiculous Emperor Soulouque.

Finally, the advent, December 22, 1858, of an energetic, intelligent, and loyal President, General Geffrard, was the occasion of new negotiations, and Mgr. Monetti, a prelate of great merit, sent in 1860 by the Sovereign Pontiff, has just returned to Europe, bringing back a concordat ratified and signed.

The honor of the initiative belongs to General Geffrard himself, who, in 1859, sent to Rome a negotiator happily chosen, M. Faubert. Better acquainted with his own country than any one, the President well knew that all the population remained attached to the Catholic faith, with remarkable perseverance, despite the efforts of Protestant missionaries, facilitated by the bad example of the Catholic clergy, reduced to thirty-three priests, French, Corsican, Italian, and Spanish. He comprehended that the reform of the clergy depended on the hierarchical relations with Rome and the establishment of a seminary. The Holy See, as persevering in carrying the faith to this population as the latter was in desiring it, corresponded to these views.

On the 3d of December, 1860, Mgr. Monetti landed at Jacmel with several missionaries, amidst a joyous ovation of the inhabitants, already informed of the signature of the treaty with Rome by the President's speech at the opening of the Session, August 29, 1860. All the National Guard was under arms, a lighted taper in the right hand, and a musket on the left arm. From Jacmel to Port au Prince, the distance is twenty-two leagues, by difficult roads. The Prelate was received, December 11, by the General, ministers, magistrates, and people, with extreme enthusiasm. (The *République*, a Haytien journal, December 13, 1860.)

The enthusiasm equalled the ignorance and corruption. There were no sacraments without pay. The churches were full; but, in a parish of fifty thousand souls, occupying more than ten leagues, there was but a single priest, and of a hundred and twenty-four children baptized, but four legitimate children only! From December 3, 1860, to April 6, 1861, Mgr. Monetti visited the parishes, reanimated the zeal of the priests, and distributed the sacraments, while a French missionary preached Lent at Port au Prince, and others instructed the children, and gave to the people the unheard-of spectacle of gratuitous ministration to the dying.

The Senate and House of Representatives congratulated the President on having signed the concordat, which they regarded as the corner-stone of the civilization of the Republic.

This concordat (*Moniteur haïtien*, December 8, 1860) is composed of eighteen articles. It declares (Art. 1) the Catholic religion that of the majority, and recognizes its rights. An archbishopric is to be erected at Port au Prince, and several dioceses established on the island (Art. 2). The pay of the clergy, the appointment of canons, curates, and vicars, the establishment of religious orders, the free correspondence with the Holy See, the respect for canonical laws, the administration of large and small seminaries, the participation in that of the parochial funds, with a council of notables, are secured to the bishops by Arts. 6 – 14, 17. The bishops are appointed by the President, and instituted by the Holy See, and *if the Holy See thinks fit to postpone or not to confer this institution, it informs the President of Hayti, who, in the latter case, appoints another ecclesiastic.* (Art. 4.)

The bishops and members of the clergy are under oath. (Art. 5.)

More than one civilized country might take this so provident and loyal concordat as a model.

After the exchange of ratifications, Mgr. Monetti stayed long enough at Port au Prince to congratulate President Geffrard on the anniversaries of December 22 and January 1, to busy himself with the success of the reform of the clergy, and to address to the faithful, on the occasion of Lent, a touching and useful charge, followed by an exhortation to the priests themselves. Finally he signed, February 6, 1861, a regulation in pursuance of the concordat, which fixes the number of the dioceses at five, makes the number of the parishes equal to that of the communes, and fixes the salary of the clergy. (*Moniteur haitien*, March 30, 1861.)

Nearly at the same epoch, in the beginning of this year, the return of the Bulgarian nation to the Catholic Unity consoled the Holy Father. The foundation of five dioceses, and the signature of a concordat, after four years of unfruitful efforts, on a large island of the Caribbean Sea, where are deposited the ashes of Christopher Columbus, are not so important events; they are, notwithstanding, the proofs of a reviving fecundity of the faith, and the hope of a better future promised to a land which deserves, despite its wretchedness, our particular interest in many points of view, since it was French, is free, and has again become Catholic.

VI.

(Book VI. p. 226.)

Treaty of Peace between the King and the Allied Powers, concluded at Paris, May 30, 1814, and which preceded the Congress of Vienna.

Art. 1. His Most Christian Majesty, sharing without reserve in all the sentiments of His Britannic Majesty in relation to a kind of commerce repulsive to the principles of natural justice, and the enlightenment of the times in which we live, doth pledge himself to unite all his efforts with those of His Britannic Majesty in the coming Congress, to cause the abolition of the negro slave-trade to be decreed by all the powers of Christendom, so that the said trade may cease universally, as it shall cease definitively, and in any event, on the part of France, after a delay of five years; and that, moreover, during this delay, no trafficker in slaves shall import or sell them elsewhere than in the colonies of the state of which he is the subject.

VII.

(Book VI. Chap. III. p. 262.)

Catholic Missions in Africa (1860, 1861).*

Algiers. 170,000 Catholics; 3,000,000 Mussulmans; 40,000 Jews; a dozen conversions a year; about 300 infants baptized *in articulo mortis.*

Tunis. 12,400 Catholics; 2,000,000 Mussulmans; 40,000 Jews; one conversion in a year; 671 baptisms of children of infidels *in articulo mortis.*

Tripoli in Barbary. 28,000 Catholics; 2,000,000 Mussulmans; 50 children baptized; a few secret conversions.

Lower Egypt. 24,000 Catholics; 300,000 Copts; 2,000,000 Mussulmans.

Upper Egypt. 3,300 Catholics; more than 4,000,000 heretics; 3,000,000 infidels. Religion is making some progress among the Copts, and conversions appear on the point of becoming still more numerous.

Gallas. 1,200 Catholics; 10,000 heretics; 30,000 Mussulmans; 1,000,000 infidels. The inhabitants are beginning to become accustomed to Europeans; roads are being opened.

Cape of Good Hope (West). 5,500 Catholics; 40,000 heretics; 55,000 infidels. Progress is insensibly made. There have been recently some conversions, even among the Mahometans.

East Cape. 5,000 Catholics; 50,000 heretics; 150,000 infidels.

Upper and Lower Guinea and Senegambia. 4,000 Cath-

* I am indebted for this note to M. Ducros, Secretary of the Council of the Propagation of the Faith.

olics; 50,000,000 inhabitants. There is an apprentices' establishment at Dakar, where 70 children are being taught the trades of printer, bookbinder, blacksmith, joiner, shoemaker, turner, tailor, and weaver; at Gaboon, there is an establishment for study and agriculture; there are several workshops for girls.

SIERRA LEONE. Everything remains to be done in this mission, whence death swept away, in the first month, the bishop and the priests who accompanied him.

ZANGUEBAR. The missionaries propose chiefly to evangelize the negroes from the interior, whom they will ransom and keep in the mission establishment. These negroes will then go voluntarily to the Isle of Bourbon to complete their moral and religious education, and thus form a class of reliable laborers in the colony.

BOURBON. A mission for 60,000 Indians and Chinese idolaters.

SEYCHELLES. 8,000 Catholics; 1,000 heretics; 500 infidels. Religion is now flourishing in these islands, which for a whole century remained without priests, and absolutely destitute of all spiritual aid.

ABYSSINIA. In 1858, King Negoocia sent to Rome and Paris a deputation composed of his cousin Hedji Zacayi, the Abbé Emnaton, Abyssin, and M. Lepère de Lapeyreuse, secretary and interpreter. This deputation expressed to Rome the sentiments of attachment and veneration of King Negoocia for the chair of St. Peter, and declared to the Holy Father that this king would embrace Catholicism as soon as the political state of the country permitted; meanwhile he would permit in his states the free exercise of Catholicism. The Lazarists have a mission in this country.

MADAGASCAR. The Jesuits have establishments here; — 1st, at Resource, there is a special school for arts and trades and agriculture, designed to provide the small islands, and above all the mainland, with honest workmen of all kinds; 2d, at Nazareth, the nuns of St. Joseph de Cluny bring up young Madagascar girls, to whom the young workmen of Resource may ally themselves to form Christian families on their return to their country; 3d, on Madagascar itself, at the station of Nossy Faly; 4th, on the little islands of Mayotte, Nossi-Bé, St. Mary, Great Comora, Mohely, and Anjouan. These islands are possessed by fanatical Mussulmans, and the faith is planted there with difficulty.

VIII.

(Book VII. Chap. II. p. 352.)

Bull of Pope Benedict XIV. (December 20, 1741.)

To our Venerable Brethren, the Bishops of Brazil and the other Provinces, both in America and the West Indies, subject to our dearly beloved son in Jesus Christ, John, King of Portugal and Algarve.

Benedict XIV., Pope.

Venerable brethren, the apostolic salutation and benediction.

The immense charity of the Prince of Shepherds, Jesus Christ, who came to transmit to men a fuller life, and to give himself up as a victim for the salvation of many, inflames us also, his unworthy representative on earth, with an ardent desire to give our life after his example, not only for his faithful servants, but for all men without exception. The general government of the Catholic Church, imposed on our weakness, constrains us, it is true, to fill and direct in the city of Rome itself, according to the usage and regulations of our fathers, this Apostolic See towards which men flock daily from all sides, in order to watch there with a more attentive eye over the affairs of the Christian republic, and to bring to its ills a more opportune and salutary remedy. It is refused to us to fly towards those distant and scattered countries, and to lavish there on souls ransomed with the blood of Jesus Christ, all the cares of our ministry, our blood itself, did God accord this grace to our desires. Nevertheless, as we would not that a single one of all the nations under heaven should have to complain of being forgotten by the apostolic providence, authority, and beneficence, we call on you, O venerable brethren, who are joined to this same Holy See, to cultivate in common with it the vineyard of the God of armies, to share our solicitude and vigilance, so that, your task becoming easier and more fruitful from day to day, you will win at the end the crown of immortality destined to those who have fought valiantly.

None of you is ignorant of all that has been undertaken for religion by our predecessors and the Catholic princes, faithful and devoted to the Christian cause, the labors which they have endured, the sacrifices which they have imposed on themselves with a free and generous heart, to send to men wandering in darkness, and sitting in the shadow of death, holy workers whose good examples and salutary preachings might co-operate with the assistance and gifts of piety in lighting the torch of the orthodox faith in these countries, and introducing them to the knowledge of the truth. You doubtless know also the benefits, the graces, the favors, and the privileges which they still accord to-day, in order that these allurements may win them to the Catholic religion, and that by persevering in this way they may attain salvation through the good works of charity.

What bitter grief, therefore, has pierced our paternal heart, when, reperusing the wise counsels of the Roman pontiffs, our predecessors, and their constitutions, which prescribe, under the gravest penalties, that infidels shall not be subjected to outrages, bad treatment, the weight of chains, and death itself, but shall be accorded aid, protection, and favor, we have learned that still to-day *men calling themselves Christians (and this happens chiefly in the Brazilian provinces) are so far forgetful of the sentiments of charity diffused in our hearts by the Holy Spirit, as to reduce to servitude the unhappy Indians, the peoples of the eastern and western coasts of Brazil, and other regions.* They confound in their barbarity both those who are destitute of the enlightenment of faith, and those who have been regenerated in the waters of baptism. *Much more, they sell them as vile herds of slaves, they despoil them of their goods, and the inhumanity which they display towards them is the principal cause of turning them away from employing the faith of Jesus Christ, by making them look upon it only with horror.*

Desiring to bear a remedy to these evils, as far as we are able, with the help of God, we have hastened, in the first place, to arouse the ardent piety of our dearly beloved son in Jesus Christ, John, the illustrious king of Portugal and Algarve, and to make appeal to his zeal for the propagation of the faith. With that filial respect for us and the Holy See which distinguishes him, he has promised to send on to the spot to all the officers and ministers of his states, to inflict the severest penalties, conformably to the royal edicts, on such of his subjects as shall be convicted of acting towards the Indians differently from what is required by Christian gentleness and charity.

We next entreat your Fraternities, and exhort them in the Lord not to tolerate, to the detriment of your name and your dignity, the slightest relaxation in the vigilance and solicitude of your ministry, which the present circumstances demand of you; uniting your own efforts to those of the king, prove to all how much more powerful and efficacious is the zeal of charity, burning in the priest who is shepherd of souls, than the labors of secular ministers in procuring the happiness of the Indians and bringing them to the true faith.

Moreover, by the tenor of these presents, we renew and confirm, by our apostolic authority, the apostolic letters sent in the form of brief, May 28, 1537, by Pope Paul III., our predecessor of happy memory, to John, then Archbishop of Toledo, and Cardinal of the holy Roman Church, and those which Pope Urban VIII., also our predecessor, and of more recent memory, addressed, April 22, 1639, to the defender of the duties and collector-general of the tributes of the Apostolic Chamber. Walking in the steps of our predecessors Paul and Urban, and wishing to suppress the impious attempts of these men, who, far from attracting the infidels to embrace the true faith by all means of Christian charity, as they ought, turn them aside and alienate them from it by acts of inhumanity, we recommend your Fraternities, and, in your person, your future successors, to publish and placard the royal edicts yourselves, or by others, as well in the provinces of Paraguay and Brazil, extending to the Rio de la Plata, as in the other countries and places situated in the East and West Indies. We wish that the execution of these should be hastened by means of an efficient force, and that all should co-operate in securing their observance, on the one hand, with the ecclesiastics and seculars themselves, of every state, sex, condition, and dignity, especially those enjoying any authority and consideration; on the other, all the orders, congregations, and societies, that of Jesus in particular, and all the institutions of mendicants and non-mendicants, monks, regulars, and military orders, especially the Brothers Hospitallers of St. John of Jerusalem. *All infraction of these regulations shall be, by the very fact, smitten with excommunication latæ sententiæ*, which cannot be raised, save *in articulo mortis*, and after a preliminary satisfaction, either by ourselves, or, in the course of time, by the Roman pontiff then existing, *in order that in future no one may be audacious enough to reduce the said Indians to slavery, to sell them, to buy them, to exchange them, to give them away, to separate them from their wives and children, to despoil them of their goods, to transport them from one place or country to another, to deprive them, in fine, in any way whatsoever of their liberty*, and to retain them in servitude, or to second those who act thus in authorizing them by teaching and preaching, and in aiding them under a thousand false pretexts by counsels, protection, assistance, or any other co-operation. To put an end to all these disorders, we enjoin you to punish with excommunication all rebellious infractors, who will not obey each of you in all these points, and to employ through your chief the other ecclesiastical censures and penalties, and all the remedies in law and fact which seem opportune to you, so as to maintain a certain order in these measures, by redoubling these censures and penalties, and having recourse, if need be, to the secular arm. And we accord to each one of you, and to your future successors, the full and entire power to act in consequence.

IX.

(Book VII. Chap. II. p. 358.)

Bull of Pope Gregory XVI. (November 3, 1839.)

Elevated to the highest degree of apostolic dignity, and filling, although without any merit on our part, the place of Jesus Christ, the Son of God, who, by the excess of his charity, deigned to become man, and to die for the redemption of the world, we consider that it belongs to our pastoral solicitude to make every effort to divert Christians from the traffic which is made of negroes and other men, whoever they may be.

As soon as evangelical light began to be diffused, the unfortunates who had fallen into the harshest slavery, in the midst of the numerous wars of this epoch, felt their condition become ameliorated; for the Apostles, inspired by the Spirit of God, taught the slaves, on the one hand, to obey their temporal masters as Jesus Christ himself, and to be heartily resigned to the will of God; but, on the other hand, they commanded the masters to show themselves kind towards their slaves, to accord to them what was just and equitable, and not to treat them angrily, knowing that the Lord of both is in heaven, and that with him there is no respect of persons.

Erelong the law of the Gospel establishing in a universal and fundamental manner sincere charity towards all, and the Lord Jesus having declared that he should regard as done or refused to himself all the acts of beneficence and mercy which should be done or denied to the poor and obscure, it naturally followed that the Christians not only regarded their slaves as brethren, especially when they became Christians, but that they became more inclined to give liberty to those who rendered themselves worthy of it; which was accustomed to be accomplished particularly at the solemn feast of Easter, as is related by St. Gregory of Nyssus. There were even found those who, inflamed with a more ardent charity, *threw themselves into chains to ransom their brethren*, and an apostolic man, our predecessor, Pope Clement I., of most holy memory, certifies to having known a great number who did this work of mercy. For this reason, the darkness of heathen superstition being wholly dissipated with the progress of time, and the customs of the most barbarous peoples being softened, thanks to the benefit of the law working by charity, things came to the point that several centuries ago there were no longer slaves among the greater part of Christian nations.

Nevertheless, it is with profound grief that we say it, *there have since been seen, even among Christians, men who, shamefully blinded by the desire of sordid gain, have not hesitated to reduce to servitude, on distant lands, Indians, negroes, and other unhappy races*, or else to aid in this ignoble crime, by instituting and organizing the traffic in these unfortunates, whom others had loaded with chains. Numerous Roman pontiffs, our predecessors of glorious memory, did not forget to reprimand, according to the whole extent of their charge, the conduct of these men as opposed to their salvation, and blighting to the name of Christian, for they saw clearly that *this was one of the causes which most strongly retained the infidel nations in their hatred of the true religion.*

To this end tend the apostolic letters of Paul III., of May 29, 1537, addressed to the Cardinal Archbishop of Toledo, under the fisherman's seal, and other much more extended letters of Urban VIII., of April 22, 1639, addressed to the collector of duties of the Apostolic Chamber of Portugal, — letters which direct the gravest reproaches against those who dare reduce to slavery the inhabitants of the East or West Indies, sell them, buy them, kill them, exchange them, give them away, separate them from their wives and children, despoil them of their goods, carry them away or send them to foreign places, or deprive them in any manner whatsoever of their liberty; retain them in servitude, or lend aid, counsels, assistance, and favor to those who do these under any color or pretext whatever; or again preach or teach that it is lawful, and, in fine, co-operate in any manner, whatsoever it may be.

Benedict XIV. later confirmed and renewed these pontifical prescriptions, already mentioned by new apostolic letters to the bishops of Brazil and all other regions, dated December 20, 1749, by means of which he aroused the solicitude of the bishops with the same end.

Long before, another of our more ancient predecessors, Pius II., whose pontificate saw the empire of Portugal extend into Guinea and the negro countries, addressed letters bearing date October 7, 1462, to the Bishop of Ruvo, who was about to set out to exercise the holy ministry in these countries with the greatest fruit; but in which he took occasion to blame Christians most severely who reduced the neophytes to slavery. Finally, in our days, Pius VII., animated by the same spirit of charity and religion as his predecessors, zealously interposed his good offices with those in power to put an end entirely to the slave-trade among Christians.

These prescriptions and this solicitude of our predecessors have served not a little, with the aid of God, to defend the Indians and the other peoples whom we have just named against the barbarity of conquests and the cupidity of Christian traders; but the Holy See is far from rejoicing as yet at the full success of its efforts and zeal, since, if the negro slave-trade has been in part abolished, it is still exercised by numerous Christians. Therefore, in order to put away such an opprobrium from all Christian countries, after having maturely deliberated with several of our venerable fathers, the cardinals of the holy Roman Church, assembled in council, according to the steps of our predecessors, in virtue of the apostolic authority, we earnestly warn and admonish in the Lord all Christians, of whatever condition they may be, and enjoin on them that *no one shall dare in the future unjustly to annoy Indians, negroes, or other men, whoever they may be, to despoil them of their property or reduce them to servitude, or to lend aid and favor to those who abandon themselves to such excesses*, or to exercise this inhuman traffic, by which the negroes, as if they were not men, but veritable and impure beasts, reduced like them to servitude, without distinction, contrary to the rights of justice and humanity, are bought, sold, and devoted to suffer the hardest labors, and on account of whom dissensions are excited, and almost incessant wars fomented among nations by the bait of the gain proposed to the first kidnappers of negroes.

Therefore, by virtue of the apostolic authority, we reprove all the aforesaid things, as absolutely unworthy of the name of Christian, and, by the same authority, we absolutely prohibit and interdict to all, ecclesiastics or laymen, to dare sustain this trade of negroes as permitted under any pretext or color whatsoever, or to teach in public or private, in one manner or another, anything contrary to these apostolic letters.

And in order that these letters may come to the knowledge of all the world, and that no one may pretend ignorance of them, we decree and order, that they be published and placarded according to custom, by one of our officers, at the doors of the basilic of the Prince of the Apostles, the Apostolic Chancellor's office, the Palace of Justice, Mont Citorio, and at the Field of Flora.

Given at Rome, at St. Mary Major, under the Seal of the Fisherman, November 3, 1839, in the ninth year of our pontificate.

Countersigned:

LOUIS, CARDINAL LAMBRUSCHINI.

THE END.

Cambridge: Stereotyped and Printed by Welch, Bigelow, & Co.

www.ingramcontent.com/pod-product-compliance
Lightning Source LLC
LaVergne TN
LVHW021149110826
845150LV00005B/1174